Legalize Blackmail

Walter E. Block

STRAYLIGHT
PUBLISHING

Straylight Publishing, LLC
Chalmette, Louisiana USA

Book design by Gregory W. Rome

For Murray N. Rothbard—
my mentor, my teacher, my friend, my inspiration

Introduction

Preface

Acknowledgments

Part I. The Case for Legalizing Blackmail

Part II. Critiques of the U.Penn. Symposium

Part III. Critiques of Other Scholars' Views on Blackmail

Introduction

I was skeptical when Professor Block first talked to me about this book. "Legalizing blackmail? That doesn't sound like a good idea," I thought. "Could anyone really be in favor of this?" But I gave him a chance, and Professor Block brought me around.

As with every subject he approaches, he challenges the received wisdom about blackmail from end to end, using only libertarian principles and reason to show that legal prohibitions against blackmail are incompatible with a principled philosophy of freedom. In this volume, Professor Block dismantles the best arguments in favor of outlawing blackmail advocated by some of the most prestigious legal and academic minds ever to write on the subject. In the process, he has authored the definitive work on the libertarian case in favor of blackmail legalization.

This is certainly not to say that blackmail is a good thing. Professor Block does not advocate it, but neither does he believe its practitioners are criminals. After all, one can legally ask someone for money and one can gossip. Why should someone who asks for money in lieu of gossiping land in jail? He also draws a sharp distinction between blackmail and extortion, which he argues should remain forbidden.

Give this book a chance. At the very least, you'll have some fantastic cocktail party conversation. Or you might walk away with a new way of looking at the world and a newly sharpened set of tools for analyzing the rest of your beliefs.

Gregory W. Rome
Chalmette, Louisiana
October 2013

Preface

Bill Cosby was in the news a few years ago when it came to light that his illegitimate daughter had demanded money from him under the threat of revealing to the newspapers her birth status and relationship to him. This was characterized as blackmail, a criminal offense, and there was at one time the possibility of actual criminal sanctions being imposed upon Mr. Cosby's daughter.

But blackmail, as such, consists of two separate acts, each of which is and ought to be legal. First, there is a request or a demand for money. Surely it is a legitimate act for a daughter to ask her father for money. Generalizing, it is even licit for strangers to ask one another for funds; there are entire industries devoted to precisely this practice. Second, there is the "threat" to reveal embarrassing information about the target of the blackmail: to tell the world of Bill Cosby's fathering of an illegitimate child. However, had his daughter disclosed this information without offering him the option of paying her off not to do so, no law would have been violated. And this is as it should be, since such disclosure is a paradigm case of free speech. It constitutes mere gossip, certainly a legal activity.

How, then, can two legal acts, when performed in tandem, be converted into an illegal one? Legal scholars have divided into two camps on this issue. Both agree that the amalgamated act should be prohibited, even though they concede that each constituent element should be legal.

One group, the utilitarians, maintains that when both occur as part of a larger complex act, negative social repercussions ensue. The other group, the deontologists, avers that there is something philosophically wrong in the double act which does not occur in either one of them, separately.

In contrast, I maintain that both groups are in error—that it is impossible for two separately legal acts to be rendered into an illegal one, and, therefore, blackmail should be legalized. Of course, blackmail must be sharply distinguished from extortion. In the former case, the threat is to do something legal—e.g., reveal embarrassing information. In the latter, it is to do something patently illegal, such as assault, or even kill the victim.

Legalize Blackmail consists of previously published articles on the subject of libertarianism and blackmail. It is a very unpopular view that followers of the freedom philosophy have: blackmail legalization. This is not a very pressing issue for the mainstream media. An end to prohibition of this complex act is not likely to occur any time soon. Thus this book is not all that much concerned with practicality; rather, it is an attempt to ferret out the issue of justice. But the road to the free society is paved with many obstacles. Hopefully, *Legalize Blackmail* will provide one small paving stone in that direction.

It is an onerous task I have set myself. After all, I am making the case on behalf of legalizing blackmail! To say that this is an unpopular position in legal philosophy is the understatement of the century. Thus, the message is repeated, and repeated again, and then opponents of the argument for legalization are taken to task. These commentators include some of the most prestigious scholars in the philosophy of law, including Richard Posner, Leo Katz, Russell Hardin and Richard Epstein, among many others.

Although I am highly critical of the University of Pennsylvania Law Review's compilation on blackmail, I warmly appreciate its editors' preface to that volume, entitled "Instead of a preface." Here it is, with their permission, in its entirety:

> A whole symposium about an exotic crime like blackmail? Why? Only because it has come to seem to us that one cannot think about coercion, contracts, consent, robbery, rape, unconstitutional conditions, nuclear deterrence, assumption of risk, the greater-includes-the-lesser arguments, plea bargains, settlements, sexual harassment, insider trading, bribery, domination, secrecy, privacy, law enforcement, utilitarianism and deontology without being tripped up repeatedly by the paradox of blackmail. How so? And what paradox? Read on…

This preface was written by Leo Katz and James Lindgren, as an introduction to their Symposium on blackmail. That compilation of articles appeared in the University of Pennsylvania Law Review (Vol. 141, No. 5, May 1993) and its preface now serves, as well, as part of my introduction to the present book, *Legalize Blackmail*.

I would add to their very long and inclusive list a few more concepts that we trip over when we discuss the "paradox" of blackmail: extortion, political philosophy, libertarian theory, threats, free speech, gossip, defense, offense, the non-aggression principle (NAP), truth, falsity, lying, information, the first amendment to the Constitution, cheating, morality, fraud and rights—although I full well acknowledge their list is a very accurate one. I think theirs is a splendid introduction to their own compilation, and to mine on behalf of *Legalize Blackmail* as well. That is why I quote it in full.

There is another reason I want to include their preface, or non-preface, in my introduction to this book of mine: that issue of the University of Pennsylvania Law Review contains a dozen essays on this subject, all of which I think are profoundly mistaken, even though written by leaders in the fields of legal theory, political philosophy, and law and economics. All of these essays, plus many more, are criticized in the present volume. As it happens, practically the only thing I agree with in their Symposium is this (non) preface of theirs.

Section I of *Legalize Blackmail* introduces the topic. Section II is devoted to a refutation of the articles appearing in the University of Pennsylvania's symposium: it is a critique of both the utilitarian and deontological cases in support of the present legal prohibition of blackmail. In section III we consider and reject the views of still other scholars who support the blackmail legal status quo. We conclude in section IV with a call for legalization.

Most people shrink in horror from the very mention of blackmail. In the lexicon of the average person, it joins phenomena like as murder, rape, theft, Nazis and pure evil. Arthur Conan Doyle of Sherlock Holmes fame calls it murder of the soul. He says of his demonic character Milverton: "I would ask you how could one compare the ruffian, who in hot blood bludgeons his mate, with this man who methodically and at his leisure tortures the soul and wrings the nerves in order to add to his already swollen money-bags?" There is, in other words, if this is not already crystal clear, a very low rung in hell reserved for blackmailers, far below even that one occupied by those who use physical violence in their crimes.

However, according to the libertarian philosophy, criminality applies, only, to the threat or initiation of violence against person and legitimately owned property. Say what you will against blackmail (a demand for money or other valuable consideration coupled with the threat, not to violate the NAP but rather to gossip about secrets), no violence is ever threatened or engaged in. Therefore, blackmail may not be very nice, but it should not be considered a crime. This sounds horrid and unlikely. I go further, it sounds like the ravings of a veritable madman. However, gentle reader, dig deep into the present volume. Encounter its arguments. I challenge that you will be forced to retreat from that particular point of view. You may never come to favor this practice; I don't either. But you will no longer view it as criminal behavior. That is the thesis of this book.

Walter E. Block
New Orleans, Louisiana
August 30, 2013

Acknowledgments

Because this is a compilation of previously published articles, I am most indebted to my coauthors and the journals that published the articles in the first place for giving me permission to reprint them. In no particular order, many thanks are due Robert McGee, Hans-Hermann Hoppe, Stephan Kinsella, Gary Anderson, and David Gordon. My thanks also go out to the University of Hawaii Law Review, Irish Jurist, the Journal of Libertarian Studies, Business Ethics Quarterly, the Seton Hall Law Review, the Vermont Law Review, the New York Law School Law Review, the Thomas Jefferson Law Review, the University of Tulsa Law Review, the University of British Columbia Law Review, the Loyola of Los Angeles Law Review, the Florida State University Business Review, and Criminal Justice Ethics. Finally, I would like to thank my research assistants. Without all of them—coauthors, journals, and my research assistants together—this book would not have been possible.

The articles collected here have appeared in print in the following places and are reprinted with permission:

Chapter 1   *Trading Money for Silence,* originally published in the University of Hawaii Law Review, Vol. 8, No. 1 Spring 1986, pp, 57–73.

Chapter 2   *A Libertarian Theory of Blackmail,* originally published in Irish Jurist, Vol. XXXIII pp. 280–310 (1998).

Chapter 3   Walter Block & Robert W. McGee, *Toward a Libertarian Theory of Blackmail,* originally published in Journal of Libertarian Studies 15, no. 2 (Winter 2001).

Chapter 4   *Blackmail as a Victimless Crime,* originally published in Bracton Law Journal, Vol. 31, pp. 24–44.

Chapter 5   Walter Block, Stephan Kinsella, and Hans-Hermann Hoppe, *DeLong and the Second Paradox of Blackmail,* originally published in Business Ethics Quarterly, Vol. 10, No. 3, July 2000, pp. 593–622.

Part I.
The Case for Legalizing Blackmail

Chapter 1
Trading Money for Silence

I. INTRODUCTION

When the term "blackmail" was first used in 1722, it had a specific and exact meaning. Its legal meaning was precise; it prohibited actions, which were clearly at variance with the most basic and cherished of all human rights—the right to remain unmolested in one's person and property.

The Waltham Black Act of 1722 was passed as the result of the depredations of a gang of deer thieves called the Waltham Blacks, operating near the town of Waltham, England, who blackened their faces. Moreover, this gang undertook the quaint practice of sending letters "demanding venison and money, and threatening some great violence, if such their unlawful demand should be refused."[1] Hence the term "blackmail."[2] This law was clearly meant to punish demands for a victim's money or wealth coupled with threats to inflict violence on person or property.[3]

If the law prohibiting blackmail began with a clear and limited mandate, it was soon expanded through judicial determinations and legislative enactments. The law of blackmail began proscribing threats to do that which one

---

[1] *See* W.H.D. Winder, *The Development of Blackmail*, 5 MOD. L. REV. 21, 34–35 (1941). *See also* C. R. Williams, *Demanding with Menaces: A Survey of the Australian Law of Blackmail*, 10 MELB. U.L. REV. 118, 122–23 (1975).

[2] *See* Winder, *supra* note 1, at 24 (This term also has been traced to piracy: "Blackmail was originally the tribute exacted by free-booters in the northern border countries to secure lands and goods from despoilment or robbery.").

[3] *See Id.* at 21 ("[I]n those forms which require the presence of 'menaces' there had to be originally, and until fairly recently, something like a threat of personal violence or of violence to property.").

would otherwise have a full and complete right to do—such as to publicize true information about another.[4]

In common parlance, the concept of blackmail has come to be used very loosely compared with its original meaning, and is now applied to practically any commercial transaction disapproved of by the speaker. For example, the OPEC price hike of 1973 was widely castigated as "economic blackmail." The legal definition of blackmail has also been significantly broadened. This article shall attempt to chronicle the widening of the legal definition of blackmail. Section II attempts to show that the ever more encompassing behavior prohibited under modern blackmail legislation has been inimical to the public good and has transgressed canons of justice, logic, and rights to free speech and has endangered, not protected, persons and property rights. Section III explores whether one can legitimately threaten to tell secrets one would otherwise have the right to reveal—unless one is paid to desist. Section IV discusses cases (1) where the "victim" approaches the blackmailer, (2) where the threat is to expose a victimless crime, and (3) where the threat is to expose a real crime.

---

[4] *See* Williams, *supra* note 1, at 140. The Criminal Law Revision Committee held that

> there are some threats which should make the demand amount to blackmail even if there is a valid claim to the thing demanded. For example, we believe that most people would say that it should be blackmail to threaten to denounce a person, however truly, as a homosexual unless he paid a debt. It does not seem to follow from the existence of a debt that the creditor should be entitled to resort to any method, otherwise *noncriminal*, to obtain payment.

Id. (emphasis added).

II. THE CHANGING DEFINITION OF BLACKMAIL

Originally, blackmail in the common law was confined to threats of violence, or other violations of the rights of person or property.[5] In *Rex v. Parker*,[6] for example, a creditor was found guilty of blackmail for forging a letter in an attempt to recover money owed him. This is consistent with the limited construction since forgery is itself equivalent to an assault on property, and hence an action which is per se proscribed.[7] Similarly, a threat made at gunpoint that the victim would "suffer the consequences,"[8] and threats to burn down

---

[5] *See* Williams, *Blackmail (pt. 1)*, 1954 CRIM. L. REV. 79, 87:

> As has been seen, there can in general be no stealing where the property is handed over as the result of threats, unless the threats are of force or false imprisonment. ... [T]he common-law doctrine has never been extended beyond threats of physical force or false imprisonment; thus a person who obtains goods by threats of accusation of immorality would not be guilty of larceny.

See also Winder, *supra* note 1, at 42:

> The Act of 1734 recites that "many of His Majesty's subjects have of late frequently been put in great fear and danger of their lives by wicked and ill-disposed persons assaulting and attempting to rob them" and declares to be felony the conduct of such persons who "with any offensive weapon or instrument, unlawfully and maliciously assault, or shall by menaces, or in or by any forcible or violent manner, demand any money, goods or chattels, of or from any other person or persons with a felonious intent to rob or commit robbery." In its original context there can be no doubt that "menaces means such menaces as, if the demand accompanying them be complied with, robbery is committed: the words "with intent to rob" make this clear and they give effect to the declared object of the Act, There can be no intent to rob unless the handing over of the property demanded amounts to robbery. Therefore, "menaces" in section I meant present threats of immediate battery if the property were not delivered up to the accused.

[6] 74 J.P. 208 (1910), cited in A.H. Campbell, *The Anomalies of Blackmail*, 219 LAW Q. REV. 382, 391 fn.18 (1939).

[7] In the narrow definition of blackmail, threats of force against persons or property are the only proscribed threats. But are such threats always illegitimate? Surely not! Suppose for example, that the father of a kidnapping victim threatens the kidnapper with personal physical violence unless he releases his child. As long as the threatened violence is not out of proportion to the original crime (the kidnapping), there would appear nothing untoward in such an extortionate demand. For the remainder of this paper, however, unless otherwise indicated, we shall assume that threatened (or carried out) acts of violence are all initiatory and hence unjustified, not retaliatory, or in response, and hence possibly justified. For a discussion of the proportion of punishment and retaliation, *see* MURRAY ROTHBARD, THE ETHICS OF LIBERTY 85–95 (1982).

[8] *See, e.g., State v. Morgan*, 50 Tenn. 262 (1871).

the prosecutor's premises[9] were deemed to be violations of law. On the other hand, a threat of a civil suit in order to facilitate the collection of a debt was ruled not actionable: "A threat to do what one has a legal right to do is not, as a general rule, duress and will not support an action for damages."[10]

Thus blackmail was originally limited to the use of a threat of violence, or rights violations, in order to obtain valuable considerations. The concept of blackmail was soon extended, however, to include threats that did not entail physical abuse or the violation of rights.

As early as 1776, the extortion (blackmail) of money by verbal "threat to accuse a man of unnatural practices" was held to be criminal.[11] Similarly, the draftsmen of the (Blackmail) Act of 1823 extended the definitions of blackmail from "demands coupled with a threat of violence to the person or to property" to the utterance of "verbal threats to accuse another of serious crime."[12] In the modern day, the concept of blackmail has been extended to include the threat of anything that might discomfort a person. This change is so thorough that many legal commentators and much modern legislation even fail to acknowledge the traditional distinctions between threats of vio-

---

[9] *See, e.g., Rex v. Smith*, 169 Eng. Rep. 350 (Ch. 1850).

[10] *See Shelton v. Lock*, 19 S.W.2d 124, 126 (Tex Civ. App. 1929).

[11] *See* Campbell, *supra* note 6, at 382–83. *But see* Winder, *supra* note 1, at 24 ("At first, therefore, blackmail implied a threat of violent injury to property and according to the Oxford dictionary was not used, by extension, in its modern sense until the nineteenth century. The first example given of its modern use is from the year 1840.").

[12] *See* Williams, *supra* note 1, at 135.

lence, threatened accusations of a serious crime, and threatened accusations of embarrassing misconduct.[13]

Rex v. Tomlison[14] was considered to be the first case to extend significantly the concept of blackmail.[15] Tomlinson was convicted of demanding money under the threat of telling a man's wife and friends of his alleged immoral behavior with another woman, Lord Chief Justice Russell of Killowen stated:

> I should have regretted if the Court had felt compelled to confine the construction of the word 'menaces' in the way suggested [limited to injury to person or property], with the result of excluding such conduct as that of the prisoner from the purview of the criminal law. ... [I]t may [also] well be held ... to include menaces or threats of a danger by an accusation of misconduct, though of mis-

---

[13] See, e.g., Joseph M. Livermore, *Lawyer Extortion*, 20 ARIZ. L. REV. 403, 403 fn.2 (1978) (discussing the Arizona Revised Criminal Code: "In addition to the conventional proscription of threats of physical injury, property damage, criminal conduct, and reputational injury, a general clause forbids threatening 'any other act which would not in itself materially benefit the defendant but which is calculated to harm another person materially.'"). *See also* C.R. Williams, *Blackmail (pt. 2)*, [1954] CRIM. L. REV. 162, 168 ("(I]t is rightly treated as blackmail to attempt to obtain money ... by the threat to accuse of discreditable conduct.").

Moreover, there are numerous cases which have cemented the widened comprehension of blackmail. See, e.g., *Thorne v. Motor Trade Ass'n*, 1937 A.C. 797, 817, where Lord Wright states, "I think the word 'menace' is to be liberally construed and not as limited to threats of violence but as including threats of any action detrimental to or unpleasant to the person addressed. Stated Lord Atkin in this case:

> If the matter came to us for decision for the first time I think there would be something to be said for a construction of "menace" which connoted threats of violence and injury to person or property, and a contrast might be made between "menaces" and "threats" as used in other sections of the various statutes. But in several cases it has been decided that "menace" in this subsection and its predecessors is simply equivalent to threat.

Id. at 806.

See also Rex v. Boyle & Merchant, [1914] 3 K.B. 339, 343, where Lord Reading, C.J., stated: "We do not think that the meaning of the word 'menaces' in the section is so restricted. Whatever may have been the view in earlier days under the older statutes and decisions a wider meaning has been given to the word by later decisions."

[14] (1895) 1 Q.B. 706.

[15] *See* Winder, *supra* note 1, at 37–38 ("[I]t was not until *R. v. Tomlinson* in 1895 that there was indisputable authority for interpreting 'menaces' in a wide sense.").

conduct not amounting to a crime, and that it is not confined to a threat of injury to the person or property of the person threatened.[16]

This history supports the conclusion, on the one hand, that while the traditional, limited concept of blackmail is indeed criminal behavior, deserving the full punishment of law, the additional behavior proscribed by the modern, extended concept of blackmail is generally legitimate and non-criminal and should be legalized, however immoral it may be.[17] As the modern conception of blackmail prohibits both threats of violence as well as other threats, we cannot wholly condemn it.

The difficulty is that there is now no single word which describes only the original narrow concept of blackmail (a threat of criminal conduct) and no single word to describe what has been added to this concept (a threat, which does not itself violate rights). Blackmail and extortion are used synonymously to describe the wider, modern concept of blackmail (threat for money which either violates rights or does not).

There is always a risk in offering a stipulative definition. "The world will little note, nor long remember," such efforts. Nevertheless, in this confused situation, this is the path we have chosen. We shall use the term "extortion" to refer only to a demand for money made on the basis of a threat of physical violence or other clearly criminal behavior.[18] We shall reserve the appellation

---

[16] (1895) 1 Q.B. at 708–09.

[17] *See, e.g., State v, Stockford*, 77 Conn. 227, 58 A. 769 (1904) (Any words or acts calculated and intended to cause an ordinary person to fear injury to his person, business, or property are sufficient to constitute a punishable threat.); *Rex v. Pacholko*, (1941) 2 D.L.R. 444 (Saskatchewan Court of Appeal found that any threat of injury to character is equivalent to blackmail.); *Rex v. Robinson*, 168 Eng. Rep. 475 (Ch. 1796) (defendant demanded property, threatening to accuse a man of murder).

[18] For a discussion of the history of blackmail, *see In re Sherin*, 27 S.D. 232, 130 N.W. 761 (1911) (Extortion is derived from the Latin word "extortus," which means to twist or wrench out.).

"blackmail" for those threats which, in the absence of a demand for money, would be considered legal.[19]

There is a vitally important distinction to be drawn between those who threaten violence to persons or property in order to obtain money from other people, and those who only threaten to exercise their legitimate prerogatives unless such funds are forthcoming.[20] This distinction can and must be drawn.

Now it may be that both blackmail (threatening to exercise one's own rights) and extortion (threatening to violate the rights of other people) are, or should be, criminal acts. If so, this conclusion should be based on analysis, not assumptions, or mere definition.[21] By distinguishing "blackmail" and "extortion," we are at least in a position to argue that one is legitimate, the other not.

---

[19] According to the Model Penal Code adopted by the American Law Institute:

A person is guilty of theft [by extortion] if he obtains the property of another by threatening to:

(a) inflict bodily injury on anyone or commit any other criminal offense; or

(b) accuse anyone of a criminal offense; or

(c) expose any secret tending to subject any person to hatred, contempt or ridicule, or to impair his credit or business repute; or

(d) take or withhold action as an official, or cause an official to take or withhold action; or

(e) bring about or continue a strike, boycott, or other collective unofficial action, if the property is not demanded or received for the benefit of the group in whose interest the actor purports to act; or

(f) testify or provide information or withhold testimony or information with respect to another's legal claim or defense; or

(g) inflict any other harm, which would not benefit the actor.

MODEL PENAL CODE 223.4 (Proposed Official Draft 1962).

Based on our definitions, and subject to the considerations as discussed below, only (a) is extortionate. The remainder should be considered merely blackmail.

[20] *See* MURRAY ROTHBARD, MAN, ECONOMY, AND STATE 443 (1962) ("*[B]lackmail* would not be illegal in the free society. For blackmail is the receipt of money in exchange for the service of not publicizing certain information about the other person. No violence or threat of violence to person or property is involved.") (Emphasis original). *See also* WALTER BLOCK, DEFENDING THE UNDEFENDABLE 53–58 (1976).

[21] *See* Harry Hibschman, *Can "Legal Blackmail" Be Legally Outlawed?*, 69 U.S.L. REV. 474 (1935). The editors of this article note, "The phrase 'Legal Blackmail' … involves … a contradiction of terms." *Id.* at 474 ed. note.

III. CAN ONE THREATEN WHAT ONE HAS A RIGHT TO DO?

An overwhelming majority of courts and commentators agree that a threat to disclose embarrassing information if money is not paid can be illegal even though the disclosure itself would not be.[22] There is, however, limited support for the view that blackmail as we have defined it, should be legalized. Lord Justice Romer in *Hardie & Lane v. Chilton* [23] expressed this view:

> I cannot find that the defendants have done anything of which complaint can be made in a Court, whether of civil or criminal jurisdiction. In my opinion the evidence shows at the most no more than that the defendants in good faith proposed and agreed to abstain from doing something that they could lawfully do, on the

---

[22] For a general discussion of this point, *see* Williams, *supra* note 13, at 162–63; Williams, *supra* note 1, at 129–30.

[23] (1928) 2 K.B. 306.

condition that the plaintiffs made a payment that they could lawfully make.[24]

This minority position derives additional support from Professor Livermore, who claims, "that one may threaten to do what one is legally entitled to do to enforce that claim."[25] And again, the obverse: "There is no sound reason to allow lawyers to threaten what is legally unavailable to them to influence actions of others."[26] If lawyers are to be prohibited from threatening that which they cannot do, then the presumption is that they should be allowed to threaten that which they can legally do.[27]

So we have two schools of thought as to whether blackmail should be illegal. The overwhelming majority of the profession holds that it should be. Under this view, two rights can make a wrong. This conclusion is troubling. First, it would appear that the burden of proof should be on the side that is making

---

[24] *Id.* at 335–36.

As one commentator on *Hardie & Lane* has written:

In the present case the threat involved no legal injury to (the trader). There was nothing contrary to public policy in expelling him or abstaining from so doing on condition that he paid a sum of money. But the fact that a thing perfectly legal in itself is not consistent with legal views of morality or public policy is often the dominating factor, which causes a transaction to be found illegal. The (association) merely proposed and agreed to abstain from doing something that they could lawfully do, on condition that (the trader) made a payment which he could lawfully make, and there was no illegality in making the payment the consideration for the abstention. Nor was the letter in this case a demand with menaces without reasonable and probable cause, within the meaning of sec. 29(1), though I rest my judgment on the surer ground that it was not uttered without reasonable and probable cause.

The real principle, in my view, may be expressed thus: Anyone who, without contravening morality or public policy, offers and agrees to receive, as an alternative to an act, which he may lawfully perform, money which the other party may lawfully agree to pay as a consideration for such forbearance, is not guilty of a criminal offence.

Lecture, *Blackmail and Innocent Pressure: Interesting Middle Temple Moot*, 73 LAW J. 224, 225 (1932).

[25] Livermore, *supra* note 13, at 406.

[26] *Id.* at 409.

[27] *Id.* at 411 (A "lawyer would, of course, remain free to threaten legal action which is available to his client.").

a counter-intuitive claim. And there can be hardly anything more counter-intuitive than the claim that two rights can make a wrong. And yet the majority opinion does not explain how this can be so.

Second, given that the action is legal, then it can be legally implemented without recourse. That is, the would-be blackmailer can avoid the legal proscription by actually revealing the secret or embarrassment—so long as he does not ask for money for his silence. But if he does implement the threat without first offering his silence in return for payment, the blackmail victim may be far worse off as a result of the criminalization of this act. If blackmail were legalized, the victim would have the option of paying money in order to avoid what for him would be a worse fate, the publication of his secret.[28] With blackmail illegal, the victim's welfare is paradoxically diminished.[29]

Two influential cases involved the question of a cartel's right to discipline a violator of price fixing arrangements, and to fine the chiseling firm in lieu of expelling or boycotting it. In *Hardie & Lane v, Chilton*,[30] decided in 1928, the court held that the trade association did not breach the law by threatening to publicize a member's misconduct.[31]

Seven years later in *Thorne v. Motor Trade Association*,[32] a price-fixing violator was offered the option of paying a fine as an alternative to being boycotted (stop-listed) by the cartel. The House of Lords held that since the trade

---

[28] For a ringing affirmation of this principle, *see* Rothbard, *supra* note 7, at 121–27. *See also* Block, *supra* note 20, at 53–54.

[29] See Livermore, *supra* note 13, at 406:

Anomalously, it would be permissible to destroy reputation by bringing suit but not to allow the defendant to avoid that destruction by paying the claim. Not only would this mean a net loss to the privacy that the extortion status is, in part, aimed at protecting, but it would also involve significantly expanded litigation costs and burdens on efficient utilization of judicial resources.

[30] (1928) 2 KB. 306.

[31] A commentator on *Hardie & Lane* analyzed the courts reasoning and wrote:

[W]here a trade association was entitled by its constitution to put on a stop list the name of a person who had infringed its rule forbidding the sale of articles at other than the fixed prices, the association might, instead, lawfully adopt the more lenient course of asking the person to make a payment of money by way of compromise, and such money could be accepted and was not recoverable as if paid under duress.

Blackmail and innocent Pressure, supra note 24, at 225.

[32] 1937 A.C. 797.

association had a right to place the violator on the stop list, it also had a right to demand a money payment as an alternative. Stated Lord Atkin:

> It appears to me that if a man may lawfully, in the furtherance of business interests, do acts which will seriously injure another in his business he may also lawfully, if he is still acting in the furtherance of his business interests, offer that other to accept a sum of money as an alternative to doing the injurious acts. He must no doubt be acting not for the mere purpose of putting money in his pocket, but for some legitimate purpose other than the mere acquisition of money.[33]

In addition, Lords Wright and Roche held that were the fine too high, or "unreasonable," then the Motor Trade Association would have been guilty of extortion.[34]

The Thorne case may thus be interpreted as giving support to our contention that blackmail ought to be legalized. After all, the accused blackmailer, the secretary of the MTA, was found innocent. But Thorne furnishes only the weakest support for this position. The requirement that the fine be "reasonable" is a significant limitation on the blackmailer's ability to charge a market price for his services.[35] In addition, the defendant was held not guilty only because the MTA was deemed to have been acting "for some legitimate [business] purpose other than the mere acquisition of money." This, too, restricts the conduct of blackmailers. As well, it is nonsensical, for the major purpose of business is the "mere acquisition" of money. Certainly the MTAs objection to the price-cutter stemmed from its fear that such a practice would reduce the money that could be otherwise acquired. Not much furthers business interests apart from the acquisition of money.[36]

Let us consider one last version of this majority view before closing this section. In Campbell's view:

---

[33] *Id.* at 807.

[34] *Id.* at 817–18, 824.

[35] Williams, *supra* note 13, at 171 ("[It] appears to be somewhat anomalous, for in no other instance of an absolutely justifiable threat is there authority for saying that the matter is affected by the amount asked as the price for abstaining from carrying out the threat.")

[36] To the extent that the businessman acts in any other way, for example by renting a more plush office than strict considerations for bottom line, profit maximizing would require, to that degree he is acting as a consumer, not a businessman.

> If X and Y are rival candidates for an appointment and X offers to withdraw his name if Y pays him money, doubtless X is offering to surrender a material advantage, which he might legitimately enjoy. But if X threatens to reveal some secret failing of Y's to the appointing board unless Y pays him money, is X not a blackmailer? Yet he had the right to reveal Y's secret to the board, and if the revelation resulted in the rejection of Y and the appointment of X this would be a furthering of X's legitimate material interests and might even be in the public interest. *The real point is not whether X had an interest, which he could legitimately enjoy but whether he had an interest, which he could legitimately surrender, or offer to surrender, in return for money.* There may well be interests, which a man can legitimately enjoy himself, and rights and liberties which he can legitimately exercise in furtherance of these interests, but which he cannot legitimately transfer to another, e.g. his interest in and right to the consortium of his wife and there may well be interests and rights and liberties which he can enjoy and exercise himself, but which he cannot legitimately covenant not to enjoy or exercise, e.g. he has an interest in pursuing his trade and a liberty to pursue his trade or not as he pleases, but he cannot validly covenant, save within certain limits, to refrain from pursuing his trade. *And in most cases of blackmail we are dealing with interests, which may be legitimately enjoyed and liberties, which may be legitimately exercised but whose surrender, or attempted surrender, for money is not only void but is a crime. The question we have to answer is not: Had the accused an interest, which he could legitimately enjoy, but: Had the accused an interest which he could legitimately surrender for money?* [37]

This statement is based on the premise that one can own or enjoy a right but cannot sell or transfer it. The argument stands or falls with this questionable premise. Campbell, unfortunately, provides no reasons or justification for this basic assumption. He merely asserts it.

The one example he vouchsafes us: that a man cannot legitimately transfer interest in and rights to the consortium of his wife[38] does not prove Campbell's basic premise. The issue in the debate over blackmail is not whether the right to disclose information can be transferred to another, but rather whether one can seek money in exchange for not exercising the right.

---

[37] Campbell, *supra* note 6, at 388–89 (emphasis added).

[38] *Id.* at 389.

Thus in the context of marital rights, the question is not whether the right to consortium can be transferred to another, but rather whether one can take money in exchange for not exercising the right. The question is unresolved to our knowledge.

At least the example of the consortium of the wife had a certain shock value. But what are we to make of the assertion that a person "has an interest in pursuing his trade and a liberty interest to pursue his trade or not, as he pleases, but he cannot validly covenant, save with certain limits, to refrain from pursuing his trade?" If a person really has a right to pursue his trade, why can he not accept a payment not to pursue it?

IV. BLACKMAIL CASES

Having outlined the rudiments of the case in favor of legalizing blackmail, one may apply this analysis to a series of cases to contrast this position with the more orthodox one on this subject.

A. Victim Approaches Blackmailer

Let us first consider several cases where it is not the blackmailer who approaches the "victim," but rather the "victim" who approaches the blackmailer.[39] In these cases, the victims clearly prefer to pay money rather than have their "blackmailers" exercise some legal right. In *People v. Dioguardi*[40] a stationery business was struck by four unions in an attempt to organize the employees. The labor pickets made it impossible for the firm to conduct business. The owner approached McNamara, a teamster official, and offered him money to end the labor troubles. McNamara agreed, making a proposi-

---

[39] See Rothbard, *supra* note 7, at 125, where Rothbard raises this point in opposition to the outlawry of a blackmail contract:

> Suppose that ... instead of Smith going to Jones with an offer of silence, Jones had heard of Smith's knowledge and his intent to print it, and went to Smith to offer to purchase the latter's silence? Should that contract be illegal? And if so, why? But if Jones' offer should be legal while Smith's is illegal, should it be illegal for Smith to turn down Jones' offer, and then ask for more money as the price of his silence?

See also Herbert J. Stern, *Prosecutions of Local Political Corruption Under the Hobbs Act: The Unnecessary Distinction Between Bribery and Extortion*, 3 SETON HALL L. REV. 1, 7 (1971) (concerning businessman (victim) who "himself makes the solicitation").

[40] 8 N.Y.2d 260, 168 N.E.2d 683, 203 N.Y.S.2d 870 (1960).

tion for payment. After he and his codefendant Dioguardi were paid off, the pickets vanished and labor peace ensued.[41]

As a result, McNamara and Dioguardi were indicted, tried and convicted of extortion under a then current New York statute which defined extortion as the "obtaining the property of a corporation from an officer ... thereof, with his consent, induced by a wrongful use of ... fear."[42] The defendants argued that their behavior did not constitute a threat to do an unlawful injury because if their proposition had been rejected they would have done absolutely nothing. In the view of a student commentator: "Clearly, defendants failed to consider § 858 of the Penal Law which expressly brings a threat 'not to do something' within the scope of extortion."[43] The commentator further stated:

> Might not any refusal to act unless paid (as with doctors, lawyers and plumbers) in response to a request for help be extortion? A doctor or lawyer says simply 'I will not remove your troubles unless I am paid.' There is no implication of power to continue the victim's troubles and the victim knows it. But when a labor official says, 'I will not remove the pickets unless I am paid,' a logical inference arises (which in the instant case was encouraged by the defendant) that he has the power to maintain the picket—the very thing the victim fears. The two situations are distinguished by the presence in the latter of power and a threat, express or implied, to use it wrongfully. Therein lies the wrongful use which turns an otherwise lawful act into extortion.[44]

But this analysis overlooks the fact that the union pickets were entirely legal. It is of course true that the doctor or lawyer was not the cause of the victim's troubles in the first place, and has not the power to continue them. It is also true that the union officials were the cause of the victim's difficulties in the first place, and can cause them to continue, merely by refraining from any further activity. Yet their conduct during the labor dispute was within their

---

[41] *Id.* at 266–67, 168 N.E.2d at 687–88, 203 N.Y.S.2d at 875–76. For a discussion of this case, see Decision, *Criminal Law-Extortion-Defendant Need Not Initiate the Fear*, 27 BROOKLYN L. REV. 346, 346–51 (1961).

[42] 8 N.Y.2d at 275, 168 N.E.2d at 693, 203 N.Y.S.2d at 883 (quoting N.Y. PENAL LAW § 850).

[43] *Criminal Law-Extortion*, *supra* note 41, at 349.

[44] *Id.* at 349 fn.13.

powers under the various United States labor laws and their power to continue these labor problems merely by doing nothing was also lawful.[45]

Suppose that the unionists, when approached by the businessmen, had recoiled in horror from any suggestion that they relinquish their lawful picketing in return for anything so gross as money. Suppose, that is, they had realized that by falling in with the businessman's suggestion, they would be themselves subject to charges of extortion. Under these conditions, would the position of the unionists have been illegal? Certainly not! They would have been completely within their rights to continue the picketing activities permitted them by law. Would the businessman have been better or worse off? To ask this question is to answer it. Obviously, the businessman would have been worse off, how else to explain the fact that he approached the unionists, and agreed to pay for labor peace? How can this power of the unionist be used "wrongfully," if, as a result of its use, the supposed victim of extortion is made better off?

In the arena of labor relations, threats to engage in legal protest are either forbidden outright or at the very least highly suspect. We have found only two English blackmail cases where labor threats were found to be unequivocally legitimate. In *Hardie & Lane v. Chilton*,[46] it was stated in dicta that a cook may ask for a rise in wages in exchange for not giving notice of termination. And as Lord Wright stated in *Thorne v. Motor Trade Association*: "[A] valued servant may threaten to go to other employment unless he is paid a bonus or increased wages.[47]

It is not possible to reconcile these two statements with the findings of extortion in *Dioguardi*.[48] The cook or the "valued servant" who threatens to leave for greener pastures does no more wrong than do the picketing unionists. If the unionists have the right to strike, but not to surrender this right for money, why should the cook or servant with a right to quit be able to surrender it for money? Suppose the cook's employer approaches her and asks that she return to his employ for money considerations. If she agrees, logic demands that she too be considered an extortionist. Of course, the quitting cook and striking union engage in vastly different behavior. But the point is that both their activities should be lawful.

---

[45] It may be true that the power given them by the labor legislation is improper, but that is beyond the scope of this article.

[46] (1928) 2 K.B. 306.

[47] 1937 A.C. 797, 820.

[48] *Id.*

B. Victimless Crimes

We now turn to a consideration of several extortion cases, which fall under the rubric of victimless crimes. The first grouping to be considered features a demand for money on the part of the accused blackmailer, and a threat to expose the "victim" of a contravention of heterosexual mores. Charges of blackmail have been made for threats to reveal a brothel visit,[49] a clergyman's sexual activities,[50] a husband's infidelity,[51] and threats to make a criminal complaint for allegedly indecent assault.[52]

The general analysis used by the courts in these cases focused not on the question of whether accused had threatened some illegal conduct but rather on the question of whether he or she was entitled in law to the money demanded or at least that were thought so in good faith.[53] This approach misses the important issues that were raised in these cases. The model developed in this paper presents a quite different view. Under this model, it is immaterial what the accused demanded, let alone whether the accused felt justified in making this demand. The only issue is whether the threatened conduct was legal.

"[T]he threat is to do an act that is itself lawful. Nor is there any wrong merely in demanding payment of a sum of money. A man is at perfect liberty to importune a gift. The demand made is therefore lawful in itself."[54] Two legal rights do not make a legal wrong. The accused in all these cases are indeed guilty of blackmail, which should not be criminal. They are innocent of extortion, which should alone be a crime.

---

[49] *See, e.g., Regina v. Hamilton*, 174 Eng. Rep. 779 (N.P. 1843) (threats to tell father, brothers, friends and newspaper that woman visited the brothels).

[50] *See, e.g., The Queen v. Miard*, 1 Cox C.C. 22 (Midland Cir. 1844) (threats to tell the Archbishop of Canterbury, other bishops, and the newspapers of clergyman's sexual indiscretions).

[51] *See, e.g., Rex v. Tomlinson*, (1895) 1 Q.B. 706 (threats to tell wife and friends); *Rex v. Bernhard*, (1938) 2 K.B. 264 (threats to tell wife and newspaper).

[52] *See, e.g., Rex v. Dymond* (1920) 2 K.B. 260 (threats to bring charges against a mayor for allegedly placing his hands up a woman's clothes in a public park).

[53] *See, e.g., Miard*, 1 Cox C.C. at 24 (jury instructed to determine whether the demand "was made at a time when the party making it really and honestly believed that she had good and probable cause for so doing"); *Dymond*, (1925) 2 K.B. at 265 ("It is for the jury to decide whether there was reasonable or probable cause for making the demand and it is not for them to decide whether the accused believed that she had reasonable or probable cause for making it.").

[54] *Dymond*, (1925) 2 KB. 260.

The analysis should be the same for cases related to threats concerning homosexuality and other allegedly deviant acts. Because of the social ramifications of charges of such behavior, the cases have generally held that threats of this type are illegal when in conjunction with demands for money.[55]

The decisions in these homosexual cases are flawed in the same way as the previous cases. Is it or is it not lawful to actually accuse someone of sodomy and other "unnatural" practices? It is lawful. If so, there is no crime, for, as we have seen, there is no reason to reject the view that what may be legally threatened also may legally be kept silent—for a fee.[56] Certainly, the victim is better off by having this option. With blackmail, he has a choice: to allow his secret to be told, or to pay up, and be spared the embarrassment.

The orthodox theory, upon which these cases are based, comes in for some sharp criticism. In the view of Professor C. R. Williams, relying on the belief of the perpetrator in the rightness of his act is entirely subjective in nature:

> The adoption of a wholly subjective test, making the accused's criminality depend upon his own view of the propriety of his actions, is a surprising departure from the approach taken in others contained in the Crimes (Theft) Act. It is a requirement of offences such as theft, obtaining property by deception and robbery that the accused be shown to have acted 'dishonestly.' The standard to be taken for determining what constitutes dishonesty is objective. Whether the accused has acted dishonestly is a question to be determined by the jury, applying 'the current standards of ordinary decent people.' Thus a modern Robin Hood who asserted quite sincerely that he believed he was acting honestly in robbing from the rich to give to the poor would have no defense to a charge of theft or of robbery. This is because 'ordinary decent people' do not believe it to be honest to rob from the rich to give to the poor. However, if Robin were to be charged with blackmail, it would seem that his beliefs would give him a defense. The subjective nature of the test is well illustrated by the case of *R. v. Lambert*. ...

---

[55] For a review of early cases finding such threats to be sufficient basis for conviction, *see* Winder, *supra* note 1, at 26.

[56] *See* Williams, *supra* note 5, at 80. *But see* Hogan, *Blackmail: Another View*, 1966 CRIM. L. REV. 474, 474 ("[A] demand against a threat to expose ... sexual deviance [is] every bit as bad as a demand against a threat to do bodily harm.").

The acquittal of the accused in *R. v. Lambert* because he subjectively believed he was entitled to demand money in such circumstances seems surprising and unsatisfactory. More extreme examples can easily be imagined. We live in times when members of terrorist organizations often act in the name of some higher morality, which they assert, quite sincerely, justifies both their aims and any methods they choose to adopt to achieve those aims. If such people were to engage in activities, which would, viewed objectively, be said to constitute blackmail, could their own beliefs, however, extreme, afford them a defense? One commentator has described the view that they could as 'scarcely conceivable,' yet such a result seems to follow with remorseless logic from the wording of the section. In his book, The Law of Theft, Professor J. C. Smith has suggested that such a result may be avoided by saying that a person can only believe he has reasonable grounds for making a demand when he believes that reasonable men would regard the grounds as reasonable. However attractive on policy grounds such a view may be, it is submitted that the words of the section are clear, and no objective requirement can be spelt out of them.[57]

The final sets of cases that can be grouped under the rubric of victimless crimes involve demands for the repayment of debts arising out of gambling. And here, there is happily almost a unanimous belief in the proposition that one may threaten public posting, or other such negative publicity, in order to recover a gambling debt—without being held guilty of extortion."[58]

Any time the law treats demands accompanied by menaces and threats as non-criminal, that is an advance for the cause of liberty. But it will not do to make too much of this rare unanimity in celebration of the rights of free speech. These cases are only very limited support for the concept of legal blackmail. A welter of restrictions hems in the would-be blackmailer: This threat must arise out of a "legitimate business interest" and might well not apply to "a casual bet made between two private persons."[59] No more than the amount actually owed may be demanded and he cannot make any threats other than posting. The blackmailer can only enforce debts owed to himself,

---

[57] *See* Williams, *supra* note 1, at 142–43. *See also* Bernard Mackenna, *The Theft Bill-II, Blackmail: A Criticism*, 1966 CRIM. L. REV. 467, 468–69.

[58] *See generally* Campbell, *supra* note 6, at 388–96; Williams, *supra* note 1, at 129–30.

[59] *See* Campbell, *supra* note 6, at 394–95.

which arise out of a "merely void and not illegal transaction."[60] All in all, this is hardly a stirring victory for the forces of reason and justice to blackmailers.

C. Accusations of Real Crimes

We now turn to blackmail attempts in which the "victim" is threatened with a charge of criminal behavior. This is serious business because if the threat is carried out, the "victim" faces a potential term in prison, in some cases for many years. But there is no difference in principle between being threatened with exposure as a real criminal, and as a perpetrator of a victimless "crime."

Acts such as sodomy carried stiff penalties, at least in bygone eras. And in the modern day, drug-related criminals can receive large fines and lengthy jail sentences.

Threatening to accuse someone of a crime is considered legitimate on all sides. We are analyzing rather the propriety of refraining from accusing someone of a crime for a fee. And this is an entirely different matter. It is certainly legal to threaten to accuse someone of a crime, provided it is not motivated by being paid off for one's silence. If the accused is actually guilty, then the accuser is considered a public benefactor, not an extortionist. But if the threat is made in order to elicit a payment from the guilty party, then the preponderance of legal opinion is that the accuser is indeed guilty of extortion.

There is also some legal precedent and support for the view that one may threaten to prosecute for a crime, and offer the "victim" the option of paying him off for withdrawing without being considered guilty of menacing (extortion).[61] Most commentators have drawn a sharp distinction between the threat of a civil and a criminal suit. Although the mainstream opposition to the threat of criminal prosecution is very strong, most commentators advocate the legitimacy of a threat of civil suit for recovery of owed money.[62]

In our view, this distinction should have no legal relevance whatsoever. Since it is entirely legitimate to bring suit in civil court or to assist in the prosecution of a crime, it ought to be legal to threaten to do so. And if this

---

[60] *Id.* at 393

[61] *See, e.g., State v. Burns*, 161 Wash. 362, 297 P. 212 (1931) (demand can not exceed the amount actually owed).

[62] *See* Winder, *supra* note 1, at 31 ("It was held to be no offence at common law to obtain money by means of a threat to bring a penal action and the ratio decidendi would apply also to a threat to prosecute for any crime.").

were so, it ought to be lawful to offer the "victim" the option of payment for the dropping of a suit of either type.[63]

Moreover, one cannot overlook the indirect effect of the blackmailer in reducing crimes.[64] Not that it was ever necessarily any part of the intention of the blackmailer to play so public-spirited a role. But as Adam Smith concluded, it is "not from benevolence" that many economic actors accomplish beneficial, but unintended goals. And so it is with the blackmailer.

How does this work? Consider the following example: A writes to B saying, "Pay me $100 or I will tell the police I saw you shoplifting." Assuming A saw B shoplifting he is not only legally entitled to inform the police, but he has a moral duty to do so. Nonetheless, A commits an offense because although the action threatened is justifiable the demand as an alternative to it is not.[65]

Let us assume that the effect, at least marginally, of declaring A's blackmailing behavior criminal will be that he is less likely to engage in it. If so, there will be less pressure placed upon the real criminal, B, the shoplifter. A has two motives for opposing B: financial considerations (the blackmail) and public spiritedness (turning B over to the police purely for the emotional satisfaction of stopping crime). If blackmail were illegal, A might act against B out of public spiritedness, but presumably he would not blackmail B. If blackmail were legalized, however, there will arguably be more pressure placed upon the real criminal. While it is true that some of the formerly public-spirited might lose their sense of civic responsibility, and take up the profession of blackmail, this too would tend to reduce the activity of real criminals. It might be less effective in that the blackmailer might offer the

---

[63] See Williams, *supra* note 1, at 128:

> [T]he effect upon the recipient [of a threat of civil suit] would be much the same as a threat of criminal proceedings. In such a case what the victim generally fears most is public exposure of his improper conduct, and such exposure takes place equally in civil as in criminal proceedings.

See also Williams, supra note 13, at 166:

> It may also be pointed out that the distinction between threatening civil proceedings (which is allowable) and threatening criminal proceedings (which is not) is somewhat artificial when what the victim most dreads is exposure. Exposure follows as much from the bringing of civil proceedings as from the launching of a criminal prosecution.

[64] For the argument that blackmailers indirectly benefit society, *see* Kurt H. Nadelmann, *The Newspaper Privilege and Extortion by Abuse of Legal Process*, 54 COLUM. L. REV. 359, 360–61 (1962).

[65] Williams, , *supra* note 1, at 127.

criminal a "lighter-sentence," i.e., an option preferable to incarceration. On the other hand it might be more effective in crime prevention if the blackmailers are more efficient at ferreting out such crimes.

The point is that blackmailer is like a parasite on the criminal. In this case A preys on B, and the more he does so, the less shoplifting and other such crime there will be. The law of economic incentive applies to shoplifters as well as blackmailers.

V. CONCLUSION

Let nothing said above be interpreted as affirming the propriety or morality of blackmail.[66] This practice has not been claimed to be ethical. The thesis of this article is merely that blackmail is not akin to theft, not an invasive act, nor threat thereof, nor an initiation of violence, nor a violation of rights—and that therefore it should not be prohibited through force of law.

Our present blackmail statutes do not protect the persons or property of the so-called victims of blackmail. Society would be better off, and human rights more secure, if our blackmail legislation were terminated.

---

[66] See Rothbard, *supra* note 7, at 127:

> When I first [articulated a] right to blackmail ... I was met with a storm of abuse by critics who apparently believed that I was advocating the morality of blackmail. Again—a failure to make the crucial distinction between the legitimacy of a right and the morality or esthetics of exercising that right!

Part II.
Critiques of the U.Penn. Symposium

Chapter 2.

A Libertarian Theory of Blackmail: Reply to Leo Katz

This chapter will attempt to analyze the law prohibiting blackmail from a libertarian perspective. Libertarianism is a political philosophy; as such, it is a theory of the just use of violence. From this viewpoint, the just use of violence is only defensive: one may employ force only to repel an invasion—only to protect one's person and his property from external threat—and for no other reason.

According to Rothbard:

> The libertarian creed rests upon one central axiom: that no man or group of men may aggress against the person or property of anyone else. This may be called the 'nonaggression axiom.' 'Aggression' is defined as the initiation of the use or threat of physical violence against the person or property of anyone else. Aggression is therefore synonymous with invasion.'

> If no man may aggress against another; if, in short, everyone has the absolute right to be 'free' from aggression, then this at once implies that the libertarian stands foursquare for what are generally known as 'civil liberties': the freedom to speak, publish, assemble, and to engage in ... 'victimless crimes.[1]

At the outset it may be claimed for this philosophy that it falls well within American legal and cultural traditions. Who, after all, advocates the initiation of coercion against innocent people? Thus the presumption is that if a law incarcerates people who have neither initiated nor threatened violence, it is out of synchronization with our legal mores.

The central question of this paper, then, is whether blackmail constitutes an invasive act or threat, and should be prohibited under the libertarian axiom, or not, and should thus be legalized. My thesis is that the latter is correct: blackmail to be sure embodies a threat but it is only to do that which one has a right to do. For example, I demand money from you as the price of refraining from gossiping about your penchant for rubber duckies in your bathtub. If

---

[1] MURRAY N. ROTHBARD, FOR A NEW LIBERTY 23 (1978); *see also* HANS-HERMANN HOPPE, A THEORY OF SOCIALISM AND CAPITALISM: ECONOMICS, POLITICS AND ETHICS (1989).

your secret got out, it would prove embarrassing to you, but I have a free speech right to be a gossip.

States Rothbard: "*[B]lackmail* would not be illegal in the free society. For blackmail is the receipt of money in exchange for the service of not publicizing certain information about the other person. No violence or threat of violence to person or property is involved."[2]

In sharp contrast is extortion, which superficially resembles blackmail. In both cases, a threat is made, coupled with a demand (usually for money, but it might include sexual or other services, etc.) But in the former case, as we have seen, the threat is to do something licit, e.g., indulge in free speech. In the latter, the threat is anything but legal. For example, I might threaten to kill you, or kidnap your children, or firebomb your house, unless you give me some valuable consideration.

With this introduction, let us consider Katz[3] who maintains that blackmail ought to be legally proscribed. His reasoning furnishes an illuminating contrast with that of libertarianism.

I. CASES AND MATERIALS

Katz starts off by considering the case of Busybody threatening to tell Philanderer's wife about the latter's affairs, unless he is paid $10,000. He acknowledges that

> if Busybody had actually revealed Philanderer's affairs, or if he had threatened Philanderer with doing so but not mentioned the money, or if he had asked for the money but not mentioned what he was going to do if he didn't get it—if he had done any of these things, he would not be guilty of any crime whatsoever. Yet when he combines these various actions, a crime results—blackmail.[4]

Katz asks why this should be so, but before he answers, he attempts to eliminate a wrong answer: the thought that "blackmail is essentially a crime of

---

[2] MURRAY N. ROTHBARD, MAN, ECONOMY, AND STATE 443 (1993).

[3] Leo Katz, *Blackmail and Other Forms of Arm-Twisting*, 141 U. PA. L. REV. 1567, 1567–1615 (1993).

This article is part of a compilation of no fewer than 13 pieces, all of them united in the supposition that blackmail should be against the law. Not a one of the authors represented here is representative of the libertarian position on the matter.

[4] *Id.*

information, that it invariably involves the threat to disclose an embarrassing fact about the victim."[5]

In this, Katz is absolutely correct. Blackmail involves *any* licit threat, coupled with a demand for money. For example, I may be considering selling a car, and you buying it from me, whereupon I declaim, "If you don't give me $10,000 (demand for money), I won't give you this car (threat)."[6] But this is no more than the "threat" made during every business transaction; and, as every commercial arrangement also calls for some sort of payment, we have a delicious reductio ad absurdum in the making: all exchange is really blackmail, and should be prohibited, at least by those, such as Katz, who advocate the outlawry of this practice.

Now consider a series of cases offered by our author as instances of blackmail. They involve no informational aspects, but he sees them as illicit. What are they, and how would a libertarian react to each?

1. "Pay me $10,000, or I'll call on my men to strike." This is extortion, not blackmail, because that which is being threatened is itself illegitimate. Here, we assume that the union leader is only authorized to promote a strike when it is in the best interests of the rank and file that he do so, not in order to feather his own nest. This being the case, his demand for $10,000 passes from legitimate blackmail to illegitimate extortion.[7]

2. "Pay me $10,000, or I'll flunk you on the exam." This too is extortion, since the threat is an improper one. Here, the contractual violation, like that between the union leader and its members, concerns the professor and the university's board of trustees. Presumably, the faculty member was hired, among other things, to award grades on the basis of student learning as measured by exams, not for the purpose of enriching himself in this manner.[8]

---

[5] *Id.*

[6] Katz explicitly acknowledges this statement, but refuses to call it blackmail. *Id.* at 1603.

[7] Rothbard, *supra* note 2, at 129–30 analyzes a similar case in terms of bribery and payola. In his view, the corrupt union leader of Katz's, e.g., the bribee, but not the corporate victim or who is forced to become the briber, would be guilty of illegal behavior; this would be due to contract violation with the members of the labor organization. In the present paper we characterize such behavior as extortion, but this term is inclusive of all illicit threats, such as that which occurs in Rothbard's bribery case.

[8] On the other hand, under the libertarian legal code it would be perfectly legal for a university to pay low salaries, with the explicit understanding that professors could enhance their incomes by selling grades for money. As long as the students were made aware of this rather unique system, no fraud would have been perpetrated upon them. As a practical matter, of course, this scheme would not likely succeed, but that is a very different issue.

3. "Pay me $10,000, or I'll cause some really bad blood at the next faculty meeting." This is mere blackmail, since the professor has every right to create "bad blood," which we here interpret as saying something nasty about someone.

Katz claims that the next few cases are controversial, indicating he thinks these are not.[9] Yet, as we have seen, there is disagreement on two out of the three cases.

4. "Pay me $10,000, or I will seduce your fiancé." Again we have a case of (legally) innocuous blackmail, not illegitimate extortion. Had the threat been to rape the fiancé, the latter category would apply. But seduction, presumably of an adult woman, amounts to no more than turning on the charm, being nice, buying flowers, etc. Surely this is not against the law, nor should it be. But if not, then to threaten this act should also be considered legal.

5. "Pay me $10,000, or I will persuade your son that it is his patriotic duty to volunteer for combat in Viet Nam." Again, this time on the assumption that your son is an adult (otherwise, he would scarcely be accepted by the military) this is just a matter of threatening to engage in free speech. Unless you are contractually obligated to stay away from the man's son (that is, the father has paid you, and you have agreed to stay away), then your threat, no matter how morally reprehensible (or not), should not be legally proscribed.

6. "Pay me $10,000, or I will give your high-spirited, risk-addicted 19-year-old daughter a motorcycle for Christmas." On the assumption that her age is equal to or past that of legal consent, it would certainly not be an indictable offense to give her the vehicle; how, then, can it offend any rational law to threaten to do that which one has a *right* to do (again, no matter how reprehensible)?

7. "Pay me $10,000, or I will hasten our ailing father's death by leaving the Catholic church." A similar analysis applies. Leaving Catholicism is not and cannot be illegal. Threatening to do so, even from the lowest of motives, therefore, cannot be legally prohibited either.

Yes, Katz is entirely correct in pointing out that "the disclosure of embarrassing facts" is not the central issue, nor is it even necessary that money be demanded.[10] Sexual favors will do quite well to establish blackmail. But apart from that, there is a deep chasm between us.

This author next introduces a series of what he categorizes as "collateral problems."[11] Let us consider them in the order he establishes.

---

[9] Katz, *supra* note 3, at 1567.

[10] *Id.* at 1568.

[11] *Id.* at 1569.

A. Warnings.

Abigail is a very successful competitor of Mildred's for parts in plays. If Mildred threatens Abigail with exposure of her infidelities as a means of eliminating her competition (Variation I) there is no doubt this is blackmail (but not extortion). But suppose Mildred informs (e.g., warns) Abigail that she has sent a letter to her husband, disclosing these peccadilloes, which will be delivered at the time of the audition. Abigail can intercept this mail, but only during the audition. Is this blackmail?

In the libertarian perspective, both are lawful activities, in that neither threatens or uses force. But in the latter example, although Mildred is still trying to attain the same goal, no threat is made, so it does not formally match the conditions of blackmail, as does the first.

B. Omissions

Here, Katz attempts to distance from blackmail the ordinary bargain, or commercial relationship, where the seller threatens to omit giving the buyer the commodity unless he is paid for it.[12] He gives three cases of threatened omissions which are candidates for doing this. I cite them, and give the libertarian response to each:

1. "[T]he potential employer who offers an applicant a secretarial job if she will sleep with him." Here, the threat is that the woman will not get the job unless she succumbs to the boss's advances, e.g., the job will be omitted. But since she has no right to the job in the first place, this is blackmail, not extortion.

Alternatively, this can be looked upon as merely the offer of a dual job, secretary and prostitute.[13] This is akin to offering other dual positions, such as that of cook and bottle washer, or secretary and treasurer, or dean and professor, or handyman (carpenter, plumber, etc.), or groundskeeper (gardener, masonry, etc.) It is a dramatic example only because of the unclear legal status of prostitution, and heightened sensibility about sexual harassment.

2. "[T]he American who offers to marry a foreign heiress, unable to secure citizenship, if in exchange she will fund some of his financial ventures." Here we have the straight offer of a trade, money for a marriage of convenience. The threat is typical in such arrangements: unless you give me what I want, I won't give you what you want. That Katz can mention this in an article

---

[12] *Id.* at 1570.

[13] For the case on behalf of legalizing prostitution (but *not* in favor of this activity *per se*), *see* WALTER BLOCK, DEFENDING THE UNDEFENDABLE (1985).

ostensibly devoted to blackmail further strengthens our contention that there is no legally relevant difference between blackmail and ordinary commercial interaction.

3. "[T]he outgoing governor who offers to endorse his aspiring replacement in exchange for a financial token of gratitude." We have already analyzed a similar case, that of the corrupt[14] union official. As in that instance, the governor is "selling" something that does not belong to him: his endorsement, which is, presumably, supposed to be based on the merits of the competitors, not their willingness to offer a bribe.

C. Manipulative Crimes

States Katz:

> Oscar implores Alonzo not to go on a concert tour of the Soviet Union, in protest against the Afghan war. Alonzo is unrelenting. Oscar threatens to destroy the one and only violin on which the eccentric Alonzo is willing to play, unless he promises not to go. Alonzo just laughs. Eventually, Oscar sets fire to Alonzo's violin, and Alonzo has to cancel his tour. Oscar's acts were not, of course, spurred by the sheer joy of torching Alonzo's violin. No doubt he is guilty of the comparatively minor offense of maliciously destroying someone else's property. But given the purpose of his actions, is he not also guilty of blackmail? After all, had his threat succeeded in dissuading Alonzo from making the trip, he clearly would be guilty of blackmail. How can making good on that threat improve Oscar's moral, and legal, position—especially when it secures for him the very advantage which the threat was originally meant to secure![15]

First, we are focusing solely on legal issues in this paper, not moral ones; we must therefore tread cautiously on that issue. Second, I agree that making good on the threat can scarcely improve Oscar's legal position. Surely, it is of lesser moment to threaten to kill someone than to actually do it. Third, note the difference between Katz and myself on the burning of the musical instrument. Katz characterizes this as "the comparatively minor offense of maliciously destroying someone else's property." I see this as the essence of the

---

[14] For the case that all union officials are necessarily corrupt, *per se, see* Walter Block, *Labor Relations, Unions and Collective Bargaining: A Political Economic Analysis*, 16 J. SOC. POL. AND ECON. STUD. at 477–507 (1991).

[15] Katz, *supra* note 3, at 1571 (footnotes omitted).

piece, the threat which elevates (or, rather, lowers) this whole episode from one of blackmail to downright extortion. I do not see this as "minor" at all. Nor need the punishment, if it is to fit the crime, be limited to the value of the violin. We might also contemplate incorporating the costs of the foregone concert tour.

D. Buybacks

States Katz:

> Anatole steals a Rembrandt from the Metropolitan Museum. He sends a letter to the museum which reads: "Pay me $10,000, or you'll never see that Rembrandt again." The museum buys back its painting for $10,000. Anatole is clearly guilty of theft for taking the Rembrandt. But what about the second transaction? Is it a simple sale (as one German court held) or blackmail? ("Pay me $10,000 or else …" certainly sounds like blackmail.) More generally, is Anatole morally better or worse for not having held on to that painting, but instead having sold it back for a fraction of its market price?[16]

First, it is by no means clear that the museum was the rightful owner. If, as I suspect, it is a government, or state funded museum, that it bought that painting with stolen (e.g., taxed) dollars.[17] This being the case, no crime was committed by relieving the museum of its ill-gotten property.[18] Second, let us stipulate, just for the sake of argument that it was a private, hence, legitimate museum. Anatole, then, is guilty not of blackmail, but of extortion. But what about the second transaction? In order to delete any odor of impermissibility, let us suppose that the writer of that letter ("Pay me $10,000, or no Rembrandt") merely found it. Better yet, let us assume that he, like Ragnar, forcibly took it from Anatole, the thief, with the intention of returning it to its rightful owner. Is he entitled to more than a voluntary reward? ("Here is your painting back, now, please, give me a reward for returning it.") If we borrow a leaf of what international law has to say about finding boats, or retrieving them from pirates, then this letter writer is due a "salvage" payment, typically

---

[16] *Id.* (footnotes omitted).

[17] This statement need not imply that all taxes are theft. But even in the classical liberal vision of limited government, where the state is confined to armies, courts and police, museums are an improper interference with economic liberty. Tax payments to underwrite such expenses would clearly be illegitimate, and hence akin to theft.

[18] *See* the Ragnar Danneskjold episode in AYN RAND, ATLAS SHRUGGED (1957).

one third the value of the recovered ship, and thus far more than $10,000. So Anatole is only guilty, in the first instance, of extortion, but is guiltless for writing that follow up letter.

E. Self-sacrifice

In this section Katz treats us to three (sets of) fascinating legal cases.[19]

First, there are Matilda, Leopold, Genevieve and Ferdinand, who all threaten to kill themselves in various ways or risk death unless someone else does their bidding. They are indeed all engaging in blackmail, and thus should be deemed innocent, since what they threatened (various forms of suicide) they had every right to do. If not true under present law, this is the case at least under the libertarian legal code, since none of the four threatened or invaded other people, only themselves.

Second, there is Angelica, a pedestrian, who wants to reserve a parking space for her friend who is due to arrive imminently. Boniface has his eyes on the same spot. As he tries to drive his car into the empty space, Angelica plants herself squarely in front of him and announces "Over my dead body."

"You're kidding," replies Boniface, "you are threatening to die for the sake of a parking space?"

"Exactly."

"Well, I won't be blackmailed. I'm going to park here anyway."

"You mean you are threatening to run me over with your car unless I move?"

"Exactly."

"Well, I won't be blackmailed. I'm staying."

Thereupon Boniface drives in, and Angelica jumps aside at the last minute.[20]

The problem here is that two different entities (Angelica, Boniface and his car) cannot possibly occupy the same space at the same time. The libertarian solution to all such problems is to determine who is the owner of the property right under dispute, and then to resolve the matter as he wishes.[21] If there were a parking space in a private lot, the resolution would be easy. If the owner says that the first person with a car to arrive there has the parking right, then Angelica, it turns out, had engaged in extortion. (She used force to

---

[19] Katz, *supra* note 3, at 1571–73.

[20] *Id.* at 1572.

[21] This is to leave the market to determine whether the property owner's decision was a wise (profitable) or unwise (unprofitable) one. The libertarian legal code only determines justice, not wealth enhancement, an entirely different matter.

gain her ends.) If the owner takes the position that the first person with or without a car to arrive there has the parking right, then Boniface, it turns out, had engaged in extortion. (He used force to gain his ends.) Similarly, if one believes in the legitimacy of public streets, sidewalks and parking spots, then the government must make this determination. Only if we know whether it is operating on a rule which allows people to "save" spaces for friends in cars can we determine who has utilized force against whom.[22]

Third, there are two cases from Greek mythology. In the first, Odysseus is faking madness so that he won't have to go to war. Palamedes places his infant son so that Odysseus will have to act rationally in order to save him, thus revealing his fitness for war. This was clearly an illicit act, since no matter whether or not the father is culpable, the son certainly is innocent. To put him in danger is to initiate violence against a non-aggressor, a clear violation of the libertarian legal code.

In the second case, Katz seems to have strayed from the main point. This time Achilles is refusing to take part in a fight, hiding out in the guise of a girl. Odysseus orders a sudden loud trumpet call to battle, and Achilles, going on instinct, picks us a spear, thus coming out of the female closet, so to speak. But here there was no threat or violence used. Thus, there was neither blackmail nor extortion. All that occurred was a bit of sharp detecting. If Achilles was legally obliged to wage war (say, he had signed a contract to do so), then the trick was used to a good end. If not, not.

F. Brutal Honesty

Hortense knows two embarrassing secrets about Thaddeus: marital infidelity and corrupt finances. In her initial demand for money, she mentions only the first secret. He refuses to pay. Then, she reveals knowledge of the second secret. Asks Katz, "Has her greater honesty improved her moral position, or has her increased threat only aggravated it?"[23] The answer from this side of the net is that since, presumably, it is immoral to blackmail, her second attempt worsened her ethical position. As far as her legal position is concerned, however, a threat to be a gossip should be allowed by law since this is merely a legitimate exercise of free speech and not a crime. A request for money to

---

[22] But this is hardly unique. If we see two men, A and B, both fighting over a wallet, we cannot tell who is in the right (and is the victim) and who is in the wrong (and is the aggressor) until and unless the property rights can be established. *See* on this MURRAY N. ROTHBARD, THE ETHICS OF LIBERTY 51 (1982).

[23] Katz, *supra* note 3, at 1573.

maintain silence is like any other commercial arrangement. To do this twice instead of once should make no legal difference.

II. BLACKMAIL IN RELATION TO "PLAIN VANILLA" COERCION

Having set the stage, our author now moves into his second section. Here, he adumbrates his theory of crime, which he will later attempt to use to shed light on the blackmail conundrum. Considering the utterance "Your money or your life," Katz starts off well by focusing on the crucial question: "what is the difference between a threat—which is deemed coercive—and an offer which is not."[24] But his reply, as he doesn't seem to appreciate, is actually in two parts, each inconsistent with the other. The first is in sharp variance with libertarianism: "The answer is that offers enlarge your opportunity set whereas threats shrink it."[25]

Katz goes so far as to cite Nozick in his footnote 11 as "A classic source in which [Katz's] distinction between offers and threats is explored."[26] This is injudicious, in view of the devastating and eviscerating critique of Nozick's "drop dead" principle offered by Rothbard

> For his criterion of a 'productive' exchange is one where each party is better off than if the other did not exist at all; whereas a 'non-productive' exchange is one where one party would be better off if the other dropped dead. Thus: 'if I pay you for not harming me, I gain nothing from you that I wouldn't possess if either you didn't exist at all or existed without having anything to do with me.' …
>
> Let us then see how Nozick applies his 'non-productive' … criteria to the problem of blackmail. Nozick tries to rehabilitate the outlawry of blackmail by asserting that 'non productive' contracts should be illegal, and that a blackmail contract is non-productive because a blackmailee is worse off because of the blackmailer's very existence (84–86). In short, if blackmailer Smith dropped dead, Jones (the blackmailee) would be better off. Or, to put it another way, Jones is paying not for Smith's making him better off, but for *not* making him *worse off*. But surely the latter is *also* a productive

---

[24] *Id.* at 1574.

[25] *Id.*

[26] *Id.* at 1574 fn. 11.

contract, because Jones is still better off making the exchange than he *would have been* if the exchange were not made.

But this theory gets Nozick into very muddy waters indeed; some (though by no means all) of which he recognizes. He concedes, for example, that his reason for outlawing blackmail would force him also to outlaw the following contract: Brown comes to Green, his next-door neighbor, with the following proposition: I intend to build such-and-such a pink building on my property (which he knows Green will detest). I won't build this building, however, if you pay me X amount of money. Nozick concedes that this, too, would have to be illegal in his schema, because Green would be paying Brown for not being worse off, and hence the contract would be 'non-productive.' In essence, Green would be better off if Brown dropped dead. It is difficult, however, for a libertarian to square such outlawry with any plausible theory of property rights. ... In analogy with the blackmail example above, furthermore, Nozick concedes that it would be legal, in his schema, for Green, on finding out about Brown's projected pink building, to come to Brown and offer to pay him not to go ahead. But why would such an exchange be 'productive' just because Green made the offer? What difference does it make who makes the offer in this situation? Wouldn't Green still be better off if Brown dropped dead? And again, following the analogy, would Nozick make it illegal for Brown to refuse Green's offer and then ask for more money? Why? Or, again, would Nozick make it illegal for Brown to subtly let Green know about the projected pink building and then let nature take its course: say, by advertising in the paper about the building and sending Green the clipping?[27] Couldn't this be taken as an act of courtesy? And why should merely *advertising* something be illegal? Clearly, Nozick's case becomes ever more flimsy as we consider the implications.

Furthermore, Nozick has not at all considered the manifold implications of his 'drop dead' principle. If he is saying, as he seems to, that A is illegitimately 'coercing' B as B is better off should A drop dead, then consider the following case: Brown and Green are competing at auction for the same painting which they desire. They are the last two customers left. Wouldn't Green be better off if Brown

---

[27] Shades of Katz's Mildred and Abigail 'warning' case.

dropped dead? Isn't Brown therefore illegally coercing Green in some way, and therefore shouldn't Brown's participation in the auction be outlawed? Or, *per contra*, isn't Green coercing Brown in the same manner and shouldn't *Green's* participation in the auction be outlawed? If not, why not? Or, suppose that Brown and Green are competing for the hand of the same girl; wouldn't each be better off if the other dropped dead, and shouldn't either or both's participation in the courtship therefore be outlawed? The ramifications are virtually endless.

Nozick, furthermore, gets himself into a deeper quagmire when he adds that a blackmail exchange is not 'productive' because outlawing the exchange makes on party (the blackmailee) no worse off. But that of course is not true: as Professor Block has pointed out, outlawing a blackmail contract means that the blackmailer has no further incentive *not* to disseminate the unwelcome, hitherto secret information about the blackmailed party.[28]

The second part of Katz's explication of the distinction between threat and offer, in contrast, is on firm (e.g., libertarian) ground:

The threat permits you to choose which of many things you are entitled to you will give up. The offer permits you to choose which of many things you are entitled to you will, if you want to, exchange for something else which you are not entitled to. The robber coerces because he offers to sell you back what he has first unlawfully taken from you—the chance to go on living.[29]

Let us use Rothbard's insights, and put matters in terms more congruent with Katz's terminology. In the Brown-Green-pink building, auction-painting, or suitor for girl examples, if we use Katz's first enlarging or shrinking the "opportunity set" criterion, we would have to conclude that Brown is criminally threatening Green, not making him an offer. For in each case, because of Brown, Green's "opportunity set" is shrunken, not enlarged. But it is highly problematic to consider Brown a robber in any of these cases, and a theory of blackmail which rests on this vision of criminality cannot be a valid one. Expanding or contracting "opportunity sets" is irrelevant to misconduct. The key, rather, is the libertarian axiom of non-aggression.

---

[28] Rothbard, *supra* note 22, at 240–42.

[29] Katz, *supra* note 3, at 1574.

On the other hand, Katz is on firm ground with his second criterion, the one which speaks of entitlements. Here, Brown never in a million years even came close to making Green choose giving up anything to which he was entitled. Green wasn't entitled to live in a "pink building free" zone. Green wasn't entitled to the painting. Green wasn't entitled to the girl.

Katz's second criterion is entirely consistent with, even equivalent to, the libertarian theory of crime, which focuses entirely on the initiation or threatened violence against person and legitimately owned property. Property entitlement is the bedrock upon which the libertarian theory of crime rests. Unfortunately, as we shall see, Katz seems wedded both to his first, illegitimate, "opportunity set" criterion and to his second appropriate, libertarian, "entitlement" one.

Let turn now to a consideration of several cases posed by Katz in order to illustrate his theory(ies) of crime;

> 1. A illegally blocks the public sidewalk, so that pedestrians can pass only by walking in the street. In order to pass, B walks in the street, knowing that there is a substantial danger of being struck by passing traffic. He is struck and injured by a negligently driven automobile.

> Did B assume the risk of injury and is he therefore barred from recovering from A? Keeping in mind the robbery analogy, one soon sees why the answer should be no. A illegally narrowed B's choices, much as the robber narrowed those of his victim. A forced B to buy back—by exposing himself to the risk of being hit by a car—something that was already his, namely the right to walk down the street.[30]

Here we see Katz trying to ride two horses at once. On the assumption that it is illegal to block a public sidewalk, A is indeed at fault, but not because he "narrowed B's choices." As we have seen from Rothbard, Green can narrow Brown's choices until the cows come home and will nevertheless commit no illegal act. On the contrary, the reason A is at fault is because he improperly (according to our assumption) took away a property right of B's, namely his right to walk down the street.

But why need we assume that this was an illegal blockage? Don't people also have the right to stand on the sidewalk? My wife and I along with Charles Koch and his wife were standing on a sidewalk, peacefully, minding our own

---

[30] *Id.* at 1575–76.

business, chatting quietly, when along came an inebriated lout, demanding that we step aside for him. Were we wrong to refuse and thus force him to detour around us into the street?

If it is a private sidewalk we are talking about (such as can be found in a shopping mall or Disney World) then it is the owner who is entitled to determine who has precedence. If his ruling is in favor of the walker, then Katz is correct; but if in favor of "first come first served," then A, who was there first, is guiltless. If the sidewalk in question is a public one, then, perhaps, the person who is blocking it is protesting the lack of privatization. In the libertarian legal code, this person would be in the right, and B would have to take his chances with vehicular traffic, since sidewalk provision is not a legitimate government function.

2. In the second case, a caterer at the very last moment raises his contractually agreed upon price; the party giver reluctantly acquiesces, but later claims duress. Katz hews to the libertarian line: this was indeed a robbery, in that the hostess was forced to give up something she (contractually) owned—the lower initial price.

3. Here, the police, contrary to a court ruling of unconstitutionality, threaten a traveler who fits the Drug Enforcement Agency's courier profile, that unless he consents to a search for drugs, they will detain him until they obtain a search warrant. Katz claims this is an illegal search and seizure on the ground that traveler has been in effect robbed of something he owns, namely, "the right not to be detained."

There are many things in this analysis which offend libertarian sensibilities. First, drug use is a victimless crime, in that it does not involve what Katz in another context correctly calls "impermissible boundary crossings," or "discernible invasions."[31] (If Katz sees this as a necessary condition for criminality, why does he refrain from applying that insight to the present case?) Therefore, *anything*[32] done by the Drug Enforcement Agency, or the police who do their bidding, is illegitimate. We certainly don't need fancy theories about criminality to reach that conclusion. Second, on the assumption that the police are dealing with a real criminal—e.g., a rapist, murderer, etc.—the Supreme Court ruling that police may not stop and question suspicious looking characters is itself improper. True, if they do so, and the detainee is proven innocent, then the police themselves are liable for an improper border cross-

---

[31] *Id.* at 1576.

[32] That is, apart from disbanding.

ing, but that is entirely another matter.[33] There is, then, no "right not to be detained," for criminals, that is.

4. "The prosecutor has inadmissible but conclusive evidence demonstrating that the defendant is guilty of murder. He also has admissible but flimsy evidence implicating him in a rape. The prosecutor does not believe the defendant committed the rape. Nonetheless, desperate to put someone he knows to be a murderer in jail, he threatens the defendant with a rape prosecution unless he pleads guilty to some lesser charge (let's say, the aggravated battery of the fellow he murdered) the fearful defendant consents. But his consent is no more valued than the robbery victim's. The defendant is being asked to buy back (by pleading guilty to aggravated battery) relief from a trial, which the prosecutor is not entitled to launch anyway (given the frivolousness of the rape charge.)"

This analysis, I claim, is nonsense on stilts, albeit predicated on modern day jurisprudence. It takes rather a warped and corrupt notion of justice to favor the murderer's side in behalf of hyper convoluted notion of procedural rights. From whence springs the absolute right not to be charged of a crime on the basis of flimsy evidence? To be sure, there is such a thing as malicious prosecution, and the prosecutor in this case may well have left himself open to such a charge. But if his detestation of murder is greater than his fear of being found guilty of such an act, he will proceed. In any case, why is there such a thing as inadmissible evidence? No doubt, we do not want our police torturing defendants into confessing. But if this occurs, why should the murderer be let go, instead of the policeman charged with the crime of torture? Why, in general terms, should we treat procedural error with the freeing of the criminal, instead of punishment for the evil doer? None of this makes any sense from a libertarian point of view, which takes a harsh view of criminals who violate property and personal entitlements. Katz pays lip service to the latter idea, but fails to carry through on it.

Katz next considers the attempts of several other authors to explain the prohibition of blackmail.[34] Let us consider each of them in turn, Katz's commentaries on them, and then offer a response.

1. Epstein

In Katz's view, Epstein's main contribution is to focus attention on Blackmail, Inc., a corporation which would come into being upon legaliza-

---

[33] If the detention is of a few moments, it would fall under *de minimis* rules. If for days or weeks, this is equivalent to kidnapping.

[34] *Id.* at 1576–82.

tion.[35] Its business would be to acquire embarrassing information, and then to blackmail people with it. Apart from the crime of blackmail per se, this would lead blackmailees,[36] as it does drug addicts, into still other crimes in order to pay for their "fraud habit."[37]

Katz criticizes this theory on three grounds. First, it is wedded to informational blackmail, and cannot be applied to non-informational examples such as the threat to call a strike, sell the daughter a motorcycle, etc. The problem here, from the libertarian perspective, as we have seen, is that there is no warrant to call several of these examples blackmail, let alone extortion. Thus, we side with Epstein vis à vis Katz on this point.

Second, Katz taxes Epstein on the latter's account that hiding embarrassing facts about oneself amounts to fraud. Again, we give the nod to Epstein. Yes, fraud is equivalent to theft, but merely keeping one's own business private cannot be considered a crime.[38] Later, in his analysis of Feinberg,[39] Katz waxes eloquent about privacy rights.[40] Here, he appears to be attacking the notion. One discerns a bit of a contradiction.

Katz enters another sticky wicket when he asks: "Is the reason we are upset with the blackmailer who promises not to reveal a fellow employee's homosexuality (for a fee) that we would in fact like him to tell the employer what he knows?"[41] Although Katz does not vouchsafe us an answer to this question, one can easily imagine his answer to be "Hardly." That is, Katz is disturbed by the blackmailer because he sees his act as despicable.

But this is a very unreasonable basis for a legal system. As for the "revulsion"[42] one feels at the practice of blackmail, many people feel an equal amount of revulsion, if not more, for homosexuality. Does this mean we should ban the latter activity as well, according to Katz? This would certainly not follow from a libertarian point of view, as homosexuality, at least that between consenting adults in private, does not constitute a border crossing, and hence should be legal.

Third, Katz takes Epstein to task for unduly weighting the fact that blackmail will lead to "other" crime, so that the blackmailee can pay off

---

[35] Richard Epstein, *Blackmail, Inc.*, 50 U. CHI. L. REV. 553 (1983).

[36] Following Rothbard, I refuse to call them "victims" since blackmail (but not extortion!) is a voluntary trade, and in all such cases there are mutual gains, at least in the *ex ante* sense.

[37] Katz, *supra* note 3, at 1578.

[38] Rothbard, *supra* note 22, at 78–79.

[39] JOEL FEINBERG, HARMLESS WRONGDOING (1988).

[40] Katz, *supra* note 3, at 1580.

[41] *Id.* at 1567.

[42] *Id.* at 1578.

Blackmail, Inc. He does so on the ground that even if true, this isn't the real reason for our "revulsion" at blackmail.[43] However, he contends that Epstein's empirical account is "very plausible." In doing so, Katz fails to reckon with Block and Gordon,[44] who criticized Epstein[45] on the ground that the legalization of blackmail can actually *reduce* real crime.

2. Nozick

Here we come to a section of the paper that is more than just passing curious. Katz accurately describes Nozick's contribution to the blackmail literature, and then masterfully refutes it.[46] Blackmail, for Nozick, should be banned because the blackmailee would be better off if the blackmailer dropped dead; e.g., the blackmailer is reducing the "opportunity set" of the blackmailee.[47] Katz's critique is that Nozick's theory is both over and under inclusive. It is over-inclusive because a lot of innocent activity is swept into the category of illegality. States Katz, "The silver medalist at the Olympics would be better off if the gold medalist didn't exist."[48] The only problem is, in making this point, he contradicts his own reliance on the Nozickian notion of crime, as diminution of "opportunity sets."[49]

Why is Nozick under-inclusive? Because his theory "does not cover the kind of blackmail in which the blackmailer promises to perform some beneficial act in return for the payoff."[50] This sounds like a voluntary mutually beneficial trade, not something to be outlawed.

3. Feinberg

In his analysis of Feinberg, Katz takes the position that the blackmailer "is asking the victim to buy back what the victim, morally speaking, already owns, like the right to keep his homosexuality secret."[51]

---

[43] *Id.*

[44] Chapter 13, this volume..

[45] Epstein, *supra* note 34.

[46] Katz, *supra* note 3, at 1578–79.

[47] ROBERT NOZICK, ANARCHY, STATE AND UTOPIA, (Basic Books 1974).

[48] Katz, *supra* note 3, at 1579.

[49] *Id.* at 1574.

[50] *Id.* at 1579.

[51] *Id.* at 1580.

Let us pause a moment and consider what kind of a world it would be if people really owned the right to keep homosexuality secret.[52]

It would mean, for one thing, that anyone else who saw them engage in this practice would be a thief. That is, if C as much as saw Mr. A and Mr. B kissing, C would at that moment cease to be an innocent person. Instead, C would now be guilty of the crime of stealing, for he now knows something that is the private property of A and B. For another thing, all detectives, and detective agencies, would be forthwith and summarily jailed. For the essence of detecting is to unearth other people's secrets. But if each person owns all secrets which pertain to him, any detective who makes a discovery is *per se* an aggressor. Take that, Arthur Conan Doyle!

And not only detectives; this also applies to investigative reporters, news hounds, gossip columnists, etc. Further, no one would be able to take anyone else's picture without permission, and this applies to police doing so to speeding motorists. The jails will be overfull in the Katzian world.

States Rothbard on this matter:

> But is there really such a right to privacy? How can there be? How can there be a right to prevent Smith by force from disseminating knowledge which he possesses? Surely there can be no such right. Smith owns his own body, and therefore has the property right to own the knowledge he has inside his head, including his knowledge about Jones (that he is a liar, thief or homosexual). And therefore he has the corollary right to print and disseminate that knowledge. In short, as in the case of the 'human right' to free speech, there is no such thing as a right to privacy except the right to protect one's property from invasion. The only right to 'privacy' is the right to protect one's property from being invaded by someone else. In brief, no one has the right to burgle someone else's home, or to wiretap someone's phone lines. Wiretapping is properly a crime not because of some vague and wooly 'invasion of a "right to privacy,"' but because it is an invasion of the property right of the person being wiretapped.[53]

---

[52] The same analysis would apply to marital infidelity, or financial cheating, or any other embarrassing act.

[53] Rothbard, *supra* note 22, at 121–22.

4. Lindgren

In Lindgren's theory, the blackmailer improperly seizes "bargaining chips," the secrets of the blackmailee, which are the latter's property, and uses them against him.[54] One complaint of Katz against this viewpoint is that it is under-inclusive: it cannot account for the non-informational cases: "Pay me $10,000—or I will cause bad blood at our club, seduce your fiancée, persuade your son to enlist," etc.[55] The problem here is, as we have seen, that these cases do not violate the libertarian axiom of non-aggression.

However, Katz quite properly castigates Lindgren on the ground that "[t]he bargaining chips which he finds the blackmailer guilty of misappropriating seem like a very unreal sort of commodity, made of the most diaphanous of tissues. It is hard to see the principle that elevates this very metaphorical kind of misappropriation to the level of a robbery."[56]

III. A PUZZLE ABOUT PUNISHMENT

In this section Katz launches himself into a long, and seemingly irrelevant, but very interesting disquisition on the punishment fitting the crime. His main interest is evaluating the theory that "Harm is in the eye of the victim," who should therefore determine the level of imprisonment.[57] For example, if a would-be rape victim prefers death to dishonor, should her murderer or rapist receive a stiffer penalty? Ordinarily, the former is punished more severely; but to the extent we incorporate the victim's preferences, this would be reversed.

Unfortunately, while Katz is willing to seriously entertain this preference based approach, for a whole host of real crimes (although he ultimately rejects it), he gives the back of his hand to the victimless variety. He states, "Excepting odd cases like prostitution and drugs, what a victim wants cannot count as an injury."[58] It is somewhat strange to characterize prostitution and drugs, two of our larger industries, as "odd cases" while dealing with a whole host of made up mind boggling puzzlers without dismissing them on this ground. It is logically inconsistent to seriously consider the tastes of victims, no matter

---

[54] James Lindgren, *Unraveling the Paradox of Blackmail*, 84 COLUM. L. REV., 670 (1984).

[55] Katz, *supra* note 3, at 1581.

[56] *Id.*

[57] *Id.* at 1584.

[58] *Id.*

how "idiosyncratic,"[59] while ignoring those with a desire for addictive drugs or commercial sex.

IV. THE PUNISHMENT PUZZLE RESOLVED

Why, despite the superficial plausibility of seriously taking into account the idiosyncratic tastes of victims in sentencing, does Katz think we should nevertheless reject the preference based approach?[60]

According to him, this is because of a bifurcation between the views of the individual victim and those of the judge, who represents all of society. The former cares only about the level of harm; it matters not one whit whether this comes about as a result of commission or omission. The latter, in contrast, "will generally deem the omission innocent and the act culpable," and, as well, will be less harsh with negligent wrongs than intentional ones, remotely caused wrongs than proximately caused ones.[61]

And why is this? Because the latter in each of these three sets is "more invasive!"[62] His evidence for this is that it would be worse (because more invasive) to steal an extra redundant kidney from the inside of a person who has another, fully functioning one, than to take a yet to be implanted kidney out of a refrigerator, even if its intended recipient dies as a result.

Now Katz's concern about invasiveness certainly strikes a libertarian chord. Remember, this is at the very essence of the non-aggression axiom. But surely it is a greater rights infringement to cause a death by stealing the kidney in the refrigerator from the would-be recipient who has none, than it is to invade the body of a person who has two "through a completely risk free and painless procedure."[63] After all, a death will occur in the second case, not the first. Yes, other things equal, the presumption is that an attack on the person is worse than an attack on his property, and rifling through property in his immediate vicinity is a more serious crime than doing so with his possessions far removed. But other things are not always equal. And further, the statement "You have more of a claim to the things in your immediate vicinity than to those further away" sounds more like an attack on absentee ownership than a libertarian protection of property rights.[64]

---

[59] *Id.*

[60] *Id.* at 1590–95.

[61] *Id.* at 1590.

[62] *Id.* at 1591.

[63] *Id.* at 1590.

[64] *Id.* at 1592.

Nor does Katz's example of torture fully resonate. Yes, perhaps, he has put his finger on why in the west we do not torture prisoners, even though many might prefer it to a lengthy jail sentence. Certainly this was the reaction when a young American was given 5 lashes in Singapore for a misdemeanor. But the Singaporeans, obviously, do not hold this view, thus rendering it less than obviously true on an intuitive basis. Nor is it fully reasonable, even in the west, that people who torture their victims ought not to be treated in the same manner.

If his torture example does not work, his "straightforward analogy in government assistance for the poor" is really tortured.[65] He says that we would rather give welfare in the form of medical care, food stamps, etc., than in the form of money (which they would prefer), not because we are necessarily paternalistic, but, in effect, because "we believe that they only have a claim on our providing them the particular things usually granted as aid-in-kind."[66] What is the connection between these remarks and invasiveness? It would appear to be that Katz thinks it invasive not to give the poor things to which he thinks they have a claim. But why do they have a claim to *anything* from the rich, let alone the particular things to which Katz thinks they do?[67] A more serious problem is that welfare, whether in money or in kind, is the paradigm case of invasiveness: it takes money from taxpayers against their will. How can he use any supposed shortcoming of this program as an example of invasiveness when its very existence is an instance of that quality? This argument applies as well to his championing of tax progressivity as less invasive.[68]

Nor does his example of sentencing criminals constitute much evidence in support of his underlying contention that "harms are to be objectively rather than subjectively judged!" so as to reduce invasiveness.[69] Katz argues that if we were really concerned to equalize (e.g., be objective and non-invasive with regard to) the suffering of inmates, we would treat more harshly

---

[65] *Id.* at 1593.

[66] *Id.*

[67] Katz gives no reasons for this stance, but it would presumably be because he has an affinity for egalitarianism, or he believes that this actually helps the poor. As for the former, he should reread Nozick's ANARCHY, STATE AND UTOPIA, which he several times cites in other contexts, which constitutes one of the best antidotes to egalitarianism ever penned. As to the latter, he might consult Murray's LOSING GROUND: AMERICAN SOCIAL POLICY FROM 1950 TO 1980 (1984).

[68] *See* MURRAY N. ROTHBARD, POWER AND MARKET: GOVERNMENT AND THE ECONOMY (1970).

[69] Katz, *supra* note 3, at 1594.

the happy go lucky person; Katz maintains that we do not because in effect this would be too subjective and hence invasive.[70] An alternative, more reasonable explanation is that we simply cannot tell, scientifically, who is naturally cheerful and who is morose. Any attempt to discern this (once captives found out what was going on) would all but preclude jailbirds similar to those (like Zero Mostel) in the movie "The Producers." Further, we must continue to protest the equation of non-invasiveness with egalitarianism.

If we were really concerned with non-invasiveness, moreover, we would not focus too heavily on the punishment of criminals. Instead, we would devote our attention to making the victim whole.[71] Remember, they are actual victims of real crime. In the libertarian philosophy, it is *their* welfare, not that of the criminal, which is the main concern.

Katz's last example concerns the burglar, Smithy, the victims Bartleby and Bartholomea, and their two vases.[72] His point, again, is that we should penalize the criminal based upon the objective not the subjective value of the vases; his underlying reasoning is that this is less invasive.

Katz's closing argument is as follows:

> If we took the position that what we are really after in assessing the wickedness of the theft is the victim's subjective sense of loss, then presumably the theft of a thousand dollars from a millionaire is a less serious affair than the theft of the same amount from someone less wealthy. And that would certainly seem odd.[73]

Yes, indeed, that would seem odd—but Katz is logically precluded from drawing any such conclusion. For this author is on record in support of progressive taxation, and this is precisely the ground upon which this system is supported.[74] That is, there is declining marginal utility of money, such that the loss of $1,000 hurts a millionaire less than the gain of it benefits a poor man; if we take the money from the latter and give it to the former through redistributive progressive taxation, "social welfare" (that which is obtained by adding up the welfare of the two of them) therefore increases. If this is sauce for progressive taxes, why should this not be so for the analysis of theft?

---

[70] *Id.* at 1595.

[71] *See* ASSESSING THE CRIMINAL: RESTITUTION, RETRIBUTION AND THE LEGAL PROCESS (Randy E. Barnett & John Hagel III eds.) (1977).

[72] Katz, *supra* note 3, at 1594–95.

[73] *Id.* at 1595.

[74] *Id.* at 1593.

There is an alternative explanation (to invasiveness) as to why we should prefer objective to subjective punishments, even though value is at bottom subjective, not objective.[75] And that is because it is impossible to scientifically compare utility interpersonally.[76] This, not the supposed non-invasiveness of our society, is a far better explanation of what objectivity we have.

Let us conclude this section. Libertarians are very sympathetic to non-invasiveness. It lies at the very heart of our philosophy. But Katz, through a welter of highly inventive, weird, exotic and fascinating cases relies on the supposed thread of non-invasiveness which exists, now, in our present institutions. This must ring false, however, to any libertarian, since many of the institutions he cites (welfare, punishment, taxation) are often paradigm cases of the presence of invasiveness. To deduce non-invasiveness from invasiveness is a task beyond even the inventive powers of Katz.

V. BLACKMAIL PROPER

After this tour through the legal philosophy of punishment, Katz now returns to blackmail. He maintains: "In both puzzles the defendant's accommodation of the victim's preferences aggravates rather than improves his moral position. In both puzzles the defendant is considered worse, not better, for having gone along with the victim's choice."[77]

We have previously given good and sufficient reasons for calling this very statement into question. Now, we will suppose, just for the sake of argument, that it is true. It still does not follow that a mere immorality can serve as the basis of a criminal act. This is the nub of Katz's problem: how to invest an act which has not one single iota of criminality in it with illegality of the invasive variety. This is why he brings in criminality, his "puzzle," even though he admits that the blackmailer is guilty of no *per se* criminal behavior. It is an attempt to smuggle into the pristine (in the legal sense, that is) world of blackmail the invasive act of the criminal.

Katz only succeeds in confusing matters with his example of Anatole, the thief of the Metropolitan Museum's Rembrandt who then tries to sell this picture back to them. Our author asks us to forget about the fact that this is a stolen painting, and to concentrate on the second act in the play, the one where the blackmailer tries to "steal" $10,000 from the Museum in return for

---

[75] LUDWIG VON MISES, HUMAN ACTION (1966).

[76] Murray N. Rothbard, *Toward a Reconstruction of Utility and Welfare Economics*, San Francisco Center for Libertarian Studies, Occasional Paper #3 (1977).

[77] Katz, *supra* note 3, at 1595.

this objet d'art. Previously, we objected on the grounds that the Museum probably wasn't the rightful owner anyway, and that even if it were, it would still owe a salvage fee to Anatole. Now, just for the sake of argument, we will suppose that Katz's scenario makes sense, and cannot be toppled on these grounds. Still, he has not succeeded in deducing a crime from an immorality, since the holding of stolen good is still a crime. Katz validly concludes that blackmail is a crime in this one case, only because this crime, not immorality, appears in the premise. On no fewer than four separate occasions in the paragraph beginning on page 1596 and ending on page 1597, Katz characterizes Anatole's holding of the painting as "noncriminal." But repetition cannot alter reality. The threat in blackmail is non-criminal gossiping. The threat in Anatole's "offer" of the return of the stolen painting for the $10,000 is to hold onto stolen property. If this is not a crime, then nothing is.[78] In our terminology, Anatole is an extortionist, not a blackmailer.

But this does not begin to exhaust Katz's difficulties. He uses immorality, not invasiveness, as the springboard for his charges of blackmail, but he is not at all clear on what is immoral. Katz never gives us a criterion, or a definition nor examples. One would have expected at least the latter, given this authors penchant for numerous and mesmerizing cases in point. If immorality is his bedrock, he is building his blackmail edifice on a foundation of shifting sand.

Second, Katz would have to withstand any number or reductios ad absurdum, and he cannot contend with even a one of them. What else is or has ever been considered immoral? Premarital sex, open marriage, polygamy, pornography, gambling, homosexuality, overeating, impoliteness, sloth, greed, not contributing to charity, nose picking, suicide, smoking tobacco, using addictive drugs, breaking wind, drinking alcohol, immediately spring to mind. But then, with his theory, the threat of any of these things would have to be outlawed, surely not a welcome conclusion. However immorality is defined, we would surely wish to distinguish between it and invasive criminal behavior.

Katz appears to have a reply to this charge:

> If for instance Anatole's threat to the museum had not been to sit on the Rembrandt forever but merely to be surly to the museum director, that threat too would involve a wrong, but altogether too minor a one to turn the transaction into blackmail.[79]

---

[78] See Rothbard, supra note 22, at 51 ("The criminal has no natural right whatever to the retention of property that he has stolen.").

[79] Katz, supra note 3,. at 1597.

But this opens up more problems than it solves. For not only does Katz base his theory of blackmail on an undefined immorality, even within that category it would appear that there are serious immoralities (which do entail blackmail) and minor ones (which do not). Needless to say, just as Katz nowhere articulates his perspective on immorality, he never draws the line between serious and trivial violations thereof.

Be that as it may, Katz is now ready to apply his insights to the various types of blackmail, and we will continue to follow his lead.

A. The Canonical Problem

Here, it will be remembered, Busybody asks for $10,000 for his silence about Philanderer's infidelities. Katz, based on his long discourse into punishment theory, characterizes this as follows;

> Busybody is putting Philanderer to a choice between two wrongs. Busybody will either commit the theft—the unconsented-to taking of $10,000—or the revelation of Philanderer's infidelities. Why is the payment of $10,000 unconsented-to, given that Philanderer is paying voluntarily? It is unconsented-to because it is made with the threat of something wrongful, the revelation. But how is the revelation wrongful when it is not in fact prohibited by the criminal law? It is wrongful because it is immoral, even though not criminal or even tortious. To be sure, it is not a major immorality by any means, but simply 'swinishness.' Indeed it wouldn't even be immoral if it had been made out of friendship with the cheated wife. It is immoral only because, if it were to be done, it would be done for purely retaliatory reasons—retaliation for Philanderer's refusal to pay. But now comes the most formidable objection: if revealing the infidelities is only a minor immorality, then how can the taking of money which the victim prefers to that minor immorality be anything more than a minor immorality itself? That's where our solution to the punishment puzzle comes in. The lesson of the punishment puzzle was that when the defendant has the victim choose between either of two immoralities which he must endure, the gravity of the defendant's wrongdoing is to be judged by what he actually did (or sought to achieve), not by what he threatened to do.[80]

---

[80] *Id.*

49

In a previous life, Katz must have been a broken field runner of no little talent; one can see, if one looks carefully, at the swiveling of the hips at a prodigious rate as he attempts to evade the logic and implications of his views. But the truth of the matter is that even if what Busybody did was immoral, no amount of twisting and turning can render this invasive criminal behavior. Period. And, as Katz himself is on record[81] as identifying a la Nozick "impermissible boundary crossings," or "discernible invasions" as the necessary characteristics of a crime, it is a complete mystery as to how he can regard mere blackmail in this light. The blackmailer never invades, or threatens to invade, anyone's boundary.

Suppose there were a case where the "defendant (does not have) the victim choose between either of two immoralities which he must endure." Would this let the blackmailer off the hook in Katz's view? Such a situation is easy to construct.[82] Suppose that Philander had somehow gotten wind of the fact that Busybody had the goods on him, and was about to spill the beans to his wife. Philanderer then approaches Busybody, not the other way around, and begs him to keep quiet, offering $10,000 for Busybody's silence. Here, Busybody is not the initiator of the offer; Philanderer is. Here, Busybody is not at all forcing his "victim (to) choose between either of two immoralities which he must endure." Rather, the "victim" is making this offer to the blackmailer. According to the analysis offered by Katz, this case could not be considered one of blackmail. And yet this is just as much the canonical blackmail case as the one depicted by Katz.

B. Blackmail and "Plain Vanilla" Coercion

Again, Katz characterizes the blackmailer as attempting to "take money without the owner's consent."[83] But this is seen to be false when we consider the deal initiated by the blackmailee, not the blackmailer. In our scenario, the blackmailee is practically begging the blackmailer to blackmail him, rather than engage in free speech gossip about him. How this can be converted into "without consent" can only be considered a product of a lawyer's facility with language.

---

[81] *Id.* at 1576.

[82] Rothbard, *supra* note 16, at 124–25.

[83] Katz, *supra* note 3, at 1599.

C. Omissions

Omissions, too, can be considered blackmail. According to Katz, "Not throwing the drowning stranger a life vest is at least mildly immoral, though generally not criminal. Hence, not surprisingly, it sounds like blackmail for the defendant to say to the drowning victim: "Pay me $10,000 or I won't throw you that life vest."[84]

But not contributing to charity is also immoral, one presumes. Hence, if I told you that unless you give me $10,000, I won't contribute to charity, I would be summarily relegated to the hoosegow by Katz.

Is it really invasive not to do something you are not contractually obligated to do? Hardly. So Katz must either leave us his quasi-libertarian concern with invasiveness, or change his tune on blackmail.

Moreover, the canonical commercial transaction fits this omission format. For does not the salesman always (implicitly) make this "threat" to the customer: "Pay me $10,000, or won't sell you this car?" If so, Katz's theory is shown yet again to be wildly over-inclusive. There would be an awful lot of people cooling their heels in jail for engaging in such economic "crimes."

D. Sexual Favors

Asks Katz, "What about the employer who offers an applicant a secretarial job if she will sleep with him?"[85] His conclusion is that this is blackmail, since "the employer is putting the victim to a choice between two moral wrongs—a retaliatory non-hiring, or non-consensual sex."

There are grave problems here. What about the woman who approaches a male employer and offers to work for him in not one but two capacities: secretary and prostitute. He would appear guilty of blackmail, no matter what his reply. For he would be putting her in a position where she would have to accept one of two immoral states of the world. If he refuses, the immorality would consist of her not being hired (the "non-hire"). If he accepts, he would be immorally involving her in prostitution, which Katz would undoubtedly regard as non-consensual, even though she made the proposal. And for her very offer, she, too, would be considered culpable of this crime. For then she would be demanding of him that either he hire her on this basis (which Katz, at least, is on record as regarding as immoral), or not working at all (which Katz is also on record as regarding as immoral—this is the "non-hire.")

---

[84] *Id.*

[85] *Id.* at 1600.

Suppose another case. A man offers marriage to a woman if she will 1. sleep with him; 2. sleep with him, but not in the missionary position. On the ground that all sex is non-consensual (which seems to be Katz's position), case 1 constitutes blackmail. On the ground that the missionary position is the only moral one, the man is additionally guilty of blackmail. Jail over-crowding, here we come.

E. Suicide

> We are ambivalent on the question of whether the prisoner who goes on hunger strike in support of some demand or other, or the husband who threatens to commit suicide if his wife leaves him ought to qualify as blackmailers. We are ambivalent because we are ambivalent on whether the threatened wrong represents any wrong whatsoever.[86]

If I read this correctly, the uncertainty stems from the fact that Katz does not know whether or not suicide is more immoral than, say, surliness. The strikes one as odd, since suicide is typically a paradigm case of immorality. This author's analysis is unsatisfactory, in that it intimately relies not only on morality which is never defined, but on a certain level of morality, "a *de minimis* threshold"[87] which seems to have escaped even him. One may perhaps be excused for thinking that this sounds rather like a poker game where one of the players makes up the rules as he goes along, to fit the hands he happens to be dealt.

F. Brutal Honesty

In this case Hortense increases the blackmail pressure on Thaddeus by not only threatening to expose his infidelity, but now, also, his financial peccadillos. Katz thinks this leaves the level of her blameworthiness untouched, since this "is largely determined by the demanded advantage and not the threat" which remains unchanged (Hortense offers Thaddeus a two for one deal: the same price to keep both secrets as to keep one).[88] I persist in thinking that since she only engages in (two) blackmail(s), and not extortion, she is legally blameless. Since I am not at all clear on the immorality charge, I will leave it to experts such as Katz.

---

[86] *Id.*

[87] *Id.*

[88] *Id.* at 1601.

G. Prior Theories[89]

1. Lindgren

Katz thinks that Lindgren's test is not over-inclusive, since "What is usually described [by the latter] as playing with someone else's bargaining chips will invariably turn out to involve the threat to commit some ... swinishness unless one is paid off."[90] But it is under-inclusive in that not all instances of "swinishness pass the bargaining chip test."[91] Here, much as it pains me to side with Lindgren[92] I must take his side at least partially against that of Katz. Contrary to him, many people would consider it the height of "swinishness" to "encourage someone's son to volunteer for combat duty in Vietnam." Katz, however, is shielded from my full opposition since I cannot measure levels of "swinishness," at least not without help from him, which is not forthcoming. So who knows if this is swinish or not. Presumably, it is, for Vietnam war opponents, but not for advocates. Strange to have a possible jail sentence (for the "crime" of blackmail) turn on considerations of this sort. Certainly, this would not pass muster under Hayek's [93] "rule of law."[94]

2., 4. Feinberg and Epstein

Katz's reexamination of Feinberg and Epstein depends upon the former's idiosyncratic sense of immorality.[95] Having already commented on that, we shall do so no more.

3. Nozick

Katz claims that Nozick's "existence" test really functions so as to distinguish commissions from omissions, and that since most immoral conduct (whatever that is) involves an act, the latter has stumbled onto a pretty good proxy for blackmail. After Rothbard's critique of Nozick, one would have

---

[89] Katz is reasonably inclusive as to the prior theories of blackmail he considers. Too bad, then, he did not comment on any of the theories which interpret blackmail as a non-crime.

[90] Katz, *supra* note 3, at 1601.

[91] *See Id.*

[92] *See* Chapter 13, this volume.

[93] FRIEDRICH A. HAYEK, THE CONSTITUTION OF LIBERTY 397–411 (1960).

[94] For a libertarian critique of Hayek's political philosophy, see Rothbard, *supra* note 22, at 219-28 and Block, *supra* note 21.

[95] This is what Rothbard, *supra* note 22, calls Nozick's "drop dead" criterion

thought that nothing worthwhile was still standing of this philosophical edifice. In any case, an act is by definition an omission of a failure to act. Thus, it doesn't seem as if this distinction would give us much forward momentum in our attempt to shed light on blackmail.

VI. AN OBJECTION

In this section, Katz deals with an objection to his thesis.[96] Suppose, instead of Anatole stealing a Rembrandt from the museum, he had taken $100,000; but rather than asking for a "reward" of $10,000, he had simply deducted this amount, and returned only $90,000.

In the view of most people, this triumph of form over substance would make no difference. Our evaluation of both acts would be identical. However, for Katz it is of crucial importance; similarly, Katz analyzed the Mildred Abigail example differently as alternative means of blackmail were chosen. (Based on this, one imagines that Katz would also treat as dissimilar the case where the blackmailee approaches the blackmailer.)

Katz attempts to explain his position by recourse to two cases put forth by Judith Jarvis Thompson. In the first, the trolley conductor has the choice between allowing his vehicle to follow its original track, and kill five people, or steer onto another path, and kill only one (the brakes are not working, so he cannot simply stop.) Katz gives it as "nearly unanimous opinion" that the latter course of action is preferable; after all, five lives are saved at the expense of one, yielding a net balance of plus four.[97] But in the surgeon case, there are five patients on the verge of death, for lack of a heart, liver, etc. Along comes another patient with a full complement of organs; the surgeon kills him, and distributes these amongst the other five. Again, five lives are saved at the expense of one, yielding a net balance of plus four. But this time "opinions are nearly unanimous" that this would be illegal.[98]

Katz now states:

> Let's now consider a hypothetical that combines elements from both of the foregoing cases. Think again of the unstoppable trolley. Imagine that the driver can't make up his mind about what to do, and thus ends up running over the five, rather than the one. Miraculously, he doesn't kill them, but only hurts them badly. Never-

---

[96] Katz, *supra* note 3, at 1603–05.

[97] *Id.* at 1604.

[98] *Id.* at 1605.

theless, they are certain to die from their injuries *unless* furnished with certain transplant organs. ... Suppose now the driver deeply regrets not having turned the trolley and announces: 'It would have been all right had I turned the trolley and thereby killed the one for the sake of the five. I hesitated because I wanted to give the matter more thought. Upon reflection, I have decided it would indeed have been better to have killed the one to save the five, and I want to make up for my earlier omission. The victim really isn't entitled to protest: He is giving up nothing other than what I would have been entitled to take from him anyway.'[99]

Katz takes this to be evidence of the triumph of form over substance. If this consideration can work here, it can be applied as well to Anatole and the Museum. This, at least, is his defense for his form over substance analysis of that case. But there is an alternative explanation.[100] It is that the trolley conductor has only a choice between killing one or five people; no matter what he does, he will have to violate the rights of at least one person. The surgeon, in contrast, faces no such dilemma. He *need* not engage in the border crossing of *anyone*. True, five patients will die if he refrains from the initiation of aggression against an innocent victim, but if he refuses, he can at least be comforted by the fact that he followed the libertarian axiom.

And the same applies to Katz's trolley conductor who later changed his mind. First, it seems to be a bit of a stretch to say of the person who was spared when the five were killed that he is "giving up nothing other than what I would have been entitled to take from him anyway." The conductor was hardly *entitled* to kill this pedestrian; rather, he could not *avoid* doing so. Second, and more important, for the trolley driver, the *first* time around he *had* to kill someone by invasion; that is the essence of the dilemma. But the second time, after the conductor had reconsidered, he no longer *has* to engage in a border crossing. He could do nothing and allow his first five victims to die, the exact position occupied by the surgeon.

VII.A FURTHER OBJECTION

Say what you will about Katz, you must at least admit he is clear about what he is doing. No shilly-shallying and purposeful obfuscation for him. It is at least possible to achieve real disagreement with Katz, no mean accom-

---

[99] *Id.*

[100] I am indebted to Matthew Block for helping to put this point into focus for me.

plishment. He admits, in black and white, that his theory of blackmail depends on his (and our?) ability to tell the difference between "a sufficiently grave piece of obnoxiousness" and "of nothing more than garden-variety meanness."

And that makes blackmail, says Katz:

> [A] very odd kind of offense: As the defendant's threat edges up on, but stays shy of, some ill specified magical threshold, he is merely considered a crafty, nasty, unsavory, slightly immoral negotiator. Once he passes that threshold, his blameworthiness suddenly soars into the stratosphere—soars, that is, to the level of a regular blackmailer. That sort of radical discontinuity must seem both alarming and implausible.[101]

If this "radical discontinuity" were all that were wrong with his explanation, that alone would be sufficient to disqualify it from being a full and accurate account of blackmail. Who, after all, can make such fine, not to say meaningless, distinctions? But this does not at all end his problems. He has still not explained why we should regard any immoral albeit legal threat as that of an outlaw. *That* is the most serious drawback to his analysis.

Katz spends the next few pages claiming that as such radical discontinuity can be found in physics, chemistry, political elections, psychology, computers, anthropology, game theory, negligence law, the *mens rea* of knowledge, intention, and finally, alumni loyalty. But as this phenomenon is not really at the heart of the libertarian critique of Katz, we pass by these claims, all of which are really irrelevant to the issue of blackmail in any case.[102]

VIII. IMPLICATIONS, RAMIFICATIONS, SPECULATIONS

A. Crimes vs. Torts

Katz first draws an implication from his blackmail theory to the distinction between torts and crimes. As for the libertarian this is an invalid distinction, we shall not pursue him on this matter.[103]

---

[101] Katz, *supra* note 3, at 1605
[102] *Id.* at 1606.
[103] *Id.* at 1607–11.

B. Unconstitutional Conditions

As employed by Katz, this concept applies to a governmental grant of a favor (e.g., a subsidy) predicated on a condition that would not otherwise obtain (e.g., that the recipient not "air ... his political convictions").[104] As there would be no such governmental favors granted to anyone in a libertarian society, we again will not take Katz up on this matter.[105]

C. Nuclear Deterrence

Katz poses the question, If it is immoral to drop a nuclear bomb on someone, is it also immoral to threaten or intend to do so?[106] As stated, this query falls outside of the realm of libertarianism, which encompasses only legality, not morality. We can instead ask, if it is invasive to drop a nuclear bomb on someone, is it also a rights violation to threaten or intend to do so? The answer, at least as offered by Rothbard is a resounding "Yes."[107] The negative effects of such weapons cannot by their very nature be confined to guilty parties; they must necessarily impact innocent people, and are thus contrary to the non-aggression axiom. Intentions to the side,[108] threats of nuclear war also fall outside the realm of licit behavior.

Katz is inclined to argue to the contrary "if the policy really does what it purports to do, deter nuclear war."[109] But surely, if true, this would not be the first time on record that illicit threats had utilitarian effects. Or, to put this the other way around, just because an action has effects that some consider salutary does not mean it was not an improper border crossing. For example, banning homosexuality might well reduce the incidence of AIDS; still, to throw people in jail for adult consensual sex is a violation of their rights, something not to be tolerated in the libertarian society. Or, black male teenagers are disproportionately over represented in crime statistics. Were we to

---

[104] Rothbard, *supra* note 22, at 60 n. 1.

[105] But what of the limited government libertarian, who will eschew subsidies but will certainly allow for some government employment? May the state impose conditions on its civil servants, such as that they stay out of politics? This, presumably, would depend upon the stipulations of the agreement (the constitution) under which the government operates. But there would certainly be no blanket objection to such a stipulation.

[106] Katz, *supra* note 3, at 1613.

[107] *Id.*

[108] If people could be jailed for their unexpressed un-carried-out intentions, most of us would have long ago been incarcerated.

[109] Rothbard, *supra* note 16, at 190–91.

engage in preventive detention for this entire age-sex-race cohort, from, say, ages 13 to 19, the level of rapes, murders and robberies would undoubtedly decrease. But to do so would be a grave injustice, at least according to libertarianism, if not Katzianism; for this would involve the initiation of violence against innocent people (the overwhelming majority of black male teens who do not engage in criminal wrongdoing.) Similarly, a threat to do this would also constitute a serious inequity. Or, a ban on interracial dating, sex and marriage might well reduce the resentment, and increase the utility of (particularly) white males and black females, and all others who oppose this practice. Yet, according to the libertarian philosophy, such activity is well within the rights of all who engage in it.

Katz maintains that the installation of a spring gun which automatically shoots intruders is legally wrong if it actually is employed in that manner, since no one is "entitled to defend property by the use of deadly force."[110] Let us assume he is correct in this. Yet, he argues that the mere establishment of this mechanism, that is, the *threat* to shoot the burglar is not legally impermissible, since the "successfully demanded, not the threatened contingency, determines the level of blameworthiness of the defendant's conduct."[111] Here, the successfully demanded behavior is the "non-intrusion onto one's property," and since this is not morally blameworthy, neither is the threat which attains this goal.

About all that one can say of this is that it is indeed a logically consistent application of Katz's blackmail theory. But suppose I blackmail you into doing something good. For example, you are an overweight rubber fetishist, who is ashamed only of the latter. I threaten that unless you go on a diet, I will disclose your secret. Since a diet, by stipulation is good for you, the presumption is that I am not acting immorally.[112] This being the case, Katz could not condemn this as blackmail. Yet, it has all the earmarks of Katz's canonical case of blackmail, if ever there was one.

IX. THE LOGIC OF THE ARGUMENT

It has been a pleasure chasing down Katz. Although I disagree with him on many things, I am aware in reading him of dealing with a lively mind, one

---

[110] Katz, *supra* note 3, at 1613.

[111] *Id.*

[112] As a libertarian, I am by definition limited to engaging in legal analysis, and precluded from engaging in the moral variety; thus, I can only entertain this line of thought for argument's sake.

determined to "pursue … [the] ripple effects odd assumptions in one area can have in an entirely different area."[113] It is a delight to deal with someone willing to confront the logical implications of his theory, *wherever* they lead.

Nevertheless, I must conclude that the libertarian position on blackmail, that it should be decriminalized, remains unscathed, Katz's best efforts to the contrary notwithstanding.

---

[113] Katz, *supra* note 3, at 1614.

Chapter 3.

Toward a Libertarian Theory of Blackmail:

Rejoinder to Fletcher

I. INTRODUCTION

As we will attempt to apply the legal code of the libertarian political philosophy to the issue of blackmail, we do well by starting off defining our terms.

Rothbard notes that this "legal code, simply, would insist on the libertarian principle of no aggression against person or property, (and) define property rights in accordance with libertarian principle."[1]

Under this system people would be free to do whatever they wished, without limits, except that they would have to respect everyone else's right to be free in the same sense. They could do this if and only if they refrained from initiating violence, or the threat thereof, against another person or his property.

Blackmail is the request for money or other valuable consideration, coupled with an offer, typically, to refrain from exposing a secret embarrassing to the blackmailee. Since it is legal to request money, and it is lawful to make offers, one would think that a complex act composed of both of these elements would also pass muster under our system of jurisprudence. But such is not the case. On the contrary, blackmail is considered a crime.

More broadly, blackmail is the request or demand for money or other valuable consideration, coupled with any offer or threat, the carrying out of which involves no criminal behavior. For example, instead of offering to refrain from exposing a secret embarrassing to the blackmailee, one could offer to refrain from attempting to seduce the blackmailee's fiancé. Alternatively, one could threaten to seduce his fiancé, unless he were paid off not to do so. Since seduction is not a criminal act, nor is a request or demand for money, again we arrive at the same paradox: if two acts are legal, separately, how can they become illegal when combined?

Whether in the broad or narrow interpretation, blackmail must be sharply distinguished from extortion, which it superficially resembles. In the latter case, there is the same request or demand for funds or other valuables.

---

[1] MURRAY N. ROTHBARD, THE ETHICS OF LIBERTY 235 (1982). This is based on homesteading virgin land and, thereafter, voluntary commercial acts such as trade and gifts. *See* on this HANS-HERMANN HOPPE, THE ECONOMICS AND ETHICS OF PRIVATE PROPERTY: STUDIES IN POLITICAL ECONOMY AND PHILOSOPHY.

But now, instead of an accompanying threat to do, or offer to refrain from doing something legal, it is to engage in criminal behavior. For example, the extortionist threatens to blow up your house, or kill your children unless he is paid, or to refrain from doing so, upon receipt of a payoff.

Perhaps the following depiction will clarify matters:

	Blackmail	**Extortion**
Demand	money (legal)	money (legal)
Threat	to tell secret (legal)	to kill children (illegal)
Request	money (legal)	money (legal)
Offer	to remain quiet (legal)	to refrain from killing children (illegal)

This state of affairs, two legal "whites" combining to constitute a legal "black," has been considered a paradox by several commentators. Fletcher argues to the contrary "that blackmail is not an anomalous crime but rather a paradigm for understanding both criminal wrongdoing and punishment."[2]

Why? Our author asks: "Why should an innocent end (silence) coupled with a generally respectable means (monetary payment) constitute a crime?"[3] He argues that "This supposed paradox ... is not peculiar to blackmail." And why not? Because "many good acts are corrupted by doing them for a price." This, right off the bat, is in sharp contrast with libertarianism, since paying for something is not *per se* invasive. Therefore, from this perspective, if it is legal to do X, it is also legal to pay for X; there may conceivably be a moral "corrup-

---

[2] George P. Fletcher, *Blackmail: The Paradigmatic Case*, 141 U. PA. L. REV. 1617, 1617–38 (1993).

[3] *Id.* at 1617.

tion" involved in making a payment for something, but there can be no legal defilement.[4]

How does Fletcher defend this contention? He offers three examples. One: "There is nothing wrong with government officials showing kindness or doing favors for their constituents, but doing them for a negotiated price becomes bribery."[5]

For purist libertarians, there shouldn't be any politicians in the first place; this is because government itself, in the absence of a contract (constitution) signed unanimously, is invalid. The politicians themselves are the anomaly. Therefore, the question of their being bribed does not arise.

In the more moderate version of this philosophy, there is indeed room for the state. Here, government has certain legitimate roles, typically limited to courts, armies and police. Politicians and bureaucrats may indeed do "favors for their constituents" but these are severely truncated. They would be restricted to defending person and property against invasion.[6] Certainly, no "favors" of the usual pork barrel or subsidy variety would be tolerated. Politicians would have far less to do than at present.

However, suppose the friendly neighborhood cop protected a citizen from a mugger, and then turned around and charged him for this service. This would certainly be untoward, but would not at all indicate that otherwise good acts can be corrupted by money payments. The unlawful behavior, here, would not be bribery, but contract violation. In any reasonable police arrangement, a "no tipping" policy would be strictly enforced, lest it set in train motivations which would undermine the whole operation.

But similar adaptations prevail in the non-political arena. For example, a disc jockey is hired to play records which in his expert opinion are the "best." If financial considerations from record companies play any part in his choices, the entire radio station will come under suspicion. Therefore, the firm is likely to contractually bar any bribes for its disk jockeys. But suppose it

---

[4] Some acts *cannot* be done for a price. For example, there can be no such thing as the purchase of true friendship. But this is not a legal "cannot," rather a logical one. That is, if a relationship is purchased, the English language functions so as to logically preclude the possibility that it is true friendship. Alternatively, if there is a true friendship, it, by its very nature, could not have been purchased by either of the friends. But this is very different than the view expressed in the text.

[5] Fletcher, *supra* note 2, at 1617.

[6] In the more radical version of libertarianism, these functions, like all others, would be privatized; a competing defense industry composed of police, army and court firms would play this role.

did not. Presume, that is, that the radio station publicly announced,[7] perhaps in view of the fact that the wages it offered were being seriously reduced, that its disk jockeys would henceforth be free to accept bribes, and choose records on this basis. The station would have to take its chances with its customers—listeners and advertisers—but since nothing in this scenario is equivalent to the initiation of violence against person or property, no libertarian law would have been violated. Of course, a private police firm might engage in this commercially risky practice as well. If so, this is but further evidence of the fact that financial payments do not render invalid otherwise licit acts. Now assume that a government were so constituted as to allow and encourage side payments to its civil servants. As long as this were open and above board, while certainly peculiar, this practice, too, would not be legally improper. This indicates that it is not the side order payments, themselves, which render this practice improper, but rather its behind closed doors (e.g., fraudulent nature).

Fletcher's second case in point is that "Sex is often desirable and permissible by itself, but if done in exchange for money, the act becomes prostitution."[8]

The response here is simple. Prostitution should be legalized, forthwith. It is a victimless crime.[9] In some political jurisdictions it is already legal, such as rural Nevada, the Netherlands, etc.[10]

Fletcher's third example is "Confessing to a crime may be praiseworthy in some circumstances, but if the police pay the suspect to confess, the confession will undoubtedly be labeled involuntary and inadmissible."[11]

This is a rather weird scenario. Ordinarily, our concern is with police torturing suspects into confessing, not paying them to do so. Were this all there

---

[7] So that there could be no question of fraud.

[8] Fletcher, *supra* note 2, at 1617.

[9] It is not a victimless crime in the sense that no one can rationally object to it, nor be hurt by it. But the same can be said of practically anything. For example, suppose I open up a grocery store. No more innocent an occupation can be imagined. Are there any "victims?" Certainly, there are: at the very least, the employers and employees of already extant and thus competing groceries. Just as in the case of prostitution, or drugs, some of these people may become despondent, even kill themselves or others. But opening a grocery store, for all that, is still a victimless activity, for what we mean by a crime with victims is one where initiatory violence is used against innocent people. Neither grocers nor prostitutes fit this particular bill.

[10] This does not mean that prostitution would be allowed everywhere. As long as restrictive covenants and other forms of market zoning are allowed, such activities will be confined to areas where they cause few negative externalities. Bernard H. Siegan, *Non-Zoning in Houston*, 13 J. L. & ECON. 71 (1970); BERNARD SIEGAN, LAND USE WITHOUT ZONING.

[11] Fletcher, *supra* note 2, at 1617.

were to it, however, it would be unobjectionable. I didn't really steal that TV. But if the cops pay me $1,000,000, hell, I'll "confess" to it. Mutual gains from trade, and all that.

But this isn't really all there is to it. The problem is, under these assumptions, the real thief will get away; the police will no longer look for him, as they have me in custody, the "confessed" robber. Thus, this devolves into our answer to the favor giving politician: it is another example of a contract violation. The reason we hire police is to catch criminals; if they "buy" convictions, they are violating their contract with us.

These three examples having failed in their task, we are forced to conclude, then, that the ordinary common sense insight remains standing, despite Fletcher's best anti-market efforts to undermine it: if an act is legal, doing it for a payment cannot render it criminal.

1. Ten Cases

Fletcher's method in the remainder of his paper is to highlight ten legal cases and then use them as a vantage point from which to consider various theories of blackmail.[12] Let us follow in his footsteps.

Here are the 10 cases:

1. Crime case: D[13] threatens, if not paid, to report V's suspected crime to the local prosecutor.

2. Tort case: V rams his car into D's. D threatens to sue if V does not compensate D for the resulting damage.

3. Hush money: D threatens to reveal a damaging truth, say a sexual peccadillo, about the celebrity V unless the latter pays "hush money." The threat is supported by incriminating pictures.

4. Late employee: D, V's employer, threatens to fire V if he does not get to work on time.

5. Lascivious employer: D, V's employer, threatens to fire V unless he sleeps with her.

6. Baseball case: D offers to sell V a baseball autographed by Babe Ruth with knowledge that V's child, who is dying, would receive solace from having the ball. D demands $6,000 for the ball

---

12 *Id.* at 1618–20.

13 D, presumably, stands for defendant, or possible blackmailer, while V stands for victim. I have no problem with using D for defendant, but as I do not consider blackmail a crime, I cannot consider the person being blackmailed as a victim. Instead of that terminology, I use the more neutral "blackmailee."

7. Dinner kiss: D says to V: "If you do not go to dinner with me, I will not kiss you." Alternatively, D says to V: "If you do go to dinner with me, I will kiss you."

8. Tattoo case: D tells his friends that unless they pay him money, he will have his entire body tattooed.

9. Political embarrassment: V is a black political candidate. D is a black activist with anti-white views, whose connections to V are an embarrassment to V. D goes to V and tells him that unless he is paid off, he will speak out and repeatedly declare his support for V, thereby sabotaging V's electoral chances.

10. Paid silence: Same story as in 9, but V goes to D and offers him $20,000 to "lay low" until after the election.

What I would like to do at this time is to compare and contrast Fletcher's evaluation of these cases with my own.[14] But one must step carefully here, for Fletcher divides them into the categories: the crime of "blackmail" and "no crime," while my categories are: the non-crime of "blackmail" and the crime of "extortion."[15] If we were each to stick to our own categorizations, the baseball scorecard would look like this:

	Fletcher	Block	Agreement?
1. Crime	blackmail	blackmail	no
2. Tort	no crime	blackmail	yes
3. Hush money	blackmail	blackmail	no
4. Late employee	no crime	blackmail	yes
5. Lascivious employer	blackmail	blackmail	no
6. Baseball	no crime	blackmail	yes
7. Dinner kiss	no crime	blackmail	yes
8. Tattoo	no crime	blackmail	yes
9. Political embarrassment	blackmail	blackmail	no
10. Paid silence	no crime	blackmail	yes

---

[14] Fletcher, *supra* note 2, at 1618–20.

[15] *Id.*

My reasoning, it will be remembered, is that if what D threatens or offers is (or rather should be under the libertarian code) *per se* legal, then we have the non-crime of blackmail. On the other hand, if what D threatens or offers is (or rather should be under the libertarian code) *per se* illegal, then we have the crime of extortion. For me, whether or not money changes hands is strictly irrelevant. Let us now consider each of these cases in detail.

1. Is it, or should it be legal, for D to report V's suspected crime to the local prosecutor? In order not to deal with a straw man, we assume the worst case scenario for the libertarian point of view. That is, we posit that V did not in fact engage in the forbidden action, and that D full well knows this. Under these circumstances, it should still not be illegal for D to exercise his free speech rights, because they do not constitute an invasion.[16] And, having threatened to say something he has every right to say, unless he is paid, this act must be considered licit blackmail, not illicit extortion.

How can we categorize falsely accusing someone of a theft? The appropriate terminology would be libel. This, in turn, is usually considered a crime, but would not be by libertarians. Explains Rothbard;

> Smith has a property right to the ideas or opinions in his own head; he also has a property right to print anything he wants and disseminate it. He has a property right to say that Jones is a 'thief' even if he knows it to be false, and to print and sell that statement.[17]

The usual argument against this line of reasoning is that if D falsely claims that V is a thief, he has ruined D's reputation; the real robber, then, is D, for making such a statement. The problem here is that V's reputation consists of the thoughts of many people about him, not his own about himself, and thus cannot be owned by anyone else, least of all the person to whom it

---

[16] Does this means that anything goes? That anyone may say anything he wishes at any time? No. Certain types of speech constitute invasions. For example, if I hold a gun on you and yell "Your money or your life!" this is a paradigm case of initiatory aggression, even apart from actually pulling the trigger. (If I am sufficiently larger and/or stronger than you, I will not even need a gun). Similarly, if your son is at sea where he cannot be reached, and I tell you that I hold him captive and ask for funds to secure his release, this too is an example of "mere" speech constituting a criminal border crossing.

[17] Rothbard, *supra* note 1, at 126.

refers, V. Therefore, D, in "taking away" V's reputation, has not seized from V anything that V can legitimately own.[18]

But isn't it worse to make libelous statements to the police and courts? They, after all, can lock you up, or, worse, impose the death penalty on the basis of such "free speech." On the contrary, in the libertarian world each person is responsible for his own acts. If the police or courts foolishly trust the statement about V by D, it is their responsibility. They will have engaged in an unwarranted border crossing, and when the truth gets out, they will have to pay the appropriate penalty.[19] Doing this is *a fortiori* no worse than an incitement which leads to death or injury. Rothbard illuminates:

> Should it be illegal ... to 'incite to riot?' Suppose that Green exhorts a crowd: 'Go! Burn! Loot! Kill!' and the mob proceeds to do just that, with Green having nothing further to do with these criminal activities. Since every man is free to adopt or not adopt any course of action he wishes, we cannot say that in some way Green determined the members of the mob to their criminal activities; we cannot make him, because of his exhortation, at all responsible for their crimes. 'Inciting to riot,' therefore, is a pure exercise of a man's right to speak without being thereby implicated in crime.[20]

The point is, that if a man has a right to incite, he certainly has a right[21] to bear false witness to the police or courts. Even on a mere utilitarian basis, he is likely to do far less harm, for there experts will be taking his testimony, as opposed to members of an unruly mob.

2. Should it be legal for D to threaten V with a law suit, unless he pays for the damages inflicted on D's car? Yes, it should be always legal for anyone to launch a law suit against anyone else. Therefore, to threaten to do so would constitute legitimate blackmail, not extortion. True, there is such a thing as malicious prosecution, where the plaintiff can be successfully sued for launching annoying lawsuits. But to bring suit is not *per se* a rights violation; therefore, threatening to do so should be legal.

---

[18] For a further elaboration of this point, including a demonstration that, paradoxically, reputations would be safer in a libertarian world than they are now, *see* WALTER BLOCK, DEFENDING THE UNDEFENDABLE 59–62; Rothbard, *supra* note 1, at 126–7.

[19] This is an unusual claim. Typically, officials of the justice system are protected from the error of their ways. This would not be so under libertarianism.

[20] Rothbard, *supra* note 1, at 80.

[21] We are, throughout this article, concerned only with legal rights, not moral rights.

3. Should it be legal to threaten to reveal an embarrassing secret, unless one is paid off not to do so? (Alternatively, should it be legal to remain silent about this secret, for remuneration?) The answer from the libertarian perspective is a definite Yes, since publicizing this secret, e.g., gossiping about it, is itself legal. How can threatening to do something that would not violate the law if carried out be criminal?

4. Should it be legal for D, V's employer, to fire V if he does not get to work on time? Of course it should. It is always legitimate to fire an employee for any reason at all, at any time, assuming that there is no long run contract in force. Since it is lawful to do this, it must of necessity be licit to threaten to do this.

5. Should it be legal to fire an employee who refuses to sleep with the boss? Precisely the same analysis applies to this case as to the previous one. If the employer has a right to fire a worker for any reason, then this applies whether men of good will would likely support the reason (as in the "late employee" case) or not (as in the present one). Any attempt to show a relevant difference is doomed to failure. Fletcher makes this attempt by citing Feinberg to the effect that the lascivious employer is guilty of "exploitation."[22] But one man's exploitation is another man's voluntarily agreed upon contract. Why is it necessarily more exploitative (whatever that weasel word means) to agree to sleep with the boss than to come to work on time? For some people, surely, it will be less onerous to do the former than the latter, although such slothful types will likely be in the minority.

There is simply no reason for the law to accept certain voluntary contracts between consenting adults (ones stipulating that the worker has to appear at the office on time), while rejecting others (those stipulating a dual job, such as cook and bottle washer, or, more controversially, prostitute and secretary). If prostitution itself should be legal, then so should a job which combines that profession with any other, such as, say, nursing, or teaching.[23]

6. Should it be legal for D to sell V a baseball card for $6,000, so that a dying boy can have solace? Fletcher categorizes this as non-criminal,[24] as do I. In my case, since there is no physical invasion of person or property involved in the "threat" to withhold the good unless the seller is paid, it is a licit act. But what of our author? Why doesn't Fletcher adopt a point of view consistent with his analysis of the lascivious employer? It is morally obnoxious in the

---

[22] Fletcher, *supra* note 2, at 1619, fn. 6.

[23] I personally regard such behavior as morally reprehensible, but that is entirely a different matter. *See* Walter Block, *Libertarianism vs. Libertinism*, 11 J. LIBERTARIAN STUD. at 117–28 (1994).

[24] Fletcher, *supra* note 2, at 1619.

minds of most people to combine the jobs of secretary and prostitute, the reason, presumably, he called this a crime. But this applies also (equally?, more so?) to "taking advantage" of a young child on his deathbed.

7. Should it be legally allowable for D to offer a kiss to V as a reward (penalty?) for going to dinner with him? The "threat," here, is that if V refuses the culinary invitation, the kiss will be withheld. This is just one in the vast number of "capitalist acts between consenting adults" that people involve themselves in.[25] Since it does not imply the initiation of aggression, the libertarian will have no trouble in passing on this as legal. But again Fletcher, who also regards this as "no crime," has some explaining to do.[26]

Why is this any different than the case of the lascivious employer? If we alter the players a bit, and change the sexual act from a kiss to intercourse, it would appear that we have the same example once again. Surely these changes of degree are irrelevant to the principle of the matter. The majesty of the law should, presumably, take no notice of the difference, except for degree of punishment. If so, how comes Fletcher to take one side here, and the other, there?[27]

8. Fletcher and I both agree that people should be allowed to threaten their friends that they will tattoo themselves all over if they are not paid.[28]

9., 10. This is really the same example as far as I am concerned. In example 9, the radical black activist seeks money from the black politician to stay out of the latter's campaign; in example 10., the politician offers money to the radical black activist to stay away. For the libertarian, both are instances of blackmail, and should thus be considered legal. A contract is a contract; it matters not one whit who initiates it in terms of legality.

For Fletcher, matters are otherwise.[29] He designates the blackmailer initiated example as "blackmail," and the blackmailee initiated one as "no crime." Again, he has a bit of explaining to do.

Let us now look at all 10 cases as a whole. I regard each and every one of them as an instance of blackmail, since none of the ten threats, if carried out, would be (better yet, should be) illegal. None of them were extortionate, since no threat of killing, maiming, etc., if valuable considerations were not forthcoming, ever appeared. Fletcher disagrees on cases 1, 3, 5, and 9.[30] But we are in accord that it is irrelevant whether the demand is in terms of money, sexual

---

[25] *See* Robert Nozick, Anarchy, State and Utopia.

[26] Fletcher, *supra* note 2, at 1619.

[27] *Id.*

[28] *Id.*

[29] *Id.* at 1619–20.

[30] *Id.* at 1618–20.

favors, or other valuable considerations. Furthermore, we agree that there is no "principled distinction" to be made between the threat to disclose unwelcome information (3. hush money) and firing a worker (5. lascivious employer).[31] We do not concur, however, on the issue of the threshold.[32] The difference between a kiss and sexual intercourse is of no moment, I maintain. If these favors are attained through legitimate non-invasive means (no use or threat of force or fraud), either is permissible; if not, not. Libertarianism is black and white on this issue: either the threat is invasive or not; if so, it constitutes extortion, if not, blackmail.[33]

2. Threats and Offers

In this and the next few sections of his paper, our author examines these ten cases through various types of eyeglasses. Fletcher is on strong ground when he refuses to buy into the notion that all threats should be outlawed, and all offers legitimized.[34] As he correctly points out, "not all threats ... are criminal; for example, the threat to sue in the tort case (no. 2), is considered permissible. So too the threat in the tattoo case (no. 8)." Further, one can never the forget Marlon Brando, in "The Godfather" movie, making his victims "an offer they cannot refuse." With "offers" like these, who needs threats?

It is thus hard to accept his view that "[a]n all too facile resolution of these cases is that they contain threats that D has the right to make."[35] An "offer" or a threat to cut your throat unless you abide by my commands is illicit, since I have no right to cut your throat. An offer or a threat to sue you unless you abide by my commands should be legal, since I do have a right to launch a lawsuit against you.

Moreover, Fletcher is on weak ground when he accepts the notion that "Coercion is immoral because it deprives the victim of an option she would

---

[31] *Id.* at 1620.

[32] *Id.* at 1621.

[33] Libertarians, of course, along with everyone else, are aware that there is a continuum between aggression and non-aggression. If I bring my fist to within one inch of your nose with "bad intentions," this is clearly an initiation of violence, even though I have not hit you (yet). On the other hand, if I shake my fist at your from one mile away, this is clearly not. Well, at what precise point does a (legally) meaningless gesture become a "clear and present danger?" This is a grey area for all philosophical viewpoints.

[34] Fletcher, *supra* note 2, at 1621.

[35] *Id.*

have had, and this deprivation interferes with her autonomy, i.e., her freedom of action."[36]

Coercion of this sort may well be immoral,[37] but it certainly should not be illegal. If it were, his theory would be wildly over inclusive, as it would drag into its clutches most if not all competitive activity. For example, the successfully competing grocer will cost you profits, and eventually, perhaps, drive you into bankruptcy. If so, this will deprive you of an "option" you would otherwise had, apart from his action, and this will undoubtedly interfere with your "autonomy, i.e., (your) freedom of action." That is to say, you will have far fewer resources, because of this grocer's "coercion."

Nor is his reliance on "the baseline of normalcy" at all convincing.[38] For here, "we may regard proposed changes for the worse as threats." But we have already seen that the new grocery store would comprise a change for the worse for you. Therefore, according to Fletcher, this would be a threat and, thus, presumably, outlawed. Preposterous.

This leads Fletcher to a another philosophical blunder. He says:

> Suppose that D sells sports memorabilia and the normal asking price for the ball autographed by Babe Ruth is $600. If V has an expectation and a right to buy at $600, then D's setting the price ten times higher constitutes a threat to withhold the ball unless V pays the exploitative price. It is as though D threatened to take the ball away from V if V did not pay an additional $5400.[39]

Right now, as I am writing this, I am in the process of trying to arrange for a trip from Little Rock, Arkansas to Rome, Italy, in order to give a speech there. I had expected that the price would be about $650. I have just learned, much to my consternation, that the actual cost will be in the neighborhood of $1300, roughly double the amount of what I regard as normal.[40] In effect, I am V, and the airline, D. Did I have a "right" to buy at $650 merely because I had an "expectation" that this would be the price? Seemingly, according to Fletcher, I did have that right. Therefore, the airline's "setting the price (twice as high) constitutes a threat to withhold the (ticket) unless I pays the exploita-

---

[36] *Id.*

[37] Who knows, since this author has given us not criterion on the basis of which to judge?

[38] Fletcher, *supra* note 2, at 1622.

[39] *Id.* at 1622 fn. 11.

[40] True, I don't have to pay it, but I have to go through the embarrassment of telling my host in Italy, who had asked me to arrange travel from this end, that he will have to pay an additional $650.

tive price. It is as though (the airline) threatened to take the (ticket) away from (me) if I (or rather my host) did not pay an additional $650." One shudders at such a conclusion. For this is by no means limited to philosophical speculation. Fletcher is seriously putting forth a theory of criminal behavior. This means, did he but have his way, the airline executives would be accused of blackmail, and face a fine or a term in the pokey.[41]

This reasoning also leads Fletcher to a misconceived support for Nozick's fallacious "productive activity."[42] After Rothbard's utter evisceration of this concept, it is difficult to understand why anyone would still utilize it. Rothbard points out that Nozick

> concedes, for example, that his reason for outlawing blackmail would force him also to outlaw the following contract: Brown comes to Green, his next-door neighbor, with the following proposition: I intend to build such-and-such a pink building on my property (which he knows Green will detest). I won't build this building, however, if you pay me X amount of money. Nozick concedes that this, too, would have to be illegal in his schema, because Green would be paying Brown for not being worse off, and hence the contract would be 'non-productive.' In essence, Green would be better off if Brown dropped dead. It is difficult, however, for a libertarian to square such outlawry with any plausible theory of property rights. ... In analogy with the blackmail example above, furthermore, Nozick concedes that it would be legal, in his schema, for Green, on finding out about Brown's projected pink building, to come to Brown and offer to pay him not to go ahead. But why would such an exchange be 'productive' just because Green made the offer? What difference does it make who makes the offer in this situation? Wouldn't Green still be better off if Brown dropped dead? And again, following the analogy, would Nozick make it illegal for Brown to refuse Green's offer and then ask for more money? Why? Or, again, would Nozick make it illegal for Brown to subtly

---

[41] I also have certain expectations about my wife, children, friends, employers, etc., which, not to put too fine a point on it, are not always fully satisfied. (In contrast, I am perfect, and always satisfy any expectations that anyone has ever had of me. Thus, according to Fletcher, I, alone, would not be subject to the penalties accorded to blackmailers.) As for these other people, if they don't watch out, I'll sic Fletcher on them, and they will face jail time. Well, maybe I had better not make this threat, or Fletcher will accuse me of criminal blackmail. Come to think of it, I hereby retract this threat.

[42] Fletcher, *supra* note 2, at 1622 fn. 11.

let Green know about the projected pink building and then let nature take its course: say, by advertising in the paper about the building and sending Green the clipping? Couldn't this be taken as an act of courtesy? And why should merely advertising something be illegal? Clearly, Nozick's case becomes ever more flimsy as we consider the implications.[43]

Another difficulty with predicating the analysis on "the normal situation" is that this elevates the status quo into a sort of legal litmus test. If, for example, in the hush money case (no. 3), it is normal for the information to be suppressed, then, according to Fletcher, this would be one of criminal blackmail. However, he also concedes that "if the normal situation is that the information leaks out," then the very opposite result obtains.[44] Come again?

But wait! Perhaps I am being unfair to this author. After all, at the end of this section, he turns around an criticizes this very notion of normalcy, dismissing it as "insuperably ambiguous," and sums up: "the distinction between threats and offers is not likely to get us very far."[45] This constitutes strong evidence that I am indeed misreading Fletcher. But I persevere in my error, if error it be: if Fletcher is not using something like the "normal situation," or Nozick's horrendously misbegotten notion of "productive activity,"[46] then how on earth is he able to determine that the "hush money" case (no. 3) is one of criminal blackmail? If gossip is the norm, and it sure is in certain circles, then this criterion would point in the diametric opposite direction.

3. Third Party Chips

In this section, Fletcher comments upon the work of Lindgren.[47] But he starts off on the wrong foot, stating that Lindgren has written a "comprehensive study [that] reviews the literature, pans all competing theories."[48] Lindgren[49] is not at all as comprehensive as Fletcher seems to think; it ignores a

---

[43] Rothbard, *supra* note 1, at 240–42.

[44] Fletcher, *supra* note 2, at 1623.

[45] *Id.*

[46] Hardin states: "Richard Posner says blackmail ... has no social product and should therefore be criminalized. This is a very odd conclusion. Much of what I do has no social product (for instance, I consume, I waste time), but surely it should not be criminalized." Russell Hardin , *Blackmailing for Mutual Good*, 141 U. PA. L. REV. at 1787–1816.

[47] Fletcher, *supra* note 2, at 1623–26.

[48] *Id.* at 1623.

[49] James Lindgren, *Unraveling the Paradox of Blackmail*, 84 COLUMBIA L. REV. 670 (1984).

whole host of libertarian articles critical of the blackmail as paradox perspective, maintaining, instead, that there is no paradox and that blackmail should be considered a legal (albeit not necessarily a moral) market activity.

Fletcher for the most part is sympathetic to Lindgren, noting that the latter's theory applies most directly to what Katz calls "informational blackmail," e.g., cases 1 and 3, crime and hush money.[50] Fletcher goes so far in helping Lindgren as to try to shoe horn the latter's theory so as to make it apply to the lascivious employer (no. 5) and political embarrassment (no. 9) cases.[51]

But then he lowers the boom. In his first critique argues that in both the political embarrassment and paid silence cases (no. 9, no. 10) "D plays with a chip that seems to belong to someone else," and yet V "is not the victim of blackmail if he initiates the transaction."[52] I suppose my "intuition" is very different from Fletcher's and that of the "most people" he reports on in this regard. Take the hush money case (no. 3). If V were to approach D, and plead with him to keep secret V's marital infidelity for a fee, my reading of the man on the street is that he would say that this, too, is blackmail. Certainly Rothbard's Green-Brown example comes out much the same way no matter who takes the first step. Why should it matter who opens the negotiations when V, by stipulation, has a "gun" being held over him in any case?

Moreover, there can not be property rights in information. If information is the chip, then anyone who knows it, legitimately owns it. If I see the potential blackmailee coming and going from a woman's home across the street from me at odd hours of the night, to say that I do not own this information is to say that I do not own the evidence of my own eyes.

His second critique is a telling one against Lindgren. Here, Fletcher argues that in the baseball case (no. 6);

> She (the seller) drives a hard exploitative bargain, but one that is neither criminal blackmail nor any other form of crime. The windfall profits derive from her taking advantage of something that does not belong to her, namely, the child's and parent's consumer surplus in possessing the ball. She is bargaining with a chip that does not belong to her, and for Lindgren, that should be enough to render her demand criminal. Since by common agreement it is not criminal, there must be something awry in Lindgren's argument.[53]

---

[50] Leo Katz & James Lindgren, *Instead of a Preface*, 141 U. PA. L. REV. 1565, 1565–67 (1993).

[51] Fletcher, *supra* note 2, at 1624.

[52] *Id.*

[53] *Id.* at 1625.

There are only two difficulties here. The first, somewhat off the main point, is, how can a commercial interaction which is voluntary for buyer and seller be "exploitative." Surely there would be consumer surplus on both sides, even at the higher price. If there were not, the two parties would not have both agreed to consummate the transaction. Second, "chip ownership" is a lot more "flexible" than Fletcher seems to think. It is always open to Lindgren to assert that the baseball seller really owns the child's and parent's consumer surplus. With an ambiguous term such as "chips," anyone may say anything he likes. Which leads to the real problem, the slipperiness of the concept.

Third, Fletcher criticizes Lindgren for utilizing "a notion of extra-legal moral rights."[54] If Fletcher had gone on to state that these were a concoction, something created out of the whole cloth with no justification, he would have been on firm footing. After all, anyone can create rights de novo, and then brand as criminals those who violate them. For example, I hereby declare, as a matter of law, the "right" to be free of left handed red heads. We can now hunt down these people, mercilessly, secure in the knowledge that we are upholding this new "right."

Instead, however, Fletcher accepted these Lindgren-created other-people's-chip "rights," and argued that even if they were valid the criminal law does not uphold these as legal rights. My response is, this is legal positivism run amuck. Yes, happily, the law has not yet entrenched Lindgren. For once, the criminal law is correct in not recognizing "chip rights." But, contrary to fact conditional, suppose it did, as Fletcher seemingly accepts. Then wouldn't it be proper to penalize those who played with others' chips?

Fletcher's demurs. His reason? He asserts: "We do not penalize cheating on exams, committing adultery with other people's wives or husbands, or even stealing numerous forms of intellectual property."[55] But isn't cheating on an exam a form of fraud, and shouldn't we punish fraud? Why should stealing intellectual property occupy a different legal category than other types of property? We certainly throw embezzlers in jail. And, as for adultery, there were certainly times in history when this was treated as a crime. That this no longer obtains is more an effect of governmental monopolization of the marriage contract than that the law should not punish crime. That is to say, were we to have erected a wall between marriage and state of the sort that some advocate for church and state, it is the rare contract, probably, that would stipulate a jail sentence for adultery. Governmentally imposed marriage contracts do make adultery a crime, but this has become a dead letter law. In any

---

[54] *Id.* at 1623.

[55] *Id.*

case, it cannot be used to make Fletcher's (contrary to fact) point against Lindgren.

4. Dominance and Subordination

Having cleared the decks, so to speak, of "all" contending theories, Fletcher is now ready to regale us with the correct solution. It turns out that this is a variant of the Marxian critique of hierarchies based on dominance (bad) and subordination (victim status).

A key element of this insight is that the blackmailer can keep "coming back for more." This is illustrated in the difference between the crime (no. 1) and tort (no. 2) cases. According to Fletcher,

> if V pays D an amount necessary to settle the tort dispute between them, D must release his claim. He cannot thereafter come back to V and demand more. But if V pays D money to suppress a criminal investigation, D retains the option of coming back for more. ... Living with that knowledge puts the victim of blackmail in a permanently subordinate position.[56]

A difficulty is that mere domination cannot be necessarily be a crime. In the Marxist lexicon, the employer always dominates the employee; does that mean that the boss always blackmails the worker? One would suppose so, at least in Fletcher's Marxist world. In the feminist lexicon, the female is always subordinate to the male; does that mean that all women are always and ever being victimized by the blackmail of men. One can only suppose so, in Fletcher's feminist world. In the black "studies" lexicon, the black is always subordinate to the white; does that mean that all people of African extraction are always and ever being victimized by the blackmail of those with a Caucasian background? Again, one can only suppose so, in this particular world view.

But this is only the tip of the iceberg. If A is more in love with B than B is with A, then B can get more from A than A can get from B. This may, conceivably, result in B blackmailing A (heck, it could also result in B extorting from A, almost anything is possible in these made up scenarios), but need it do so, as is logically implied by Fletcher? Hardly.

Something like this domination–subordination relationship will occur, more generally, in any case where X wants what Y has more than Y wants what X has. Usually, a price change will alter this, and, presumably, sweep

---

[56] *Id.*

away the blackmail. For example, if the demand for apples is greater than the supply thereof, suppliers will "dominate" (e.g., criminally blackmail) the demanders, until price rises so as to equate the two sides of the market, and stop this nefarious activity.

Having established this criterion, at least to his own satisfaction, Fletcher now moves on to a consideration of how it can shed light on his ten cases.

It would appear that dominance and subordination illuminates the hush money case (no. 3). The key seems to be that even after V pays off D, V will still never have a moment's peace, because D can always make new demands in the future. According to Fletcher: "This is the essence of the blackmail—not in the transaction itself, but the relationship of dominance implicit in taking the first step of inducing the victim to pay money for her own protection." [57]

One minor point, to begin with. Fletcher seems to resent the idea that people would be forced to pay for their "own protection." But even under present circumstances, it is people's tax money that is used in (very small) part, for this purpose. Unfortunately, much of the proceeds earmarked for this purpose are used not to protect the victims of crime,[58] but rather to ensure procedural niceties to protect the "rights" of criminals.

Now for the major point. Fletcher would appear to have inverted the usual time dimension of criminality. In the traditional case, crimes take place in the past and are punished in the future. Here, there is an inversion: the blackmailer is guilty not for any action he has already taken, but for those he might take in the future. Fletcher worries that "Even if D says that she is surrendering the pictures and the negatives, there is no assurance that copies have not been made" and might conceivably be brought to bear eventually.[59] Citing Altman, Fletcher bewails the fact that "there cannot be any guarantee that a first payment will not be followed by more demands."[60] What a way to run criminal law—on the basis of what people might do in the future. On this ground, we are all due for a spell in the pokey. For example, I might punch

---

[57] *Id.* at 1627.

[58] Real crime, that is, physical invasions against person or property, not blackmail.

[59] Fletcher, *supra* note 2, at 1627.

[60] *Id.*

you in the nose, next Tuesday. Shall I be incarcerated now for this "crime?" This would appear to be the logical implication of the Fletcher analysis.[61]

A slightly more sympathetic interpretation of Fletcher would have it not that he advocates putting people in the slammer, now, for what they might do in the future, but putting them in jail for presently having an illicit "hold" over someone. For example, the blackmailer who has just been paid off, still has a "hold" over the blackmailee. The former can always "com(e) back for more."

But this is over inclusive. There are lots of people who have a hold over the head's of other people, or who have something "on" others, who are still walking around free, and quite properly so. For example, parents have something on their young kids, in that they can always abandon them; later, adult kids have an implicit threat hanging over their now aging parents: the very same one. To return to our friends the Marxists, in their view, there is a employer's sword of Damocles hanging over every worker: he can always be fired. In like manner, the feminists and black "studies" theoreticians make similar claims vis-à-vis males and females, white and blacks. The doctor with a good bedside manner (and a record of successful operations), the heroin seller, the husband who is nice to his wife (or mean to her in the case of masochism), all set up dependencies, and thus have an implicit threat to hang over the heads of the people with whom they deal, e.g., the sick patient, the addict, the wife. According to Fletcher, they would all be guilty of blackmail. No, this interpretation will scarcely keep any[62] of us out of jail, if we accept this analysis.

Fletcher thinks that:

> So long as V shows up on time, D can make no additional threat of dismissal" (discussing the late employee case (no. 4), and that, in contrast, in the lascivious employer case (no. 5), if "V sleeps with D, he places himself in her power. The initial submission establishes a

---

[61] This is eerily reminiscent of the Coase-Posner-Demsetz "Law and Economics" approach which determines property rights not on the basis of the past, but predicates it upon speculations as to what people might do in the future. Specifically, it will tip the balance in favor of those whose future acts are expected to most raise economic wealth. *See* RICHARD A. POSNER, ECONOMIC ANALYSIS OF LAW; Ronald Coase, *The Problem of Social Cost*, 3 J. L. & ECON. 1 (1960); Harold Demsetz, *Ethics and Efficiency in Property Rights Systems*, in TIME, UNCERTAINTY AND DISEQUILIBRIUM: EXPLORATIONS OF AUSTRIAN THEMES (Mario Rizzo, ed.).

[62] All people are either whites, or males, or employers, or parents, or spouses, or friends, or children, or members of other, similarly "exploitative" groups.

relationship of dominance and subordination that encourages further sexual demands.[63]

I just don't see the difference. Why, just because V sleeps with D once, is he (sic!) more beholden to do it again? And how does V, the late employee, escape the clutches of D, the boss, just because he comes to work on time? Where is the difference in principle? One can as easily envision the very opposite case, where the blackmailer in the late employee (no. 4) case escalates the threats (perhaps into a full blown demand for sex or money paybacks), and where the boss in the lascivious employer case (no. 5) pulls back after one sexual escapade. Neither "victim" is totally bereft of defensive resources. The "late employee" can complain to the president of the company, or to the corporate or governmental harassment officer, but the worker subjected to the bosses unwanted sexual overtures has the very same options. I can certainly imagine the scenario as depicted by Fletcher. But why is this the only realistic one? That it must be so seems a weak foundation upon which to build a theory of crime.

I must concede to Fletcher that the baseball case (no. 6) comes reasonably close to fitting his theory,[64] but not even it fits perfectly. Our author maintains: "Once the parent purchases the baseball, the seller D can demand nothing further."[65] I have previously suggested that this is not true in the general case, in that anyone can always demand anything of any victim in the future. However, at first glance it would appear that the parent does not put herself (sic!) in any worse position in this regard because of the purchase of the baseball. But upon further reflection, even this is not true. For the "exploitative" baseball seller, thanks to this very sale, will now see a weakness in the buyer that was not apparent beforehand. Namely, this dying child is in a very precarious position, and the loving parents are willing to do whatever it takes to make its last few weeks enjoyable ones. Therefore, the exploitative blackmailing seller can perhaps interest these parents in more stuff for their dying kId. Maybe a Michael Jordan sweatshirt, this time around. The possibilities are endless, at least while the kid is still alive. Like a shark with the scent of blood

---

[63] Fletcher, *supra* note 2, at 1627. Fletcher's political correctness is not merely annoying, it is a threat to clear communication. In this case, he is positing that a female is blackmailing a male to attain sexual favors. This is so much the reverse of the usual situation that one has to stop and think, every time one mentions this case, to make sure one still understands it correctly. Yes, there is a movie which made the rounds several years ago predicated on Fletcher's premise, but this is clearly a rare man bites dog story.

[64] Although I would hardly call it a "troublesome" case. *Id.* at 1627.

[65] Fletcher, *supra* note 2, at 1627.

in its nostrils, this seller now "has a hold over" the hapless parents, which would not have been available but for the sale.[66]

Fletcher's theory, similarly, shows further unraveling when he considers the dinner kiss (no. 7) case. He boldly asserts that "dominance requires something more than withholding a kiss."[67] Says who? I ask. In addition to rereading Marx, Fletcher ought to avail himself of some of the more outlandish writings of psychologists and psychiatrists, particularly of the "New Age" variety. Surely, the imaginative powers of a person like Fletcher are not beyond positing a scenario where a person commits suicide because of the lack of a kiss. If so, then of a certainty the ability to offer or withhold this physical interaction would put the "kisser" in a position of dominance.

Nor does he fare any better when it comes to the tattoo case (no. 8). Fletcher is unwise enough to assert that "no one can dominate someone else by asking for money to do or not to do that which is in one's recognized domain of freedom."[68] Here, Fletcher should make himself aware of the phenomenon of the "Jewish mother." This individual recognizes no such domain of freedom, for her son, at least. If a male Jew were to threaten his mother with total body tattoos, she would be putty in his hands. Surely, he could "dominate" her, to the extent, that is, that this could ever occur, given her secret weapon.[69]

However, in the course of his disquisition on tattoos, Fletcher gives the entire game away. His "smoking gun" statement is:

> The [tattoo] case resembles the problem of the landowner who threatens to build a wall on his own property that will deprive his neighbor of light. The neighbor has no easement to interpose against the landowner, and if the latter thus demands payment to forgo building the wall, the demand is within the landowner's rights; there is no blackmail in demanding payments to do or not to do that which one has a right to do. For the neighbor to complain of subordination to the whims of the wall builder, he would have to have some legitimate interest that is put in jeopardy by the repeated

---

[66] Let us not enquire too closely as to how great a hold the seller has over the parents, and whether this is of greater moment than the "hold" held over the head of the philanderer by the gossip. The impossibility of interpersonal comparisons of utility renders all such speculation invalid.

[67] Fletcher, *supra* note 2, at 1627.

[68] *Id.* at 1627–28.

[69] Guilt.

demands for payment (emphasis, and material in brackets, by present author).[70]

About this, a few comments. First, this resembles nothing so much as the "spite fence" case, or Rothbard's flaying of Nozick for his "productive exchange" concept with the Green–Brown pink building example.[71] Evidently, in making this statement, or, rather, to the degree that he really accepts this, Fletcher has changed his mind on these matters. Second, and even more telling, Fletcher has conceded the entire libertarian case in favor of legalizing blackmail!

Consider again his canonical case (no. 3) of hush money, in light of the italicized sentence in the previous quote. It is the libertarian contention that D has the right to reveal damaging truths about a sexual peccadillo of the celebrity V. No one on the other side of this debate really denies this. States Katz:

> [I]f Busybody had actually revealed Philanderer's affairs, or if he had threatened Philanderer with doing so but not mentioned the money, or if he had asked for the money but not mentioned what he was going to do if he didn't get it—if he had done any of these things, he would not be guilty of any crime whatsoever. Yet when he combines these various actions, a crime results—blackmail."[72]

Even Fletcher himself admits that there "is nothing wrong with the separate acts of keeping silent or requesting payment for services rendered."[73]

But, if "there is no blackmail[74] in demanding payments to do or not to do that which one has a right to do;" and people have a right to gossip, to remain silent, and to request or demand funds for doing services; and if silence is a service; then it follows ineluctably that people have a right to engage in blackmail.[75] And if this is true, it takes the merest of logical deduction to reach the conclusion that this practice ought to be legalized. Once one agrees

---

[70] Fletcher, *supra* note 2, at 1628.

[71] Rothbard, *supra* note 1, at 240–42.

[72] Katz, *supra* note 49, at 1567 (emphasis added).

[73] Fletcher, *supra* note 2, at 1617. Of course, he takes this all back with his discussion of good acts being "corrupted by doing them for a price," *Id.*, but that is another matter. We can hardly expect logical consistency from those who argue in favor of criminalizing blackmail, after making the concession quoted in the text.

[74] For Fletcher, this means there is no *criminality*.

[75] That is, that blackmail is a legitimate market transaction, not a crime.

with the Fletcher quote I have labeled the "smoking gun," it is only a failure to follow through with the syllogism that can lead anyone to a conclusion other than this libertarian one.

Fletcher, needless to say, does not see things quite this way. Instead, after taking this detour, he reverts back to his old patterns. He now tries to apply his dominance and subordination test to the political embarrassment and paid silence cases (nos. 9 and 10). But this criterion applies no matter who initiates the deal! That is, in both the political embarrassment (no. 9) and the paid silence (no. 10) cases, the D can keep "coming back for more" money, and thus is "dominant" over the "subordinate" V; and yet Fletcher characterizes the former as (criminal) blackmail and the latter as no crime. How can he, when his criterion operates, equally, in both cases? The politician is in a subordinate position, whether he approaches the political activist, or the reverse occurs.

5. Punishment as the negation of dominance

Having "now generated a coherent and convincing fit between the principle of dominance and these specific cases," Fletcher moves on to show that this principle "explain[s] not only why blackmail is undesirable but also why it is conventionally regarded as a crime."[76]

And why is this? It is because punishment, at the end of the day, can be fully justified neither on utilitarian grounds, nor on the basis of Kantian ones. Instead, according to our author,

> The failure of the state to come to the aid of victims, as expressed in a refusal to invoke the customary institutions of arrest, prosecution and punishment, generates moral complicity in the aftermath of the crime. The state's failure to punish also reaffirms the relationship of dominance over the victim that the criminal has already established.[77]

In effect, then, all crimes are but further instances of Fletcher's dominance and subordination motif. It cannot be denied that this is a necessary condition for crime. One could hardly have a violation of legitimate law with-

---

[76] Fletcher, *supra* note 2, at 1628.

[77] *Id.* at 1634.

out someone dominating someone else, thus rendering them subordinate.[78] But this certainly isn't necessary. As we have seen, and as common sense so fully attests, life is full of non-criminal hierarchies, where dominators outrank subordinates. In the orchestra, the conductor dominates the musicians; in sports, the players are subordinate to the coach; in academia, the professor dominates the students; in family life, the children are subordinate to the parents; in work, employers dominate employees; in construction, the architect is dominant over the builders; in commerce, the customer is always right. Are we to throw our whole society in jail?

But this does not fully exhaust the difficulties with Fletcher's perspective. For one thing, the state need not be the only institution of capture and punishment.

For another, even assuming the legitimacy of (only) government punishment, this still leaves open whether this should be restricted to clear cut crime such as murder and rape, or also include blackmail (as distinct from extortion). Nothing adduced by Fletcher inclines us to the latter opinion.

Fletcher continues at the same old lemonade stand, worrying that the blackmailer can keep coming back for more from the victim, and thus "has a hold over" him in the future.[79] He waxes eloquent about the fact that "Rape victims have good reason to fear that the rapist will return, particularly if the rape occurred at home or the rapist otherwise knows the victim's address. Burglars and robbers pose the same threat."[80]

While, to be sure, this is a great concern, one would have thought it to be secondary; secondary, that is, to the first and only crime, the actual rape. The point here is that there was only one crime committed in these cases, the one which actually took place. The fears that this engenders about a repeat performance,[81] while important, are only peripheral. The main problem we have

---

[78] In a real puzzler, Fletcher himself specifically rejects this claim: "It would be difficult to maintain that all crimes are characterized by this feature of dominance. We can say, however, that this relationship of power lies at the core of the criminal law. It is characteristic of the system as a whole." Fletcher, *supra* note 2, at 1635. But if the essence of blackmail consists of dominance and subordination, and if blackmail is "the paradigmatic crime," this feature of dominance must be at least a necessary condition of crime. Even I am willing to admit that this is so; it is strange that Fletcher would not.

[79] Fletcher, *supra* note 2, 1634–35.

[80] *Id.*

[81] States Altman: "[T]he criminal nature of making repeated demands does not explain why the first demand should be criminal[, and] ... we condemn and prohibit blackmail even when future demands are unlikely or impossible." Scott Altman, *A Patchwork Theory of Blackmail*, 141 U. OF PA. L. REV. at 1655–56 (1993).

with the rapist or burglar is that he committed the crime. Even if, somehow, no fears were ever created about the future,[82] the rape or burglary itself would still not disappear. It is hard to avoid the conclusion that Fletcher is led to placing undue overemphasis on the fears engendered by the crime, and under-emphasis on the crime itself, because of his dominance and subordination theory.

6. Objections

Here, reasonably enough, Fletcher considers objections to his thesis. Unfortunately for him, this section only succeeds in worsening his difficulties. It emerges even more clearly how deeply wedded he is to the concept of future fears of dominance, even at the expense of the actual (past) crime itself. For example, he admits that homicide does not fit his model, because the victim is now dead, and thus beyond, presumably, any fears.

One would have thought, to the contrary, that homicide would have been the best example of the perpetrator dominating a subordinate victim. Here, the criminal goes so far as to actually annihilate his prey. Instead of focusing on this primordial fact, gets lost in speculations about how much fear a murder will create in the minds of the "decedent's loved ones."[83] Suppose that the victim was a hermit, and that the murder was never discovered! That would not at all change the reality of the crime, although it could not at all increase fears of any future homicides. That this irrelevancy should change matters for Fletcher is further evidence that his thesis is problematic.

The second objection he considers is irrelevant to present concerns. It is clear as a bell to the present author that punishment would indeed "counteract the criminal's dominance over the victim."[84] The third is of interest, in that we have made it ourselves: that dominance is an insufficient account of the criminality of blackmail, since it may be justified, e.g., as in the case of voluntary hierarchy. Unfortunately, Fletcher does nothing to deflect this charge; instead, he contents himself with reiterating the importance of the "ensuing relationship between D and V," and the "aftermath" of the crime, all but ignoring the crime itself.

Lastly, Fletcher deals with the challenge of Why not "wait for the second demand to ascertain whether the blackmailer intends to exercise his pow-

---

[82] Assume that the victim was psychologically secure, or that the world ended right after the crime took place, or that the criminal was killed

[83] Fletcher, *supra* note 2, 1635 fn. 45.

[84] *Id.* at 1637.

er?"[85] He rejects this on the ground that "the relationship of dominance and subordination comes into being as a result of the victim's making the first payment or engaging in the first coerced act of submission." Yes, indeedy do, that is exactly how he has defined the concept, as a "state of anticipation."[86] But this is merely to reiterate his own position, not to seriously answer the charge that it is surely illicit to hold people guilty of a crime which they might commit, in the future.

Yes, as Fletcher asserts, "the existence of criminal sanctions give [the blackmailee] the possibility of asserting a counter threat of going to the police."[87]

But this option would also obtain were we to legalize blackmail. For in this case, the presumption is that a legally binding blackmail contract would be signed, which would stipulate the entire amount of the payment. If the blackmailer demanded more, he would then be guilty of contract violation.

Thus, if Fletcher is concerned with arming the blackmailee with a weapon, he need not stick to his own viewpoint. He could instead embrace the libertarian position of criminalizing only uninvited border crossings of invasions.

---

[85] *Id.* at 1637–38.

[86] *Id.* at 1638.

[87] *Id.*

Chapter 4.
Blackmail as a Victimless Crime: Reply to Altman

The legal theory of blackmail is the veritable puzzle surrounded by a mystery wrapped in an enigma. Consider. Blackmail consists of two things, each indisputably legal on their own; yet, when combined in a single act, the result is considered a crime. What are the two things? First, there is either a threat or an offer. In the former case, it is, typically, to publicize on embarrassing secret; in the latter, it is to remain silent about this information. Second, there is a demand or a request for funds or other valuable considerations. When put together, there is a threat that, unless paid off, the secret will be told.

Either of these things, standing alone, is perfectly legal. To tell an embarrassing secret is to do no more than gossip. To ask for money is likewise a legitimate activity, as everyone from Bill Clinton to the beggar to the fundraiser for the local charity can attest. Yet when combined, the result is called blackmail and it is widely seen as a crime.

But that is just the puzzle. The mystery is that over a dozen attempts to account for this puzzle have been written, and not one of them agrees to any great extent with any other. It is as if there are a plethora of witnesses to a motor vehicle accident, each not only disagreeing with all the others but each telling a completely different story. The enigma is that with the exception of a corporal's guard of commentators, no one has seen fit to assert the contrary: that two legal "whites" cannot make an illegal "black."

Th   is is precisely the point of the present paper. Here, there will be no attempt to account for this puzzle-mystery-enigma. On the contrary we shall maintain that since it is legal to gossip, it should therefore not be against the law to threaten to gossip, unless paid off not to do so. In short, blackmail is a victimless crime, and must be legalized if justice is to be attained.

What is the relevance of a paper of this sort? If it is limited to arguing the case for blackmail, its appeal will be somewhat circumscribed. The political realties are such that blackmail prohibitionism is not likely to be overturned any time soon. Such an essay might still have some value, but mainly as an exercise in logic or perhaps to promote antiquarian interest in the history of legal philosophy. Fortunately, however, there are in addition many practical implications of the views to be explored in this paper.

Exhibit A in this contention is the entire preface to University of Pennsylvania Law Review's symposium on blackmail. It reads as follows:

A whole symposium about an exotic crime like blackmail? Why? Only because it has come to seem us that one cannot think about coercion contracts, consent, robbery, rape, unconstitutional conditions, nuclear deterrence, assumption of risk, the greater includes the lesser arguments, plea bargain, settlements, sexual harassments, insider trading, bribery, domination, secrecy, privacy, law enforcement, utilitarianism and deontology without being tripped up repeatedly by the paradox of blackmail? How so? And what paradox? Read on...[1]

Consider sexual harassment in this regard. In the view of those that would prohibit the behavior, a *quid pro quo* is illegitimate; e.g. it is improper to hire an employee on the condition that she goes to bed with you.

But what is this if not blackmail? That is, there is no difference in blackmail between "go to bed with me or I reveal your secret" on the one hand, and "go to bed with me or I won't hire you (or will fire you)" on the other. Take the case of Nevada where prostitution is legal. There, presumably, I may make a woman the following offer: come and work for me as a secretary and there will be "sexual services" that you must provide for me in this contract.

If this sort of *quid pro quo* is harassment, and you believe that prostitution ought to be legal, and you oppose the legalization of blackmail, have you not committed a logical contradiction? Whether or not this is true, such a consideration at least shows that the debate over blackmail has ramifications and implications for a much wider realm of activity than and that of Katz and Lindgren[2] are eminently correct in linking the two.

Consider but one more case mentioned by these two scholars: insider trading.[3] Here, too, there is a kinship with blackmail. For what are insider trading but a sort of *quid pro quo*: you sell me your share of stock for an agreed upon price, but I have some hidden secret knowledge unbeknownst to you that I obtained in a totally legal manner (I am, for example, the geologist who first spotted the new copper deposit).

This is neither the time nor the place for a full exploration of the parallels between blackmail and the activities mentioned by Katz and Lindgren.[4] Suffice it to show that there is more riding on the debate over blackmail *per se*, to

---

[1] Leo Katz and James Lindgren, *Symposium: Instead of a Preface* 141 U.PA.L.REV. 1565, 1565 (1993).

[2] *Id.*

[3] *See* Robert W. McGee and Walter Block, *Information, Privilege, Opportunity and Insider Trading* 10 N. ILL. U. L.REV.1 (1989).

[4] Katz and Lindgren, *supra* note 1, at 1565.

which we now turn, than first meets the eye.In order to put flesh on these bare bones, we will consider in detail, the views of Altman, as a foil. This author starts off with an interesting observation: "people who disagree about many legal and moral questions usually favor punishing blackmailers."[5] This cannot be denied, as we have seen. But Altman's inference form this fact, that it "suggests room for overlapping consensus on this issue" is only one plausible conclusion. The other is that all of these people are mistaken; e.g., the reason they cannot agree as to why blackmail should be outlawed is that this is an unreasonable position.

Let us try to make this point in another way. Elsewhere Altman states:

> We might more easily solve the legal and moral puzzles if we stop insisting that one principle must explain every aspect of blackmail. I recommend abandoning the search for a unified explanation. Probably no single flaw justifies condemning and prohibiting all and only blackmail transactions...Because blackmail is varied, different reasons might support condemning and prohibiting different forms.[6]

Yes, blackmail does have several different variations. Typically what is threatened is the release of information embarrassing to the blackmailee. But other threats are possible too. For example, Katz offers the following:

> Pay me $10,000—or I will: cause some really bad blood at the next faculty meeting...seduce your fiancée, Persuade your son that it is his patriotic duty to volunteer for combat in Vietnam... Give your high-spirited, risk addicted 19-year-old daughter a motorcycle for Christmas, ... hasten our father's death by leaving the Catholic Church.[7]

If the threats are varied, so too is the demand; usually it is for money, but it could also be sexual favors, or any other valuable consideration. Moreover, blackmail typically consists of a threat, ("Pay me x or else...") but it could also constitute an offer ("I'll perform the service for you of keeping quiet about your secret for y"). That is, the blackmailer commonly approaches the blackmailee, but sometimes the reverse takes place.

---

[5] Scott Altman, *A Patchwork Theory of Blackmail*, 141 U. PA.L.REV. 1639, 1639 (1993).

[6] *Id.* at 1640. This is eerily reminiscent of the philosophical analysis of Ludwig Wittgenstein. *See* LUDWIG WITTGENSTEIN, PHILOSOPHICAL INVESTIGATIONS (G.E.M. Anscome, trans., 1953).

[7] Katz, *supra* note 1, at 1567–68.

Upon initial examination, Altman's hypothesis sounds reasonable. After all, given that blackmail is a house with many rooms, each "room" might be accounted for in a different way. But how can the variations call for a different explanation, when they all have something in common, by virtue of which they are called blackmail?[8] Namely, what is threatened (or offered) is entirely legal, and what is demanded or requested is likewise within the law.

I. BLACKMAIL AS COERCION AND EXPLOITATION

Despite the foregoing considerations, Altman presses ahead. His first stab at the problem is the claim that blackmail is different than the ordinary commercial transaction in that "Blackmailers sell secrecy, a product many of them would give away if unable to bargain. Grocers would not give away food if they could not demand payment."[9]

There are problems here. First of all, why is it at all relevant to anything that a seller would give away his wares for free if he were somehow unable to consummate a deal? How does this help the case of prohibitionism? Secondly, Altman's case is not a telling one, because some (many?) grocers do "give away food if they could not demand payment." I refer, here, to "day old" food, which is often given to the poor, or to homeless shelters or some such. There are some who even give away freshly baked bread, sometimes in the form of money, e.g., charity, and other times directly, also as a charitable donation. True, a grocer would not long continue in business if no one ever paid him for his wares, but no less can be said for the blackmailer.

Nor is this an end to the difficulties, for Altman further attempts to drive a wedge between blackmail and ordinary commercial arrangements: "Both grocer and customer benefit from the opportunity to bargain. On the other

---

[8] Strictly Speaking there is a third dimension here. The person who condemns the act, as criminal must regard the conflation of these two events as evil or reprehensible. Otherwise, there is no way of distinguishing blackmail from ordinary trade. For in the latter case, each party also makes (a legal) threat and (a legal) demand for money or some other valuable items. Take the rather pedestrian case of a newspaper vendor and his customer. The former says to the latter: "Give me a pound (demand for money), or I won't give you this newspaper (threat)" The latter says to the former, "Give me a newspaper (demand for consideration), or I won't give you this pound (threat)." But most people do not condemn the sale and purchase of newspaper, so this is not considered blackmail.

[9] Altman, *supra* note 5, at 1640.

hand, the possibility of blackmail transactions primarily benefits blackmailers."[10]

Now this is more than just merely curious. No doubt both grocer and customer benefit from their deal, How could it be otherwise, at least in the *ex ante* (anticipations) sense. We know this from the fact that the bargain was consummated. If the grocer preferred the money he was offered to the produce from which he had to part, it is equally true that the consumer opted for the foodstuffs over and above the money foregone. But the same is true for the blackmailer and blackmailee. If the blackmailer preferred that everyone hear the blackmailee's secret to the money he received to keep quiet about it, he would have "blabbed."

From the fact that he forbore, we are entitled to deduce that he preferred the money to the option of engaging in his free speech rights to engage in gossip. But no less applies to the blackmailee. He chose to pay the blackmailer for his silence, instead of keeping the money it cost him to buy this service. Were matters different, had the blackmailer asked for too much, the person with the secret would have said "Publish and be damned!" Similarly, had the grocer wanted to charge too high a price, the consumer would have said, "Take your provisions and @!#$%#$% them!"

The two cases are as parallel as they can be. And what is this about "blackmail transactions primarily benefits blackmailers?" There is no warrant in either the grocery or the blackmail case, to determine by how much either party gained. Blackmail no more primarily benefits blackmailers than grocery sales primarily benefit buyers. Or sellers. Further, to say, as does Altman, that "blackmail transactions primarily benefits blackmailers" is to concede that they at least partially, or more accurately, secondarily benefit blackmailees! And this concession is totally at variance with his main point that blackmail is a crime because it "exploits" its so-called victims. There are no victims; this is a "victimless crime." No one is exploited. Both parties to this transaction gain, as is true of all voluntary commercial arrangements.

1.1 Coercion

In this section, Altman wrestles with the concept of coercion and then links it to blackmail.

---

[10] *Id.* at 1641.

Now we all know what coercion means. There is a hard and fast line between your fist and my nose,[11] and whenever that barrier is breached,[12] coercion has taken place. In order for this to be the case, property rights must be
established. That is, it must be clear that the proboscis at the end of my face is
indeed my nose, owned by me, and that the implement you are about to strike
me with, your fist, is actually your possession.

But this is an easy case. Very few people would quarrel with this example
of coercion. The situation is somewhat more difficult when it comes to possessions. Rothbard states:

> Suppose we are walking down the street and we see a man, A, seiz-
> ing B by the wrist and grabbing B's wristwatch. There is no question
> that A is here violating both the person and the property of B. Can
> we simply infer from this scene that A is a criminal aggressor, and
> B is his innocent victim? Certainly not, for we don't know simply
> from our observation whether A is indeed a thief or whether A is
> merely repossessing his own watch from B who had previously sto-
> len it from him.[13]

Coercion, then, is equivalent to a taking of someone else's legitimately
owned property, and/or a physical interference with his person, or the threat
thereof.

How does Altman fare in his attempt to deal with this concept? Not too
well. He expresses the opinion that "Professional blackmailers might turn to
kidnapping rather than journalism."[14] That is, if the intended blackmailee
proves obdurate, and will not fork over the requisite cash, and since while
"some blackmailers could sell their information elsewhere, they could rarely
do so as profitably," and since it does the blackmailer no good to "reveal the
information," he might as well turn to something else in the same line of
work, e.g., kidnapping.

---

[11] There is a gray area, too, in that when your fist comes within one inch of my nose, headed in
my direction, that is clearly coercive, even though no physical contact has (yet) taken place. On
the other hand, if you shake your fist at me from 300 yards away, that is not (yet) coercive.
Where the precise line between one inch and 300 yards should be placed is a continuum problem, with no fixed solution.

[12] Without my permission, that is. Voluntary sadomasochism between consenting adults
should not be considered coercive.

[13] Murray N. Rothbard, The Ethics of Liberty 51 (1982).

[14] Altman, *supra* note 5, at 1641.

But there is all the world of difference between kidnapping and blackmail. The former involves an uninvited border crossing, or coercion e.g., the initiation of violence against innocent people. The latter, it cannot possibly be over emphasized, involves nothing of the kind. Instead, it is a threat to do something that the threatener has every right to do, namely, engages in gossip.

Moreover, it is a strange sort of indictment to level at someone that he "might turn to kidnapping." Anyone might do practically anything in the future! Pigs might fly, Altman himself might turn into a murderer, and aliens might abduct us. If I don't get the raise to which I think I am entitled, I myself might turn to kidnapping. If this is the basis upon which Altman intends to tarnish blackmail, the case for legalization is to that extent very secure despite his best efforts.

This author's understanding of this concept is flawed in yet another way. He states: "the removal of important available options to alter someone's actions is coercion."[15]

This is not at all the case. Suppose one of your most important options is to be friends with me. And I threaten you as follows: "Unless you do X I won't be your friend." Here, I have removed an important option of yours in order to alter your action from what they would otherwise have been. But have I coerced you? To ask this is to answer it.

In his scatter shot approach to the problem, Altman finally hits the target, in yet another try. But he does so in a way, which further illuminates why his previous attempts were failures and helps him not one whit in his overall bid to explain on rational grounds and justify the illegality of blackmail. He states: "Many blackmailers coerce ... because they propose to reveal information they are obliged not to reveal."[16]

He might just as well have said, "Many automobile repairmen coerce, because they pad their bills, or use shoddy merchandise instead of the higher quality goods they are contractually obliged to employ." Both are plausible, but neither gets to the point. Yes there are many tradesmen and professional who cheat and cut corners; but this does not impact negatively on their activities *per se*. We should not penalize all automobile repairmen, only those guilty of fraud. Similarly, we should not jail all blackmailers, only those who, in Altman's words, "reveal information they are obliged not to reveal."

Why, it may be asked, might a blackmailer be properly obligated not to reveal secret information or even sell his silence about it? One possibility is that the information was attained illegitimately, e.g., by use of real coercion that is, violence, force, trespass, etc. In this case it is not the blackmail that is

---

[15] *Id.* at 1642.

[16] *Id.* at 1642, note.

illegitimate, but rather the means to attain the ammunition for it. Here, the licit blackmail is poisoned by the illicit prior act.

Let us consider an analogy. Suppose I rob a bank and then buy a toy for my child with the proceeds. In ordinary circumstances, my second act in this little two-act play—the purchase of the toy—is an unexceptionable. That is to say, there is nothing wrong with a plaything for my child. However in this case the acquisition is poisoned by the fact that it was obtained through unlawful means, robbery.

There is another reason why a blackmailer may be legitimately obligated not to reveal secret information: he contracted not to do so. That is, were blackmail legal, and I had the 'goods' on you, but agreed to keep quiet about it for a fee, whereupon I told all anyway, I should be penalized to the fullest extent of the law. But as the wrong here is contract violation, not blackmail, this hardly helps Altman's case.

The author's next attempt to besmirch the ancient, honorable and (should be) legal practice of blackmail is a further elaboration of his concern about removing options. Here, he considers the case of the person who proposes to throw the drowning swimmer a rope for a fee.[17] He then supposes that demanding money for this service were somehow impossible. Then, if the person on shore would have done the good deed anyway, the monetary demand "removed the otherwise available [option] of being saved without promising cash," But since removing options is tantamount to engaging in coercion, and coercion is illegal, then demanding money in this circumstance is akin to criminal blackmail.

Of course, there is a perfectly good English word, which fully expresses what is meant by removal of options. It is loss of wealth or poverty. But such an expression will not help Altman's case. Who, after all, would want to outlaw every case where a man's action reduces someone else's wealth? If I compete successfully with your grocery by opening my own, across the street I will have decreased your economic well-being. But only a demagogue would advocate jailing me for that. So, instead, Altman characterizes impoverishment emanating from such a cause as a loss of "freedom."[18] This is an attempt to smuggle in a phrase relevant to the law where options language would not suffice. This attempt must be resisted, lest we incarcerate people who threaten loss of friendship, or grocery competition if they do not get their way.

Altman worries that "if each of us took every opportunity we have to threaten others everyone would be worse off including even those who some-

---

[17] *Id.* at 1643.

[18] *Id.* at 1643, note.

times benefit by making threats."[19] He does not seem to realize that we already do this, everyday of our lives. Katz points out a pretty common one: "I won't sell you N, if you don't pay me Y'," and notes, "most contracts involve the threat of an omission" of this sort.[20] He might well have said "all."

Nor can we see our way clear to agreeing with the author on noise pollution. Again, he confuses threatening real coercion of the involuntary property border crossing variety with the threat of what would be entirely legal if carried out. According to Altman: "At every moment someone would be demanding payment not to make noise or to do some act for which we all depend on others each day."[21]

This is neither the time nor the place for a full-blown legal analysis of noise and noise pollution. [22] Suffice it to say that under a private property rights regime, people would own the right to emit noise based on homesteading. [23] This means, for example, that if the airport "got there first." and had been accommodating take off and landing traffic, and that if you then arrived on the scene and demanded the quiet of the tomb, you should have no case in law.

On the other hand, if the airport were built in the middle of a quiet residential area already in existence, it would be guilty of the equivalent of a criminal trespass. Any airport (or factory, or steel mill, or symphony orchestra for that matter) which threatened (unless paid off to desist) the peace and quiet of property owners who had already homestead "quiet" rights would thus be guilty of extortion, not blackmail, for it would be threatening that which it had no right to carry out. So, let people threaten to do things they have every right to do; let them do this "'til the cows come home;" it will not disarrange society by even one iota. But let not a single threat be heard, without a punitive response from the police and courts, when it consists of doing something illicit.

But this does not end the difficulties we see in this section. As a parting shot, Altman unburdens himself of the following remark:

---

[19] *Id.* at 1643.

[20] Katz and Lindgren, *supra* note 4, at 1603.

[21] Altman, *supra* note 5, at 1643.

[22] *See* MURRAY N. ROTHBARD, THE ETHICS OF LIBERTY (1982); Walter Block, *Ethics, Efficiency, Coasean Property Rights and Psychic Income: A Reply to Demsetz* 8 REV. AUSTRIAN ECON.61 (1995).

[23] *See* HANS-HERMANN HOPPE, THE ECONOMICS AND ETHICS OF PRIVATE PROPERTY: STUDIES IN POLITICAL ECONOMY AND PHILOSOPHY (1993).

> A norm against asking to be paid for what one is willing to do for free does not prevent beneficial bargains because it never disallows anyone from receiving a minimum asking price. Because a general rule against threats benefits everyone at little social cost, it should be regarded as a prima facie moral rule no less than rules against theft and physical violence.[24]

There are problems here. As we write this, Michael Jordan is in the process of dispatching the *Miami Heat*. We don't know this man, personally, but we are willing to speculate that he loves the game of basketball. We imagine, further, that were the world constituted in such a way such that he could not be paid enormous sums for leaping 40 feet in the air and slamming the ball into the basket, he would still be "willing to do it for free." If so, then according to Altman, Michael Jordan should be slapped in jail, forthwith, if he has the audacity of demanding any salary, let alone the multimillion dollar contracts to which he has become accustomed. Why? Because this would constitute a threat not to play unless he is paid, and we can't have people running around making threats of this sort, now can we?

Altman seems unacquainted with what economists call psychic income or producer surplus. If Michael Jordan would have been willing to play for £10,000, but instead gets £30,010,000, then his producer surplus is thirty million. Yes, to be paid only £10,000 for his services (a common annual salary in the early years of the NBA) would not "disallow (Jordan) from receiving a minimum asking price" of £10,000, but it seems a bit harsh to accuse him of criminal blackmail for receiving any more than this. It is easy to see why Gerry Reinsdorf, president of the Chicago Bulls might appreciate this economic analysis, but hard to understand how this "benefits everyone at little social cost." Surely Michael and his agent would not at all be happy with it.

One last point on this. We have been charging all throughout this paper that Altman confuses blackmail, a "threat" to do that which one has a right to do, with "theft and physical violence." Nowhere is it clearer that he does just that than in this quote.

1.2 Exploitation

We move, now, to the topic of exploitation, which Altman defines as "benefiting at another person's expense from her difficulties."[25] This, in turn,

---

[24] Altman, *supra* note 5, at 1643.

[25] Altman: supra note 3-p.1644.

means "obtaining a better deal in negotiation than one would have obtained for the same good or service had that person lacked the difficulty."

There is nothing wrong with this definition. Many societies use the word in this way. Indeed, it has a long Marxist pedigree behind it. People can define words in anyway they want. But when an interpretation is going to serve as the basis of criminalizing behavior, some semblance of caution would seem to be indicated.

Defined in this way, virtually the entire institution of free enterprise appears to be indictable.[26] For the essence of the market is to "take advantage" of the needs of other people—by supplying the very goods and services they require most desperately! This is practically the sole private financial incentive to invent a cure for AIDS, cancer, etc.

The people suffering from these ailments are, presumably, the most desperate potential consumers of all. Imagine if things were otherwise; that is, suppose that the market system were not predicated on "exploitation' as defined by Altman. Then, instead of allocating resources heavily in the direction where people found themselves in the greatest of "difficulties," more money would be spent on fripperies. Jerry Maguire, a recent hit film became famous for the expression "Show me the money." This is precisely the moral compass of capitalism: for the "money" leads unerringly in the direction of the greatest misery, and this serves as the best guideline the world has ever known for alleviating the greatest distress. Were we seriously to entertain putting into effect Altman's perspective, we would render our economy very much less efficient than it is today.

That we spend a significant amount of what most people would consider inessential is due to several things; diminishing marginal utility (the more food, clothing and shelter you have, the less valuable is any additional increment; the fewer lipsticks, jewels and violins you have, the more important they become), risk (the more money allotted to cancer research, the less likely the marginal dollar is to uncover the cure, since, presumably you first finance the best prospects), and subjectivity (one person's luxuries are another person's necessities).

Altman does not seem to understand this when he says "charging higher than free value for scarce tickets to a sporting event does not exploit the buyer because there is no reason to think the buyer's desire to attend stems from an

---

[26] As part of this indictment, Altman avers, "Blackmail victims ... can be driven to irrational or criminal behavior." *Supra* note 5, at 1644. But this is over-inclusive. Many phenomenon lead to these results. Probably, rap "music" renders irrational many teenagers. Some men are, undoubtedly, driven to criminal behavior by wives nagging for luxury goods. Should we have preventative detention for rap singers and nagging wives?

hardship."[27] For most people, he is undoubtedly correct. But there are those fanatics[28] who will go without shelter and all but a modicum of food to see their favorite athlete or movie star. On what basis can our author deny they are "exploited" by high-ticket prices?

Altman then asserts, "Charging poison victims who face imminent death more for medication than one would charge less desperate purchasers of the same drug exploits their hardship."[29] He does not seem to realize that those societies which allow free enterprise (anyone can charge anything he wants for his own property no matter how improper interventionists like Altman think it is) are far more likely to have medicines which save lives than ones which embrace socialism, regulationism, interventionism and other interferences with the free economy such as those advocated by that author. If I faced imminent death for want of a medicine, other things equal, I would rather take my chances in the U.S., or Switzerland or New Zealand or Hong Kong or Singapore, which are relative bastions of free enterprise[30] than in any of the countries run on the fascist model favored by Altman. So much for mere utilitarian considerations, which, perhaps, are not worth the ink expended on them.

On a deeper philosophical level, then, Altman's viewpoint is flawed because, once again, it is unable to distinguish between violation of the person and property rights, on the one hand, and being politically correct, on the other.

Further, Altman focuses on mere prices; why are we quibbling about them?

Either something is lawful or it is not and to focus on the price charged for it, as the determinant of its legality, is to push the clock backward to medieval times, when scholars and Theologians would debate the "just price." Altman bases the criminality of an act on the price paid for it; surely this is mistaken. What the rapist and the murderer do is *per se* unlawful; the price they do it for (e.g. as in Murder, Inc.) is totally irrelevant. But in Altman's analysis of blackmail, price takes center stage. This is but one more bit of evi-

---

[27] Altman, *supra* note 5, at 1644.

[28] Sports "fans" is derived from this concept.

[29] Altman, *supra* note 5, at 1644–45.

[30] Several attempts have been made to measure economic freedom and rank countries based on how much of it they have. For example, *see* JAMES GWARTNEY, ROBERT LAWSON, AND WALTER BLOCK, ECONOMIC FREEDOM OF THE WORLD: 1975-1995 (1996); Bryan T. Johnson, Kim R. Holmes & Melanie Kirkpatrick, 1998 Index of Economic Freedom (Heritage Foundation and The Wall Street Journal, 1998).

dence showing the philosophical chasm between real crimes such as murder and rape vis-à-vis victimless ones such as blackmail.

Another difficulty, this time on a practical level, is that it is by definition impossible for a third party to ever know if blackmailers "demand more for silence than the price for which they could have sold the information."[31] How can the forces of law and order, charged with eliminating crime, know whether the price charged is higher than this hypothetical level?

Altman makes much of the point that "blackmailers frequently demand repeated payments for their silence."[32] So what? As every economics student knows, stocks can always be converted into flows, and vice versa, through the intermediation of an interest rate and the concept of present discounted value. Landlords, too, typically demand repeated payment for their services. Are they to be confined to the prison Altman reserves for blackmailers on this ground?

2. Patching theories together

Having disposed of the preliminaries, Altman is now ready to put things together. He terms it coercion to "prevent...the wrongful act of another."[33] Suppose I see you poised over a baby carriage, knife held high, in the process of plunging it into the body of the occupant. I lasso your striking arm, thus saving the life of the baby and preventing you from murdering it. Have I "coerced' you? This seems to be an altogether unusual, not to say perverse, use of language. Coercion, more naturally and accurately, applies to the use or the threat of force against an innocent person, not stopping a person in the act of committing a crime. It is the person in the act of killing a helpless baby who is the coercer; this appellation hardly applies to the person who stops him.

On the basis of this premise, however, Altman claims "blackmail is often worse than revealing embarrassing information. Revealing embarrassing information, although it alters options, does not usually coerce. It does not coerce because the purpose of the revelation is not usually to induce the person to do anything."[34]

But this is fallacious. Suppose I have come to know that you take a bath with a rubber duck, and this would prove highly embarrassing to you should I publicize this perversion of yours. So much so that you would he prepared to pay me a top offer of £10,000 to keep quiet. However, you conceal from me

---

[31] Altman, *supra* note 5, at 1645.

[32] *Id.*

[33] *Id.*

[34] *Id.* at 1640.

just how devastating the release of this information would be to you,[35] and manage to buy my silence for a mere £2,000. Altman says blackmail is worse than gossip. But in this case, if I gossip about you, you lose what you value at £10,000. If I merely blackmail you, you lose only £2,000. Blackmail may be worse to Altman, but not to you,

But, our author would object, the blackmailer puts you in fear of being beholden to him forever. However, in the free society, where blackmail contracts would be legal, we would sign a contract stipulating my silence forever, for a payment of this £2,000. Thus, if after you had paid that amount I came back to you and asked for more money—for what I had already been paid to do in full—and you feared that I would keep doing this every year for the rest of your life, you would now have something to hold over my head: a lawsuit for contract violation. This is something not available to the blackmailee under the present legal regime.

Altman is also wrong in claiming that gossip is not usually intended to persuade it's subject to change his behavior. Traditionally, before political correctness came along, and even nowadays to a great extent, gossip was always used as a form of non-criminal sanctions to induce people to follow societal mores. If I gossip about you and your rubber duck, and you are sufficiently humiliated by it, you will tend to stop this deviant practice. Other rubber duck users, whose evil ways have not yet been ferreted out, will have an incentive to cease and desist from this horrid practice.

But these considerations will not suffice to "solve the longstanding problems of blackmail,"[36] because they "alone cannot explain the immorality" of this practice. For that, we must resort to the "patchwork," to which our author now turns.

2.1 Non-Coercive Blackmail

Altman considers the case of the "newspaper publisher who proposes to publish information if not paId." He castigates this as "morally corrupt" on the grounds that "most newspaper publishers have assumed an obligation to make publication decisions based on judgments about news worthiness."[37]

But newspaper publishers are not licensed. They are thus not obligated legally to do any such thing. If it is a moral obligation, how can this be true only of most newspaper publishers? Surely, the obligation would then rest on all those who take up this occupation. The only way to make sure of Altman's

---

[35] Quaere: Are you exploiting me?!

[36] Altman, *supra* note 5, at 1645.

[37] *Id.* at 1647.

statement is to assume that this obligation stems from a contract which most, but not all publishers have signed. But this gets us out of the realm of blackmail and into the realm of contract violation, where we belong.[38] Further, if word got out that a newspaper was basing publication decisions upon side payments, and not news worthiness, the odds are that it would go bankrupt very quickly.

Next Altman offers us the case where Susan accidentally films Allan, a Hasidic Jew, eating pork.[39] She can sell the video to win a contest for £100. Instead, she offers her only copy of this evidence to Allan for that exact amount, thus not exploiting him.

We are here back to "just price" doctrine. Before determining whether an act is moral or not, we must first determine whether or not the "price is right." One yearns to say in response, if an act is licit it is licit at whatever the price; if it is not, a different price will not make it so.[40]

But Altman is made of sterner stuff than his analysis, strictly speaking, would imply. For although he refuses to characterize this purchase as unmoral, he "nonetheless support[s] a law prohibiting Susan's behavior... for prophylactic reasons."[41] And what are these? "This situation is probably rare, and difficult to distinguish from serious moral wrongs."[42] But this is most un-

---

[38] Altman, *Id.* at 1648 fn., rejects such remedies on the ground that "victims can be induced over time to pay for secrecy than it is worth to them." In effect, he is saying that if the blackmailee values the secret at £2,000 he might still be willing to pay £10,000 to keep it under wraps. Either this is arrant nonsense, or the blackmailee has made a mistake in calculation. Contracts, obviously, cannot help with the latter problem, in this area or in any other.

[39] Altman, *supra* note 5, at 1647–48.

[40] A man approaches a woman and asks if she will go to bed with him for £1 million. A virtuous woman, her initial (unspoken) reaction is to refuse with indignation. However, upon more sober reflection, contemplating, no doubt, just how large a sum of money this is, she agrees. Whereupon he asks her if she will perform this service for £10. At this point, she cast a withering glance at him in refusal, and haughtily asks, "What kind of woman do you think I am?" The man's response? "We have already established what kind of woman you are; we are now merely haggling over the price."

[41] Altman, *supra* note 5, at 1648.

[42] *Id.*

satisfactory. It means that poor Susan, guilty merely of "market price only blackmail." will be incarcerated for doing absolutely nothing wrong.[43]

Next Altman tackles head on the issue of payer-initiated blackmail, one of the most powerful arguments on behalf of its legislation. This is because if the blackmailee first approaches the blackmailer and offers to pay for the latter's silence, it constitutes prima facie evidence that the former benefits from the arrangement. In the intuition of most people, blackmail at least of this type should he legalized. And with so powerful an entering wedge, why should any variety of blackmail be exempt from decriminalization?

Our author, perhaps glimpsing this abyss, pulls back sharply. He begins by conceding "that payers would not offer to pay for silence unless they had reason to think the other party planned to reveal the information. If so, permitting such bargains roughly reflects the acceptability of non-coercive blackmail."[44]

This is an important concession because once one allows the concept of "non-coercive blackmail" to gain currency, it will be hard to keep a straight face on its present prohibition. If it is non-coercive, why should the law prevent it?

Reaching deeply, Altman comes up with an answer to this conundrum:

> Evidentiary and definitional problems with payer initiation can undermining any power it has to separate coercive from non coercive transactions, some bargains appear payer-initiated because the payer initially suggests the deal. But the payer might only learn of the other party's intent to reveal the embarrassing information after that party discloses this intent in order to elicit an off or payment. Because this case cannot easily he distinguished from genuine

---

[43] Altman is much mistaken moreover, in singling out commercial arrangements of this sort as "market price only." On the contrary, all voluntary trades, all capitalist acts between consenting parties, of necessity, are concluded at market prices. For that is all that is meant by a market price: one agreed upon by a buyer and a seller. Altman is confusing this with the idea of making a sale at a zero profit, the proper characterization of the Susan-Allan deal. To see this as " probably rare" is mistaken. No trade, no human action (purposefully) occurs at zero profit. In every acquisition of any kind, there is always an attempt to improve one's lot; to make the future a more preferable one than that which would have obtained in the absence of the bargain. On this, see LUDWIG VON MISES, HUMAN ACTION. But the difference between the preferred future as a result of the act, and the dispreferred future, which would ensue without it, is profit. This stretches all the way from complex multinational trade deals to the simplest of human activities. For example, the reason you are now reading this (or any other) article is because you expect to earn a profit by so doing.

[44] Altman, *supra* note 5, at 1649.

payer initiation, permitting payer initiation can insulate paradigmatic blackmail cases from punishment.[45]

Let us see if we understand this by use of an analogy between sexual and
blackmail relationships. Especially in the eyes of third parties, there is not
always a clear and sharp distinction between seduction and rape. Therefore,
not just one but both practices should be deemed illicit. This seems to be what
Altman is saying, as can be shown with the following transposition:

> Evidentiary and definitional problems with [sex] can undermine
> any power [the law] has to separate coercive from non coercive
> [coitus,] ... Because this case [of seduction] cannot easily be distin-
> guished from genuine [rape], permitting [voluntary sexual con-
> gress] can insulate paradigmatic [rape] cases from punishment.
> Therefore, we should outlaw not only [rape] but also [seduction]
> between consenting adults.

This is spurious. If there is indeed a valid distinction to be made between
evil "paradigmatic blackmail" and inoffensive "non-coercive blackmail," as
even our author concedes, then only the former should be prohibited, not the
latter, even if it is difficult to distinguish between them in practice. As the old
saying goes, "Better that 1,000 guilty men should be set free than that one innocent one be incarcerated." And this is on the assumption that "paradigmatic
(non-payer initiated) blackmail" is indeed akin to rape. But, as we have taken
pains to show, and Altman has not so much even attempted to refute, even the
supposed evil payee initiated blackmailer does no more than to threaten that
which he has every right to do, namely, gossip.

On the other hand, Altman does adopt a modest stance.[46] He admits "the
criminalization of blackmail makes some potential blackmail victims worse
off."[47] And again: "Like any market intervention, its wisdom depends in part
on the number of consumers benefited compared to the number of consumers hurt as well as on the magnitude of the effects."[48] Further, "I can hardly
insist that I am right about either the frequency of wrongful blackmail or the
practicality of such defenses" (claiming that the "blackmailer somehow could
not easily have demanded additional payments.").[49]

---

[45] *Id.*
[46] *Id.* at 1650.
[47] *Id.*
[48] *Id.* at 1659.
[49] *Id.* at 1650.

This is unsatisfactory on two grounds. First, this resort to blatant utilitarianism is intellectually bankrupt. Interpersonal comparisons of utility are invalid. We simply have no way of telling "how much" some people are hurt and helped by legislation. Second, even if it were somehow possible to discern these comparative values, to make utilitarian considerations of this sort the touchstone of the law is to eschew justice.[50] Third, *there are no blackmail victims.* Whether payer or payee initiated, the commercial transaction of blackmail makes both parties to it better off at least in the *ex ante* sense. There would hardly be an agreement, otherwise. That the blackmailer gains there can be no doubt. But the blackmailee also benefits, since he values the payment he must make as less important than the secret being publicized. He is paying for silence, and contemplates that he is getting his money's worth, otherwise he would not pay.

2.2 A Less Controversial Patchwork

With this introduction to his patchwork theory, Altman now pauses for breath and recapitulation. He claims that his explanation of blackmail is essentially a moral one. Previously he focused on the "coercive and exploitative" aspects of this activity.[51] Now, he will defend the outlawry of blackmail on several new ethical grounds. The problem with this agenda is that so many things are, or have been considered to be by some, immoral.[52] Included is homosexuality, heterosexuality, masturbation, fornication, addictive drugs, greed, envy, sloth, premarital sex, intermarriage, etc. If we accept Altman's notion that blackmail ought to be legally proscribed because it is thought immoral, and we want to be logically consistent, then we would have to ban all these other practices as well.

---

[50] Joe is slob who values his own life. There are many gourmets, aesthetes, artists, connoisseurs and other such types who have a sadist cast of mind. They would simply love to see innocent person Joe tortured to death. Even if their utility is seeing this foul deed done vastly exceeded Joe's loss in undergoing it (remember, we are now assuming that interpersonal comparisons of utility are intellectually coherent), it would still be unjust for the law to allow it, let alone compel it—the logical implication of Altman's remark.

[51] Altman, *supra* note 5, at 1661.

[52] In the absence of a clear definition of immorality or morality, it is difficult to distinguish between these two states of affairs. The only "help" on this vouchsafed us by Altman, *Id.* at 1639, is we as a society "do not agree on what constitute morality." True to this lack of understanding of morality, Altman is often forced to express himself in a very tentative manner: e.g. "many people believe," "most people believe." *Id.* at 1652. It is strange to predicate an entire theory on such shaky foundations.

Let us in any case, consider the immoralities discussed by our author.

2.2.1 Rights and Duties

One of them is that "all acts of blackmail breach obligations."[53] In order to determine if and to what extent this is so, we must enquire as to the genesis of duties. One possible source is etiquette: one is obliged to use the correct fork, etc. Another is morality: it is unethical to be envious. Both of these considerations yield duties, but neither will serve as a rational basis of law.

A more reasonable cornerstone is contractual: I can obligate myself to pay you £10 for a book if I agreed to do so. To take the book and to give you anything less than this amount of money would be theft. Then there are those duties properly imposed upon me whether I agree to them or not: I must keep my fist off you nose, my hands out of your pockets, and my fingers away from your neck. Failure to live up to these obligations constitutes assault, robbery or murder.[54]

Where does the obligation, which will be breached by blackmail fit into all of this? It certainly violates social mores. Blackmail simply is not done in the finest of drawing rooms. If ever we were told exactly what immorality is, we could say for sure whether blackmail is contrary to it; as it is, we can only accept this as a presumption. However, even if true, this is insufficient to establish the case for outlawry.

What about contracts? Yes, if you and I signed an agreement precluding you from blackmailing me, and now you do so, you ought to be penalized to the fullest extent of the law. But in the absence of such an event (which is totally irrelevant to blackmail *per se*), there is nothing in the act of offering to keep silent for a fee, which violates any obligations such that it should be legally proscribed on that ground. Nor can this conclusion be drawn from the case of duties incumbent upon us whether we have agreed to abide by them or not. Blackmail simply does not constitute an uninvited border crossing as do theft, murder and rape.

2.2.2 Third Party Interests

"[I]f I tell you that I will inform your neighbors that your father was a war criminal unless you pay me a large sum, I have committed a serious wrong

---

[53] *Id.* at 1653.

[54] This assumes, of course, that you have not invited me (and even paid me) to punch you in the nose (as occurred in the movie, Dirty Harry), or kill you (as in the case of Dr. Kevorkian). Such cases of voluntary sadomasochism do not constitute violation of obligations.

even though I have not used anyone else's rights or settled anyone else's disputes inappropriately."[55] This attack on Lindgren[56] is well conceived. No one can own information (so far) given to him or her. If they could, it should be illegal for teachers to charge a fee for imparting knowledge. This should be given to the students for free, as they already (in justice) really own it. However, it is hard to see why threatening to tell someone's secret is a "serious wrong" given that it is not a serious wrong to actually tell it. It is, further, difficult to follow Altman given that the son of the war criminal voluntarily agrees to pay for silence, perhaps even makes the initial offer, in order to forestall gossip about his father.

2.2.3 Promoting Virtues.

Altman[57] criticizes several authors[58] who justify the prohibition of blackmail on the ground that this promotes virtue. However, our author does so not because this is a nonsensical argument, but based on the claim that these theories are incomplete. He states: "Nonetheless as part patchwork, each adds a good reason for condemning some blackmailers."

But to say this is to give up on a theory of why blackmail should be outlawed. Here, in effect, blackmail of type A should be prohibited for reason A1, blackmail of type B should be prohibited for reason B1, and so on. One problem here is that there is no one overarching reason to consider all blackmail illegal. Notice, we do follow this pattern with regard to any other crime; arson, murder, rape and theft are all illegal for one reason and one reason alone: they all violate people's rights in their properties and/or in their persons. A more basic problem, however, is that, as we have seen, each of the reasons A1, B1, etc., do not sufficiently account for prohibition.

Should the law promote virtue? Well, it is virtuous not to kidnap, and the ban on this activity certainly reduces the incidence of this particular crime, so, score one point for this theory. However, as in the case of immorality, so many, many other things are also virtuous: cleaning your plate, being solicitous, and brushing your teeth. Let the law intrude into all such areas, and it will become even more of a shambles than at present.

Consider now this example:

---

[55] Altman, *supra* note 5, at 1654.

[56] James Lindgren, *Unraveling the Paradox of Blackmail*, 84 COLUM. L. REV., 670 (1984).

[57] Altman, *supra* note 5, at 1654–55.

[58] Wendy J. Gordon, *Truth and Consequences: The Force of Blackmail's Central Case*, 141 U. PA. L. REV. 1741 (1993); Waldron (unpublished).

> [I]f I discover that a neighbor is a movie star living in secret to avoid the throngs of adoring fans who make her life difficult, it would be immoral and appropriately criminal to demand payment to forego telling the tabloids.[59]

Suppose the tabloid found out this fact for itself. Should it be prevented from publishing? This seems to be the implication of our author's position on the matter, yet it flies in the face of everything we know and love about press freedom. If newspapers cannot publish anything that might be inconvenient for anyone, are negative book and movie reviews, and intellectual critiques such as the one you are now reading to become verboten?

On the other hand, if, more reasonably, it is legitimate for the tabloid to print the movie star's address, why cannot the gossiper impart that information to the journalist? (How else are journalists to know what is going on if no one can tell him or her anything?) And if the gossiper can indeed do this, why cannot he be paid not to do so? It would certainly save the actress a lot of time, effort and aggravation if she could pay the snoop off and keep him quiet.[60]

Next, consider Altman's critique of Waldron's "complicity" theory of blackmail prohibition.[61] ("Blackmailers who demand payment to keep silent about evil acts are complicit with evil.") Altman refuses to abandon his opposition to legalized blackmail even though "Some supposed victims are vicious people who deserve to he exposed and punished."[62] And this is for two reasons. "First, not all blackmail victims are vicious people deserving punishment." Our reply here is that there are no blackmail "victims." All blackmailees (the neutral descriptive terminology) engage in a voluntary transaction. If anything, they are beneficiaries of the blackmailer, as they value his silence

---

[59] Altman, *supra* note 5, at 1655.

[60] The real reason movie star's lives are uncomfortable is due to public sidewalks, streets and roads, where *hoi polloi* can congregate, gazing at their betters with impunity. In the totally free society, where all such property is privatized, movie stars and other high-profile people will be as well protected everywhere as they are now in their gated and exclusive communities. On the other hand, given that we do not now enjoy the benefits of full free enterprise, why should rich people like our movie actress be singled out for special protection not available to others, or, if so, only at a high price? That is to say, if the actress want to be free of the attention of her "adoring" fans, why doesn't she move to a gated community, or to a high rise apartment house with a staff of doormen and bouncers? In that way, she could attain a modicum of privacy unavailable to her, presumably, in her present domicile.

[61] Altman, *supra* note 5, at 1654.

[62] *Id.* at 1655.

more than the money they pay (otherwise, they would not have agreed to the deal).

Certainly, the blackmailee is in a far better position with a blackmailer willing to sell his silence for a fee than in the hands of a gossiper, who will let the cat out of the bag no matter what. From the point of view of the black-mailee, at least the blackmailer has the decency to allow him to buy his way out of being exposed; the gossiper offers no such consolation.[63] As well, even on Altman's own terms, why doesn't he advocate legalization in those few cases where even he admits that the blackmailee is indeed "vicious?"

Altman's second critique of Waldron is as follows:

> [P]eople who deserve punishment are wronged if harmed by some-one not entitled to carry out the punishment. The fact that wrong-doers do not deserve pity does not prevent condemning those who act badly toward them. For example, it is both illegal and prima facie immoral to steal from a thief.[64]

We do not know what "prima facie immoral" means since Altman has never given us an explanation of this term. That it is deemed illegal to steal from a thief we have no doubt; our question is should this be so?[65]

Consider once again Rothbard's wristwatch example.[66] What follows from it is that if A is really the rightful owner of the wristwatch, he may justly seize it from B. That is, it is not only true that he would have been justified in de-fending it from B's initial attack, when B first stole the watch from A, but also that he is later (not in "hot pursuit") justified in seeking out and finding A, and then relieving him of his ill gotten gains. If so, then we have to qualify Altman's assertion. Yes, it is presently illegal to steal, and, who knows, it may even be immoral to do so; however it should not be illegal to seize stolen property from a thief, for one may merely be repossessing one's own property.

But we can go further. If it is licit for A to retake his own watch from B. the thief, it is also legitimate for A to hire C to do this in his behalf. This seems to be unobjectionable. How about if C does this on his own initiative? This, too, would appear to be a reasonable extension of the view we are devel-oping, since B, the thief, by definition, has no proper legal title to the watch.

---

[63] WALTER BLOCK, DEFENDING THE UNDEFENDABLE at 55 (1985).

[64] Altman, *supra* note 5, at 1655.

[65] Brown discusses blackmailing criminals as a form of punishment. Jennifer Gerarda Brown, *Blackmail as Private Justice*, 141 U. PA. L. REV. 1935 (1993).

[66] Rothbard, *supra* note 22, at 51.

But we can go even further! Forget about whether it is legal, or moral, or should be legal to steal from a thief. Is it even possible to do so? And the answer emanating from this quarter is that it is not. That is to say, given that the thief paradigmatically can have no legitimate property title to the stolen goods now in his possession, and given also that theft is the taking of rightfully held property, then it is not a logical impossibility to steal from a thief. One cannot steal from a crook. One can only relieve him of his booty.

Let us put this in another way, since it is so contrary to received opinion on the matter. In Altman's view, if someone not entitled to carry out a punishment nevertheless does exactly that, then the punishee, even if he deserves what he gets, is still wronged. But the police, courts and jailers of a nation are certainly "entitled to carry out that punishment." Under democratic theory they are merely the (albeit indirect) agents of the citizenry. If so, then why may not the individual himself seize his own property back from the thief? If the citizen can delegate this authority to the state, he may surely keep it for himself.[67]

If you kidnap my child and I see you walking down the street with him, and I grab him back from you, am I to be jailed as having "wronged" the "victim?" (Remember, in Altman's view, the "wronged' victim is the kidnapper from whom I seize back my child; the person "not entitled to carry out the punishment" is me, the parent who grabs back his kid.) This would appear to be the thicket into which Altman has enmeshed himself. Thus, even if blackmail is a legal wrong, which it is not, it should still be lawful to blackmail a thief.[68]

2.2.4 Domination

In this section,[69] Altman offers a devastating critique of Fletcher.[70] The latter saw the particular evil of blackmail that the payee could always come back to the payer and demand more money. Altman states:

---

[67] Some might say that through the constitution the citizen has already delegated this authority to the police power of government, and thus may not always keep it for himself, any more than he can eat his cake and have it too. For a disabusement of this position, see LYSANDER SPOONER, NO TREASON (1870).

[68] Given that there are no positive obligations other than contractual ones, the blackmailer has no duty to turn the blackmailee over to the police.

[69] Altman, *supra* note 5, at 1655–56.

[70] George P. Fletcher, *Blackmail: The Paradigmatic Case*, 141 U. PA. L. REV. 1617, 1617–38 (1993).

> [T]he criminal nature of making repeated demands does not explain why the first demand should be criminal[, and] ... we condemn and prohibit blackmail even when future demands are unlikely or impossible.[71]

That is, for example, in the case where the blackmailee dies soon after the first payment, and thus can no longer be blackmailed, most people would still condemn the first instance of this commercial interaction.

This point is symptomatic of the University of Pennsylvania symposium dedicated in its entirety to defending the outlawry of blackmail.[72] In virtually every case where one participant disparages the theory of the other, the critic is invariably correct. This leads to one of two explanations. The first is that like some N.B.A, teams, the contributors to this volume are better on "Offense than Defense." The second, more pertinent to our present discussion, is that it is very easy to attack the mistaken view that blackmail should be a crime, and difficult to defend this erroneous position. We lean toward the latter explanation.

2.2.5 Waste and Subsidiary Harms

This is a brief but curious section of the paper. As in the previous one, Altman ransacks several other defenses of blackmail prohibitionism, this time of the consequentialist variety.[73] Included here are Isenbergh, Ginsburg and Schechtman,[74] Shavell, and Posner. Each of them claims that blackmail has one or another distasteful consequences, but Altman pithily observes: "these insights alone ... do not account for the strong intuition that blackmail is a wrong to the victim."[75]

Instead of concluding that these failures further weaken the case for the status quo in this regard Altman takes the very opposite position. It is as if "correct" arguments for our author's perspective strengthen it, but flawed or inconsistent ones do too. Heads Altman wins, tails his opponents (including the present authors) lose. We would hate to play poker with this man!

He says in his own defense against this charge: "We should not reject partial accounts merely because they fail to explain one case or another. They

---

[71] Altman, *supra* note 5, at 1655–56.

[72] 141 U. PA. L. REV. (1993).

[73] Altman, *supra* note 5, at 1656–57.

[74] Douglas H. Ginsburg and Paul Shechtman, *Blackmail: An Economic Analysis of the Law,* 141 U. PA. L. REV. 1849 (1993).

[75] Altman, *supra* note 5, 1656–57.

might be valuable elements in a theory when paired with moral accounts that apply to other examples."[76] But here he does himself an injustice. If his own critiques of competing theories were a little less thorough, he could perhaps rely on this line of argument. But after reading them, none of his opponents have much of a leg to stand on. Thus, Altman cannot now turn around and make use of the very argument, which he has previously annihilated to promote his awn conclusions. The point is, these are not really partial accounts; instead they are, mistaken accounts, as Altman himself has so witheringly shown. That he nevertheless is willing to weave them together to form a "patchwork" on behalf of blackmail prohibition perhaps shows only how desperate he is to defend this conclusion.

3. Other market transactions

In this section Altman tries to defend himself against the charge that he is over-inclusive.

First up in the batter's box are "rescue bargains" (e.g. I toss a rope to a drowning victim after demanding all his money to do so). If we are prohibiting blackmail on the ground that it exploits its "victims" (e.g. the blackmailees), should we not also outlaw a commercial transaction to save a desperate person's life at exorbitant prices for this reason? Altman says no: "That rescuers demand high payments for their services does not prove that they coerce or exploit."[77] Now, Altman does not have to convince us. We are on record with the view that coercion and exploitation cannot take place unless there is the threat or use of physical force or fraud against an innocent property. We agree that no rescue bargain, at any price, can be rendered illegitimate under such a criterion. But Altman, with very different views on compulsion, cannot logically avail himself of these arguments.

The only avenue open to him is to show that on his own account of coercion, the blackmailer, but not the rescuer, is guilty. Here is his first attempt: "Unlike many blackmailers, these rescuers provide a service they would not otherwise provide."[78] But this surely is incorrect. For the blackmailer too, provides a service, silence, he would not otherwise have provided. This is a valuable consideration as shown by the high price the blackmailee is willing to pay for it. Nor can Altman hide behind the argument that the blackmailer would otherwise have not provided this silence. On the contrary, were he not paid off to be quiet, presumably the blackmailer could well have "spilled the beans."

---

[76] *Id.* at 1657.

[77] *Id.* at 1658.

[78] *Id.*

Perhaps because of the psychic enjoyment the human animal has at the prospect of relishing other's discomfort, many axe the people who can "dine out for free" for many months because they are the source of titillating gossip.

Altman's second attempt to extricate himself from these difficulties is as follows:

> Unless the rescuer charges a higher price for a rescue of equal difficulty when the rescuer finds that the victim faces imminent suffering or death, the rescuer has not taken advantage of the victim's hardship.[79]

Unfortunately, this will not work either. Altman himself admits, "Some rescuer negotiations, like most blackmail obligations, involve coercion and exploitations."[80] In the case of blackmail (which for Altman is part exploitative and part not) he takes the former part as the general rule and throws out of court the entire concept because of it. In the case of rescue bargains, however, Altman takes the very opposite track. Again, he admits there is an exploitative aspect, but this time he ignores it in behalf of the non-exploitative aspect.

States Altman: "One might think that the principles justifying blackmail laws would also justify criminalizing some demands for payment by rescuers."[81] Yes, one might indeed think that. But no, Altman squeezes out of this requirement of logic because there are "practical reasons ... not to criminalize such demands,"[82] and this after he had just finished lambasting consequentialists in his treatment of waste and subsidiary harm.[83]

Altman cannot have it both ways. Either "practical considerations" indicate we should legalize all blackmail, whether "exploitative" or not, in which case we should also decriminalize all rescue bargains; or they do not, in which case we should not legalize either of these contracts, Altman has not succeeded in showing a relevant difference between the two and thus is not entitled to treat them differently.

Amazingly enough, Altman sees this point, and yet still insists on prohibiting all blackmail, while allowing all rescue bargains:

---

[79] *Id.*

[80] *Id.*

[81] Id.

[82] Id.

[83] *Id.* at 1656–57.

> Criminalizing blackmail deters some individuals from purchasing silence at a price that they would be happy to pay and in contravention of no moral or legal obligation. Permitting rescuers to demand payment sometimes leads needy people to pay for rescues they might have had for free, and to pay prices inflated by their desperation.[84]

Arguing with Altman is to attempt the impossible.

Nothing daunted, Altman gives three reasons for his stance:

> (1) we cannot easily distinguish particular threats from particular offers; (2) we suspect that coercion and exploitation are far more common among blackmailers than among rescuers; and (3,) the risk of deterring rescue is more dangerous than permitting immoral rescue bargains, while the risks of permitting coercion and exploitation in the sale of secrecy seem more serious than the harms of deterring bargains for silence. *The distinctions are not those of principle. They result from the practical balancing typical in legal decision-making.*[85]

Well, at least Altman can agree with us that there is no difference in principle between hard rescue bargains and blackmail. (We would say between any bargains and blackmail. We certainly don't agree about the incidence of illegitimate activity—our position being that no exploitation or coercion takes place in either case.

But let us take Altman at his word. Surely he will agree with us that black male teenagers commit crimes (real crimes, that is) at rates far in excess of their proportional representation in the population. Surely, then, the risk of not engaging in preventative detention for this group of people is greater than that of allowing "exploitative" bargains for silence. If it is a matter of principle, then this age sex cohort is safe from so unjust an act. But if it is a matter of the "practical balancing in legal decision-making," these young people are in grave danger.[86]

Consider now the last case and the analysis thereof offered by Altman:

---

[84] *Id.* at 1659.

[85] *Id.* (emphasis added).

[86] According to the old saying, "No man's life or liberty is safe while the legislature is in session." If we adopt the Altmanian insights, this becomes, "No man's life or liberty is safe while the legal decision-making is in session."

Imagine that everyone wrongly believes Rich is a member of the Ku Klux Klan. Bob discovers evidence showing that the rumor is false. Bob tells Rich that he will share the evidence in exchange for one million dollars. This proposal is likely to he coercive and exploitative. In this regard it resembles blackmail. But prohibiting the proposal could be problematic. Some exculpatory information is discovered intentionally and through some effort. I would hesitate to enact criminal laws that could deter discovery and disclosure of exculpatory information. In this regard Bob's proposal is more like a rescue proposal than a typical blackmail proposal.[87]

Our response is that all blackmail is actually rescue. The blackmailer is "rescuing" the blackmailee from the gossiper, himself in this case.[88] If Altman is serious about legalizing all voluntary rescue contracts, no matter how odious anyone thinks them, and wishes to be logically consistent, he must also change his mind and now advocate the decriminalization of all voluntary blackmail contracts, again, no matter how odious.

4. Conclusion

Wittgenstein[89] used the example of a very long rope composed of many strands, none of them, however, substantial enough to stretch for its entire length. Altman is arguing, analogously, that the case in behalf of banning blackmail is composed of many arguments (e.g. strands), none of which alone can justify this conclusion, but all of which, together, are sufficient to this task. Our reply is two-fold. First, this may apply to rope, but not to the philosophy of law. In the latter case we seek one overarching explanation, not dozens, or even several. Second, even if we accept the "rope" analogy, we must still insist that each strand be acceptable on its own merits, and that none of them be incompatible with any another.

Altman exposes the fallacies of many if not all of these strands, and then somehow thinks he can weave a sound rope out of them, No! Borrowing from a related context Altman's rope is as weak as its weakest strand. Nor is the

---

[87] Altman, *supra* note 5, at 1660.

[88] Superficially, this sound like a Mafia protection racket: the criminal will "protect" you from himself for a (large) fee. But there is a real difference between the two cases: the blackmailer has an absolute right to engage in gossip, the threatened activity. In contrast, the hoodlum has no right at all to do that which he threatens to do in order to get you to pay "protection" money.

[89] *Supra* note 6.

entire rope any stronger for being composed of many pieces, none of them valid.

Chapter 5.

DeLong and the Second Paradox of Blackmail

One so-called paradox of blackmail concerns the fact that "two legal whites together make a black." That is, it is licit to threaten to reveal a person's secret, and it is separately lawful to ask him for money; but when both are undertaken at once, together, this act is called blackmail and is prohibited. A second so-called paradox is that if the blackmailer initiates the act, this is seen by jurists as blackmail and illicit, while if the blackmailee (the person blackmailed) originates the contract, this is commonly interpreted as bribery and is not illicit.

But these are paradoxes only for legal theorists innocent of libertarian theory. The authors use that perspective to reject the claim that blackmail should be unlawful. If this act were legalized, then both paradoxes would disappear, precisely their contention.

I. INTRODUCTION

Zeno, the ancient Greek philosopher, was the author of a number of famous paradoxes, including this one: how can the rabbit ever catch the turtle? The turtle has a head start but the rabbit is faster. Zeno reasoned that since the hare would hop to the place the tortoise had last occupied, he would never draw even, for in that time the latter could move (very slightly) forward. So the slower animal would still be ahead of the faster one. The process could be repeated again and again, in ever smaller and quicker steps. But each subsequent step takes some amount of time, and there are an infinite number of such steps. It would therefore seem to take an infinitely long time to complete the infinite number of steps needed to catch up to the turtle.

Thus if we accept the premises of the argument, there is no way in which the bunny could ever catch up to his racing competitor. And yet we also believe, from common experience, that the rabbit could overtake the turtle; hence the paradox.[1] The solution to the paradox, of course, is to call into question the basic premise of the argument, which amounts to the assumption that an infinite number of steps, no matter how small in duration, cannot be accomplished in a finite amount of time. As any student of calculus knows,

---

[1] *See* ANTHONY FLEW, A DICTIONARY OF PHILOSOPHY at 262 (2d ed.) (defining "paradox").

however, an infinite series can have a finite sum.[2] Each smaller gap between tortoise and hare also requires a smaller time, and the sum of this infinite series of ever-smaller time intervals is a finite time interval, at the end of which the hare reaches, and passes, the tortoise. Once it is realized that Zeno's argument rests on a false assumption, the paradox of how the faster animal can catch the slower disappears.

According to some scholars, the crime of blackmail provides a famous paradox in the legal field. It is licit to gossip about someone else's secret (e.g., marital infidelity), and it is legal to threaten to publicly reveal such information. It is also permissible to ask that person for money. But the combination of the two acts, each of which, on its own, is legal, is illegal. That is, there is a prohibition against threatening to reveal this secret unless you are paid. This is called blackmail, and is widely considered criminal behavior, and thus is uniformly outlawed today. [3] Yet it seems paradoxical to outlaw an action the component parts of which (threatening to reveal information; asking for money) are separately legal. As Lindgren summarizes the paradox, "Why do two rights make a wrong?"[4]

A second paradox regarding blackmail has also been identified by some theorists. If the unfaithful spouse approaches the gossip and offers to pay him not to disclose the infidelity, that would be considered legal. As DeLong explains, "it is not unlawful for one who knows another's secret to accept an offer of payment made by an unthreatened victim in return for a potential blackmailer's promise not to disclose the secret."[5] It is considered paradoxical that the sale of secrecy is legal if it takes the form of a bribe, yet is illegal where the sale of secrecy takes the form of blackmail. Why should the legality of a sale of secrecy (secrecy agreement) depend entirely upon who initiates the transaction? Why is bribery legal but blackmail not?

---

[2] C.H. EDWARDS, JR. & DAVID E. PENNEY, CALCULUS AND ANALYTIC GEOMETRY, chapter 12 (1982).

[3] In modern criminal codes, blackmail is usually defined as a special type of extortion, theft, or other offense, despite the fact that blackmail and extortion are clearly distinguishable, since extortion involves a threat to perform an unlawful act while blackmail involves a threat to take otherwise legal action. *See, e.g.,* Louisiana Revised Statutes, Title 14 § 66 (1998), defining one type of extortion as "A threat to expose any secret affecting the individual threatened or any member of his family or any other person held dear to him." *See also State of Louisiana v. Felton*, 339 So. 2d. 797, 800 (1976), explaining that the general scope of the crime of extortion is intended to include what is commonly known as "blackmail."

[4] James Lindgren, *Blackmail: An Afterword*, 141 U. PA. L. REV. 1975, 1975 (1993).

[5] Sidney W. DeLong, *Blackmailers, Bribe Takers, and the Second Paradox*, 141 U. PA. L. REV. 1663, 1664 (1993).

The second paradox arises, then, because both the bribe taker and the blackmailer are paid money for their silence. Both the bribe giver and the blackmailee are thus presumably ill treated.[6] Yet one type of secrecy agreement (blackmailer-initiated) is proscribed by law, and the other (bribe giver-, i.e. blackmailee-, initiated) is not. As a real-world example, consider the fate of Autumn Jackson, who was convicted of extortion for threatening to tell the tabloids that she was entertainer Bill Cosby's out-of-wedlock child unless he paid her $40 million.[7] Many commentators noted with irony that if Jackson had first filed a paternity suit and then settled the suit in exchange for money and silence—essentially, being bribed—no crime would have been committed.[8]

Most mainstream commentators believe both of these situations to be paradoxical; first, the fact that two rights (a threat to gossip and a request for money for silence) can make a wrong, and second, that the legality of a secrecy agreement depends entirely upon who initiates it. For them, it is taken as a given that blackmail should be illegal. This leaves them with the task of resolving the apparent paradoxes generated when blackmail is illegal yet its component parts are not, and when blackmail is legal when it takes the form of bribery and illegal otherwise.[9]

Theorists who support the outlawry of blackmail have thus spilled much ink generating contorted arguments trying to resolve these paradoxes. They endeavor mightily to explain why it makes sense to outlaw blackmail while not outlawing its component parts, and why it matters who initiates the exchange. As DeLong notes, contemporary theories attempt to justify blackmail and resolve its paradoxical nature "by arguing that blackmail exchange only appears to be mutually beneficial, but is in fact either wrongful or wasteful. They justify the law prohibiting blackmail as a way of preventing this exchange from taking place."[10] These arguments are often couched in terms of economic efficiency or similar notions.

As we will argue, these attempts are doomed to failure. There is an inconsistency involved in outlawing blackmail, if bribery, gossiping, and asking for

---

[6] We prefer the term "blackmailee" to "victim" for the reasons give below.

[7] "Autumn Jackson begins 5 year jail sentence for Cosby extortion plot," CNN Interactive, April 23, 1998 <http://cnn.com/US/9804/23/briefs.on/autumn.jackson/index.html>.

[8] *See, e.g.,* Walter E. Williams, "Was it extortion or merely free speech?", Tuesday, August 26, 1997 <http://www.jacksonvilledailynews.com/stories/1997/08/26/xjmmjbnt.shtml>.

[9] As Fletcher notes: "When a [legal] paradox is uncovered, we can restore consistency in our legal structures ... by finding or constructing a distinction ... that dissolves the paradox." George P. Fletcher, *Paradoxes in Legal Thought*, 85 COLUM. L. REV. 1263, 1269 (1985).

[10] DeLong, *supra* note 5, at 1664.

money are permissible. With respect to the second paradox in particular, the subject of this paper, it is impossible to justify the discriminatory treatment of blackmail and bribery. The way to resolve the alleged paradoxes is not to attempt to distinguish the undistinguishable, but to recognize that blackmail should be legal.

If it is true that blackmail should be legal, the paradoxes vanish and there is nothing to explain.[11] It is legal (and we contend that it should be) to gossip about other people, even concerning their infidelities.[12] It is not against the law to threaten to gossip, nor to demand or request money. If it is legal to bribe someone, to pay them for silence, it should not matter whether the blackmailer or briber (blackmailee) approaches the other to initiate the transaction. If it is licit to make a threat, is should not be a crime, either, to decline to carry it out, for a fee. In short, blackmail does not involve aggression, i.e. the initiation of force. It therefore does not violate individual rights, and the state is consequently not justified in using the force of the law to outlaw this non-aggressive action.[13]

It is the claim of most commentators on blackmail that the blackmailee is indeed a victim. This is exactly why they support the outlawry of blackmail and futilely attempt to resolve blackmail's paradoxes rather than simply admit

---

[11] It would be no paradox if one claimed that "2+2=5." All attempts to resolve the contradictions emanating from such a statement would be doomed to irrelevancy. Our claim is that the "paradoxes" of blackmail—both of them—resemble such cases. By recognizing that blackmail indeed should not be illegal, one realizes there is no paradox to resolve. Only by accepting a false political notion (that blackmail should be illegal) does one generate a paradox that needs resolving. Note that other apparent legal paradoxes can be resolved by the use of the libertarian sword to cut the Gordian knot. For example, it seems paradoxical that is legal to give sex away for free but not to sell it (prostitution). It seems paradoxical that it is legal to accept a job offer at a very high wage, or at no wage (e.g., an intern who works for free), but not at some wage in-between zero and the minimum wage. It seems paradoxical that alcohol is legal while marijuana is not. The solution is not to attempt to justify the unjustifiable, but to simply admit that anti-prostitution laws, minimum wage laws, and anti-drug laws are immoral and should be repealed.

[12] Of course, some gossipers can incur liability if the gossip amounts to defamation. Laws against defamation (libel and slander) are problematic as well from a libertarian perspective, although a discussion of this topic is beyond the scope of this article.

[13] There is less to this distinction than meets the eye. I can "request" money from you in the most threatening circumstances; e.g., holding over your head my intention, unless you pay, to gossip about your embarrassing secrets. Alternatively, I can "demand" money from you in the least threatening of situations: I demand $20 from you as the cost of a ticket to the concert; unless you pay, I will deny you admission. (In this article, we will occasionally use the singular terms "I" and "my" for simplicity of illustration.)

that blackmail should be decriminalized. In this paper, we use the term "blackmailee" to refer to the person being blackmailed, rather than "victim," for two reasons.[14] First, referring to the blackmailee as a victim begs the question of whether blackmail should be illegal, by presupposing the blackmailee truly is a victim. Second, as we shall argue, the blackmailee is a beneficiary of the blackmailer, not a victim, in that he would far prefer his secret be in the hands of the blackmailer than the gossip.[15] For in the former case, at least there is the possibility that he may buy silence. (And if so, it must of necessity be at a price below the value placed on the secret by the blackmailee; otherwise, the deal would not be consummated.[16]) In the latter, the secret will be publicized, no matter how much he would have been willing to pay for silence.[17]

It is our contention, therefore, that blackmail should not be a crime. If there is any paradox, it concerns only why so many otherwise astute commentators on the law should have not only failed to see this, but have written vociferously to deny it. In what follows we critique various economic theories that attempt to resolve the paradoxes of blackmail, with a focus on the second paradox. We will show that it is, indeed, inconsistent to outlaw blackmail while permitting bribery, and will argue that the blackmailee is not properly considered as a victim of the blackmailer.

---

[14] We shall also refer to the agreements resulting from either blackmail or bribery as secrecy agreements. We shall distinguish between the two different types of secrecy agreements, where necessary, by referring to them as blackmailee-initiated secrecy agreements (bribery) or blackmailer-initiated secrecy or blackmail agreements (classic blackmail).

[15] The person gossiped about may be referred to as a "gossipee" or "subject of gossip."

[16] *See, generally*, MURRAY N. ROTHBARD, MAN, ECONOMY, AND STATE, chapters 1.5.A and 2 (1993); LUDWIG VON MISES, HUMAN ACTION, chapters IV.4 and X (3d ed.).

[17] Moreover, even if one ignores the fact that the blackmailee is a beneficiary of the blackmailer, the blackmailee is not "victimized" in a way that justified outlawing blackmail. The only type of victimization that justifies the use of the legal force and thus outlawing the victimizing activity, is aggression. But the act of blackmail does not involve aggression and thus the blackmailee is not a victim.

II. A CRITIQUE OF SOME ECONOMIC THEORIES OF BLACKMAIL

A. The Economics of Secrets

1. Internalizing Externalities

The so-called "economic" analysis[18] of blackmail explains (and justifies) its outlawry as an attempt to maximize wealth. This is problematic on the face of it. For one thing, the conventional economic considerations of profit and loss hardly apply to courts and legislatures. In the ordinary case of candles, ships, and sealing wax, if the entrepreneur does not act in a manner which maximizes wealth, he faces loss of profit and eventual bankruptcy. It is difficult to see how this could apply to the official bodies charged with law making.[19] For example, it could be argued that many policies would increase overall utility or wealth, such as re-instituting slavery, censoring all anti-Christian or pornographic publications, or outlawing frivolous time—and money—wasting activities like collecting Beanie Babies.[20] Yet it does not follow that it is proper to institute such policies (and, indeed, libertarians would oppose such policies, and Austrian economists would deny that such wealth-maximization claims are true or even meaningful).

---

[18] This is a bit of a misnomer. It implies that all economists see wealth maximization, not justice, as the main desiderata of the law. Worse, the implication is the utilitarian one that there is essentially *no difference* between wealth and justice.

[19] To be sure, this applies in a somewhat attenuated manner to politicians. They can be voted out of office for various reasons, including failure to adequately represent their electorates. But the political process is so vastly less efficient than its economic counterpart so as to render this almost a difference in kind, not merely degree. In the former, the political vote takes place only once every four years; in the latter, the dollar "vote" occurs each day. In the political arena, apart from referenda, we are forced into a package deal: candidate A, who represents policies a1, a2, a3, etc., or candidate B, with b1, b2, b3, etc. We can never "fine tune" our choices, and select, for example, a1, b2, a3, b4, etc. And this is to say nothing of judges, who are insulated from the process at one further remove. The only control the populace has over them is indirectly, via the politicians who appoint and approve of them.

Even worse for the analogy, economic trades represent "capitalist acts between consenting adults" in the felicitous phraseology of Nozick (1974, p. 163). Here, there is always unanimous agreement between all (e.g., both) trading partners. In contrast, the political sphere is one of force and compulsion, where the minority must go along with the wishes of the majority against their will.

[20] Although either of the authors would be pleased to receive a Ludwig von Mises beanie baby.

Another problem with supporting blackmail outlawry on economic grounds is that blackmail contracts would appear to satisfy the usual conditions for *ex ante* gains from trade. Each party to the transaction, necessarily, benefits from a blackmail agreement, that is, from both blackmail and bribery. The blackmailer values the money received from the blackmailee more than the psychic income which could be obtained by blabbing; the blackmailee, for his part, regards the silence of the blackmailer more highly than the money he must pay to obtain it. This is the classic path toward wealth maximization. One would think, given their focus on this benefit, that advocates of the "economic approach" would embrace the legalization of blackmail with enthusiasm. Yet the very opposite is the case.

What is the complaint of the "economists" who defend the legal ban on blackmailer-initiated blackmail agreements? They resort to the notion of externalities. As explained by DeLong:

> In economic terms, both blackmail and noncriminal bribery are exchanges that internalize an externality. The risk of negative externalities arises whenever one person (a "menace") has the power to act in a way that would inflict harm on another person (a "victim") without violating any legal rule and without incurring legal liability to pay compensation for the harm. Because the law does not require the menace to take the victim's loss into account in deciding whether to act, the menace may act in ways that create net social costs. [21]

DeLong attacks the "economic approach" on the ground that blackmail and bribery are, in fact, the ways to internalize externalities. In a very powerful analysis of this subject, DeLong [22] brings blackmail under the purview of forbearance exchanges. Selling the service of silence when one has a right to speak is but one among many instances in which menaces, who have a legal right to harm their victims, are nevertheless constrained to desist. As long as the value they place on the pleasure of engaging in the harm is less than that placed on it by the victim, a bargain can typically be struck.

For example, suppose I am legally allowed to maintain my tree at its present (and even growing) height. Yet it blocks my neighbor's view. I legally "menace" him with this tree. He may offer me $1,000 to top it off, say, at 40 feet. If I value the money more than the extra height for the tree, we can both

---

[21] DeLong, *supra* note 5, at 1665–66 (footnote omitted).

[22] DeLong, *supra* note 5, at 1666.

be made better off. In this way the external diseconomy I impose upon him is internalized.[23] As DeLong states:

> A frequent subject of forbearance exchanges is secrecy: actual or potential menaces sell promises of secrecy to actual or potential victims. Examples include an attorney's promise not to disclose the confidences of a client, a departing employee's agreement not to disclose the trade secrets of an employer, a settling litigant's agreement not to disclose what she learned during civil discovery, *or a blackmailer's agreement not to disclose the secret of her victim."* [24]

Thus, the economists who argue that blackmail should be banned based on the risk of negative externalities overlook the fact that both bribery and blackmail are types of forbearance exchanges. Both bribery and blackmail are sales of the service of silence when one otherwise has a right to speak. Selling the service of silence when one has a right to speak is but one among many instances in which menaces, who have a legal right to harm their victims, are nevertheless constrained to desist. Thus, such forbearance exchanges serve to *internalize* externalities.

2. Problems with Neoclassical Monopoly Theory

Insightful as it is, however, DeLong's placing of blackmail under the rubric of forbearance contracts is marred by his acceptance of the neoclassical economist's distinction between monopoly and perfect competition. States DeLong:

> The market power of a seller of secrecy depends upon whether she knows the secret at the time of the sale. At the time of the fee agreement, for example, the attorney has not yet learned the client's secret. If she sells her services in a competitive market, she must bid against others who might also offer secrecy. The price she will charge for confidentiality—the portion of the fee necessary to compensate her for this promise—will be a function of her opportunity cost in forgoing the future ability to disclose the secret. In the case of the attorney, it will usually be small.

---

[23] DeLong is correct in crediting Coase as furnishing numerous examples of forbearance exchanges.

[24] DeLong, *supra* note 5, at 1666 (emphasis added).

> By contrast, the departing employee, the litigant, and the black-
> mailer have learned the secret before the sale. A menace who has
> learned her victim's secret is a monopolist because her disclosure
> alone is sufficient to harm to victim and she is the only person who
> can sell protection from that disclosure. The price she will charge
> usually tends to be function of the harm that disclosure would
> cause the victim rather than a function of her opportunity cost in
> forgoing the disclosure.[25]

In other words, those who learn the secret ahead of time are "monopolists," as opposed to those, like attorneys, who are not told the secret until first
agreeing to keep it secret. These "monopolists" would thus tend to charge a
higher price for silence than those who agree to silence before knowing the
secret.

There are several difficulties here. First, the reason the departing employee, the litigator, and the blackmailer are in a better position vis-a-vis the
potential blackmailee than is the attorney vis-a-vis the potential client has
nothing to do with monopoly and competition. Instead, as DeLong recognizes, it depends upon the time dimension. More specifically, the client who
holds a secret is in a position to contractually tie up the attorney, in effect to
swear him to secrecy as a precondition of hiring him. This has absolutely
nothing to do with the number of lawyers available. There may be only one,[26]
but this is irrelevant. As long as this lawyer stands to lose, and lose heavily[27] if
his client's secret gets out, the secret-holding client has little to fear.

Further, although some of the leverage of the secret-holder depends upon
timing, this is at best a sufficient, not a necessary condition. For suppose there
were a firm called "Blackmail, Inc."[28] Its mission is to ferret out people's embarrassing secrets (through detective work, following people around, lurking
in hotels in the afternoon, and the like) and then to charge them for keeping
silent about this purposefully-acquired information. Blackmail, Inc. need not
have the goods on anyone, initially; if its employees uncover hitherto concealed facts later on, this will be perfectly satisfactory from their point of
view. Thus "time of sale" is hardly all important. Nor does it much matter how

---

[25] DeLong, *supra* note 5, at 1667 (footnotes omitted).

[26] In which case only the structuralists would call it a monopoly; as long as there were no legal
barriers to entry, the behaviorists would characterize an industry with even only one firm in it
as competitive.

[27] E.g., by being disbarred for violating attorney-client privilege, as discussed in further detail
below.

[28] *See, generally,* Richard Epstein, *Blackmail, Inc.*, 50 U. CHI. L. REV. 553 (1983).

many such firms exist. One or two will do quite nicely, but so will hundreds or thousands, for those who think nose counting lends insights into the competitiveness of markets.

Then there is the fact that once the lawyer hears the secret, he is no longer in a "competitive market." At least according to the advocates of blackmail outlawry, the attorney is just as able to blackmail his client as is any other blackmailer. Lawyers know their clients' intimate secrets, often ones that would expose the latter to a risk of jail. No matter what the initial bid, now that the attorney knows the client's secret, he can blackmail him with impunity. As nothing in the DeLong analysis would prevent such an occurrence, it must be at least incomplete, on this one ground alone. There must be something more to the story.

At the very least, the client, in becoming such, must thereby attain some countervailing power. We suggest it is at least in part the ability to counterblackmail any blackmailing lawyer by complaining to the bar association about him.[29] By spreading the news about the attorney's blackmailing attempts, the attorney's reputation can suffer, and he can lose clients and livelihood, and be disbarred. Further, the blackmailee-client could sue the attorney for damages for breach of contract.

The problem that this analysis poses for advocates of blackmail criminalization, however, is that it implies that there can be substantial disincentives for a blackmailer to engage in repeat blackmail. Many blackmailers, not just attorneys, can suffer monetary and other damage if they lose their reputation; and any blackmailer is conceivably subject to legal damages for breach of the secrecy agreement. In a society having a proper legal system, an attorney or other blackmailer may be liable for even more severe penalties or punishment, such as a jail sentence. Nor need such a sentence be limited to only a few months, as mentioned by Sir Arthur Conan Doyle's Sherlock Holmes (see below). For broadcasting a secret very harmful to the client blackmailee, while under contractual obligation to do no such thing, the penalty might be much more severe, since it would have to be commensurate with the harm suffered by the blackmailed client.[30] Even without the prospect of corporal punishment or detention, however, the danger of repeat blackmail is not a

---

[29] DeLong—*supra* note 5, at 1690-91, n. 65)—later shows he is aware of this possibility, but does not apply it to this case.

[30] On libertarian punishment theory, *see* MURRAY N. ROTHBARD, THE ETHICS OF LIBERTY, ch. 13 (1998); N. Stephan Kinsella, *A Libertarian Theory of Punishment and Rights*, 30 LOY. L.A. L. REV. 607 (1997); N. Stephan Kinsella, *New Rationalist Directions in Libertarian Rights Theory*, 12:2 JOURNAL OF LIBERTARIAN STUDIES at. 313–26 (1996).

serious risk and therefore not a strong reason in support of blackmail outlawry.[31]

Another difficulty with the neoclassical monopoly analysis concerns the fact that "the departing employee, the litigator and the blackmailer" need not necessarily be the only ones in each of these categories. There may be, for example, several employees, litigators and blackmailers. If so, there will be more than one person "who can sell protection from that disclosure."

In addition, DeLong's analysis of opportunity costs is problematic. Yes, the price paid by the blackmailee will undoubtedly be a function of how important it is to him that light is not shed on his secret doings, on the blackmailee's wealth, and also on the cost to the blackmailer of disclosing this information (both positive and negative).[32] But there is no reason to believe that this price will not depend upon these first two considerations in the case of the attorney. Nor does it logically follow that even when there is only one seller of silence, the price will depend mainly on the importance placed upon the secret by the blackmailee. Why can't opportunity costs loom large in this calculation? This seems reasonable if the blackmailer is somehow involved in the secret, or fears being labeled a blackmailer, or is bluffed by the blackmailee into thinking that silence is less important than it really is.

DeLong adds a lagniappe to his analysis of monopoly and the gains from trade:

> If the seller is a monopolist, however, as in the typical case of blackmail, then the price of confidentiality may capture almost all the utility that the victim would obtain from the exchange. Thus, in the typical situation in which the blackmailer "bleeds" the victim repeatedly, the exchange is only *slightly* beneficial from the victim's point of view. [33]

---

[31] Many advocates of blackmail outlawry base part of their argument on the claim that were blackmail legal, the blackmailer would "come back for more" money after a blackmail contract had been signed, or that he would continue to "bleed" the blackmailee repeatedly. *See, e.g.,* George P. Fletcher, *Blackmail: The Paradigmatic Case*, 141 U. PA. L. REV. 1617, 1626 (1993), which zeroes in on "the prospect of repeated demands" as generating an impermissible "relationship of dominance and subordination."

[32] The positive costs include being implicated in the negative publicity; the negative costs (benefits) concern the psychic income obtained by the blackmailer in turning gossip, should the blackmailee balk at paying.

[33] DeLong, *supra* note 5, at 1667 fn.13.

This opens up a Pandora's box of objections. Why call the blackmailee a "victim" if he *benefits*, no matter how "slightly" from an exchange? Surely, a better appellation would be "beneficiary." Second, it is impossible to tell who gains more or less from any trade, let alone who gains precisely how much—in fact the concept of one party gaining "more" or "less" than another in a trade is literally meaningless—because of the impossibility of interpersonal comparisons of utility.

These difficulties with neoclassical monopoly theory aside, however, De-Long admits:

> Even though it may involve such monopoly power, however, a confidentiality agreement is presumptively beneficial to both parties. Any price the parties agreed upon would be less than the cost to the victim of suffering disclosure and more than the value to the menace of making disclosure. Therefore a confidentiality exchange, in the absence of other effects, would increase social utility, since each party would be better off after the exchange than before it. [34]

Thus, despite the foregoing confusion regarding the neoclassical conception of monopoly and perfect competition, even DeLong acknowledges that confidentiality agreements, of which blackmail contracts are an example, are mutually beneficial to *both* parties, blackmailer as well as blackmailee.

B. Blackmail and Efficiency

Even from the "law and economics" viewpoint, therefore, a blackmail agreement is presumptively beneficial to both parties, even if it be conceded that such an agreement involves "monopoly power." That is, "in the absence of other effects."[35] Unfortunately, according to the law & economics crowd, these "other effects" are all too present, and undermine the argument for laissez-faire capitalism (the legitimacy of all non-invasive contracts such as blackmail).

States DeLong, on behalf of the "economists:"

> [T]he confidentiality agreement may be allocatively inefficient because third parties would have valued disclosure of the secret more than the victim values secrecy. In a world of third parties, incomplete information and transactions costs, a confidentiality exchange

---

[34] *Id.* at 1667–68.

[35] Id.

might be inefficient despite both parties' willingness to enter it. First, confidentiality may create its own externality by being more costly to third parties than beneficial to the two contracting parties. Second, the exchange might be wholly unnecessary because the menace would not have disclosed the secret in its absence. Third, the possibility of such an exchange might lead the parties to make strategic, nonproductive investments in bringing it about or preventing it. Finally, because the relationship between the menace and victim constitutes a bilateral monopoly, the exchange might be so costly to negotiate and enforce that the gains from the exchange would be exceeded by transactions costs. [36]

As DeLong incisively notes, however, these criticisms are also true of the bribe taker, and yet the latter is legal. [37] These concerns do not help to justify the anomalous distinction between blackmail and bribery. And yet more remains to be said about the deficiencies in the "economist's" arguments.

One problem is that their contentions are over-inclusive. If we ban blackmail on this ground, we will end up prohibiting almost all trades, if we follow through in a logically rigorous manner. Take the rather pedestrian sale of a can of beer for $1.00. Probably, in this imperfect world, there "would have been" some other buyer who valued this commodity even more highly. As well, there is probably someone who valued the money to a greater degree, that is, who would have been willing to sell a product with the same specifications for less than $1.00. In either case, this trade is "inefficient" based on the criterion employed by these unnamed "economists."

This argument can also be put forth in terms of information, to bring us closer to the case at hand. A journalist works for newspaper A at the wage of W_A; he could have been employed by B, at higher wage W_B; unfortunately, the two parties were unknown to each other, and were not able to consummate the deal. Inefficient? Yes, on the assumption that the information and transaction costs were lower than the present discounted value of the difference between W_A and W_B.

A further example. It is always possible that the husband of an adulterer might have been willing to pay even more for this information to the blackmailer than was his wife. But if so the blackmailer is a poor businessman; he didn't sell to the best customer for his wares. Such mistakes occur every day, every second, in real world markets.

---

[36] *Id.* at1668.

[37] *Id.* at 1668–69.

The implication of the "economists" (apparently accepted also by De-Long) is that just because something is economically "inefficient" we should ban it. If so, we might as well ban all markets, all enterprises touched by human hands for that matter, since they are all inefficient in this sense. Of course, when we ask, With what shall we replace them?, the ludicrousness of the scheme becomes apparent.

Efficiency, moreover, is a value-laden term; there is always an implicit goal in mind, which takes us out of positive economics and deposits us into the normative realm. Here, the economist qua economist can make no contribution whatever.

We do not argue that all commercial arrangements agreed upon by two parties ought to be legally enforced. There are, of course, exceptions. For one, A hires B to murder C. For another, fractional reserve banking.[38] But the overwhelming presumption must be that contractual agreements enhance economic welfare, so long as the contract has a lawful and possible object.[39]

The criticism of unnecessariness[40] is likewise over-inclusive. Yes, the blackmail exchange might not be beneficial to the blackmailee, if the secret would not have been revealed in any case. However, this, too, can apply to virtually every trade. You go to the store to purchase a loaf of bread. There is a small chance that the owner might have given this foodstuff away to you for free, or for a nominal price, had you but enquired. But you didn't. You just paid the sticker price. Similarly with bluffing or "puffing." In the field of real estate, there is rarely a seller who does not imply he has other anxious buyers, nor a buyer who does not indicate he has other attractive options. Are all such transactions to be labeled inefficient and legally proscribed on that basis?

We have already called into question the application of the term "monopoly" to the blackmail situation. First of all, there may be many blackmailers and many "victims" (e.g., "blackmailees"). If so, bilateral monopoly does not enter into the picture even on neoclassical structuralist grounds. Second, if "the relationship between the menace and victim constitutes a bilateral monopoly," so does that between buyer and seller, landlord and renter, and so forth, whenever there are not numerous buyers and sellers, a homogeneous

---

[38] *See* in this regard Hans-Hermann Hoppe, Jörg Guido Hülsmann, and Walter Block, *Against Fiduciary Media*, 1 Quarterly Journal of Austrian Economics at 19–50 (1998).

[39] The Louisiana Civil Code, for example, provides: "Parties are free to contract for any object that is lawful, possible, and determined or determinable." La. Civ. Code art. 1971.

[40] To-wit, the economists' second ground that a confidentiality agreement may be "allocatively inefficient" even if both parties desire to enter into it, because "the exchange might be wholly unnecessary because the menace would not have disclosed the secret in its absence." DeLong, *supra* note 5, at 1668.

good, full information, zero profits, equilibrium, and all the other unrealistic assumptions of perfect competition. Since this model *never* applies to the real world, we have here the perfect case of over-inclusiveness: this criticism applies to *every* commercial interaction without exception.

1. Blackmail-Caused Inefficiencies in Criminal Law Enforcement

Landes and Posner have offered another economic critique of legalized blackmail based on inefficiencies it introduces into criminal law enforcement.[41] They argue that government must have a monopoly of law enforcement, and that under legalization, blackmailers would interfere with optimization of these expenditures, as well as be "preventing appropriate levels of illegal activities from taking place."[42]

DeLong powerfully rebukes these authors on the ground that "the state can never have a monopoly on crime prevention, which include such diverse phenomena as neighborhood watch programs, surveillance cameras, burglar alarms, armored cars and karate lessons." [43] As well, he taxes them on the ground that their "rationale for blackmail statutes would equally justify outlawing bribery, and so fails to account adequately for current law."[44]

However, DeLong could have gone further in his denigration, and commits several errors in his own analysis. First, the DeLong who here upbraids Posner and Landes is inconsistent with the DeLong [45] who brought blackmail under the rubric of forbearance exchanges. The former DeLong accepted the argument that what the neoclassicals call monopoly was inferior to their version of competition. The latter DeLong allows Posner to get by, unscathed, in arguing for government monopolization of law enforcement, demurring only slightly in his objection that "the state can never have a monopoly on crime prevention." The implication here, though, is that if somehow the government *could* attain this status, that would be efficient. But this means that DeLong goes along with Posner's and Landes' trashing of the structuralists views of monopoly now, after he has previously accepted this perspective. The point: what is sauce for the market goose is sauce for the government gander: if monopoly leads to inefficiency in the market sector, this applies, as well, to gov-

---

[41] Richard Posner, *Blackmail, Privacy and Freedom of Contract*, 141 U. PA. L. REV. 1817 (1993); William Landes and Richard A. Posner, *The Private Enforcement of Law*, 4 J. LEGAL STUD. 1 (1975).

[42] DeLong, *supra* note 5, at 1671.

[43] *Id.* at 1670.

[44] *Id.*

[45] *Id.* at 1667.

ernment. Monopoly is monopoly is monopoly. Neither Landes, nor Posner, nor DeLong should be allowed to get away with assailing monopoly in one context while championing it in another, unless they can show a relevant difference between the two.[46]

Then there is a difficulty about the "optimal amount of crime." Let this be said once and for all, loud and clear, contrary to both DeLong and the "economic perspective" he otherwise criticizes: the optimal amount of crime is zero![47] True, the optimal amount of crime *prevention* is *not* the amount that would bring the crime rate down to zero. This can hardly be optimal, given that it might take the entire GDP (or more) to attain. But abstracting from crime *prevention* expenditures, the optimal level of *crime itself* can never be greater than zero. If it were, this would imply—at least as far as the "economists" are concerned—that the stolen goods are greater in value to the criminal than to the rightful owner, a conclusion which relies on illegitimate interpersonal comparisons of utility even for coherence.

2. Wasteful Investments of Resources

Economists such as Coase and Ginsburg & Shechtman argue that blackmail ought to be illegal in order to economize on resources.[48] Which resources? The ones which would be frittered away by would-be blackmailers in attempting to unearth embarrassing secrets, and the ones wasted by those guilty of shameful acts in an effort to keep them secret.

However, the waste-reduction theorists have neglected to take account of the resource-enhancing elements of legalized blackmail. As explained by DeLong:

> In all cases in which the menace would otherwise have disclosed the victim's secret, a blackmail exchange is at least presumptively efficient from the perspective of the menace and the victim. The victim is able to purchase secrecy, a benefit to which he is otherwise

---

[46] For an Austrian economic critique of the very concept of a non-government "monopoly," *see* Rothbard, *supra* note 16, ch. 10.3; HANS-HERMANN HOPPE, A THEORY OF SOCIALISM AND CAPITALISM, ch. 9 (1989).

[47] This is for real crime, of the uninvited border crossing variety, not victimless crime, such as sales of sex or drugs from and to consenting adults, or, for that matter, the type currently under discussion.

[48] *See, generally,* Ronald H. Coase, *The 1987: McCorkle Lecture: Blackmail,* 74 VA. L. REV. (1988); Douglas H. Ginsburg and Paul Shechtman, *"Blackmail: An Economic Analysis of the Law,* 141 U. Pa. L. Rev. 1849 (1993).

unentitled, and that would be unavailable in the absence of the exchange.[49]

DeLong[50] exposes another flaw in the arguments based on waste:

> Waste reduction theorists ignore this benefit [the ability to purchase secrecy from a blackmailer] by assuming that most blackmailers would not disclose the secret if they could not blackmail the victim. Yet this assumption is quite doubtful. Given the very low costs of disclosure to most blackmailers, the social rewards of disclosure, and the blackmailer's typical disregard for the victim's feelings, it seems likely that many if not most people who would threaten blackmail would happily disclose their victim's secret if blackmail were prevented.

The waste theory also "fails to account for the differentiation between bribery and blackmail."[51].

DeLong's critique hits the mark, but it only scratches the surface. First of all, why, just because an act is "wasteful" of resources, should it be banned? Surely, there is nothing more wasteful than watching soap operas or sports, or listening to rap music, or being a tourist, or drinking alcohol, or playing any other sport than handball; should all of these things be legally proscribed? Hardly. Second, one man's dissipation is another man's pleasure. Just because a given individual finds the aforementioned activities wasteful does not mean they are intrinsically so. Since there is and can be no objective criterion for "waste," any more than there is or can be for utility, this seems a weak reed upon which to rest criminal law.[52]

Third, there are many cases where one person acts in an "aggressive" manner, and another adopts a defensive posture. If both of them would simply refrain from their behavior, wealth would presumably be increased, at least according to the faulty criterion employed by mainstream economic theorists. For example, in football, basketball, baseball, hockey, and many other sports, there are those intent upon advancing the ball (or puck) in an entirely aggressive manner. They are usually deemed the "offense." On the other hand, there are those, many of them, equally intent that this shall not

---

[49] DeLong, *supra* note 5, at 1673.

[50] *Id.* (footnotes omitted).

[51] *Id.*

[52] *See also* the discussion in section II.A.1 above with respect to the prohibition of "wasteful" or "frivolous" activities.

occur. Millions of dollars, and much time, sweat, tears, and even blood are "wasted" on such defensive maneuvers. If only they would cut this out, *both* of them, our society would surely be the richer for it. DeLong concurs with Coase and Ginsburg & Shechtman to the effect that blackmail consists of "pointless deadweight losses and economically sterile exchanges."[53] But these examples are identical in all relevant respects to blackmail. If blackmail should be outlawed, should these other frivolities?

This, however, is only the tip of the iceberg. Gossips expend effort to try to ascertain who is doing what to whom who shouldn't be; but those who are doing these things also take precautions to keep them secret. Are we to criminalize both sides to reduce "waste?" Who else acts incompatibly with someone else? Cooks, chefs, restaurateurs; the sugar, chocolate, baking, and fast food industries all act in a way which makes us fatter and unhealthier. On the other hand, there are vegetable growers, nutritionists, doctors—to say nothing of those in the diet and exercise industries—who are struggling, valiantly, to undo the efforts of the first set of economic actors. Let us incarcerate all such people for the "crime" of acting incompatibly with one another, and thus "wasting" resources.

In like manner, insurance companies take great pains to reduce motor vehicle accidents, for which they are financially responsible; while Detroit makes cars which can go faster and faster, and are hence more dangerous, and Milwaukee brews beer to the same latter end. Divorce lawyers have an interest in marriage breakup, clergymen in the strengthening of this institution; librarians and newspaper owners in literacy, cartoonists in the very opposite; repairmen of all stripes and varieties in the breakdown of machinery, those who offer guarantees and warrantees in their soundness. Locksmiths are internally contradictory in this manner; on the one hand their reputation rests on the durability of their wares, on the other hand if they could never be breached, and no one, therefore, even tried, this industry would be bankrupt. Let us incarcerate the whole lot of these people in the name of "the economic approach."[54]

---

[53] DeLong, *supra* note 5, at 1673.

[54] Friedman argued that the gold standard is inefficient and wasteful; it involves digging up this metal in one place (the mine) and burying it in another (Fort Knox). MILTON FRIEDMAN, A PROGRAM FOR MONETARY STABILITY (1960). That is one way of looking at the matter. Another is to see these expenses as an insurance policy against governmental inflation. On this *see* Walter Block, *The Gold Standard: A Critique of Friedman, Mundell, Hayek, Greenspan*, 25 MANAGERIAL FINANCE at. 15–33 (1999). Against what is blackmail an insurance policy? Against gossip.

3. Costly Reallocative Exchanges

As discussed by DeLong, Coase "also sees the law of blackmail as assigning to the victim a 'right not to be blackmailed'" based on efficiency reasons.[55] Under the Coase Theorem, legal entitlements should be allocated to parties that value them most, to save transaction costs of reallocative bargaining. Coase assumes that the victim is likely to value the right to not be blackmailed more than the blackmailer would value the right to blackmail. Thus blackmail is inefficient and should be prohibited. There are numerous problems with this view.

In traditional jurisprudence, property rights are first vested in human beings, each to his own, one to a customer.[56] That is, I own myself, you own yourself, he owns himself, they own themselves. Then, in the Lockean tradition, each of us can mix his labor with previously unowned or virgin territory, farm animals, etc., and come to own them in this way.[57] A third source of property rights stems from trade or gifts. You homestead land and grow wheat; I domesticate a cow. We then trade milk for bread and come to own things we did not produce—but which can be traced back to legitimate title transfer.[58] All legitimate property, at least theoretically, can be understood as having taken part in such a process.[59] As Hoppe notes, "One can acquire and increase wealth either through homesteading, producing and contractual exchange, or by expropriating and exploiting homesteaders, producers, or contractual exchanges. There are no other ways."[60]

If you and I are having a dispute as to the ownership of a jacket, the judge steeped in this tradition of jurisprudence will engage in a bit of historical analysis, predicated on this theory of private property. He will look backwards, asking each of us to produce a receipt for this article of clothing (or, if we claim to have made it ourselves, then a receipt for the cloth, buttons, zipper we used in its construction). Or he will in some other way attempt to

[55] DeLong, *supra* note 5, at 1674–75.

[56] *See, generally,* HANS-HERMANN HOPPE, THE ECONOMICS AND ETHICS OF PRIVATE PROPERTY: STUDIES IN POLITICAL ECONOMY AND PHILOSOPHY (1993); Kinsella, *supra* note 29.

[57] *See, generally,* JOHN LOCKE, AN ESSAY CONCERNING THE TRUE ORIGIN, EXTENT, AND END OF CIVIL GOVERNMENT; JOHN LOCK, SECOND TREATISE OF CIVIL GOVERNMENT.

[58] *See, generally,* ROBERT NOZICK, ANARCHY, STATE AND UTOPIA (1974).

[59] *See, generally,* MURRAY N. ROTHBARD, FOR A NEW LIBERTY (1978).

[60] Hoppe, *supra* note 55, at 66.

weigh our (conflicting) claims. But he will do so guided by this traditional theory of property rights and their creation.[61]

We belabor the obvious only to show how radical a departure from this familiar territory is Coase's perspective. For him, property rights are not at all based on historical antecedents. Rather, they are established on the basis of predictions about the future! The justification of property titles, here, is not past actions, but rather the maximization of wealth in the future. If your and I are contesting the ownership of the jacket, the Coasean judge will not ask either of us to verify how it happened to come into our hands in the past. On the contrary, he will award the garment to whichever party he deems will be able to use it to increase future wealth by the greatest amount. If, for example, this is your only jacket and you will use it to ward off cold and thus save the life of a highly productive worker; and if I am awarded this article of clothing it will only sit in my closet along with the rest of my gigantic wardrobe; then, presumably, the Coasean judge will award it to you since social wealth will be maximized in this way.

How does all this pertain to our present concerns? The traditionalist will interpret ownership of a secret in one way, the Coasean in an entirely different manner. If I come to know of your predilection for taking a bath with a rubber duckie legitimately (you yourself bragged to me about this, you even gave me a picture of you in this act, when you were younger and more foolish), I then properly own this information. I may gossip about it if I choose. If you later come to be ashamed of this behavior, I can sell you my silence about it (i.e., I can blackmail you about it), or you can initiate matters and buy my silence about this episode from me (blackmailee-initiated blackmail, or, in conventional phraseology, bribery).

For Coase, however, matters are very different. Under rare circumstances, perhaps, if the judge thinks I value the right to gossip about the duckie more highly than you regard silence about it, then he may conceivably award this right to me. In the more likely case,[62] the Coase-influenced jurist will ban me from speaking about this, since you value silence about the rubber duckie more than I value the right to gossip about it. In this way, wealth will be maximized.

Coase argues:

---

[61] *See* RANDY E. BARNETT, THE STRUCTURE OF LIBERTY: JUSTICE AND THE RULE OF LAW at 109–21 (1998) (discussing the use of abstract legal principles as general guidelines used to critique and help develop concrete legal rules or precepts).

[62] Although, as we have seen, given the subjectivity of predictions about the future, no clear implication emerges from the Coase Theorem.

In a blackmailing scheme, the person who will pay the most for the right to stop the action threatened is normally the person being blackmailed. If the right to stop this action is denied to others, that is, blackmail is made illegal, transactions costs are reduced, factors of production are released for other purposes, and the value of production is increased. This is an approach which comes quite naturally to an economist. [63]

DeLong quite properly rebukes Coase for having "gotten it backwards. Laws against blackmail *prohibit* a reallocative bargain that is made necessary because the right to disclose the secret has been assigned to the menace."[64]

But this is only the beginning of the problems with Coase. Our claim is that despite what Coase specifically says, his claim is really about ownership of secrecy rights, not blackmail *per se*. Coase's theorem is preeminently a theory about ownership. Secrets can be owned (gossip can be declared illegal) but blackmail cannot itself be owned. Rather, blackmail is itself a way of *transferring* such ownership rights from one person (blackmailer) to another (blackmailee). Coase, then, not only has "gotten it backwards," he has also gotten it inside out. That is, Coase[65] is inconsistent with Coase.[66] In his 1960 article, Coase waxed eloquent about, in a low or zero transactions cost world, the irrelevancy of judicial findings regarding resource allocation (but not wealth distribution). If property was mistakenly given to the "wrong" man, the "right" one, who really valued it more and thus if put into has hands would more greatly increase wealth, could always bribe him out of it. (If I was awarded the jacket, but you valued it more, you could purchase from me. If you were given it, I would not be able to buy it from you since you value it more than me.) But blackmail is the preeminent way of transferring titles to secrets.

For not appreciating this, Coase has indeed "gotten it backwards." Typically, in such situations, there are only two parties, the blackmailer and the blackmailee. So transaction costs must perforce be low. If Coase[67] were consistent with his own Coase Theorem, he would have favored the legalization of blackmail, not its prohibition. For it is only in this way that resources may

---

[63] Coase, *supra* note 47, at 673.

[64] DeLong, *supra* note 5, at 1674.

[65] Coase, *supra* note 47.

[66] Ronald H. Coase, *The Problem of Social Cost*, 3 J. L. & ECON. 1 (1960). It is the latter from whence sprang the Coase Theorem; the former is but an application, and a mistaken one, at that.

[67] Coase, *supra* note 47.

shift from those who value it less to those who value it more—something quite important for wealth maximization in the zero-transactions costs world when the judge errs in his findings. Instead, Coase calls blackmail "moral murder," thus getting it "inside out." [68]

But even this by no means exhausts the problems with Coase's analysis. This is neither the time nor the place for a full-scale critique of this doctrine. Suffice it to say that "no man's property will ever be safe" when the Coasean court is in session. For at any time, any person can seize your car, or your jacket. He will not be treated as a thief, if he can but convince the judge that leaving your property in his hands will better increase wealth than allowing you to keep your own possessions. Comparing how two or more people value a car or a jacket or anything else is essentially a subjective exercise. No matter how fully steeped in the Coase Theorem, judges can and will disagree with each other on these matters. This being the case, no longer is there any fixed demarcation between mine and thine. Since that is the main function of property rights, it is no exaggeration to claim that under Coasean rule there will *be* no property rights. At best, there will be only a shifting pattern of temporary ownership; title is legitimate only until the next claimant comes along.

This analysis follows logically from the Coasean premise that "the value of production would be maximized if rights were deemed to be possessed by those to whom they were most valuable, thus eliminating the need for any transactions."[69] Under the Coasean rule, all justice and law break down. For example, the defendant in a rape case would have an altogether new defense available in the Coasean world: his utility in forcing sex upon the victim was greater than her disutility from the attack. Even the concept of self-ownership with which we began this section (and apologized over for belaboring the "obvious") can now be called into question. For example, given that O.J. Simpson valued his wife's life more than she valued it on her own account (let us assume that she had low self-esteem), in the real world of high transactions costs, the Coasean judge would award him the ownership rights over her. Since he is the legitimate owner, and may dispose of his *property* in any way he wishes, he is innocent of murder even if he did indeed kill her. [70]

Clearly, Coasean reasoning is unhelpful in deciding normative issues, like whether or not one has a right to not be blackmailed. Even if the victim values the right to not be blackmailed "more" than the blackmailer, this does not imply that blackmail should be unlawful. Additionally, even granting for the

---

[68] DeLong, *supra* note 5, at 1689 quoting Coase, *supra* note 47, at 675.

[69] DeLong, *supra* note 5, at 1674 fn.27, quoting Coase, *supra* note 47, at 673.

[70] *See* Walter Block, *O.J.'s Defense: A Reductio Ad Absurdum of the Economics of Ronald Coase and Richard Posner*, 3 Eur. J. L. & Econ. 265 (1996).

sake of argument the Coasean logic that high transaction costs warrant different initial rights allocations, in the blackmail context there are only two parties and transaction costs are low. Thus, instead of outlawing blackmail, it should remain legal so that secrecy can be purchased in situations where the blackmailee actually does value the secret more than the blackmailer.

4. Market Price Blackmail: The Attack on Profit

We next move to a consideration of so-called market price blackmail. The view, here, is that blackmail should be legal as long as the price charged is no higher than that which the blackmailer could have received from an alternative (non-blackmailee) bidder.[71] The presumption is that if price is restricted in this way, the blackmailer is not really taking advantage or exploiting the blackmailee; he is only covering his (opportunity) costs. The usual example is that of a journalist who can sell the story to a newspaper for a modest amount, say $100. As long as he charges the blackmailee no more than that, "market pricers" advocate legalizing such blackmail transactions.

There are several practical problems with this approach, mainly stemming from subjectivist considerations. [72] For example, "victims" (i.e., blackmailees), as well as police and courts "will often be unable to discern a true market price blackmailer … from a false" one. As well, "the subject matter of the sale, the secret itself, cannot be described to the buyer for purposes of valuation without disclosing the secret."[73]

DeLong, however, is incorrect that, if these pragmatic difficulties are overcome, "market price blackmail seems to be justifiable."[74] DeLong is wrong because the market price blackmail program suffers from a host of other deficiencies as well as the practical ones he has noted. For the initiative is really a disguised attack on the institution of profit. If the blackmailer can charge no more than his alternative cost (e.g., the price he could have obtained from the newspaper), he can earn no profit. But why should profits be illegal? To prohibit non-market price blackmail just because a higher price is charged is to confuse profit-making with extortion or invasiveness.

This is a common confusion of socialism, of course, but that pedigree alone should be enough to make one suspicious of arguments that depend

---

[71] Advocates of this doctrine include Scott Altman, *A Patchwork Theory of Blackmail*, 141 U. PA. L. REV. 1639 (1993); Nozick, *supra* note 57; and CHARLES FRIED, CONTRACT AS PROMISE (1981).

[72] DeLong, *supra* note 5, at 1675.

[73] *Id.* at 1676.

[74] *Id.* at 1675.

upon attacking the institution of profit. Many mainstream or neoclassical economic theorists seem to think that if a price incorporates profit it cannot be considered a market price. [75] Nothing could be further from the truth. It is only equilibrium prices, not market prices, which exclude profits.[76]

A more basic problem is that legalizing so-called "market price" blackmail and criminalizing blackmail beyond this point is to conflate a legal wrong with the price charged for a legal wrong. Compare murder, a real crime, not a victimless one, in this regard. Suppose A hires B to kill C for $100,000. This should be legally forbidden *not* because the price is too high, or because someone makes a *profit* on the deal, but because murder is an invasive act, an act of aggression. The act of murder would be no less invasive, by even one iota, if the price charged for the "hit" was instead $10, or $1 or even were done for free.

Indeed, the fact that the price charged is even relevant to determine whether a crime has been committed indicates that the blackmail theorists are not discussing a real crime, such as murder. If we were discussing a real crime, price would be irrelevant. Even advocates of blackmail outlawry do not seem to take seriously the idea that blackmail is really a crime. If they did, they would not bring price into it, any more than they would hand-wring over the price charged for an assassination.

III. OTHER EXPLANATIONS OF BLACKMAIL OUT-LAWRY

In addition to economic-based theories in support of blackmail criminalization, a variety of other defenses are often offered, including various appeals to emotion or intuition. DeLong, for example, who has criticized many of the conventional, economic defenses of blackmail outlawry, ends up making such an appeal in an attempt to explain what he sees as the widespread revulsion against blackmail. He very properly dismisses as a "bizarre conclusion" and a "provocation" the claim by some economists[77] that the law, as presently constituted, is best understood merely as an attempt to economize

---

[75] *See, e.g.,* DeLong, *supra* note 5; Altman, *supra* note 70; Nozick, *supra* note 57; and Fried, *supra* note 70.

[76] Profit above and beyond the pure rate of interest, that is. *See, e.g.* Rothbard, *supra* note 16, at ch. 8.1; Mises, *supra* note 16, at 289–301, discussing entrepreneurial profit and the evenly rotating economy.

[77] Mainly those clustered around the University of Chicago and the "Law and Economics" movement it has spawned.

on resources.[78] Instead, he seeks a "social meaning" and not only for blackmail but for bribery[79] as well.

DeLong[80] begins with a quote from Doyle, which bears repeating:

> "But who is he?"

> "I'll tell you, Watson. He is the king of all the blackmailers. Heaven help the man, and still more the woman, whose secret and reputation come into the power of Milverton! With a smiling face and a heart of marble, he will squeeze and squeeze until he has drained them dry. ... I have said that he is the worst man in London, and I would ask you how could one compare the ruffian, who in hot blood bludgeons his mate, with this man, who methodically and at his leisure tortures the soul and wrings the nerves in order to add to his already swollen money-bags?" ...

> "But surely," said I, "the fellow must be within the grasp of the law?"

> "Technically, no doubt, but practically not. What would it profit a woman, for example, to get him a few month's imprisonment if her own ruin must immediately follow? His victims dare not hit back."

By not commenting further on this bit of wisdom from Sherlock Holmes, DeLong indicates he thinks this is a definitive critique of legalization. Actually, this constitutes an argument in favor of *decriminalization*. For if the unhappy woman is in such a poor condition under present legal arrangements—and her well-being seems to be the entire point of the law—her plight can hardly be worsened were blackmail to be decriminalized.

In contrast, DeLong's implication is that if the blackmailee's situation is desperate under present institutional arrangements, it would be far more critical were blackmail to become legal.

Let us consider such a situation. A woman falls into the clutches of Milverton, who leads her to pay him, and perhaps, in addition, do unspeakable things in order to protect her secret. Worse, the blackmailer could keep coming back for more payments, over and above those initially agreed to; he would "bleed" her.

---

[78] DeLong, *supra* note 5, at 1689.

[79] I.e., blackmailee-initiated secrecy or blackmail agreements.

[80] DeLong, *supra* note 5, at 1688–89.

But this tug at the heartstrings will not do. Let us posit that the reason the woman is in Milverton's clutches is because she committed adultery. Is her being blackmailed so horrible a result? On the contrary, one might argue, this will teach women to think first before committing this illicit act. Were Milverton's hold over this unhappy woman to be widely publicized in the newspapers, just once, thousands of women who might otherwise have engaged in marital infidelity will now not do so. In other words, there are other things worthy of consideration in law beside the feelings of blackmailees.

Paradoxically, the position of the woman might be improved under legalization. For then, when Milverton initially approaches her, threatening her with exposure (or, when she initially approaches him, and offers to pay him for his silence), the demand is likely to be slight—how else can be explained the increasing severity of the demands, the continual "coming back for more" and "bleeding?" If so, they will sign a contract stipulating that Milverton will keep silent about the woman's secret in return for a relatively modest payment. Now, if he "comes back for more" making new demands, she has him tied up contractually. True, if she sues him, her secret will be lost. But it will no longer be true that "His victims dare not hit back." As discussed in Section II.A.2 above, the repeat blackmailer will indeed pay a severe penalty. This need not at all be limited to the "few month's imprisonment" mentioned by Doyle. Instead, if the punishment is to fit the crime, and the contract violation of the blackmailer will be a severe hardship to the blackmailee, as stipulated to by Doyle and DeLong, then the penalty imposed on Milverton will be equally harsh.[81]

But the best answer to the "Milverton" challenge is to compare the woman's plight when she is in the power of this "king of all the blackmailers" with her situation had a gossip got hold of her secret. Would the woman be in a better position? Far from it. At least Milverton, this "moral murderer," had the decency not to let the cat out of the bag before enquiring as to whether the woman would rather pay him off to refrain. But once we introduce the gossip, all is lost. If Milverton deserves to be damned to hell, then the gossip deserves to occupy an even lower rung in the nether world. But our author fails to call for the legal prohibition of gossip! How could he, given that gossip is worse for this woman than blackmail, after he has jerked our tears via Sherlock with her plight.

DeLong asks, "Why does blackmail strike us as so wrongful?"[82] and seeks an answer in terms of "social meaning," which can, in turn, be discerned

---

[81] *See* discussion and references in Section II.A.2, above.

[82] DeLong, *supra* note 5, at 1689.

through "intuition."[83] DeLong's intuition tells him that blackmail cuts off the ties between the individual and his community.

Consider, however, the case where the parent says to the child: "If you don't do your homework, you can't get on the Internet." Although this is hardly the paradigmatic case, this nonetheless fits all the criteria for blackmail. There is a demand for valuable consideration (homework, in the eyes of the parent). This is coupled with a threat (no Internet) which parents have every right to enforce.

We venture to submit that most individual's "intuition" in this case, in contrast to DeLong's, is that this is very far from Coase's "moral murder." What is threatened here is not to reveal a secret, but it indubitably "cuts off the ties between the individual and his community." The Internet, like the telephone in an earlier age, is a key element in the teenager's communication with his community. Normal intuition, very different from that of DeLong, sees this parental blackmail threat as harmless, even salutary. To place this in an even more commonplace context, my purchase of a newspaper is an exercise in mutual blackmail. I "threaten" the vendor that unless he turns over the paper to me, I will not pay him 50 cents. He, for his part, "threatens" me that unless I tender him the money, I will have to do without his product. DeLong may see this as "an oppressive relationship,"[84] but this commercial interaction is instead mutually beneficial; indeed, it forms the bedrock of our very civilization.

It might be objected that the blackmail of the parent and child or newspaper sale does not really fit this model. This is erroneous, since the essence of blackmail is the combination of a demand for money, coupled with a threat to do something which is itself lawful, and all of the reductio examples considered herein under the rubric of blackmail fit that bill. DeLong then resorts to profit bashing in an attempt to explain why we should feel a particular revulsion for blackmail. He focuses on "our condemnation of the menace's attempt to profit from her threat."[85] But why is it so disgusting to earn a profit? We have seen that the gossip, who earns no profits, renders the blackmailee's position far more precarious. If we are not ready to legally condemn the latter, logic prohibits us from doing so to the former.

Profit, in any case, is far more ubiquitous than DeLong and other profitbashers seem to realize. Strictly speaking, it is the difference in value between what we give up in taking an action, and what we receive.[86] For example, you,

---

[83] *Id.* at 1690.

[84] *Id.*

[85] *Id.* at 1691.

[86] *See* Rothbard, *supra* note 16, at ch. 8.1, 4.5.C; Mises, *supra* note 16, at 289.

gentle reader, in reading this article, are profiting, at least in the *ex ante* sense. You are giving up some of your time for this enterprise, and gaining insights into a different perspective (or perhaps seething in indignation, but enjoyably so, you masochist, otherwise you would long ago have put down this article). The difference in value to you between these two is profit. It is positive, if you are still tuned in. Profit, defined in this broad manner, rules not only the free economy, but even our everyday activities, such as eating, brushing our teeth, sleeping, and so forth. In fact, as Mises points out, "[t]o make profit is invariably the aim sought by *any* action."[87] It will take more than a socialist attack on profits to undermine the case for legalizing blackmail.

DeLong identifies "isolation from the community" as a main reason that blackmail is considered to be a crime: "Blackmail … entails a double isolation and a double crime against community."[88] But why is this so important as to render criminal an otherwise legal series of acts, e.g., blackmail? There are many people who are isolated from their communities to greater or lesser degrees. For example, monks in a monastery, nuns in a nunnery, fishermen, sailors, hunters, and farmers who live by themselves in out of the way places. The most extreme case, of course, is the hermit. Isolation may not be psychologically healthy, at least for most people, but to elevate this fact and make it the basis of law seems outlandish.

DeLong, however, equates isolation with submissiveness:

> [T]he purpose of the law of blackmail is to protect the community against the conspiratorial agreement of blackmailer and victim, which isolates the victim and subjects him to a submissive relationship with the blackmailer.[89]

This comes with ill grace from a DeLong who states: "The victim is able to purchase secrecy, a benefit to which he is otherwise unentitled, and that

---

[87] Mises, *supra* note 16, at 289 (emphasis added). Mises also states: "Profit, in a broader sense, is the gain derived from action; it is the increase in satisfaction (decrease in uneasiness) brought about; it is the difference between the higher value attached to the result attained and the lower value attached to the sacrifices made for its attainment; it is, in other words, yield minus costs. To make profit is invariably the aim sought by any action. If an action fails to attain the ends sought, yield either does not exceed costs or lags behind costs. In the latter case the outcome means a loss, a decrease in satisfaction."

[88] DeLong, *supra* note 5, at 1691.

[89] *Id.* This calls to mind Fletcher's view that blackmail establishes a "relationship of dominance and subordination," discussed *supra* note 5, at 1626.

would be unavailable in the absence of the exchange."[90] If the blackmailee "benefits," in what sense is he a "victim?" And if the blackmailee is a beneficiary of the blackmailer (certainly compared to the situation where the secret is held by an unbribable gossip), in what sense is he "submissive?" But we don't have to range widely over DeLong's article, 23 pages above, to find a contradiction. On the very page that DeLong is castigating the blackmailer for isolating the blackmailee, and making him "submissive," he also mentions the "victim's eagerness to buy secrecy."[91] If this is so, and it certainly is, from whence springs all this talk of submissiveness and victimization? Does the rape victim "eagerly" embrace the rapist? Does the murder victim "eagerly" interact with the murderer? Not a bit of it. There is a clear difference between true victims, who are never eager to be victimized, and victimless blackmailees, who benefit from the silence of the blackmailer.

Next, DeLong opines as follows:

> An often overlooked reason for outlawing blackmail is to avoid the violence that might be engendered by the victim's desperation. The intensity of a victim's reaction to blackmail may be something that the law simply wants to avoid.[92]

But this is absurd. As we have already established, the desperation of the man whose secret is unearthed by a gossip is even worse than that felt by the person in the clutches of a blackmailer. At least the latter gives you a choice. Therefore, the violence "engendered" by gossip can be expected to be even greater. We cannot but conclude, then, that gossip should be outlawed; indeed, that if we could only legally proscribe one of them, gossip or blackmail, it should be the former which is given such treatment. DeLong, however, never calls for any such public policy.

Further, if avoiding violence is the be all and end all of the law, why don't we ban unions, or the Ku Klux Klan, or the Communist Party, or the Nazis, or even soccer games? All of them are heavily associated with violence. With regard to "desperation," this can hardly be exceeded by the plight of the drug addict in need of a fix, who cannot get it because of the prohibition of narcotics, and who then turns to violence. If DeLong were correct in his surmise, we would long ago have legalized these substances.

DeLong's remarks seem puzzling when he addresses the difference between blackmail and bribery: "While blackmail is something the menace

---

[90] DeLong, *supra* note 5, at 1668.

[91] *Id.* at 1691.

[92] *Id.* at 1691 fn. 68.

does, bribery is something the victim does. The blackmailer threatens; the briber offers. Blackmail makes the victim worse off; bribery makes him better off."[93]

The puzzle is that even according to DeLong, both blackmail and bribery are the same economic interaction; the only difference between them, the only reason DeLong even calls them by different names, is the former is blackmailer-initiated, the latter is begun by the blackmailee. But the deal consummated is identical in both cases! In each, the person with the secret to hide pays the person with the secret to tell so that the latter will desist. In both cases there is a trade of money (or other valuable consideration) for silence. There is simply no other difference between the two cases. To call for the legalization of one and the prohibition of the other is difficult to understand.

Whether the farmer advertises for a golf course manager after he has decided to divert some pastureland for this new purpose, or a firm specializing in golf courses approaches the farmer to buy or rent his land, or act as his agent, makes not one slight bit of difference. In either case, the identical trade takes place. It matters not one whit who initiates the deal—at least in terms of whether it should be lawful. Yet, using the considerations put forth by DeLong, one is in danger of concluding that one of these should be allowed, the other banned. Here we have a distinction without a difference. Amazingly enough, DeLong seems to admit this point: "the focus on agent and action peculiar to the two stories[94] obscures the *substantive equivalence* of the exchanges."[95] But if blackmail and bribery are "substantially equivalent" what is the reason for banning the one and allowing the other?

IV. CONCLUSION

As we have pointed out, the various economic approaches to justify blackmail laws are flawed. The blackmailee is not a victim, but is instead a beneficiary. There is no justification for treating the bribe taker differently from the blackmailer. Other attempts to explain the blackmail crime, such as DeLong's intuitionist views that perhaps outlawing blackmail helps to minimize isolation from the community and desperation and violence, are also unsatisfactory.

Ultimately, the only way to resolve the nagging paradoxes of blackmail, is to recognize that the paradox is unresolvable. With regard to the second

---

[93] *Id.* at 1692.

[94] By this we assume DeLong means the blackmail and bribery stories.

[95] *Id.* at 1692 (emphasis added).

paradox, for example, there is simply no way to reconcile the differing treatments of blackmail and bribery. Blackmail, like bribery and gossiping and asking for money, *should* be legal. Economically, the blackmailee is a beneficiary of the blackmailer, and blackmail is economically indistinguishable from other, licit, relationships.

Morally, we must recognize that government has no right to outlaw blackmail, and we have no right to advocate this, any more than we have a right to outlaw, or advocate the outlawry of, other "capitalist acts between consenting adults."[96] The reason is that outlawing anything—any use of the state—involves using force against individuals to force them to avoid the outlawed behavior. As the use of force is presumptively criminal, its use is only legitimate when used defensively, or in response to force. In other words, as libertarians have long pointed out, the only true crimes are those that involve the initiation of force, i.e. aggression. Nothing else violates rights, i.e. justifies legal, responsive force. Thus, anything lying outside the ambit of aggression is permissible, including blackmail, since the blackmailer simply does not initiate force against the blackmailee; rather, he foregoes, for a price, his right to blab.[97] It is for this reason that blackmail and bribery should be treated alike: neither are aggressive actions.

Thus, blackmail outlawry cannot be justified, and it cannot even be explained while one mistakenly assumes it is justified. Once we realize it cannot be justified, we can seek an explanation of why society chooses to criminalize behavior that should not be criminalized. But the answer to this question is no different in kind from explanations of why all sorts of unjust policies, from taxes to conscription to licensing to anti-drug laws, are in place. Ultimately, the populace advocate or acquiesce in such unjust laws due to ignorance of sound economics, and due to unclear and unprincipled thinking about individual rights.

---

[96] Nozick, *supra* note 75, at 163.

[97] *See* Rothbard, *supra* note 16, at 443 fn.49; Rothbard, *supra* note 29, at 124–26, 245–46.

Chapter 6.

The Legalization of Blackmail: A Reply to Professor Gordon

Blackmail is the offer to refrain from engaging in an act that one has the right to perform.[1] Typically, the licit act from which the blackmailer is offering to refrain is the exercise of his rights of free speech. Alternatively, the blackmailee can initiate this agreement; he may approach the blackmailer with the offer of money or other valuable consideration as the price for the blackmailer's silence. In a 1993 article, Wendy J. Gordon hypothesized that blackmail's "central case" occurs when the blackmailer is in possession of information embarrassing or harmful to the blackmailee, and for a fee refrains from publicizing that information.[2] The present Article responds to Gordon's assertion that, for various reasons, blackmail should be legally prohibited.

A blackmail contract would be legal in a libertarian society.[3] Libertarianism is a political philosophy. The central core of Libertarianism is that an individual may do anything he wishes with his person and his justly acquired property, provided that he does not interfere with the identical rights of any other person. Free speech (as long as it occurs on one's own property) is a protected activity, and a man can expose another's secrets without invading the other's person or his property. In a libertarian society, someone could also refrain, for consideration, from revealing information about another. In such situations, the individuals would enter into a mutually agreed upon contract. The blackmailer would benefit because he values the money he receives more than the costs to him of the silence he must maintain. The blackmailee also would gain because he ranks the confidentiality he attains higher than the

---

[1] Blackmail, in MAGILL'S LEGAL GUIDE, 109 (1999). Alternatively, blackmail is the threat to engage in a licit act, unless paid off not to do so

[2] *See* Wendy J. Gordon, *Truth and Consequences: The Force of Blackmail's Central Case*, 141 U. PA. L. REV. 1741, 1746 (1993).

[3] It is difficult to overestimate the importance that blackmail plays in the political economy of our society. It pervades every nook and cranny. For example, *Newsweek* states, "[Bill] Gates cogently answered questions[,] ...a while in Washington, Attorney General Janet Reno and the head of her antitrust division, Joel Klein, were charging Microsoft with playing a game of anticompetitive blackmail to force computer manufacturers to favor its Internet browsing program." Steven Levy, *Breaking Windows*, NEWSWEEK, Nov. 3, 1997, at 46. There is no reason to couch antitrust issues in blackmail terminology; intellectually, one topic is quite a stretch from the other. That this is done in a popular magazine, however, is evidence of how deeply embedded the concept of blackmail is in our everyday thinking.

money he pays for it. Were both parties not to experience this mutual gain, the agreement would not take place.

I. THE NONEXISTENT PARADOX

In contrast to this position, and despite the mutual gains and consent on both sides, Gordon maintains that blackmail should be legally prohibited.[4] In taking this stance, Gordon begins her argument by stating that "criminalizing blackmail involves neither a paradox nor a contradiction, notwithstanding the fact that blackmail law prohibits offers to sell discreditable information that the law would permit the seller to disclose without penalty.[5] This statement, however, is a paradox because it acknowledges that people are incarcerated merely for doing what they have a right to do. Gordon demurs on this point by stating that "[i]f people do not invariably have a right to threaten to do or not do the things they are at liberty to do or not do, then blackmail's illegality is perfectly consistent with the larger pattern. Hence, the statement does not produce a paradox.[6] In this Gordon is mistaken; people most certainly have the right to threaten (or to offer) to do that which they have a right to do. Were this not the case, an individual would have the right to engage in an act, but would not be able to tell anyone about it, to publicize it, to offer or to threaten to do it, or to in any way indulge his free speech rights about it.

To buttress her point, Gordon cites the doctrine of "unconstitutional conditions," which "holds that even though the government may withhold a benefit entirely, it can nevertheless be prohibited from offering the benefit on the condition that the recipient forgo a constitutional right."[7] Why, though, should what the government may or may not do serve as the basis for law? From the libertarian perspective, the United States government itself is a lawless institution in violation of the libertarian legal code because it necessarily initiates violence against non-aggressors (for example, those who are forced to pay taxes against their will and those who are prevented from patronizing alternative defense agencies).

Gordon's contention, however, is problematic even apart from this consideration. Even supposing that the government is a legitimate institution, basing blackmail law on the fact that the government can "be prohibited from

---

[4] *See* Gordon, *supra* note 2, at 1784–85.

[5] *Id*. at 1741.

[6] *Id*. at 1743.

[7] *Id*. at 1743 fn.19 (citing Kathleen M. Sullivan, *Unconstitutional Conditions*, 102 HARV. L. REV. 1415, 1415 (1989)).

offering [a] benefit on the condition that the recipient forgo a constitutional right"⁸ amounts to legal positivism. The government, conceivably, could have taken the opposite tack by allowing itself to offer a "benefit on the condition that the recipient forgo a constitutional right."⁹ If that had been the case, Gordon would not have been forced to concede the case for blackmail legalization because, in fact, no implications for blackmail logically flow from the doctrine of unconstitutional conditions.

Gordon relies on several other considerations in coming to the conclusion that the right to act does not imply a right to notify. For example, Gordon states:

> Threatening to disclose induces action in a way that disclosure does not, so that doing and threatening can have quite different effects. This occurs in part because the two acts affect different parties: any threat the blackmailer makes will be directed to the person with the embarrassing secret, but any disclosure, will be to third parties.[10]

It is irrelevant, however, that the threat of action may focus on one set of people, while the actual action may focus on another. The real issue is whether any of these acts or threats to act constitutes an uninvited border-crossing contrary to the libertarian code. Because none of them do, all should be decriminalized, notwithstanding the undoubted distinction between acts and threats to act.

Gordon also supports her position that blackmail should be illegal by stating:

> [T]he blackmailer does more than merely threaten: He threatens to disclose unless money is paid. Regardless of whether we have liberty to threaten, the law often forbids us to commodify our liberties by selling them. Our liberties to make sexual use of our bodies cannot be bartered for cash in most states; our right to vote can neither be transferred gratuitously nor sold. The growing literature on inalienability makes clear that doing and selling are quite different issues.[11]

---

⁸ Gordon, *supra* note 2, at 1743 fn.19 (citing Sullivan, *supra* note 9, at 1415).
⁹ *Id.*
¹⁰ *Id.* at 1744.
¹¹ *Id.*

The first of these allegations is no more than another instance of legal positivism. Propriety in the law consists of precisely what the legislature mandates, no more and no less. Gordon's argument implies that the law forbids individuals from selling or commodifying their liberties, and that is the end of the matter. This is an untenable argument because the law can often be mistaken, and what the law says at any particular time or place often gives little indication of what the law should be. Moreover, Gordon's argument is particularly troubling for reasons beyond its legal positivism approach. Gordon implicitly concedes that in some states individuals are at liberty to trade sexual services for cash; she states that the law "often" (but not always) "forbids us to commodify" and that prostitution is forbidden only in "most" (but not all) states. (If so, this example certainly cannot be used to prove her point regarding the illegality of blackmail.) According to Gordon's logic, blackmail should be legalized in some states but not in others.

Gordon also erroneously relies on the prohibition of the transfer of ones right to vote. Vote buying is prohibited not because there is anything intrinsically wrong with such a state of affairs, but rather because, by stipulation,[12] individuals have agreed to live under such institutional rules. If consent is the basis for this prohibition, however, society could just as easily have consented to do the very opposite.

Gordon further argues, citing an article by James Lindgren for support, that "if an unfaithful husband pays hush money to conceal his infidelity, the blackmailer is receiving compensation while the affected wife receives neither information nor compensation."[13] This statement, however, begs the question: "How can this information ... properly belong ... to third parties?"[14] Before any commercial interaction takes place, only two people own the information: the blackmailer and the unfaithful husband, the possible future blackmailee. The husband may well owe his wife full disclosure, due to his marriage

---

[12] That this stipulation is a heroic one can be seen in the following statement:

> [T]he state has been living on a revenue which was being produced in the private sphere for private purposes and had to be deflected from these purposes by political force. The theory which construes taxes on the analogy of club dues or of the purchase of the services of, say, a doctor only proves how far removed this part of the social sciences is from scientific habits of mind. JOSEPH A. SCHUMPETER, CAPITALISM, SOCIALISM AND DEMOCRACY at 198 & fn.11(1942).

[13] Gordon, *supra* note 2, at 1744–45 fn.24 (citing James Lindgren, *Unraveling the Paradox of Blackmail*, 84 COLUM.L. REV. 670 (1984).

[14] Lindgren, *supra* note 13, at 702.

vows,[15] but the blackmailer, a total stranger, certainly does not owe anything to this unfortunate woman.

While Gordon characterizes the spurned wife as the "primary party,"[16] she has no claim against the blackmailer no matter how unfairly her spouse has treated her. To support her argument, Gordon relies on Edward J. Bloustein, who in a 1964 article stated, "'[I]n a community at all sensitive to the commercialization of human values, it is degrading to thus make a man part of commerce against his will.'"[17] This, however, is a misreading because no one is being forced to do anything against his will. Consider the possibility that the husband, learning that someone is about to reveal his secret, initiates the blackmail offer by approaching the blackmailer and offering him money in exchange for silence. This may amount to "commodification," but it is not coercive to the husband. On the contrary, the husband initiated the transaction.

Gordon also cites articles by George Daly and J. Fred Giertz,[18] Ronald H. Coase,[19] Douglas H. Ginsburg and Paul Shechtman,[20] and Richard A. Epstein[21] to support her argument that performing an act and threatening to perform an act can have quite different economic impacts. Despite this support, Gordon's point is far from proven because the argument is irrelevant to the legality of blackmail. Threats or offers are legitimate to the extent that the underlying action is (or should be) legal. An individual may properly threaten to gossip about another person's secret unless paid because the underlying free speech is legitimately protected by law. That same individual, however, may not threaten to murder or to kidnap unless compensated because those acts are rightfully proscribed.

---

[15] If the state were to separate itself from this essentially private institution, and people signed voluntary marriage contracts providing for faithfulness, then and only then would this be true, At present, whether any such conclusion may be drawn is unclear at best.

[16] *See* Gordon, *supra* note 2, at 1745.

[17] *Id.* at 1745 (quoting Edward J. Bloustein, *Privacy as an Aspect of Human Dignity: An Answer to Dean Prosser*, 39 N.Y.U. L. REV. 962, 988 (1964)).

[18] *See Id.* at 1745 fn. 25 (citing George Daly & J. Fred Giertz, *Externalities, Extortion, and Efficiency: Reply*, 65 AM. ECON, REV. 736, 997, 999–1001 (1975)).

[19] *See Id.* at 1745 fn. 26 (citing Ronald Coase, *The 1987 McCorkle Lecture: Blackmail*, 74 VA. L. REV. 655, 671–74 (1988)).

[20] *See Id.* at 1745 fn. 27 (citing Douglas H. Ginsburg & Paul Shechtman, *Blackmail: An Economic Analysis of the Law*, 141 U. PA. L. REV. 1849, 1865 (1993)).

[21] *See Id.* at 1745 fn. 28 (citing Richard A. Epstein, *Blackmail, Inc.*, 50 U. CHI. L. REV. 553, 561–65 (1983)).

II. THE CENTRAL CASE OF BLACKMAIL

Gordon introduces the model of "central case blackmail" to show that both the economic wealth maximization and the deontological moral theoretical schools of thoughts argue that blackmail should be prohibited by law.[22] Gordon explains that the "central case" occurs:

> [W]here the blackmailer acquires information for the sole purpose of obtaining money or other advantage from the victim, and where he has no intent or desire to publish the information, except as an instrument toward this purpose. The blackmailer's sole claim to this advantage rests on his possession of the information as leverage.[23]

In Gordon's view, this model, in one form or another, underlies the opposition to blackmail legalization espoused in the writings of Robert Nozick,[24] Kent Greenawalt,[25] Epstein,[26] Coase,[27] and Ginsburg and Shechtman.[28] This may well be true, at least in part. All of these authors mistakenly favor prohibitionism and may have been guided, at least to some degree, by the considerations Gordon brings to the fore. This concern with mere motives, however, is problematic. The purposes and intentions of the blackmailer should not play any role in the determination of the legal status of blackmail, let alone the central one that Gordon assigns to them. It is said that if bad intentions were enough to violate the criminal law, we would all be in jail. A similar point needs to be made on behalf of the blackmailer.

Moreover, even if Gordon somehow proves her point with regard to "central case" blackmail, this cannot be used to legally proscribe such acts. For all the blackmailer need maintain in his defense is that he is not a "central case blackmailer." Rather, he derives a psychic benefit from releasing the information, whether out of a sense of justice (for example, punishing the philandering husband) or out of a desire to establish himself as a professional black-

---

[22] *See* Gordon, *supra* note 2, at 1746.

[23] *See Id.*

[24] *See Id.*, at 1746–47 & fn. 37 (citing ROBERT NOZICK, ANARCHY, STATE AND UTOPIA 84–86 (1974)).

[25] *See Id.* at 1747 & fn. 42 (citing Kent Greenwalt, *Criminal Coercion and Freedom of Speech*, 78 NW. U. L. REV. 1081, 1099 (1983)).

[26] *See Id.* (citing Epstein, *supra* note 21, at 561–66).

[27] *See Id.* at 1747–48 (citing Coase, *supra* note 19, at 674).

[28] *See* Gordon, *supra* note 2, at 1747–48 (citing Ginsburg & Shechtman, *supra* note 20, at 1859).

mailer with a reputation for divulging information when not paid off. In neither of these cases can the unique Gordon contribution to this debate be used against such a defendant.

III. A CONSEQUENTIALIST PERSPECTIVE

A. The Economic Argument

Gordon quite correctly distinguishes between "harmful acts [people] are free to perform," and those which, presumably, they are not legally free to conduct. To illustrate this, the author states:

> For example a person who decides not to build a sun-blocking fence out of consideration for his sun-loving neighbor cannot sue to obtain a reward for his forbearance. He can choose, however, to negotiate over the fence's height, and demand consideration from his neighbor in exchange for keeping the fence low.[29]

How does blackmail fit into all of this? This act is in one sense "harmful" to the blackmailee, who would prefer that the blackmailer had never learned of his secret. On the other hand, given that his past has been uncovered, the blackmailee would vastly prefer that a blackmailer, not the inveterate gossip, discover the information. By definition, the gossip will broadcast all the information at his disposal. The blackmailer, in contrast, provides at least the chance of a mutually agreeable deal. If the blackmailer places a low enough value on his service of silence, and the blackmailee a high enough value on his secret, then a deal can be struck that benefits both parties, at least in the *ex ante* sense.[30]

Regardless of whether blackmail is harmful, revealing another's secret is an act that an individual is free to perform. No one suggests that the gossip should be incarcerated. But if one may legitimately speak, then one may also keep silent. If one has the right to keep silent, then one may be paid for keeping silent. Because blackmail consists of no more than being paid for remaining silent, Gordon logically should be compelled to favor its legalization.

Gordon evades this conclusion by referring to the notion that "[t]he blackmailer does not wish to disclose, only to extract a transfer payment."[31]

---

[29] *Id.* at 1748–49 fn. 50.

[30] Walter Block, Defending the Undefendable. 44–49 (1976).

[31] Gordon, *supra* note 2, at 1749.

Gordon rejects legalization because she defines central case blackmail so as to preclude from consideration those who are motivated by profits, not free speech.[32] Motive, however; seems to be a weak reed upon which to hang an entire theory of criminal behavior. For in Gordon's view, two people can act in an identical manner, yet one will be guilty of a crime and the other will be totally innocent of it. The first, call him the "speech blackmailer" wishes, initially, to disclose the blackmailee's secret, but is only dissuaded from making a revelation by payment for his silence. The second, call him the "profit-seeking blackmailer," has no real independent interest in exposing the history of the blackmailee; he is solely interested in receiving money. The profit-seeking blackmailer, however, asks for or accepts a payment to keep silent just as the speech blackmailer does, perhaps even an identical amount. Yet, merely because of these different intentions, Gordon condemns the one as a criminal, yet not the other. Motive is often used to determine degree of guilt; here, remarkably, motive is being used to discern presence or absence of guilt. This is too great a weight to place on so frail a foundation.[33]

B. The Irrelevance of Lawful or Beneficial Nature of the Threatened Action

For many scholars, the prohibition of blackmail is paradoxical: Two distinct acts are legal when taken separately, but are illegal when taken together. Those individuals admit that the first act—making a threat, or an offer, or giving a warning that you will speak—as well as the second act—asking for or accepting money—are both licit. They assert, however, that when combined into one single act, the two together should be prohibited by law.

Gordon, in contrast to both of those views, takes a third, distinct position. Gordon describes her view as follows:

> The initial 'paradox' involved the fact that the blackmailer threatened to do an act that was itself lawful and, by implication, beneficial. The foregoing discussion should make clear that the beneficial or harmful nature of the action threatened is irrelevant to the core economic argument against central case blackmail. In central case blackmail, the threatened action has no independent positive value for either party. What motivates the bargain instead is that the action will have a negative value to the person threatened that is greater than the null or negative value it has for the threatener. In

---

[32] *See Id.*

[33] Even Gordon herself states that "[m]otive is a notoriously difficult basis on which to build fundamental legal distinctions." *Id.* at 1771.

such a context, it is in no one's interest for the threat of disclosure to be carried out.[34]

Gordon's first error is that she equates "lawful" with "beneficial." Although the first term simply does not imply the second, Gordon slides smoothly from the one to the other, failing to recognize that the two are neither identical nor deducible from one another. There are many lawful acts that should not be considered beneficial, such as pornography, gambling, prostitution, and consuming unhealthy foods. An act need not be beneficial for it to be legal.[35]

Gordon, however, does have a response to this criticism:

> Note that the distinction here addresses the beneficial nature of the threatened action and does not separately consider its lawfulness. That is because I am assuming that in assessing the "blackmail paradox," the lawfulness of disclosure would have meaning for the economist merely as an indirect indicator that disclosure yielded more benefits than costs.

> The analysis would be more complex if we were to take into account the possibility that any criminalization of a threat to do a lawful act would itself have, negative consequences. For example, such criminalization may cause confusion or erode respect for the law. I give no attention to these possibilities since I think the criminalizing central case blackmail has no such consequences, largely because the person on the street perceives blackmail to be a wrong; therefore, criminalization of the activity evokes no sense of inconsistency.[36]

Gordon is undoubtedly correct about "the person on the street." Moreover, it is not just this presumably ignorant man who sees no logical inconsistency in "any criminalization of a threat to do a lawful act." Judging from the writers who favor the *status quo* prohibition of blackmail, one might well conclude that the mainstream professor in the law school or in the economics department also fails to see the paradox of blackmail prohibition. This paradox most certainly docs "erode respect for the law" on the part of those, such

---

[34] Gordon, *supra* note 2, at 1749.

[35] Of course, acts such as pornography and fatty food consumption are beneficial in at least some sense; in both instances, willing buyers purchased the products. The purchasers of these items must have perceived some value in them.

[36] *Id.* at 1750, fn. 55.

as this Author and a small band of commentators, who have long been protesting this perversion of the law. Indeed, one of the primary motivating forces in writing this reply is to protest that this injustice is based on a sense of inconsistency. That this should be dismissed on the grounds that the masses of people on the street or in the professorate seem to have missed the point sets a new and very remarkable standard for analysis in social science. After all, had you asked most people, even most scientists at one time, they would have replied that yes, the Earth is flat and the Sun revolves around it. Happily, these sentiments were not taken as bedrock upon which further analysis rested.

In any case, the fact that the "man on the street" has the views he does with regard to criminalizing threats to engage in legal activities is due in no small part to the efforts of Gordon and her colleagues, who have striven mightily to convince him of this very erroneous point. It comes, then, with particular ill grace, and with more than a whiff of circularity, for Gordon to now turn around and rely on the unprofessional opinions of the common man to support her own views. She and her colleagues played a great role in causing them in the first place.

Error number two is that Gordon's screed against legalization depends utterly on her assumption that the blackmailer derives not one iota of pleasure out of releasing the secret, in those cases in which the blackmailee refused to pay. Who among us, were he to enter into this ancient profession in the first place, would act in so cold-blooded a manner? Surely, it is part and parcel of the human condition to lash out at those who balk us. So, as a matter of realism, it may fairly be charged that Gordon's central case blackmailer is a null set.[37] Gordon is correct in stating that the leverage value obtained by the blackmailer who carries through on his threat when not paid, so as to make further threats more credible, "is thus not an independent positive value to the single-instance, central-case blackmailer."[38] But she seems oblivious to the possibility that there has never been and is now no such person.

Gordon, in support of her argument cites Daly and Giertz, who state, "[T]he key feature of extortion is the use of a threat to elicit a payment, not whether the threatened action is legal or illegal."[39] Gordon's argument is not

---

[37] On the other hand, this extreme case, it cannot be denied, performs a useful heuristic function, much akin to that of the perfect gas, the frictionless system in physics, and equilibrium in economics.

[38] Gordon, *supra* note 2, at 1751 fn. 56.

[39] *See Id.* at 1751 fn.60 (citing Daly & Giertz, *supra* note 18, at 757 fn. 2). Gordon asserts that, despite the fact that Daly and Giertz, in their article, address extortion by threat of violence, their model "describes the supply and demand structure of central case blackmail." *Id.*

strengthened by equating blackmail and extortion. Such an equation is problematic because the legality or illegality of the threatened act is crucially important in determining whether extortion has occurred. For example, suppose a boss threatens an employee with dismissal unless he comes in to work on time,[40] or a girl threatens a boy that she will not date him unless he takes her to a movie, or a buyer threatens a seller that he'll take his business elsewhere unless the price is lowered. Surely all these threatened acts are themselves legal, and, so, perforce, is the act of making these threats. In very sharp contrast indeed are demands for money or other valuable considerations coupled with threats to murder, maim, or rape.

C. Caveat

In making her argument, Gordon quite reasonably supports the view of William Landes and Richard A. Posner that blackmail may make a positive social contribution because the "fear of having to make blackmail payments may induce potential nonconformists to conform their behavior to majority standards."[41] However, Gordon then attempts to escape from the implications of this insight with the contention that blackmail

> will impose transaction costs that could well outweigh any beneficial disclosure resulting from blackmail attempts that misfire. Further, the possible allocative effect resulting from occasional disclosure or deterrence is not guaranteed to be beneficial. Disclosure may have a social value that is positive (for example, disclosing to the electorate that a mayor has embezzled funds) or negative (for example, making public a secret of no public import that causes deep distress in the family concerned, such as the fact that when the mayor was a child he was sexually abused by a relative). It is similarly possible that blackmail-induced conformity might involve a net cost to society.[42]

According to what she characterizes as the deontological perspective, Gordon maintains that blackmail is "unjustifiably hurting others," and thus

---

[40] *See* George P. Flectcher, *Blackmail: The Paradigmatic Case* 141 U. PA. L. REV. 1617, 1619 (1993) (outlining a series of examples in which one individual call legally threaten to do an act unless another individual performs or refrains from performing an action).

[41] Gordon, *supra* note 2, at 1752 (citing William Landes & Richard A. Posner, *The Private Enforcement of Law,* 4 J. LEGAL STUD. 1, 42–43 (1975)).

[42] *Id.* at 1752–53.

should be declared illegal.[43] The blackmailer, however, does not hurt the blackmailee. On the contrary, the blackmailer is the benefactor of the black-mailee, in that he has the power to release embarrassing information, but for-bears from doing so. Although the blackmailer does charge a fee for his serv-ices, in the view of the blackmailee, this price is lower than the possible harm of disclosure, a fact evidenced by the blackmailee's willingness to pay.

If there is any doubt of this, compare the case of the blackmailer with that of the gossip. If a gossip uncovers an individual's secret, the information will necessarily become public because, regardless of the value the person places on his privacy, the gossip's silence cannot be bought. When a blackmailer dis-covers an individual's secret, on the other hand, there is at least some chance that a bargain can be struck to ensure the blackmailer's silence. Because no one advocates jailing gossips, it is difficult to see why Gordon and her col-leagues advocate this fate for blackmailers.

A second flaw in Gordon's argument that blackmail's unjustified harm to others requires its illegality is that the argument assumes that a person who unjustifiably hurts another always should be incarcerated. This, however, is not necessarily so, at least according to the libertarian philosophy, which re-serves penal sentences for violations of the person or of property rights. For example, consider a situation in which a wife divorces her husband, not for any fault of his, but merely because she finds a more attractive younger man. The wife's action is gratuitous and, therefore, will presumably cause some de-gree of unjustified harm to the husband. If Gordon's dicta were taken literally, the wife would have to be incarcerated because her action reasonably could be expected to hurt the husband.

Gordon's assertion that the benefits of blackmail are outweighed by its transaction costs[44] is weakened by the fact that virtually any act "will impose transactions costs."[45] The real issue is not whether transaction costs exist, or whether they are imposed upon other people (they often are, as in the cases of the divorce), but instead whether the blackmailer has a right to engage in the blackmailing activities. There are two utilitarian approaches to answering this question.[46] The first, called the "macro" viewpoint, has been adopted by Gor-

---

[43] *Id.* at 1752 fn. 62.

[44] *See Id.* at 1752.

[45] Gordon's assertion also begs the question: Why single out transactions costs? Most acts are costly in terms of land, labor, time, capital and interest to say no thing of opportunity costs. In light of these varied expenses, Gordon's focus on transaction costs in this context seems arbi-trary.

[46] The reason anyone would want to adopt utilitarianism is another matter altogether. For a critique, *see generally* Hans-Hermann Hoppe, Praxeology and Economic Science (1988).

don and her peers who believe "market failure" to be overwhelmingly prevalent. The proponents of this approach ask themselves, from their own subjective perspective, which is stronger: the harm caused by the blackmail or the benefits caused by the blackmail. And, since they cordially hate blackmail, they deem it of lesser value (on the rare occasions they consider it valuable at all) than attendant costs.

The second approach, call it the "micro" viewpoint, accepts the *ex ante* evaluations of the economic actors as definitive. For example, if a person buys a coat for $100, there are considerable transactions costs associated. The proponent of the micro viewpoint, however, will conclude that the benefits of this transaction outweigh its total costs, at least in the *ex ante* sense, because otherwise the deal would not have been consummated. In the context of blackmail the "micro" viewpoint reasons that the blackmailee would not have paid the blackmailer had he not regarded the latter's silence as greater in value than the price—including its attendant transaction costs—of that silence. On the strength of this consideration alone, the "micro" evaluator, such as the economist, determines that blackmail, as with all other "capitalist acts between consenting adults,"[47] promotes social welfare.[48]

Gordon also becomes enmeshed in a defense of "harmless behavior that happens to be nonconforming," such as same-gender sexual relations.[49]. The author does not employ this discussion to support a simple straightforward libertarian defense; since this is consensual adult behavior, a victimless crime as it were with no initiation of violence against non-aggressors, it is a very paradigm case of legally permitted activity. This realization strikes far too close to home for Gordon because, had she relied upon this perspective, it would be a short step indeed to the conclusion that the blackmailer-blackmailee relationship, too, is a willing one on both sides.

---

[47] Nozick, *supra* note 24, at 163.

[48] If people voluntarily agree to any deal, the presumption is that they both gain from it, at least in the *ex ante* sense of anticipations. For example, if one individual agrees to trade his pen to a second individual for that individual's tie, it must be because the first individual values the tie more. Likewise, for the transaction to take place, the second individual must make the opposite evaluation. For an elaboration of this point, *see generally* Murray N. Rothbard, *Towards a Reconstruction of Utility and Welfare Economics,* Center for Libertarian Studies, Occasional Paper Series No. 3, at 21 (1977).

[49] Gordon, *supra* note 2, at 1753 fn. 64.

Instead, Gordon resorts to a utilitarian analysis[50] doomed at the start due to the illegitimacy of interpersonal comparisons of utility[51]—in an attempt to show that legalized blackmail would have an unjustified adverse effect upon homosexuality.[52] The author has utilized the "micro" approach: gay relationships promote utility in the *ex ante* sense, evidenced by the fact that, otherwise, at least one of the partners would terminate, or refuse to even enter into, the relationship. The objections of the more conservative[53] have no standing under this analysis[54] because they have no means of "demonstrating their preferences"[55] against such relationships. Gordon, however, could not tread down this path, for in order to do so she would have had to jettison the con-

---

[50] Utilitarianism is the philosophy most closely associated with Jeremy Benthan and John Stuart Mill. It is the view that the good, or the ethical, choice consists of the one that provides the greatest good for the greatest number of people, thus maximizing total utility. One obstacle that this view founders on is that it is impossible to meaningfully measure, and thus compare, the utility of different people. Unless utility is measurable, however, and additive, maximization is impossible. Another great difficulty is that the approach is contrary to justice. Suppose, for example, it could be shown that the Nazis gained more utility from the torture and murder of Jews than the latter lost from this process. This would hardly be just, even though it would maximize utility, and thus, seemingly, be advocated by utilitarians. *See generally* JOHN STUART MILL, UTILITARIANISM: WITH CRITICAL ESSAYS (Samuel Gorowitz, ed., 1971).

[51] *See* Rothbard, *supra* note 49, at 21. Rothbard argues that, while there are valid measurements for such things as weight, height, speed, acceleration, and temperature, there is no such thing as a unit of happiness. Therefore, while it is reasonable to say that x is twice the weight of y, it is an act of economic illiteracy to claim that x twice as happy as y.

[52] *See* Gordon, *supra* note 2, at 1753 fn. 64.

[53] Conservatives, particularly religious conservatives, object to homosexuality on the ground that it is forbidden in the bible.

[54] *See* Rothbard, *supra* note 49, at 2.

[55] *Id.*

cept of "negative externalities."[56] Much beloved of the "market failure set," Gordon calls same-gender sexual relationships "harmless." But what about AIDS, which initially was most prevalent among homosexuals, continues heavily in those circles, and has devastated, as well, members of the larger community'? Based on this consideration alone, a utilitarian case could be made that our society does not make such nonconforming behavior "too expensive,"[57] but rather too cheap.

Then there is an intractable problem: Given that much of the general public disapproves of the gay lifestyle, and many homosexuals reciprocate, which of them should cease and desist? Gordon proposes to answer this by determining "who is the least cost avoider" or, perhaps, the least changer of taste, ascribing this way of attempting to solve the problem to the typical "economist."[58]

To be sure, this is precisely the approach of the Coasean economist. But in the absence of scientifically reliable interpersonal comparisons of utility, there is simply no non-arbitrary way to resolve this debate. In their absence, moreover, it is not even a meaningful question. If the right to engage in homosexual activity depends upon so insecure a foundation, there is little hope for its defense.

Fortunately, there is a justification for gays to engage in consensual, private, adult sex. It is the "live and let live" philosophy that emerges in libertarianism. Since neither homosexuality nor heterosexuality involves *per se* invasions of other people or their property, both are licit in the free society. Neither can be justly prohibited. But this means that we have to count as invalid all notions of "externalities" and "least cost avoiders." And, if it is permissible to use in the case of sex, this applies as well to blackmail.

---

[56] Negative externalities occur whenever one person harms another and the law does not allow the victim to be compensated for this harm or to be granted an injunction to prevent it. Such harms range from railroads creating sparks that set ablaze a farmer's haystacks, to smoke pollution, to jamming radio signals. These externalities also include competition; if one individual opens a grocery store across the street from that of another individual and wins half the original's customers, this, too, can be perceived as a negative externality for which the law will not compensate. For libertarians, the key distinction is not harm to second or third parties. Rather, the distinction revolves around whether any uninvited border crossing has occurred. If a person dumps garbage on another's lawn, a trespass has occurred that the law should stop. However, engaging in competition does not involve any violation of personal or private property rights. For more on this, *see generally* Murray N. Rothbard, *Law, Property Rights, and Air Pollution, in* ECONOMICS AND THE ENVIRONMENT: A RECONCILIATION (Walter Block, ed., 1990).

[57] *See* Gordon, *supra* note 2, at 1753 fn. 64.

[58] *See Id.*

D. Imperfect Knowledge

Gordon suggests that markets are efficient and can be relied upon to sort out the aforementioned problems, stating that, "it might be argued that allowing blackmail data to be bought and sold is the best way to finesse the economic unknowns."[59] Gordon relies on two experts, Friedrich A. Hayek[60] and Coase,[61] to support this possibility. Her reliance on the former is unobjectionable; Hayek played a major role in demonstrating that markets process information with efficiency beyond the scope of government. Gordon's reliance on Coase, however, presents grave difficulties. First, the author states that "the Coase theorem teaches that in a properly functioning market, absent transactions costs, people will trade a resource until it reaches its highest value use regardless of to whom the government initially assigns its ownership."[62] For this assertion to be true, however, the loser in the lawsuit would have to possess the financial ability to bribe the winner to allow resource to flow to what Coase consider to be their optimal use.[63]

Gordon latches on to this Coasean "straw man" in an effort to undermine the implications that Hayek's analysis would have for the legalization of blackmail.[64] The author asserts:

> [I]n blackmail the transaction costs can be so high as to preclude all the affected parties from making their preferences known through the market, thus preventing transactions from reliably directing resources to their highest valued uses. For example, there may be a multitude of voters who would be willing to pay something to learn that the mayor has embezzled public funds. Yet a person who has this information cannot practicably contact this mass of possible buyers; even if he could, free rider strategic behavior could well forestall agreement, particularly when coupled with the well-

---

[59] Gordon, *supra* note 2, at 1754.

[60] *See Id.* at 1754 fn. 66 (citing Friedrich A. Hayek, *The Use of Knowledge in Society*, 35 AM. ECON. REV. 519, 524–25 (1945) (asserting that "decentralized decision making can often utilize knowledge better than centralized planning").

[61] *See Id.* at 1754 fn. 66 (citing Ronald H. Coase, *The Problem of Social Cost*, 3 J. L. & ECON. 1(1960)).

[62] Gordon, *supra* note 2, at 1754.

[63] *See* Walter Block, *Coase and Demsetz on Private Property Rights*, 1 J. LIBERTARIAN STUD. 111, 111–12 (1977).

[64] *See* Gordon, *supra* note 2, at 1754.

recognized difficulties that accompany any attempt to sell a secret
to people ignorant of its content.[65]

This reliance upon the theories of Coase, however, is not sufficient to
support Gordon's anti-legalization goals.[66] In drawing this conclusion, Gordon ignores the phenomenon of externality internalization.[67] A blackmailer
would not need to deal directly with thousands of potentially free-riding citizens and convince them to be curious of something about which they are ignorant. On the contrary, newspapers and magazines—not even those limited
to muckraking—would be more than happy to publicize a mayor's embezzlement. The publications could profit on this information through increased
subscriptions and greater advertising revenues. The blackmailer, therefore,
would not need to deal directly with a mass audience. The threat of exposure
in such venues tends to keep a damper on activities of this sort on the part of
our elected officials.

Gordon, however, does not accept this reasoning or the "micro" perspective of utilitarianism, according to which the only actors are the blackmailer

---

[65] *Id.* Gordon's strategy here reminds the reader of the argument that antitrust advocates utilized to support their position. First, the technique defines misbegotten criteria for efficiency
such as "perfect competition" in the antitrust context and Coasean theory in the present case.
In the antitrust context, the hypothetical state against which the real world is to be measured is
a state where there are millions of firms, each selling a small percentage of the total product,
which is homogenous. In addition, information is costless, there is a constant state of equilibrium, and no profits are ever made. The Coasean equivalent of this is a world with zero transaction costs.

Second, the technique criticizes the real world for not living up to these artificial standards
set by the criterion. The difficulty with this procedure is easy to see. It would be similar to defining a life-sized version of the Barbie Doll as the criteria for successful adult woman and then
fining all those human females who do not measure up to the criterion. Several authors, however, have prescribed an antidote to this stratagem in the case of antitrust and monopoly.

[66] *See* Gordon, *supra* note 2, at 1754–55 (citing Coase, *supra* note 62, 1–44).

[67] Externality internalization is the process through which the market deals with the issue of
externalities. Consider, for example, the difficulty of creating a private park in what is now a
slum area. The owner of the park will only be able to recoup his investment through admission
charges. However, if successful, the park also presumably would increase real estate values in
the surrounding neighborhood. The problem—the "market failure" of externalities—is that the
potential park owner does not own these properties and thus, is not in a position to take advantage of these benefits "external" to his park: The solution—the internalization of this externality—is for him to purchase these lands before word gets out about his forthcoming urban
park. He can do this because he is the only one who knows where he will locate this park.

and the blackmailee.[68] In contrast, the author is concerned with the macro "societal economic welfare," which requires that the entire citizenry be made aware of the mayor's peccadilloes.[69] Absent interpersonal comparisons of utility[70] though, it cannot be demonstrated that the value to the masses of the disclosure of this information will be greater than the value to the mayor of his privacy. Demanding this information dispersal in the name of justice, moreover presumes the legitimacy of a positive obligation: that the ignorant citizenry has a right, not only against the thieving mayor, which it certainly does, but also against the innocent blackmailer, that he disclose the knowledge that he alone (apart from the mayor, of course) possesses.

In light of these considerations, it is difficult to conclude that a blackmailer should be forced to share knowledge with the masses, if the mayor is willing to compensate him for his silence. Gordon argues, based on the Coase theorem, that the public allocation of "fundamental resources," such as reputation, can enhance wealth.[71] The author claims that the free market system cannot create values sufficiently well to determine whether it would be more

---

[68] This perspective is, essentially, Austrian economics. *See, generally,* MURRAY N. ROTHBARD, MAN, ECONOMY AND STATE (1962); LUDWIG VON MISES, HUMAN ACTION: A TREATISE ON ECONOMICS (1966). The Austrian School of economics is well known for its emphasis on methodological individualism. In this view, economic acts essentially occur on an individual level; groups are only amalgamations of individuals. There are no such things as groups apart from the individuals who comprise them. In the present context, from an Austrian point of view, there are only two actors in the contract: the blackmailer and the blackmailee. No one else has any standing.

[69] *See* Gordon, *supra* note 2, at 1755. Gordon asserts that, because of well-known difficulties affecting markets in information; "most of the societal benefits that could flow from disclosure are likely to be kept external to the blackmailer's decision." *Id.* at 1754–55. As a result, the author concludes, "the outcome of dealings among blackmailer, victim, and other possible buyers [of information] will prove unreliable as a guide to societal economic welfare." *Id.* at 1755.

[70] As an example of an interpersonal comparison of utility, consider the following: A values his pen at 10 utils, and B values his hat at 40 utils. Thus, both A and B regard B's hat as worth exactly four of A's pens. Needless to say, since there are no such things as utils, nor indeed, any other measure of happiness, this comparison fails on two grounds. First neither A nor B can rate items on such a scale. Second, there can be no interpersonal comparison of the items. The relevance of this explanation to the textual discussion is that Gordon is maintaining that the interests of the entire citizenry in the mayor's difficulties are greater than the mayor's interest is his own privacy. Therefore, social welfare will be enhanced if the mayor's interests are disregarded for those of the citizenry. Even apart from such specific valuations, however, there is no way to demonstrate that the mayor's privacy is more valuable to him than is the citizen's interest in obtaining the information.

[71] *See* Gordon, *supra* note 2, at 1755.

beneficial for a blackmailer to retain confidential information or to reveal it to the public.[72] Under a free enterprise system, if the blackmailee values the secret more than the price demanded by the blackmailer, he will pay and retain his privacy. If not, he risks exposure.

Gordon arrives at the opposite conclusion because she conflates the Coasean system with free enterprise or capitalism.[73] Capitalism is non-controversially defined as the totality of all voluntary trades; that is, when one person trades his rightfully owned property for that of another. Coase, in sharp contrast, specifically addresses himself to the situation in which a trade cannot take place because there is a dispute as to who possesses the rights to the property in question.[74] But in our system, only the courts, not the market, can make such determinations.[75]

In the dispute over blackmail, no real debate exists regarding who is the legitimate owner of the relevant property rights. Assuming that the blackmailer learned the embarrassing secret without violating any person or his property rights, the blackmailer may dispose of this information precisely as he wishes. On the other hand, of course, if knowledge of the secret came to him improperly (for example, through theft, torture, or kidnapping) then the blackmailer must be punished-not for blackmail, but for these other activities. Because the fruit of the poisoned tree is itself poisoned, blackmail under these conditions also would be properly illegal, but not because of anything intrinsic to that practice. Rather, blackmail should be considered illicit because of these improper antecedents.[76] For Coase, these matters would be examined

---

[72] *Id.* at 1754–57.

[73] *Id.* at 1756–67. Although Gordon reasonably enough equates "allowing. data to be bought and sold" with "markets," she identifies "markets" with "the Coase Theorem," However, the Coase theorem and the Coaseanism based upon that theorem are really an attack on markets, particularly free markets in that private property rights under gird free enterprise, and the Coase theorem is singularly antipathetic to such rights.

[74] *See* Coase, *supra* note 62, at 8–15. This Article is mainly concerned not with markets, within which trade occurs, but rather with lawsuits regarding nuisance or pollution, wherein no trade occurs, no matter what else is transpiring.

[75] Assuming that this is true, no free market actually exists that permits multiple public and private defense agencies to compete for services. The philosophy adumbrated therein is one of libertarian anarchism, or anarcho-capitalism. Under such a philosophy, all government functions, including armies, courts and police, are provided through the voluntary market place, such as through competing defense-insurance-mediation agencies.

[76] This reasoning would apply to any act that is normally legal. For example, driving a taxicab is a completely legal practice. If the driver stole the vehicle or was drunk, then operating the cab would become an illegal activity because of the underlying illicit action, which precedes the seemingly legal act.

very differently because, as an unsophisticated utilitarian at heart, he has no real theory of property rights.[77]

Gordon does not seem to realize that Coase can be interpreted in a manner consistent with her position regarding the legalization of blackmail.[78] All the Coasean judge need do is declare that the secret in the hands of the multitude of voters would be more valuable than if controlled solely by the mayor and the blackmailer, in order to reconcile Coase's principles[79] with Gordon's assertions.

Gordon is mistaken in thinking that the Coase theory cannot be utilized to reach her favored conclusion. In fact, contrary to what the author has seemingly concluded, Coase actually agrees with her views on blackmail.[80]

---

[77] In Coase's view, when a dispute arises concerning property ownership, the disputed property should vest in the person who, in a world of zero transactions costs, would have ended up owning the property in question. *See* Coase, *supra* note 62, at 38. That is, had he not been awarded it, he would have bribed the winner of a judicial decision into giving him the property under dispute. For example, Coase maintains that property under dispute should be awarded to the person who values it most highly, not to the rightful owner. In other words, for Coase, the rightful owner, to the extent that there can be any such thing is the person who values the property most strongly, not necessarily the one who purchased it or built it.

[78] *See, generally,* Coase, *supra* note 62. That Coase's writing can be read as supporting Gordon's argument against blackmail should occasion little surprise given that Coase has previously drawn the same conclusions as Gordon regarding blackmail. *See, generally*, Coase, *supra* note 19.

[79] *See, generally*, Coase, *supra* note 62. The principle of Coase in law and economics is to maximize wealth. For example, in a 1987 article he stated:

> In a blackmailing scheme, the person who will pay the most for the right to stop the action threatened is normally the person being blackmailed. If the right to stop this action is denied to others, that is, blackmail is made illegal, transaction costs are reduced, factors of production are released for other purposes and the value of production is increased. This is an approach, which comes quite naturally to an economist and was certainly the way in which I first analyzed the problem of blackmail. *Id.*

The problem with all such approach, of course, is that they founder on the lack of interpersonal comparisons of utility or wealth.

[80] *See* Coase, *supra* note 19, at 673. Coase states:

> Business negotiations (which may also cause anxiety) either lead to a breakdown of the negotiations or they lead to a contract. There is, at any rate, an end. But in the ordinary blackmail case there is no end. The victim, once he succumbs to the blackmailer, remains in his grip for an indefinite period. It is moral murder. *Id.*

It is hard to see what more Coase can possibly do to subscribe to the anti-blackmail legalization sentiments of Gordon than to characterize this practice as "moral murder."

Therefore, Gordon's attempt to use Coase as a foil against which to contrast her own position fails because he argues on the same side of the blackmail debate as does she.[81]

Gordon next argues that there are "certain fundamental resources ... whose possession can affect our ability to enjoy all other goods ... examples include life, sight, and one's standing in a community of peers.[82] Gordon believes that "[r]eputation may well be one of those fundamental resources," and reputation is precisely what blackmail threatens to harm.[83] Gordon makes the same mistake as Adam Smith[84] did when he failed to solve the diamonds-water paradox. That paradox asks how diamonds, which are useless in preserving human life, at least when compared to water, nevertheless are more highly valued on the market than that life-preserving liquid. Economists did not address this enigma until the marginalist revolution[85] of the 1870s. That revolution argued that it was illegitimate to compare the value of water

---

[81] Gordon also criticizes Coase on grounds very similar to those employed by this Author. *Cf.* Gordon, *supra* note 2, at 1757, with Walter Block, *Free Market Transportation: Denationalizing the Roads.* 3 J. LIBERTARIAN STUD. 209 (1979). Gordon states:

> [T]he celebrity is limited in his ability to protect his reputation by the amount of money he possesses or can borrow. If the celebrity does not have enough money to outbid the network, then the highest valued use of the information would now seem to be publication, even if all that has changed is the initial assignment of rights. Gordon, *supra* note 2, at 1757.

This makes it doubly difficult to understand her analysis of Coase. Gordon and this Author agree—contrary to the positions of Coase, Demsetz, and their followers—that the initial assignment of property rights can determine who will be able to outbid whom in the zero transaction costs world. Gordon focuses on the point that "[i]f the celebrity does not have enough money to outbid the network, then the highest valued use of the information would not seem to be publication, even if all that has changed is the initial assignment of rights." *Id.* This is precisely the point this Author has made against Coase and Demsetz in other articles, utilizing a "flower pot" example. See Block, *supra* note 64, at 111–15.

[82] Gordon, *supra* note 2, at 1755.

[83] *Id.*

[84] *See* ADAM SMITH, THE WEALTH OF NATIONS 132 (1965).

[85] The marginalist revolution in economics directed attention not to the total amount of anything, such as diamonds or water, but rather to the marginal amounts between which humans choose, such as a cup of water or a swimming pool of water. From this perspective, it is easy to see why diamonds are so valuable and water is not; there is very little of the former, relative to demand, while there is a great deal of the latter, *See, e.g.*, CARL MENGER, PRINCIPLES OF ECONOMICS; W. STANLEY JEVONS, THE THEORY OF POLITICAL ECONOMY; LEON WALRAS, PRINCIPLES OF POLITICAL ECONOMY.

against that of diamonds because no human being has ever been called upon to choose between them in their totality. Instead, objects should be considered from the point of view of an actual market participant, who chooses only between small (or marginal) amounts of goods and services. In other words, the value of objects should be considered as a matter of more or less, not all or none; hence, there is no such thing as a "fundamental" good.

IV. A NON-CONSEQUENTIALIST MORAL VIEW

A. Background

Moving from her economic grounds for the prohibition of blackmail, Gordon next advances several deontological[86] arguments.[87] The author claims that when blackmail occurs, "[O]ne person deliberately seeks to harm another to serve her own ends—to exact money or other advantage—and does so in a context where she has no conceivable justification for her act.[88] If this is an accurate characterization,[89] one may agree that such activity is indeed despicable, immoral, and vicious; the law, however, still should not ban it. Gordon's argument is susceptible to a *reductio ad absurdum*.[90] For example, an extremely attractive man may decide to gratuitously harm another man by alienating his wife's affections away from him—unless the husband pays the man one million dollars. To carry out his threat, the man proceeds to seduce the other man's wife. In this scenario, the seducer, who has no "conceivable justification" for his act, is deliberately seeking to harm another man to serve the seducer's goals. This is despicable, unjust, and immoral, but the man should nonetheless not be incarcerated. After all, he threatens (or actually

---

[86] "Deontological" means theoretical and morality based, as opposed to, utilitarian or pragmatic. *See* Gordon, *supra* note 2, at 1759.

[87] *See* Gordon, *supra* note 2, at 1758–74. In beginning her deontological analysis, Gordon quite rightly rejects Robert Nozick's critique that blackmail constitutes a "nonproductive" exchange by pondering whether the happening of such occurrences is "wrong in itself." *See Id.* at 1758 (citing Nozick, *supra* note 24, at 84–86); Jeffrie G. Murphy, *Blackmail: A Preliminary Inquiry*, 63 MONIST 156, 162–63 (1980)).

[88] Gordon, *supra* note 2, at 1758.

[89] This seems to be the crux of Gordon's case against blackmail. If so, the author appears to have dropped her focus on "central case" blackmail so as to concentrate on the garden variety of this act.

[90] A *reductio ad absurdum* is a critique that takes an argument to its logical conclusion to show its absurdity.

carries out) not a rape but rather a seduction, which is defined as a voluntary act between consenting adults.[91] Gordon states that "[t]he violent and unlawful nature of a threatened act may make the extortionist's moral wrong more serious ('I will break your legs' as compared with 'I will disclose your secret'), but a threat may constitute a moral wrong even if the threatened act is neither wrongful nor unlawful."[92] In actuality, however, the law should ban only extortion because it threatens illegal acts, while blackmail does not. The fact that both are immoral should not be allowed to obscure this crucial distinction. In articulating her argument, Gordon continually allows the immorality of blackmail to obscure her reasoning. For example, the author highlights the fact that to commit blackmail is "to do an act that is wrong,"[93] but fails to realize that many people consider many legal acts to be wrong, such as smoking, homosexuality, and suicide.

B. Victimization and Outrage

Gordon, citing an article by Thomas Nagel for support, further asserts that a victim necessarily "feels outrage when he is deliberately harmed."[94] The author opines that, because blackmail is a harm that presumably impugns the

---

[91] See Walter B. Williams, *The Legitimate Role of Government in a Free Society*, in THE FRANK M. ENGLE LECTURES 633, 640 (Roger C. Bird ed., 1998), Williams argues:

> The test for moral relations among people is to ask whether the act was peaceable and voluntary or violent and involuntary. Put another way, was there seduction, or was there rape? Seduction (voluntary exchange) occurs when we offer our fellow man the following proposition: I will make you feel good if you make me feel good. An example of this occurs when I visit my grocer. In effect I offer, "If you make me feel good by giving me that loaf of bread, I will make you feel good by giving you a dollar." Whenever there is seduction, we have a positive-sum game; i.e., both parties are better off in their own estimation.
>
> Rape (involuntary exchange), on the other hand, happens when we offer our fellow-man the following proposition: "If you do not make me feel good, I am going to make you feel bad." An example of this would be where I walked into my grocer's store with a gun and offered, "If you do not make me feel good by giving me that loaf of bread, I am going to make you feel bad by shooting you." Whenever there is rape, we have a zero-sum game, i.e., in order for one person to be better off, it necessarily requires that another be made worse off. *Id.*

[92] Gordon, *supra* note 2, at 1759 fn. 86.

[93] *Id.* at 1760.

[94] *Id.* at 1761.

worth of the targeted individual, it must be outlawed.[95] This reasoning, however, is problematic for several reasons. First, Gordon has not established that the blackmailee is a victim, and not a beneficiary, of the blackmailer. Second, whether the blackmailee feels outrage is irrelevant. So many people feel outrage regarding a wide array of subjects that the existence of the blackmailee's outrage in this scenario is not significant. Third, people do not necessarily feel outrage when deliberately wronged, or even when harmed. According to psychological research on the matter, people feel outrage not so much because of what happens to them, but instead because of what they tell themselves about those experiences.[96] Moreover, while people usually have limited control over their experiences, they tend to have almost total control (at least potentially) over what they think about those experiences.[97] Thus, if an individual thinks, "I can not stand to be treated unfairly," then that individual will probably feel outrage when he perceives that he has been slighted. In contrast, an individual's internal thoughts may travel along equally true but more psychologically healthy channels, such as thinking, when treated poorly, "It may be uncomfortable, but I can stand it, and indeed, I have stood far worse in the past." Such an individual is far less likely to experience outrage.[98]

C. Intent, Consequences, and the Doctrine of Double Effect

In the next section of her article, Gordon introduces a series of very fine distinctions, explaining that some deontological philosophers "distinguish between direct and oblique intention, between foreseen and intended effects

---

[95] *Id.*

[96] *See, generally,* MICHAEL R. EDELSTEIN & DAVID RAMSEY STEELE, THREE-MINUTE THERAPY: CHANGE YOUR THINKING, CHANGE YOUR LIFE (1997); ALBERT ELLIS & ROBERT A. HARPER, A GUIDE TO RATIONAL LIVING (1961). Psychotherapists of the Rational Emotive Behavioral Therapy School (REBT) put this is the form of ABC: A is an actual event that, purportedly, causes upset; for example, getting fired from one's job or losing ones girlfriend. C is the emotional consequence; for example, depression. Most commentators claim that A causes C. But the REBT theoretician claims that it is not A that causes C; rather, it is B, the person's belief about A. If he has an irrational belief (for example, that it is horrible to lose his job or girlfriend) then this is what causes the upset. In contrast, if he has a rational belief about what befalls him (for example, that such occurrences are indeed unfortunate, but he can live with them) then the A will not cause the C.

[97] *See, generally,* Edelssein & Steele, *supra* note 97; Ellis & Harper, *supra* note 97.

[98] *See* Edelstein & Steele, *supra* note 97, at 1. Edelstein and Steele explain that "[t]he way you feel emotionally, arises from the way you think. Your feelings come from your thinking." *Id.* The authors continue, "[e]vents do not directly affect our psyches the way a needle in the arm causes pain (even then the pain has gone through our brain before we can feel it)." *Id.* at 2.

or among effects that vary in their degree of 'closeness' with the intended effect."[99] Gordon attempts to use these distinctions to shed light on the puzzle presented by Guido Calabresi.[100]

At this point in her argument, Gordon discusses the Doctrine of Double Effect (DDE)[101] Gordon explains that, according to the proponents of DDE, "it can sometimes be morally permissible to do an act that has had consequences if they are outweighed by the good, so long as the harms are not directly intended."[102] This doctrine may well be a powerful tool in some contexts, but it fails to support Gordon's arguments. First, the debate over the legalization of blackmail is not concerned with what is morally permissible," but rather with what should be legal. This distinction is important because overeating, smoking, suicide, and homosexuality are all seen by many as morally impermissible, and yet, because none of them necessarily involves initiatory violence, they should not be legally proscribed. Second, no negative consequences follow from blackmail, at least as compared to gossip." The willingness, even eagerness, of the blackmailee to engage in this contractual agreement demonstrates this lack of negative consequences.

During the course of her analysis, Gordon essentially converts DDE into the "doctrine of single effect" (DSE).[103] She explains that "when one's direct intent is to do harm, beneficial side effects have little or no deontological significance" for purposes of analyzing blackmail.[104] Elaborating on this point, Gordon continues:

> Under my suggested correlative, DSE, one would ask if the actor would change his behavior if the beneficial effects were eliminated. Using that test, it appears that no significance should be given to either the lawful nature of the threatened disclosure or the potentially beneficial side effects of blackmail. Were the disclosure unlawful or impossible but the victim still capable of being frightened

---

[99] Gordon, *supra* note 2, at 1761. The point is to focus more attention on motivations, as opposed to objective results. In gangster movies, when one gang member kills another, he sometimes declares that this is "just business, it's not personal." In effect, he is attempting to obviate himself from the charge that the "harm is directly intended."

[100] *See, generally,* GUIDO CALABRESI, IDEALS, BELIEFS, ATTITUDE AND THE LAW: PRIVATE LAW PERSPECTIVES ON A PUBLIC LAW PROBLEM (1985).

[101] *See* Gordon, *supra* note 2, at 1763.

[102] Gordon, *supra* note 2, at 1763.

[103] *See* Gordon, *supra* note 2, at 1764–65.

[104] *Id.*

into paying, the typical blackmailer would extract the money anyway.[105]

Gordon's use of the phrase "were the disclosure unlawful" almost reaches the crux of the matter because, at first glance, this is precisely the point of the libertarian—the disclosure of gossip is patently not unlawful. This revelation is exactly the reason that banning the threat of that which is itself not unlawful—the disclosure of gossip—would be impermissible and, moreover, illogical.

Gordon's characterization of DSE requires the inclusion of the word "properly" so that her assertion reads as follows: "Were the disclosure to be properly unlawful but the victim still capable of being frightened into paying, the typical blackmailer would extract the money anyway. With the addition of this qualifying phrase, Gordon's DSE conclusion logically follows. Under these conditions, even the libertarian would agree that blackmail, not merely extortion, should be illegal.

Consider an illustration. You hire me, among other things, to refrain from gossiping about you (for example, I am your private secretary). You pay me good money for this service, and I agree to undertake it. Then, instead of keeping my part of the bargain, I turn against you and threaten to expose your secrets unless you pay me an additional (and very large) amount of money. Namely, I am now asking you to pay me for services for which you have already paid me (my secretarial salary). But this is the equivalent of theft.

Or consider this scenario. I blackmail you for x-dollars to keep your secret forevermore. One year later, I come back to you and demand more money as the price of my continued silence. Again, in effect, I am demanding additional money for doing what I have already contracted to do. Clearly, I am a crook.

Since stealing is a paradigm case of illegitimate behavior, at least for the libertarian, law on a deontological basis should proscribe both actions. If, then, Gordon accepts my "friendly" amendment, her views are fully congruent with libertarianism. But this means that people such as confidential secretaries and blackmailers too should be forced not to gossip, if they have contractually obligated themselves to refrain from speaking ill of the blackmailee.

Without the inclusion of the term "properly" in her discussion, Gordon's statement regarding DSE is either false or irrelevant. Gordon opines that if disclosure were unlawful, then the law would have to legally ban blackmail. In reality, though, disclosure is not (ordinarily) unlawful, and blackmail, there-

---

[105] *Id.* at 1765.

fore, should not be outlawed. Gordon rejects this analytical framework; she criticizes the blackmailer "because his intent is directed to the money, not to the disclosure or beneficial side effects that [the disclosure] might produce."[106] The ordinary tradesman, such as a butcher or a baker, however, does not care at all about the benefits his customers derive from his products beyond the fact his goods will not sell unless they are pleasing to his customers.

Gordon states "[m] y argument, by contrast, is that a threat with all immoral end can be condemned as coercive without reference to the nature of the threatened action."[107] The author fails to explain how an immoral but not coercive end possibly can be converted into a coercive one.[108] The fact that "the blackmailer's end is harm"[109] is of no consequence; the blackmailer's actions may be morally irredeemable, but they are certainly legal.[110]

D. The Property Rights Objection

As further support for the prohibition of blackmail, Gordon notes approvingly that Sir Frederick Pollack stated that "'a general proposition of English law is that it is a wrong to do willful harm to ones neighbor without lawful justification or excuse.'"[111] This assertion, however, is an example of legal positivism.[112]

Gordon mistakenly relies on malicious intent, but does not support this reasoning; for her, if there is any maliciousness involved, property rights have

---

[106] *Id.*

[107] *Id.* at 1765 fn. 109.

[108] *See* note 93 *supra.*

[109] Gordon, *supra* note 2, at 1766.

[110] Gordon would punish people solely for their motives, not their acts. If she were a judge, and two blackmailers who acted identically were brought before her, she would presumably dismiss the case against the one whose motives she favored and not against the other, whose motives she opposed. This, to say the least, runs 180 degrees counter to Hayek's "The Rule of Law." *See, generally,* F,A, HAYEK, LAW, LEGISLATION AND LIBERTY (1973). Gordon, presumably, would welcome the new hate crimes legislation, which would punish criminals not only for their acts, but also for their thoughts.

[111] Gordon, *supra* note 2, at 1767 (quoting Philip Halpern, *International Torts and the Restatement: A Petition for Rehearing,* 7 BUFF. L. REV. 21 (1957) (quoting FREDERICK POLLOCK, LAW OF TORTS (1st ed., 1887)).

[112] Legal positivism is the view that, because something is the law, it should be the law.

no relevance.[113] This would force jurists to get into the heads of defendants and begs the question of why an individual's motivations, and not his objective acts, should be made the bedrock of law. Nastiness, which has sociobiological survival value for the human race,[114] is a valuable human characteristic, fully worthy of being maintained in the panoply of our emotions. Furthermore, people have a right to act out of malicious motivation, provided, of course, that they do not violate another person or the property rights of another person.[115]

As her analysis continues, Gordon issues the following statement regarding the relevance of the legality of the information disclosure underlying blackmail:

> It is irrelevant whether or not it would be proper for the blackmailer to disclose the information, and thus destroy something the victim may value at a price even higher than the goods demanded in the blackmail transaction. For no disclosure is intended and none occurs. Whatever justification might support disclosure, none supports a threat whose only motive and effect is to extract money or compliance.[116]

---

[113] *See* Gordon, *supra* note 2, at 1766. Gordon places quotation marks around the phrase "Property Right," an act that can be interpreted as her dismissal of this concept from her analysis. *See Id.* More explicitly, she claims that, "to demand a property right as a premise for giving protection against harm is topsy-turvy," *See Id.* at 1763. This may be "topsy-turvy" in Gordon's view, but this is precisely the libertarian perspective, if her "harm" is substituted for rights violations. This is because, under the libertarian legal code, it is permissible to "harm" people in all sorts of ways (for example, competing for their customers or girlfriends), but it is always improper to violate their rights.

[114] *See, generally,* EDMUND O. WILSON, SOCIOBIOLOGY (1980). Sociobiology is the theory that, to a great degree, people act as they do because certain behavioral characteristics had survival value hundreds of thousands of years ago. For example, men are more aggressive than women because this enhanced the likelihood of survival of prehistoric pre-human tribes. A similar assertion can be made for nastiness. People presently are "nasty" because they are descended from ancestors who had this characteristic, which helped them survive earlier eras. If there were a tribe of "nice" humans, they became extinct because such a trait was not conducive to staving off extinction.

[115] It is the essence of the libertarian philosophy that people can act out of the most base of human motivation, as long as they do not physically abuse, without permission, the persons or property of anyone else.

[116] Gordon, *supra* note 2, at 1769–70.

If Gordon's basic premise (malicious motivations are the key to criminality, not objective invasive acts) could be accepted, at least some value could be placed on this assessment. There would, of course, still be the difficulty of discerning the blackmailer's motivation because no blackmailer would ever admit to being a central case blackmailer. Each blackmailer would claim at least some benefit, whether personal or for the "public good," in exposing the secrets of the blackmailee.

In any event, no actual blackmail can be defined as the "central case blackmail" because human motivations are so complex and multidimensional. Central case blackmail has all the earmarks of a theoretical construct, not an actual occurrence in the real world. The purpose of a theoretical Construct is purely intellectual or heuristic—to sharpen our thinking or to clarify categories.[117] Anyone who expects to end a theoretical construct in the real world will be sadly disappointed. Gordon not only expects to find her theoretical construct in reality, she is basing her theory of blackmail's illegality on its presence, as well as its prevalence.[118]

Moreover, it is false for Gordon to claim, even of central case blackmail that "no disclosure is intended."[119] On the contrary, disclosure is intended, if the blackmailee remains obdurate and refuses to pay. The truth of the matter is that in this "case" the blackmailer obtains no psychic benefit from disclosure; his motive is only the money, and he receives no additional benefit from seeing the blackmailee squirm. It would be much more accurate to declare that the central case blackmailer intends no disclosure unless he is balked.

Furthermore, threats intended "to extract money" are not necessarily legally improper. According to Gordon's reasoning, though, the law would prohibit both bluffing in poker and hard bargaining in commerce. Thus, Gordon's critique indicates hostility to the free market, where people can buy and sell at any agreed upon price. In contrast, she implicitly supports a form of

---

[117] An example of a theoretical construct in economics is the evenly rotating economy of Ludwig von Mises. *See, generally,* LUDWIG VON MISES, HUMAN ACTION (1949). Another example in economics is the perfectly competitive model employed by most textbook writers in the field. Examples in other fields include the frictionless world in physics and the perfect vacuum in chemistry. In mathematics, examples are the line with no width or the point with neither length nor width. These constructs are all meant as nonexistent end points and can have intellectual value even though they are not found in reality.

[118] Gordon, *supra* note 2, at 1767–69.

[119] *Id.* at 1769–70.

price controls, limited to whatever is necessary to preclude money "extraction."[120]

In a successful poker bluff (for example, your victim folds even though he holds better cards than you), no disclosure of cards is intended, and none occurs, just as in central case blackmail. Why that should occasion legal opprobrium is not clear. In chess, the sacrifice of a pawn, let alone a queen, is akin to a "bluff." Were this view to become incorporated into the law of the land, it is difficult to avoid the implication that the Game of Kings would become far less interesting.

E. Comparing Blackmail with the Ordinary Commercial Transaction

Gordon next addresses directly the libertarian view of blackmail.[121] She is one of the very few mainstream writers on blackmail to have seriously considered the libertarian perspective on this matter.[122]

Libertarians, Gordon correctly states, see no legal distinction between blackmail and ordinary commercial transactions. She disagrees with this view on three distinct grounds. First, Gordon maintains "the central case blackmail transaction is non-allocative, while the ordinary commercial exchange is allocative."[123] Her claim is that "social welfare" would decrease under blackmail, but not under ordinary trade.[124] This concept, however, is logically incoherent without interpersonal comparisons of utility, and the latter are

---

[120] *Id.* One might well argue that Gordon is doing a bit more than "implicitly" supporting price controls. When someone opposes money "extraction," he is indicating that certain prices should be illegal. For example, suppose it costs five dollars to manufacture a wristwatch, and Gordon is willing to concede that a profit of one dollar is not "extractive." If the manufacturer charges more than six dollars, the difference between that amount and six dollars would be an "extraction" of the customer. If the price is nine dollars, then the extraction is three dollars. Because Gordon opposes extraction, she must, if she is to be logically consistent, favor a price maximum (or price control) over the wristwatches of six dollars.

[121] *See* Gordon, *supra* note 2, at 1770–71.

[122] Gordon, however, is not, the only mainstream writer to address the libertarian perspective. *See, e.g.*, RICHARD A. POSNER, ECONOMIC ANALYSIS OF LAW,1817–18, 1828, 1832 (3d ed. 1986).

[123] Gordon, *supra* note 2, at 1770.

[124] *See Id.* at 1750 fn. 54.

invalid.[125] The point is that, because one person's utility cannot be compared with another's, there is no such thing as social welfare. Without this latter concept, Gordon's criticism fails.

Gordon's second criticism of libertarianism is that "the blackmailer intends to harm."[126] This, however, is frequently true: it applies to Don Rickles, every nagging wife, every scolding parent, every boss chewing out an employee, every employee bad-mouthing the firm that employs him, every teacher upbraiding a student, every pupil criticizing a professor. Even Gordon, in the present context, "intends to harm" libertarianism, at least insofar as her argument pertains to blackmail.

Gordon's third critique of the libertarian perspective of blackmail is that "the buyer of silence in an extortion transaction suffers a net harm, while the buyer in an ordinary transaction is benefited.[127] This assertion contains two errors. First, the victim of extortion is the buyer of protection against the threat of violence. In contrast, the buyer of silence is the target of blackmail. The victim of extortion does indeed suffer a net harm, but the blackmailee, as has been shown, is a net beneficiary of the blackmail transaction. Gordon herself admits this when she concedes, "the victim may value (silence) at a price even higher than the goods demanded in the transaction."[128] The second error in Gordon's third critique relates to her claim that the "buyer in an ordinary transaction is benefited." This is necessarily true in the *ex ante* sense only, not in the *ex post* sense. That is, the buyer must always anticipate that something about the purchase is worth more than the cost, but this need not be true from the historical perspective. While we usually are happy with the purchases we make, afterward, the existence of department store refunds is dramatic testimony to the fact that this is not always the case. But no less is true with blackmail. The blackmailee is by definition, satisfied with his commercial interaction in the *ex ante* sense, and usually, but not always, in the *ex post*.

---

[125] *See* Rothbard, *supra* note 49, at 21. An interpersonal comparison of utility is of the following sort: Alice likes apples more than Bill likes beans. It is one thing to say that Alice is shorter or weighs less or can run faster than Bill; there are scientific measures of distance, weight, and speed. There are, however, no units of happiness, or likes and dislikes, on the basis of which interpersonal comparisons of utility can be made. Of course, such determinations are made as a matter of everyday living. This can hardly be the basis of sound public policy, which should be based on scientific considerations, not feelings and subjective estimations of the sort made in everyday life.

[126] Gordon, *supra* note 2, at 1770.

[127] *Id.*

[120] *Id.*

1. Intent to Harm

In her analysis, Gordon offers a somewhat peculiar definition of "exploitative."[129] According to her, the term means "getting something for nothing.' Gordon claims that "most person's sense of self-respect"[130] would prevent them acting in such an improper manner and would require some degree of reciprocity in the bulk of their transactions.[131] This assertion is untrue. Israel M. Kirzner has carefully and exhaustively studied entrepreneurship.[132] According to Kirzner, the essence of entrepreneurship is precisely the ability to get something for nothing.[133] Moreover, people often wait in long lines at the opening of a new bank branch for a free toaster or at the establishment of a new restaurant in order to obtain a free hot dog. There is no reason why this is any "less desirable ... than engaging in commercial activity that involves exchange."[134] And even if it were indeed "less desirable," why should this be an issue on which the law should cast its baleful eye?

In essence, Gordon sees extraction without reciprocity as exploitation, which is "less attractive' than an exchange.[135] Blackmail, however, is a mutual exchange, not an extraction, as Gordon characterizes it. Blackmail is a mutually agreeable contract according to which one party agrees to refrain from

---

[129] *See Id.*

[130] *Id.*

[131] *Id.*

[132] *See, generally,* Israel M. Kirzner, Competition and Entrepreneurship (1973). It is no exaggeration to say that, for Kirzner, the very essence of entrepreneurship is to "get something for nothing." The entrepreneurial act is, in effect, to seize a ten-dollar bill out of thin air (by noting unmet consumer needs and acting to satisfy them).

[133] *See Id.* at 48. Kirzner States:

> The pure entrepreneur ... proceeds by his alertness to discover and exploit situations in which he is able to sell for high prices that which he can buy for low prices. Pure entrepreneurial profit is the difference between the two sets of prices. Exchanging something the entrepreneur values less for something he values more highly does not yield it. It comes from discovering sellers and buyers of something for which the latter will pay more than the former demand. The discovery of a profit opportunity means *the discovery of something obtainable for nothing at all.* No investment at all is required; the free ten-dollar bill is discovered to be already within one's grasp. *Id.* at 48 (emphasis added).

[134] Gordon, *supra* note 2, at 1771.

[135] *See Id.*

disclosing information and the second party agrees to compensate the first party for that silence.

2. Harm and Benefit

Gordon rejects the notion that "a benefit ... can be defined as ... the return of something that the other party stole only a moment before."[136] Even this is not strictly true, because if someone steals something from you, surely you would prefer that he gives it right back, rather than keep it. The former is bound to be more beneficial than the latter. Here, Gordon is correctly focusing on initial property rights; if an item is stolen and then returned, the owner is hardly better off if both occur than if neither did. Gordon's adherence to property rights analysis, however, is only superficial. Instead of looking at just ownership, Gordon offers three conditions that must be satisfied in order to determine that harm has occurred. These conditions are: (1) the thing the seller wants the buyer/victim to purchase is such that the buyer would be better off ... if the seller and his resources did not exist, (2) the buyer/victim would be better off if the transaction were impossible ... and, (3) the buyer/victim has done nothing to the other party that would give that party a corrective justice right against her.[137]

Indubitably, there are cases in which I would be better off if you did not exist, and thus your very existence is "harmful" to me, such as when two people have offered competing marriage suits for the same individual. Yes, you have harmed me by your very existence as a competitor of mine; I would be better off if you simply disappeared (an issue that should be irrelevant to law), but you have hardly violated my rights (which should be the entire focus of the legal system)

Gordon, as an illustration of the second criteria, considers a situation in which a plaintiff sues a defendant for damages created by a falling tree.[138] The author concludes, "[t]he landowner would be worse off if settling lawsuits were impossible."[139] While this seems reasonable over the long term, it is an empirical question. If the landowner is an old man who has no interest in what occurs to society after he dies, and the lawsuit will take away all of his money, and he is not likely to be a plaintiff in the future in any case, he may reasonably prefer a situation in which lawsuits are impossible.

---

[136] *Id.*
[137] *See Id.* at 1772.
[138] *See Id.* at 1772 fn. 140.
[139] *Id.*

On the basis of this idiosyncratic analysis, Gordon declares that, "the injured passerby is not harming the landowner if he extracts money in settlement or suit."[140] This assumption, however, appears rather counterintuitive because the sole function of the landowner's lawyer is to help the landowner to avoid making any payment if at all possible. Why would he want to do that if the suit were not deemed harmful to his client? Here, Gordon is again conflating harm and rights violation. Whether the victim has done anything wrong to the victimizer is totally irrelevant. If I beat you out in my marriage proposal to the woman we both love, you are the victim, and I, the victimizer. You may never have violated any of my rights beforehand such that I have a "corrective justice right" against you. Nevertheless I am entirely within my rights to press my marriage suit, even if it greatly vexes you. Gordon similarly refuses to examine the property rights in question when she states:

> [I]t does not matter whose resources the information is ... [Even if, as libertarians contend, the blackmailer "owns" the information, it is clear that the purchaser/victim is worse off in a world where the blackmailer and that resource exist. The blackmailer is therefore using that information in a way that harms the victim.[141]

In some sense, the blackmailer does harm the blackmailee because the latter would vastly prefer that the former had never come upon his secret. Mere harm, however, should not be actionable, otherwise no competition of any sort could exist, whether in commerce, sports, or anything else.

Secondly, if the blackmailee is "harmed" by the blackmailer, he would be harmed to a far greater degree if, instead of the blackmailer unearthing his secret, it is revealed by the gossip. At least the former will allow the "victim" to buy his way out of his quandary—the latter will not. Surely, then, if Gordon is willing to imprison the blackmailer, she must favor punishing the gossip far

---

[140] *Id.*

[141] *Id.* at. 1773. Only three possibilities exist regarding the rightful ownership of this information: either the blackmailer, the blackmailee, or third parties, such as a husband who would be interested in learning of his wife's infidelity. Lindgren claims that the information belongs to third parties, despite the fact that they did nothing to earn this information. *See generally* Lindgren, *supra* note 17. In Jeffrie C. Murphy's view, this knowledge properly belongs to the blackmailee. *See, generally,* Jeffrie C. Murphy, *Blackmail: A Preliminary Inquiry,* 63 MONIST 156 (1980). If this were true, gossip would be illegal because the gossipper, in effect, would be stealing this information from its rightful owner, the gossippee. No one, however, has followed this claim to its logical conclusion, which would call for the abolition of the right to free speech, as it involves gossip.

more seriously. Curiously, she entirely avoids the case of the gossip. But worse; if for Gordon it does not really matter who properly owns the secret information, then all talk of "chips"[142] is then just so much obfuscation; and so too vanishes any pretense of deontology. Contrary to her claims, Gordon's, then, is a theory of blackmail that rests entirely on utilitarian considerations. Matters of right and wrong simply do not enter into the picture.

V. CRIMINALIZATION

Having established, at least to her own satisfaction, that central case blackmail is harmful, unjustified, purposeful, wrongful, and immoral, Gordon then considers whether it should be criminalized.[143] This conclusion would appear to follow, in her opinion, from the "liberal view,"[144] at least as adum-

---

[142] Gordon, *supra* note 2, at 1777.

[143] *Id.* at 1775.

[144] *Id.* Gordon explains the "liberal view" as holding "that only the presence of harm toward others justifies criminal prohibition." *See Id.* This, however, is nonsense. One baseball team can "harm" another by winning a game, but the members of the winning team should not be incarcerated for their actions. A far better way to characterize this view would be to consider the libertarian approach, in which only the violation of personal or property rights justifies criminal prohibition. Blackmail "harms" the blackmailee compared to the situation in which the potential blackmailer merely remains silent; blackmail, however, does not harm the blackmailee compared to the situation in which the gossip has unearthed the secret. All of this is irrelevant to the libertarian because blackmail does not violate any right possessed by the blackmailee.

brated by John Stuart Mill[145] and Joel Feinberg.[146] In the author's analysis, however, the issue of whether gossips ought to be jailed never arises. Also, Gordon fails to reckon with the fact that drugs, cigarettes, gambling alcohol, pornography, prostitution, and other such victimless acts would also seem to fit the "liberal" case for prohibition. Instead of addressing the criminality of these activities, Gordon veers off into an economic discussion of blackmail.

A. The Effects of Blackmail Law on Victim Behavior and Perceptions: Character Formation

Gordon claims that "blackmail prohibition ... may encourage character-formation that discourages bad acts."[147] This is counterintuitive because criminalizing blackmail discourages blackmailers. Gordon concedes as much when she states, "criminalizing blackmail has an obvious goal of discouraging potential blackmailers from undertaking blackmail."[148] The blackmailer, though, with his ferret-like behavior, tends to strike terror into the man contemplating an immoral act. The blackmailer is, in effect, a police officer that is highly motivated and skillful because he is private.[149] Reducing the black-mailer's scope will increase such acts as cheating and philandering, at least if

---

[145] See, generally, JOHN STUART MILL, ON LIBERTY (Gertrude Himmelfarb, ed. 1988). This essay argues for liberty on utilitarian grounds; liberty is a good because it leads to the greatest amount of happiness for the greatest number of people. According to Mill, however, "[i]f all mankind minus one, were of one opinion, and only one person were of the contrary opinion, mankind would be no more justified in silencing that one person, than he, if he had the power, would be justified in silencing mankind," Id. at 16.

[146] See Gordon, supra note 2 at 1775 & fn. 151 (citing Mill, supra note 146, at 91–92). Joel Feinberg, in articulating the different viewpoints as to the moral limits of criminal law, defined the "Harm Principle" as follows: "[i]t is always a good reason in support of penal legislation that it would be effective in preventing ... harm to persons other than the actor (the one prohibited from acting), and there is no other means that is equally effective at no greater cost to other values." JOEL FEINBERG, THE MORAL LIMITS OF THE CRIMINAL LAW: HARMLESS WRONGDOING at xix (1988) (emphasis added). Feinberg then defined the "Offense Principle" as follows: "It is always a good reason in support of a proposed criminal prohibition that it is necessary to prevent serious offense to persons other than the actor and would be an effective means to that end if enacted," Id. Finally, Feinberg defined the "Liberal Position" as follows: "[T]he harm and offense principles, duly clarified and qualified, between them exhaust the class of good reasons for criminal prohibitions." Id.

[147] Gordon, supra note 2, at 1776 fn. 154.

[148] Id.

[149] See, generally, WILLIAM C. WOOLRIDGE, UNCLE SAM, THE MONOPOLY MAN (1970) (explaining how the market can supplant the government in providing for public goods).

it is assumed that the greater the likelihood of being caught, the less likely a person is to engage in the act in the first place.

In contrast, Gordon's musings focus mainly on the notion that legalization "might not only increase the threat related use of information already possessed, but might also increase the expenditures made on acquiring new information."[150] Even if this is true, it is an empirical issue and would result in only the increasing exposure of a decreasing number of bad acts. Whether the incidence of blackmail ultimately would be greater or less is difficult to say, but Gordon's original claim that "blackmail prohibition … may encourage character-formation that discourages bad acts" is clearly unproven.

B. The Effects of Blackmail Law on Victim Behavior and Perceptions: Counter Leverage

Gordon claims that blackmail prohibition gives "victims" counter leverage in that "by threatening to go to the authorities *if and only if disclosure is made,* victims can discourage blackmailers from disclosing the contested information."[151] This assumption has several problems. For one, Gordon has not yet succeeded in showing that blackmail is legally horrendous. Because she leaves gossip unscathed, there is no justification for her efforts to condemn the blackmailer. Second, the information in question is not "contested." Rather, Gordon is on record as giving upon this "contest."[152]

For argument's sake, assume that Gordon's argument is a worthwhile undertaking—that for some reason, the blackmailee must be protected from disclosure by law. Gordon thinks that the only way to accomplish this is to make blackmail illegal. This, however, is not so because the same goal can be obtained through legalization. Under a legalization scheme, the blackmailee would pay the blackmailer to keep his silence. If the blackmailer takes the payment and still threatens exposure, the blackmailee would then be able to avail himself of the courts, not for blackmail, but for contract violation. That is, while blackmail would be legal, it certainly would not be within the purview of the law to agree to this contract (silence for money) and then to turn

---

[150] Gordon, *supra* note 2, at 1776.

[151] *Id.* at 1777.

[152] *See Id.* at 1773 ("[I]t does not matter whose resources the information is … even if, as libertarians contend, the blackmailer 'owns' the information.").

around and break it (having taken the money, refuse to keep silent as so stipulated).[153]

Additionally, counter leverage, whether of the sort that our author favors or of the sort created by blackmail legalization, is itself *blackmail*. Gordon devotes an entire law review article to the iniquities and impropriety of blackmail and then champions a version of it herself. Gordon is not without a reply to this charge as she states:

> Unlike the blackmailer, who uses the threat of disclosure to force the victim to give up something ... to which the blackmailer has no right, the victim engaging in counter blackmail is using her threat to enforce her rights-to force the blackmailer to cease his wrongful behavior towards her. Since this is the victim's "own chip," and the use of the chip as leverage is neither "unproductive" nor an "unjustified harming," the victim should be permitted to make this counter threat.[154]

This rationalization, however, is insufficient; blackmail is blackmail, whether for purposes of which Gordon approves or not. If the motivation of the blackmailer is at issue, one can concoct many cases in which the blackmailer acts for what Gordon might consider good purposes." For example, consider a situation in which an individual refuses to repay a significant debt because the debt holder has no proof that any money is owed. The debt holder cannot proceed with a legal action, so instead he blackmails the recalcitrant debtor for the exact amount of money owed.

Another difficulty is that Gordon takes inconsistent positions within her article. At one point, she states, "it does not matter whose resources the information is ... [E]ven if, as libertarians contend, the blackmailer 'owns' the information."[155] Later, Gordon claims that who owns the information matters

---

[153] Under Gordon's legal dispensation, the blackmailee would not have to make the initial payment, but under that posited in this Article, he would be required to do so, In both cases, however, the blackmailee would then be safe from further demands for money. Thus, under the libertarian system, the blackmailer could legally obtain whatever funds he could bargain for, while under the present prohibition, he could not. The justification for making the blackmailer richer, and the blackmailee poorer, is that the former is the *legitimate owner* of the information that he employs to his own ends. Because Gordon explicitly refuses to challenge this claim, she should not question a logical implication made from it.

[154] Gordon, *supra* note 2, at 1777.

[155] *Id.* at 1773.

very much; in her view, the counter blackmailer owns the information.[156] Gordon's second position is correct in at least one point; all blackmailers, "counter" ones along with all the rest, own the information they use. Gordon has yet to show this does not apply in all cases.

C. The Effects of Blackmail Law on Victim Behavior and Perceptions: Anger

Gordon defends blackmail prohibitionism on the ground that it will stiffen the spines of blackmailees and make them more resistant to the threats of blackmailers. The author explains that "[i]f one assumes that acts of blackmail impose net costs on society, then the socially beneficial response to a blackmailer is to resist in order to convince potential blackmailers that blackmail never succeeds, and thus to silence their threats."[157] However, if one really wants to promote resistance, and is a utilitarian (for example, unconcerned with the niceties of justice), then one can go further. Why not make it illegal to pay blackmail? True, this, according to Gordon's perspective, would victimize the blackmailee a second time—once by the blackmailer and then by the government—but it would promote resistance.

Another difficulty is that acts of kidnapping certainly "impose net costs on society." If people never paid off kidnappers, and this were known for sure, this behavior would cease forthwith. Thus, according to Gordon's brand of utilitarianism, the state should imprison not only kidnappers, but also all those who cooperate with them by paying them off. This, it would appear, is the "honorable" thing to do.[158]

Of course, libertarian law would give short shrift to such suggestions. It is the kidnapper who violates rights, not the family member of the kidnappee who merely wants the safe return of his loved one, and is willing to pay for it. Nor is the blackmailee who pays for silence guilty of any rights violation. Nor, for that matter, is the blackmailer.

Gordon asserts that "[s]ometimes we legislate against something in order to keep our sense of outrage alive."[159] As a report of legislative activities, this is unexceptionable; surely laws against drugs, pornography, and prostitution are instances of this tendency. Gordon, however, is not merely reporting on this phenomenon, but is instead supporting it, at least in the case of blackmail. But if for blackmail, why not for these other activities?

---

[156] *See Id.* at 1777.

[157] *Id.* at 1780.

[158] *See Id.* at 1779.

[159] *Id.* at 1780.

VI. CONCLUSION

To sum up this critique of Gordon's argument for the prohibition of blackmail, central case blackmail is but a special case of this activity. Gordon's analysis, even if correct, would only teach this special case; all other forms of blackmail would still be justified. Gordon, however, has not succeeded even in this small area. The simple facts that the blackmailer derives no additional value from exposing the secret of the blackmailee and that his only motivation is pecuniary do not demonstrate that he is not the rightful owner of the informational "chip" of which Gordon speaks. Neither do these facts indicate that the blackmailer has invaded the person or property of the blackmailee. These assertions by Gordon cannot be maintained when compared to the actions of the gossip, which Gordon never mentions in her analysis.

Chapter 7.

Blackmailing for Mutual Good: A Reply to Russell Hardin

Blackmail is the demand for money, or other valuable consideration, coupled with a threat; typically, to expose information the blackmailee prefers to keep secret. For example, I threaten that unless you give me $1,000, I will tell your wife that you have been unfaithful to her. Since you value your marriage more than this amount of money, you pay me for my silence. As a result, you gain the difference between these two amounts. If my silence is worth $5,000, you benefit to the tune of $4,000. My gain is roughly $1,000 because sending a letter to your wife telling her about your peccadillo, and enclosing the pictures I have of you in the act will cost me only postage and a moment of time. As such, blackmail is like any other mutually beneficial economic transaction, at least in the *ex ante* sense.[1]

Blackmail must be sharply distinguished from extortion. They are often confused because both involve a demand for money combined with a threat. However, the threat in blackmail is an entirely legal one of engaging in free speech or gossip, whereas extortion is decidedly not licit. It consists of the threat to maim, kill, or in other ways violate personal and/or property rights. In extortion, the demand for money would typically be accompanied by the threat to murder, kidnap, or commit arson.

In addition to this distinction, Hardin draws another between different kinds of practices related to blackmail and extortion.[2] His views are not congruent with my own. In his view there are not two but three different relevant categories. First is the protection ancient Scottish chieftains sold against other marauders; this was "merely an ordinary exchange of services for services."[3] Second, "if their protection was from their own depredations, the chieftains were like the modern mafia. Their offer of a deal was extortion."[4] Blackmail

---

[1] There is an author of detective literature who appears to take a similarly benevolent view of blackmail. The heroine of the novel, Victoria I. Warshawski, has an aunt who needs an apartment in a public housing complex. The bureaucrat who can make this happen wants our detective not to probe too deeply into her own affairs. Warshawski promises to refrain, in consideration for this dwelling for her relative, and concludes on the following note: 'As I locked the office door behind me I started whistling for the first time all day. Who says blackmailers don't have fun?" SARAH PARETSKY, BURN MARKS 417 (1990).

[2] *See, generally,* Russell Hardin, *Blackmailing for Mutual Good*, 141 U. PA. L. REV. 1787 (1993).

[3] *Id.* at 1787.

[4] *Id.*

comes third and "typically lies somewhere between these [previous] two possibilities."[5]

By contrast, my view of blackmail, to use Hardin's vernacular, is "merely an ordinary exchange of services" not necessarily limited to services but including money or other valuable consideration. And what about the services given by the blackmailer to the blackmailee in return for this payment? Characteristically, services might include silence about an embarrassing secret or refraining from a legal activity such as gossiping, opening up a store in competition with one owned by the blackmailee, or building a fence on one's own property which would block the blackmailee's view.

Hardin proposes to analyze the issue of blackmail legalization based on "a moral theory," specifically "utilitarianism ... driven by concern with optimal arrangements that can be characterized as mutually advantageous."[6] This leads him to a further distinction, between blackmail, which is mutually advantageous, and blackmail, which is not. With regard to the former he states: "it seems likely that the most acceptable case for blackmail would be for mutual advantage blackmail."[7] As we have seen, both the blackmailer and blackmailee gain from their commercial interaction, otherwise a voluntary agreement between them would not take place. Nor is it true, as it is in the case of extortion, that the blackmailer begins the negotiation by taking away something that is legitimately owned by the blackmailee, e.g., "your money or your life." While the blackmailee is also asked to choose between two things, his money and the ability to keep his secret hidden, he properly owns only the former and not the latter. [8]

I. FACTS AND VALUES

Hardin begins this section with a plea to keep "normative and positive or conceptual claims separate."[9] Fair enough! This is part and parcel of any serious analysis of the law. But he derives from the rather unexceptionable premise "we cannot read values exclusively from facts"[10] the remarkable thesis "any

---

[5] *Id.*

[6] *Id.*

[7] *Id.* at 1788.

[8] There is all the world of difference between these two situations. This is a point that managed to elude the jury during the "extortion" case where Autumn Jackson sued Bill Cosby. *See U.S. v. Jackson*, 986 F. Supp. 829 (S.D.N.Y. 1997).

[9] Hardin, *supra* note 2, at 1789.

[10] *Id.* at 1791.

moral argument that concludes that blackmail is right or wrong *tout court* is specious. Blackmail, like every other kind of action or result, is right or wrong, good or bad, only as an implication of particular moral theories."[11] This would be unproblematic if Hardin would tie himself to a moral theory, which had clear implications for blackmail law. Unfortunately, he does not. Therefore, he is reduced to a sort of agnostic position: whether or not the prohibition against blackmail is just depends upon context, and there is no right or wrong context from which anyone can draw any definitive conclusion.

This perspective is buttressed with what would otherwise appear as a large concession to the case for legalization. Hardin states: "The problem with blackmail in the law is that virtually identical actions can be blackmail in one instance and not in the other. We cannot simply read from the facts of the cases that one was wrong and the other right."[12] But if this is so, then the blackmail enactment is incompatible with the "rule of law." It is like a poker game, where one player makes up the rules as he goes along. Surely, if this is so, it is a good and sufficient reason for repeal.

Hardin next moves on to the subject of plea bargaining. The district attorney offers a lighter sentence to the accused than he would obtain were he to be found guilty. Plea bargaining, it would appear, is yet another case in point for agnosticism:

> To decide whether plea-bargaining is good under some moral theory or principle requires assessment of its general effects, especially its broad systematic effects. We cannot decide the issue simply from consideration of a particular case, in which plea-bargaining is not inherently either right or wrong. But it is now legally accepted in many jurisdictions. *The difference between pleas [sic] bargaining when it is legal and when it is illegal is conventional. Illegal plea-bargaining might count as blackmail. Legal plea-bargaining would not.*[13]

Strictly speaking, plea bargaining is indistinguishable from blackmail. In both cases, a valuable consideration is demanded, under the threat of doing something entirely licit, something that everyone would agree is legitimate if it occurred in any other context. For example, money is usually the valuable consideration demanded under blackmail, and the threat is to engage in en-

---

[11] *Id.* at 1816.
[12] *Id.* at 1789.
[13] *Id.* at 1791 (emphasis added).

tirely legal gossip. In the case of plea bargaining, the demand is typically that the accused agree to serve a reduced sentence from what a guilty finding would require, and the threat is to hold a trial where the accused risks a longer sentence. Anyone, at any time, whether prosecutor or not, can legitimately ask anyone else to voluntarily serve a term in jail. Therefore, when the prosecutor asks that of the accused, he commits no crime. On the other hand, the same applies to an accusation of criminal behavior. Anyone, no matter what his status, can make an accusation of criminal behavior. It is part and parcel of free speech.[14] Therefore, when the prosecutor threatens the accused with a trial, he commits no crime. And since two legal whites, even when combined into a complex act consisting of both of them, cannot be turned into a legal black; plea bargaining is a licit act. Therefore, both plea bargaining and blackmail ought to be legal.

Hardin notes that Lindgren would nevertheless distinguish between these two cases, based on his "chip" ownership theory.[15] Hardin's response is yet another example of his unsatisfactory refusal to take a stand. Hardin says, "[t]he chief weakness in Lindgren's claim is that he simply posits the chip argument as inherently immoral. Perhaps it is."[16] Perhaps it is? One would have thought that an author with a contribution to make would have made more of an effort to come down on one side or the other of this important contentious issue.

II. INSTITUTIONAL-LEVEL ANALYSIS

> Much of the discussion of blackmail is about whether there is something inherently wrong in it, as though we could infer what the law should be from looking at the characteristics of a particular case. For an institutionalist, this approach is wrong; instead, we should determine what overall result would be better and then design the law to achieve that result.[17]

One way to characterize Hardin's view would be as a legal philosophy. Alternatively, and perhaps more accurately, this might be described as a lack

---

[14] The point here is that in the free society the prosecutor has no more rights, and certainly no fewer, than anyone else.

[15] *See*, James Lindgren, *Unraveling the Paradox of Blackmail*, 84 COLUM. L. REV. 670 (1984).

[16] Hardin, *supra* note 2, at 1791.

[17] *Id.*

of a legal philosophy. There is really no right and wrong, legal and illegal per se; rather, it depends upon "better results," but these are never specified. And this is only the beginning of the problem. Suppose that the good results were specified, e.g., they consisted of the maximization of wealth. Anything that led to maximization of wealth would be legal, and any activity that led in another direction would be illegal. This would imply compulsory cloning of Bill Gates and the prohibition of vacations, at least those in excess of the time necessary to maximize production. By taking up the "institutionalist" cudgels, and then failing to specify any criterion of "better," Hardin is safe from such criticism,[18] but only because he adds nothing to our considerations concerning the legal status of blackmail, or indeed, of any law. With regard to plea bargaining, for example, Hardin once again raises the issue, but continues to decline to vouchsafe us an opinion as to its legitimacy.[19]

In contrast, the libertarian philosophy, which underlies my own analysis of blackmail, has clear implications for plea bargaining. In the philosophy of liberty, a man may do whatever he wishes with his person and legitimately owned property as long as he respects the same rights of all other people. For blackmail, since it is not a violation of rights to ask people for money, nor to tell secrets honestly acquired, it would not be illegal to combine these two righteous acts. For plea bargaining, since there is no positive obligation for a district attorney to prosecute all possible cases, he may offer a lesser punishment to a person he strongly suspects to be guilty in order to avoid the risk of an acquittal.

Hardin launches another half-hearted attack at blackmail prohibition with the following volley: "Any claim to outlaw blackmail might seem weak if at the same time the sale of embarrassing information on another to the press remains legal."[20] This is really a devastating blow insofar as no advocate of outlawry has even attempted to rein in press freedom on so-called privacy

---

[18] Strangely, Hardin himself later offers a blistering criticism of another blackmail analyst, which could be used against himself in the present context. "Richard Posner says blackmail ... has no social product and should therefore be criminalized. This is a very odd conclusion. Much of what I do has no social product (for instance, I consume, I waste time), but surely it should not be criminalized." Hardin, *supra* note 2, at 1806.

[19] *See Id.* at 1793.

[20] *Id.* at 1793. But given the ambivalence of his underlying legal philosophy, I view with suspicion his seeming advocacy of the legalization of blackmail.

grounds.[21] The attempt to do so would involve an embarrassing *reductio ad absurdum*. Hardin says, insightfully, "We might therefore outlaw every offer to sell information to someone likely to take offense or be harmed by its publication."[22]

III. THE COMPLEX NATURE OF INTERACTION

In an attempt to elevate his focus on "outcomes" or "consequences," Hardin contrives an example he regards as "superficial." He states:

> It may be perfectly legal to own a firearm and even to fire it. It may nevertheless be illegal to kill you with it. My actions of acquiring and then firing a gun were both legitimate. How can it be illegitimate that you happen to be dead as a result?[23]

The fallacy here is due to a mis-specification of the case, not to any need to consult aftermaths or results.[24] The second action was not merely the totally legitimate one of firing a gun, but rather firing a gun at an innocent person and killing him. On the ordinary libertarian maxim of "non-invasiveness," the judge hardly needs to hear the results of such an action. It is invasive on that ground alone, even if the bullet misses or just grazes but does not kill the victim. And it certainly violates his rights if he dies.

---

[21] MURRAY N. ROTHBARD, THE ETHICS OF LIBERTY 121–22:

> But is there really such a right to privacy? How can there be? How can there be a right to prevent Smith by force from disseminating knowledge, which he possesses? Surely there can be no such right. Smith owns his own body, and therefore has the property right to own the knowledge he has inside his head, including his knowledge about Jones. And therefore he has the corollary right to print and disseminate that knowledge. In short, … *there is no such thing as a right to privacy except the right to protect one's property from invasion*. The only right "to privacy" is the right to protect one's property from being invaded by someone else. In brief, no one has the right to burgle someone else's home, or to wiretap someone's phone lines. Wiretapping is properly a crime not because of some vague and wooly "invasion of a ' "right to privacy,"' but because it is an invasion of the property right of the person being wiretapped.

[22] Hardin, *supra* note 2, at 1794.

[23] *Id.* at 1795.

[24] Without a particular theory, such as the libertarian axiom of non-aggression against non-aggressors, how are the results, outcomes, ends or consequences to be evaluated?

We need not concern ourselves with Hardin's obfuscation concerning paradoxes like flipping light switches, arrays and strategies.[25] Nor even with his very interesting point about it being "right to threaten something, which if carried out, would be wrong," such as to threaten to drop a nuclear bomb on innocent people, in order to preserve the peace.[26] That would take us too far afield. We can content ourselves with agreeing with Hardin who asks: "why one cannot threaten to do what one has the full legal right to do (such as pass relevant information to the press[?]"[27] Here, Hardin puts his finger precisely on the matter at issue. If a person can threaten things he has no right to do (drop the bomb), he can certainly threaten things that are fully legal (talk to the press). Therefore, reason would presumably lead us to accepting the legality of refraining from doing what we have a right to do (spilling the beans), even for a price (blackmail).

IV. STRATEGIC STRUCTURE OF EXCHANGE BLACK-MAIL

Next, Hardin places blackmail in the context of game theory.[28] Hardin "refers to the person blackmailed not as the victim, but as the target of the blackmail ... in order to avoid the air of persuasive moral definition."[29] He very insightfully notes that, "law can enter to stabilize the blackmail interaction ... [and] it can be used to enforce any deals the blackmailer and the target make, thereby permitting them to secure a mutually beneficial outcome."[30] So why should we prohibit this commercial arrangement that ends up providing for "mutual good?" Hardin gets into trouble mainly because there is no real justification for this conclusion; all of his attempted explanations must of necessity be erroneous. This essay now considers a few of them.

---

[25] *See* Hardin, *supra* note 2, at 1796.

[26] *Id.*

[27] *Id.*

[28] *See Id.* at 1798.

[29] *Id.* I too have refused to characterize the person blackmailed as a victim. This is because such an individual is actually the beneficiary of the blackmailer, at least when we compare his welfare to the situation where his secret is in the hands of a compulsive gossip. Instead, I have used the morally neutral term "blackmailee." But Hardin's "target" will do quite nicely.

[30] *Id.* at 1800.

1. "Perhaps blackmail is wrong primarily because we have de facto chosen not to back it with enforcement of contracts for blackmail."[31]

This is the lowest form of legal positivism. Is the law justified merely because of the way a legislature enacted it? Using this rationale one could defend any law in Nazi Germany or under Soviet Communism. This opens up the question as to why our society has chosen to make such contracts unenforceable, but it gives no answer. Worse, it is factually mistaken. At present, it is not true that blackmail contracts are only unenforceable; worse, they are also illegal.

2. The target of legal blackmail "might still view the general situation as radically unstable, because one blackmailer might soon be followed by others, each fully in the legal right. The payoff to one blackmailer would then be a sunk cost when the second blackmailer's offer is considered."[32]

This is also highly problematic. What is wrong, with paying off not just one blackmailer, but also an entire series of them? After all, if the first blackmailer provides a service like keeping silent, so do all the others. This is akin to banning any other activity wherein a succession of vendors provides a service. For example, on this ground we could compel shopping at a supermarket and outlaw patronizing a whole series of separate shops: butcher, baker, and candlestick maker, to say nothing of the green grocer and hardware store. For "one [merchant] might soon be followed by others, each fully in the legal right."[33] Moreover, "the payoff to one [retailer] would then be a sunk cost when the second [one]'s offer is considered.[34]

There is the fact that so many blackmailers tend to obviate one another. Like "too many cooks spoiling the broth," too many blackmailers ruin things for each other as well. For once a secret is in the hands of several, to say nothing of dozens of people, it is almost by definition no longer a secret. Why should the target or blackmailee be willing to pay off an entire horde of people to keep quiet if the secret is out in any case?

---

[31] *Id.*

[32] *Id.*

[33] *Id.*

[34] *Id.*

3. "Perhaps this grievous instability in the blackmail system, even when it is restricted to exchange blackmail,[35] makes it ex ante desirable to have the law prohibit blackmail."[36]

This will not do either. Why is instability grievous? Annoying? Perhaps. Although perhaps not when we reflect that the only true "stability" is death. Further, if we can outlaw something because it is unstable, blackmail is the merest tip of the iceberg. The markets for oil and agricultural products are traditionally volatile, to say nothing of the stock and commodities market. Not too many people pay attention to it, but the market for used bubble gum baseball cards is a veritable roller coaster. Should we outlaw them all on this ground? Hardly.

4. "Perhaps there is disagreement on the rightness of keeping certain information private."[37]

Strictly speaking, this cannot be true. A mere disagreement over anything could hardly account for the outlawry of an act such as blackmail. Perhaps what Hardin meant to say was that in this disagreement, one of the parties is correct, and that this view supports the legal *status quo*. For example, Gorr's view is that privacy rights ideally should legally preclude all gossip.[38] Hardin properly rejects this, but only on pragmatic grounds.[39]

However, in so doing he mistakenly buys into the relevance of the distinction between public and non-public figures regarding libel.[40] In this perspective, although full free speech rights are denied in both cases, there is a higher threshold for proving tortious slander or libel against non-public figures. This, however, seems highly contrived. Where does this distinction come from? Nobles and commoners, at least in the just society, have identical rights. Hardin correctly places himself in the camp, which demands of an "assertion [that it] would have to be inferred from more general principles," but he

---

[35] We still have not been shown that there is any other kind of blackmail, although Hardin relies heavily on this distinction.

[36] Hardin, *supra* note 2, at 1800.

[37] *Id.*

[38] *See* Michael Gorr, *Nozick's Argument Against Blackmail*, 58 PERSONALIST 187, 190 (1977); Michael Gorr, *Liberalism and the Paradox of Blackmail*. 21 PHIL. PUB. AFF. 43, 44 (1992).

[39] *See* Hardin, *supra* note 2, at 1801.

[40] *See Id.* at 1801 fn. 28.

leaves the New York Times case[41] hanging in the air as it were, an unprincipled, artificial, fabricated, legal Frankenstein.[42]

Fortunately, there is a principle upon the basis of which not only libel but also blackmail law can be based. This is called private property rights.[43] According to this doctrine, legitimate law consists of, and of nothing but, the protection of private property rights. The most important private property right, of course, is our ownership over our selves. This eliminates enslavement, kidnapping, rape, assault and battery, etc., as legitimate acts right off the bat. But there is more. Based on the Lockean homesteading principle,[44] property rights in animals, inanimate resources and land can be obtained by "mixing one's labor" with them. Then, when one owns them, he can trade them or their products with the legitimately owned property of others.[45]

How do libel and blackmail fit in to all of this? The libertarian law predicated on property rights states that the only crime shall be to violate them, whether through threat, fraud, or physical invasion, such as kidnapping or theft. Since neither the libeler nor blackmailer are guilty of any such uninvited border crossing, their activities should be legalized. We have already seen that blackmail, consisting of two separate legal "whites," cannot properly be construed as a legal "black." This is true even when the two separate activities are combined.

The private property rights basis of libel and slander legalization is equally straightforward. The typical complaint is that libel is akin to stealing, but instead of the theft of a jacket or a wallet, it concerns a man's reputation. But a momentary reflection will show that this is not so. A reputation cannot be owned by the person to whom it refers since it consists of the thoughts of other people,[46] and a man cannot own other people's thoughts. For example, I hereby libel John Smith by saying, "John Smith is a dodo bird." The argument for preventing me from this act is that, on the basis of my saying so,[47] people

---

[41] See New York Times v. Sullivan, 376 U.S. 254 (1964).

[42] Hardin, supra note 2, at 1802.

[43] See, generally, HANS-HERMANN HOPPE, THE ECONOMICS AND ETHICS OF PRIVATE PROPERTY: STUDIES IN POLITICAL ECONOMY AND PHILOSOPHY (1993).

[44] See, generally, JOHN LOCKE, THE SECOND TREATISE OF CIVIL GOVERNMENT AND A LETTER CONCERNING TOLERATION; JOHN LOCKE, An Essay Concerning the True Origin. Extent and End of Civil Government in TWO TREATISES OF GOVERNMENT 27–28 (Peter Laslett ed., 1960).

[45] See, generally, ROBERT NOZICK, ANARCHY, STATE AND UTOPIA (1974) (calling trading products a legitimate property transfer).

[46] WALTER BLOCK, DEFENDING THE UNDEFENDABLE 59–62 (1991).

[47] Well, assume I am a New York Times editorial writer.

will now avoid Mr. Smith. For example, no one will employ him or befriend him.[48] But the reason for this sudden renunciation is my doing only in the first instance. Suppose people do not believe my allegation. Then, Smith's reputation will remain intact despite my best efforts to undermine it. The only way I can succeed in my nefarious doings is by convincing others that my claims about him are correct. But if I do succeed, the changes I will have wrought will be in terms of the thought patterns of my audience. Since each of us owns his own thinking or thought patterns, and this is precisely what forms Smith's (or anyone else's) reputation. Smith paradoxically cannot own even a part of his own reputation because no part of it consists of what Smith thinks of himself. If Smith cannot own his reputation, when I take it away from him I cannot have done anything akin to stealing his wallet.

This private property or libertarian theory of law is not that far removed from what Hardin calls "mutual advantage." Apart from self-ownership and the initial acquisition of virgin territory into the capitalist nexus, all further interaction is on the basis of voluntary, mutual agreement, based on some sort of advantage, whether monetary or psychic. When I buy a newspaper for $1, or work for an employer for $50,000 per year, both parties to such trades expect them to be of "mutual advantage." If they did not, they would hardly agree to take part in them.[49] Since laissez-faire capitalism, the only system under which both libel and blackmail would be legal, is just a name for the concatenation of all such events, one would expect Hardin to embrace this system. He does not. This suggests that he does not take seriously his advocacy of "mutual advantage," or at least that he is unwilling or unable to pursue this perspective to its logical conclusion.

V. BLACKMAIL FOR MUTUAL ADVANTAGE

Hardin characterizes as a "quick conclusion" that the principle of "mutual advantage... might seem to allow [for the legalization of] exchange blackmail because such blackmail is to the mutual advantage of the parties to it."[50] Why is this wrong? "Such blackmail would, ex ante, make people generally worse off even though it would, in a particular application, make the two parties to

---

[48] Since, as everyone knows, we are all in thrall to the New York Times.

[49] In addition to barter, trade and sales or rentals of human or physical capital for money, there is also gift-giving, inheritance, gambling, etc. These are all ways in which resources may legitimately be transferred from one person to another under this system.

[50] Hardin, *supra* note 2, at 1803.

it better off."[51] Here, he has in mind the effects on third parties, or negative externalities.[52] Even on the assumption that these are not operational, Hardin attempts to show, via his theoretic game model, that blackmail can still fail to be mutually advantageous.

And why is this? Hardin informs us that in Game II, which admits to payoffs by the newspaper as well as the blackmailee, "[i]f 4, 1 is the status quo ante, then movement to 2, 2 is not Pareto efficient, because that move reduces the welfare of the target."[53] It will be remembered that 4,1 means that the blackmailer suppresses the embarrassing information, while the target does not pay. Of course blackmail, i.e., movement to 2,2, worsens the situation of the target, under these assumptions, for under this so-called status quo ante the blackmailer has suppressed the information. This is exactly what the target wants, but the blackmailer has not yet been paid for this service of providing silence.

Game II: Blackmail with payment for publication[54]

	Target Doesn't Pay	Target Pays
Blackmailer gives info to press	3,3	1,4
Blackmailer suppresses info	4,1	2,2

(1 is the best outcome, 4 the worst; the first number in each cell applies to the row player, the blackmailer, and the second to the column or target player.)

Any trade could be made to look non-Pareto optimal on this basis. For example, consider the initial position where the grocer gives me a quart of milk, and I have not paid for it. Now, he demands that I pay for it as the price of keeping it. But when he does this he worsens my position compared to the scenario with which we opened this exercise. Therefore trade, all trade, is non-Pareto optimal.

---

[51] *Id.*

[52] *See* Sydney W. DeLong, *Blackmailers, Bribetakers, and the Second Paradox*, 141 U. PA. L. REV. 1663 (1993) (offering a more developed critique of legalization along these lines); *but see*, Lindgren, *supra* note 15.

[53] Hardin, *supra* note 2, at 1803.

[54] *See Id.* at 1799.

Hardin correctly sees that 4,1, the situation where the blackmailer keeps quiet, is untenable. "[T]he blackmailer is likely to release the information eventually,"[55] presumably if he is not paid. This anyone can see. But Hardin is to be congratulated for dismissing 1,4, the scenario where the blackmailee pays and yet is double-crossed by the blackmailer as well. This is unlikely because, when the blackmailer does this, he will garner a bad reputation. Why should anyone trust him and pay him off to keep quiet when he is a blabbermouth? Where Hardin goes astray, however, is that he does not realize that blackmail legalization strengthens this tendency. Under these conditions, if the blackmailer reneges he can also be subjected to a lawsuit as well as losing his reputation or "goodwill" capital.[56]

Next, Hardin launches into a spirited and very successful attack on Lindgren's defense of the outlawry of blackmail. This is based on the claim that the blackmailer uses information and threats, i.e., "chips," which properly belong to other people. Hardin likens the blackmailer to the agent or intermediary, who knows that A and B, unbeknownst to each other, would gain from a business association with one another. He says: "I can make a great profit for myself by getting them to deal through me as an intermediary, perhaps even while keeping A and B ignorant of each other... In Lindgren's vocabulary, I profit from the use of A's and B's chips."[57]

But this is a distinction without a difference. Hardin states:

> Unlike a threat of pure harm that does not directly benefit the person causing the harm, blackmail may be a genuine case of exchange. The blackmailer may have the prospect of a significant reward for revealing her information to the press. She merely offers to sell it to someone who values keeping the information private more than the press values its publication, and who therefore might pay more for it than the press would.[58]

In other words, Game I, blackmail with no payment for publication, should be illegal, but Game II, blackmail with payment for publication, should be decriminalized. Why should it matter so much, let alone at all, whether the blackmailer has an alternative audience for his wares? There is "mutual advantage" in either instance. Is it not enough that while we are in

---

[55] *Id.* at 1804.

[56] Although, to be fair to the other side of the argument, under prohibition the blackmailer faces a jail sentence.

[57] Hardin, *supra* note 2, at 1805.

[58] *Id.* at 1805.

Game I or II, there are in both cases two licit and mutually beneficial activities, the request for money and the offer of silence, which all concede are separately legal?[59] Certainly, the blackmailer will gain from releasing the information if not paid to refrain, whether or not there is a newspaper payment.[60] Why, if there were no benefit, would he do any such thing? Hardin tries to avoid this logical implication of all human action with the weasel word "directly" in the phrase "does not directly benefit."[61] What difference does it make whether the benefit is direct or not? Why should the law turn on such an irrelevancy?[62]

Although Hardin refuses to allow legalized blackmail for Game I, at least when it comes to Game II, he is nothing short of magnificent in his criticism of the so-called "economic" analysts of this subject:

> A newspaper that pays a reporter to dig up newsworthy material on someone likely does so in order to increase circulation and advertising revenue. One might object to what the newspaper produces but it would be silly to say it is unproductive. By analogy, a blackmailer is essentially a free agent who sells the same material to that newspaper, and so also is productive.[63]

This insight notwithstanding, Hardin advocates legalization, if even only under the following narrow circumstances: "if evidential or strategic considerations made it very difficult to identify exchange [e.g., Game II] blackmail and to exempt it from coverage."[64] In effect, Hardin is saying that rape and seduction are very different, but, if it is difficult to separate them, let us prohibit both. In my view, exchange and all other types of blackmail[65] are legally the same; therefore, this issue does not arise. But even if they were somehow

---

[59] For a description of Game I, *see Id.* at 1799.

[60] *See, generally,* LUDWIG VON MISES, HUMAN ACTION (1966)

[61] Hardin, *supra* note 2, at 1805. What Hardin means is that the balked blackmailer will not financially gain from broadcasting his targets secrets in the event of nonpayment. But why should this be the *sine qua non* of the law on blackmail?

[62] *See, e.g.,* Ronald H. Coase, *The 1987 McCorkle Lecture: Blackmail,* 74 VA. L. REV. 655 (1988); Douglas H. Ginsburg and Paul Shechtman, *Blackmail: An Economic Analysis of the Law,* 141 U. PA. L. REV. 1849, 1849–75 (1993); RICHARD A. POSNER, ECONOMIC ANALYSIS OF LAW (4th ed. 1992): William M. Landes & Richard A. Posner, *The Private Enforcement of Law,* 4 J. LEGAL STUD. 1, 43 (1915).

[63] Hardin, *supra* note 2, at 1806.

[64] *Id.*

[65] But not extortion, the threat of something that is a (property) rights violation.

different, the burden of proof is always on the plaintiff. Thus, it is incompatible with libertarianism to ban acts which are not invasive, even if they are difficult to distinguish from ones which are.

Every once in a while, Hardin sounds just like a libertarian on the blackmail issue. Consider the following:

> Suppose I know how you succeed so remarkably at marketing some product, and suppose I can give this legally unprotected knowledge to a competitive firm. I make an offer to you that sound like blackmail. You put me on a generous retainer as an "advisor" and give me attractive stock options in your firm, and I keep my knowledge secret. If your competitor adopts your technique, you are immediately to fire me as advisor and, without action at all on your part, my stock options become far less attractive as your firm loses market share. In this trade-secret case, we might think there is nothing wrong with my actions. I have the legal right to go to your competitor and to negotiate favorable terms with her. All I do is give you a chance to salvage your interests by matching or topping the likely price your competitor would pay.[66]

Magnificent! A trenchant defense for the legalization of blackmail! The only problem is that this insightful piece of analysis is logically incompatible with Hardin's "mutual advantage theory." To reprise his views of only a few pages ago, Hardin is on record as maintaining that blackmail, which consists of "a threat of pure harm that does not directly benefit the person causing the harm," should not be legalized.[67] But is this not true of the trade secret holder? Surely it is. He derives no direct benefit from making the competitor aware of the marketing skills of the target firm. The only benefit he obtains is money, filthy lucre, to remain silent.

I admire Hardin's insights in the trade secret case. They furnish a powerful argument for legalization. But to show that he really means it, Hardin would have to renounce the philosophy, which he mistakenly thinks undergirds this point. For that is not one which unreservedly advocates the lawfulness of blackmail of any type or variety.

Hardin's comments about murder and dueling also present difficulties. He thinks that because at one time "killing in a duel" was not considered murder, but at present it is, the law against unjust homicide "requires a rela-

---

[66] Hardin, *supra* note 2, at 1807–08.

[67] *Id.* at 1805.

tively detailed moral theory or principle."[68] I maintain that nothing of the sort is true. Rather, this is an example of legal positivism[69] run amuck: whatever the legislators say at any given time is proper law, and if they contradict themselves over time or even reverse fields once again, all that is left for the scholar is the sociological explanation of "how a particular law came to be what it is." My claim to the contrary is that there is such a thing as just law that it is based on unchanging property rights, and sometimes legislators act in accordance with it and sometimes they do not.

Dueling is certainly a case in point. Under libertarianism, if two parties agree to fight each other, for whatever reason, the loser cannot claim to be the victim of violence. When the loser cannot claim this, then the winner cannot be considered guilty of murder if the battle ends in death, or of assault and battery if it ends with some lesser injury. If those who would prohibit dueling were logically consistent, they would also have to ban boxing, martial arts, football, rugby, soccer, handball, and even baseball.

Take boxing, for example, as the closest analogy to a duel with swords or guns. Boxers A and B voluntarily enter the ring. The latter leaves on his shield, headed for the morgue. What is the difference between this and the old-fashioned duel to the death with pistol or blade? It is only in the purpose for which the skirmish is organized. In a previous century it was honor, now it is money. Surely, this does not constitute a relevant difference for the law of murder. Or take any other athletic interaction where injury or even death occurs. What is the defense of the "killer" in any of these cases? Surely, it is that

---

[68] *Id.* at 1808.

[69] Yes, "conceptions of the right and the good change over time." *Id.* at 1808. But, contrary to Hardin, the right and the good themselves are immutably based on the libertarian axiom of non-aggression.

the deceased entered the fray knowingly and willingly.[70] But no less can be said on behalf of the victorious side in a duel.[71]

VI. BLACKMAIL IN THE PUBLIC INTEREST

Hardin offers yet another sterling defense of blackmail legalization: the Justice Department's blackmail of then-Vice-President Agnew. They would not prosecute him for taking bribes from contractors when he was governor of Maryland, if he resigned his present office. (The Department feared he would have become President had Nixon been impeached.) Hardin states, "[o]ne might conclude that it was blackmail but nevertheless a morally correct action."[72] But why the "nevertheless?" Why can it not be blackmail and "morally correct?" For Hardin, it cannot be because, despite his frequent defenses of blackmail legalization, at bottom he has bought into the notion that there is something intrinsically noxious about such contracts.

This is no mere slip of the pen for Hardin, for he indicates the same sentiment a second time. He says of the Agnew deal, "[w]as it blackmail? Were the prosecutors not simply acting in the public interest ... ?"[73] Why can it not be both blackmail and an act in the public interest? Presumably it cannot be if blackmail is intrinsically illegal. But we have been furnished with no reasons in defense of this supposition.

Hardin then uses the Sol Wachtler's case to the same end. Wachtler was the Chief Judge of the New York State Court of Appeals and "was involved in

---

[70] Or, in the cases of children who die or are injured in sports, with their parent's permission.

[71] If the king or emperor had wanted to eliminate dueling, he could have done so not by prohibitive legislation, but in a manner compatible with libertarianism. All he need have done was set an example announcing that he would not fight in any duel and that the institution had "burdened the aristocratic class." Hardin, *supra* note 2, at 1808. One objection is that, had he done so, his own position would have been rendered precarious. But this cannot be counted as an argument against the libertarian position, for the passage of this legislation would have had the same effect. Alternatively, he could have expressed it as his opinion that one of the practices of dueling should be broadened. In the good old days, the person who was challenged could choose the weapons, but this was traditionally limited to gun or cutlass. All that need be done was extend this, a bit, to allow whichever weapon the challenged person wished: chess, tiddly winks, jacks, charades, poetry reading, whatever. Since there is bound to be something in which the defense excels over the offense there would be precious few dueling challenges laid down under such a system.

[72] Hardin, *supra* note 2, at 1810.

[73] *Id.*

an ugly attempt at blackmail coupled with threats of kidnapping"[74] The U.S. Attorney's Office threatened to bring suit against him unless he resigned his post.[75] Hardin states, "[p]erhaps there was pleasing irony in the potential use of blackmail to punish a blackmailer."[76] But there are two problems here. First, this again illustrates that Hardin sees intrinsic lawlessness in blackmail. Second, our author fails to distinguish blackmail and extortion. If Wachtler threatened kidnapping, he removed himself from the realm of the former and entered that of the latter. No one has a right to kidnap anyone else. To threaten what one has no right to do must therefore be a crime. In contrast, one has a right to prosecute a judge for wrongdoing. What the U.S. Attorney did then, in sharp contrast, was to commit blackmail, not extortion.

VII. CAVEATS AND OTHER MORALITIES

In this section Hardin compounds his inability or refusal to distinguish between blackmail and extortion with a misplaced reliance on the property rights analysis of Coase.[77] Hardin uses the example of a person "aim[ing] missiles with high explosives at [his] neighbor's home" and goes so far as to characterize this as an attempt "to extort more from our joint production than merely the maximal amount of profits."[78] Thus, Hardin accurately describes extortion; he even calls it extortion. Yet he adamantly refuses to distinguish this from blackmail.

As for Coase, this is neither the time nor the place for a full-scale investigation of his denigration of property rights. Suffice it to say, for Coase there really is no such thing as property rights, at least not as they are commonly understood. In the world-view of this University of Chicago economist, things are not owned by right or on the basis of past legitimate acquisition, e.g., on the basis of homesteading, trade, or purchase. On the contrary, things are owned by A vis-a-vis B, and only on the most temporary of bases, because a judge would theoretically rule that A's use of the resources were and would be more valuable than B's. When and if the judge comes to believe that B, not A, places a higher value on it, the property would then be taken away from A

---

[74] *Id.* at 1811.

[75] *See Id.*

[76] *Id.*

[77] Ronald Coase, *The Problem of Social Cost*, 3 J. L. & ECON. 1 (1960); *The 1987 McCorkle Lecture: Blackmail, supra* note 62, at 655–76.

[78] Hardin, *supra* note 2, at 1811.

and placed in the hands of B. In other words, nobody's life or property is secure when the Coasean judge is presiding.[79]

Hardin's read on Coase is the exact opposite of the truth. Hardin maintains that, "the Coasean system has broken down" when the "missiles with high explosives [are aimed] at [his] neighbor's home ... since we are no longer in a world of consensual exchange and production."[80] But the Coasean world is not one of "consensual exchange and production." The very reverse is the case. The Coasean world is like the law of the jungle. Anyone can seize the property of another person at any time, as long as he can convince a judge that he values it more than the present owner. It is simply not true that "[a]n actor threatening a harm who derives no direct benefit from its imposition subverts social cost analysis because the Coasean framework is grounded in voluntarist assumptions."[81] This is the very opposite of the truth. As is the claim "[Coase's] whole analysis of the problem of social cost takes place, after all, in the context of a given set of rights assignments that are presumably backed by adequate state power to secure them."[82] For Coase, power is to be unleashed to undermine extant property rights.

If Hardin on Coase is faulty, the same applies to his analysis of the nuclear threat. Again, Hardin correctly identifies this as "violent extortion," but in the very next sentence characterizes this as "nuclear blackmail."[83] Whatever it is called, the same nomenclature should be applied to mutual assured destruction (MAD), notwithstanding Hardin. He refuses to do so on the ground that MAD had "good" effects, but so can real extortion, like outright robbery. For example, Jean Valjean in Les Miserables stole a loaf of bread in order to feed his family.[84] In the movie *Dr. Strangelove*, the hero had to shoot a non-threatening Coca-Cola machine in order to get change to make a phone call so he could avert a nuclear war.[85] Surely, for the utilitarian; or "mutual advan-

---

[79] As we have seen, a mans life is "merely" his most important piece of property rights. The same analysis critical of Coase applies whether we are discussing an inanimate object over which A and B are contending or the very lives of one of them.

[80] Hardin, *supra* note 2, at 1811–12.

[81] *Id.*

[82] *Id.*

[83] *Id.* at 1813. This has nothing to do with the lack of an "overarching international government," however. Probably, there will come the day when "private" gangsters issue nuclear threats; this is already a staple of adventure movies. Can reality be far behind?

[84] *See* VICTOR HUGO, LES MISERABLES 126 (1907).

[85] *See* "Dr. Strangelove: How I Learned to Stop Worrying and Love the Bomb" (Hawk Films 1964).

tage" philosopher such as Hardin, "good" ends can sometimes be achieved through "bad" means.

Next, Hardin resorts to economically impermissible, interpersonal comparisons of utility to account for the law against reckless endangerment.[86] He does so explicitly on the basis of his "mutual advantage argument."[87] But there are no measurements of happiness ("utils"). Even if there were, there is still no way to compare the happiness of different people. If somehow this could be accomplished, we would then open ourselves up to the depredations of the "utility monster." For example, his appetite for human flesh would render laws against murder obsolete. Alternatively, we would thereby unleash a new Coasean defense against the charge of rape: "I was so desperate, so needy, and she had such low self-esteem, that my pleasure in forcing her was greater than her disutility in my attack."

In the view of Hardin: "The only general argument against blackmail that can fit mutual advantage arguments must be in an institutional or *ex ante* form: *ex ante* each would prefer that blackmail be illegal because each would expect to be better off as a result."[88] Again, I part company with Hardin by 180 degrees. Both the potential blackmailer and blackmailee would prefer that blackmail be legal "because each would expect to be better off as a result."[89] Nor, as Hardin claims, is this an empirical issue. It is apodictically clear that all blackmail contracts are mutually advantageous, at least in the *ex ante* sense. Otherwise, blackmailers and targets would never agree to them in the first place. The expected advantage to all potential targets, which cannot possibly be overemphasized, is that they would prefer to pay the money rather than see their secret exposed. If this were not so, they would say to the blackmailer "[p]ublish and be damned."[90]

Hardin is quite correct in asserting, "[w]hen Joy Silverman[91] went to the F.B.I. about the blackmail threats she had received, she risked public exposure roughly equivalent to what the blackmailer threatened."[92] But with legalized

---

[86] *See, generally,* Murray N. Rothbard, *Toward a Reconstruction of Utility and Welfare Economics,* 20 San Francisco Center for Libertarian Studies, Occasional Paper #3 (1977).; LIONEL ROBBINS, AN ESSAY ON THE NATURE AND SIGNIFICANCE OF ECONOMIC SCIENCE (2nd ed. 1935).

[87] Hardin, *supra* note 2, at 1814.

[88] *Id.* at 1814.

[89] *Id.*

[90] Richard Posner, *Blackmail, Privacy and Freedom of Contract* 141 PA. L. REV. 1817, 1839 fn. 43 (1993).

[91] The woman being blackmailed by Sol Wachtler.

[92] Hardin, *supra* note 2, at 1814.

blackmail, she, as the target, would still have a hold over him, the blackmailer. If she paid and he reneged, he would be guilty of contract violation. If the secret were valuable to her (and why else would she have paid blackmail?) then the damages for this contract violation would be severe. In contrast, when blackmail is illegal she still has a hold over her blackmailer because he is in violation of the law. The point is, her situation is not worsened by legalization.

VIII. CONCLUSION

Hardin's use of "mutual advantage morality,"[93] the basis of his analysis of blackmail, has resulted in no clear implication for legalization. Based on this doctrine, not all types of blackmail should remain outlawed. This is an unsatisfactory result given that there has been no clear moral difference adumbrated between "mutual advantage blackmail" and any other kind.

---

[93] *Id.* at 1815.

Chapter 8.
Blackmail, Extortion and Exchange: Rejoinder to Posner

I. INTRODUCTION

Blackmail sounds menacing and nefarious, an activity at its heart a criminal enterprise. Indeed, in most modern countries and jurisdictions blackmail is in fact a crime, alongside murder, theft, and rape. However, this grouping of the (admittedly) illegal act of blackmail with crimes like murder is misleading on one score: blackmail *per se* is a voluntary act between consenting adults.

The leading authority in the law and economics literature on the problem of blackmail is Richard Posner.[1] He argues that the prohibition of this practice can be justified on grounds of economic efficiency. Thus, he regards blackmail as an exception to the rule that free market exchange maximizes wealth.

Posner defines blackmail as "the attempt to trade silence for money."[2] But a more accurate definition would be "*willingness* to trade money for silence." What is the difference between the two versions? In Posner's formulation, the blackmailer must initiate the deal. According to the alternative definition, the first offer can come from either of the two parties to the bargain.

This difference is subtle but nonetheless highly significant. For example, suppose that A, the adulterer, approaches B, the blackmailer, and offers him money if he, B, will not tell anyone about this secret. Posner, strictly speaking, could not even call this blackmail. Based on the second version, we would have no problem doing so.[3] It is precisely the same trade of money for silence, no matter who initiates it.

Another critical definitional issue concerns the distinction between *extortion* and blackmail. Blackmail can only be an offer, not a threat, while extortion can be only the latter. Further, extortion is the threat to do something which *should* be illegal (murder, rape, pillage), while in blackmail the offer is to commit a paradigm case of a lawful act (i.e., engage in free speech: gossip about secrets which embarrass or humiliate other people). For example, since it would be legal to reveal a secret about adultery, it should also be lawful to offer to do just that, or to accept money, when offered, in exchange for not making such a revelation. In contrast, since it is *properly* illegal to murder or rape, it should also be a criminal act to threaten such acts.

---

[1] Richard Posner, *Blackmail, Privacy and Freedom of Contract*, 141 U. PA. L. REV. 1817 (1993).
[2] *Id.* at 1817 fn. 1.
[3] Leo Katz, *Blackmail and Other Forms of Arm-Twisting*, U. PA. L. REV. 1567 (1993)

Posner argues that "blackmail is, and should be, forbidden" because "it is likely to be, on average, wealth reducing rather than wealth maximizing."[4] But if blackmail is voluntary, as Posner admits,[5] then it *must* (*ex ante*) be wealth enhancing, since each party would only agree to the contract if he receives something more valuable to him than what he gives up. That is to say, the blackmailer values the money he receives for his silence more than the disutility he receives from not being able to broadcast the secret; the blackmailee values the preservation of his secret more than what it costs him. How, possibly, could wealth *not* increase from such a contract (as it does from *all* voluntary agreements)? Our purpose here is to carefully critique Posner's model of blackmail from this perspective.

The present paper is divided into five sections. Section II closely examines the differences between blackmail and extortion, and argues that the former may (under some circumstances) represent an entirely voluntary transaction. Section III subjects Posner's elaborate taxonomy of different types of *blackmail* to close scrutiny and shows that after coercive elements are clearly distinguished, what remains is an ordinary market trade of a service for money. Section IV examines various difficult cases in which non-coercive *blackmail* may become intermingled, and subsequently confused with, theft and fraud. Finally, Section V summarizes and concludes the argument.

II. BLACKMAIL AND EXTORTION COMPARED AND CONTRASTED

Blackmail is often treated as a kind of intermediate case, partly voluntary but partly coercive. Posner shares this view. Consider the following statement by Posner about

> contracts made under duress, a class of contracts with which blackmail is often grouped. If an assailant points a gun at you, saying, 'Your money or your life,' you will doubtless be very eager to accept the first branch of this offer by tendering your money. There are third-party effects, but the essential objection to the transaction is that the victim would prefer a regime in which such transactions were outlawed, because it would reduce the probability of his receiving such unwanted offers (a qualification is discussed later). In

---

[4] Posner, *supra* note 1, at 1817.
[5] *Id.* at 1818.

this case a restriction on freedom of contract protects a contracting party ex ante.[6]

But this particular threat would represent an instance of *extortion*, not *blackmail*. Such an "offer" would not constitute a voluntary contract. The phrase "or your life" clearly implies the robber's intent to kill you, should you not submit to his threats. But from whence does his right to perpetrate such a foul deed spring? Such a right does not exist, since we have no right to murder other people. Contrast this with a different offer: "Your money or I go public with your secret adultery." If this offer is accepted, the result is a *contract*, not an instance of robbery or extortion. The U.S. Constitution guarantees free speech rights. If there is a right to speak, it logically follows that there is a right to *discuss speaking*, e.g., to talk about the forthcoming speech, warn of it, or reveal one's willingness to refrain from so doing, perhaps even for a fee.

This, however, is not the perspective adopted by Posner. Instead, he mentions "[s]imilarly, people desperately eager to pay blackmail would prefer not to be blackmailed and would therefore prefer a regime in which blackmail is forbidden."[7] In other words, in his view, blackmail is akin to extortion. But just because some people prefer not to have X, doesn't mean X is criminal. People prefer not to get fat, lose customers, lose a mate to a competitor, get beaten in sports, or experience unrequited love. This does not imply it is appropriate public policy to outlaw all of these things.

Posner clearly finds *blackmail* confusing. Indeed, he repeatedly contradicts his earlier assertion that the practice is not voluntary. Although at one point he proclaims "it is a voluntary transaction between consenting adults," only one paragraph later he returns to his original theme: "Another way of bringing out the commonality between duress and blackmail is to note that both involve threats."[8] But this observation is highly misleading. *Every* voluntary interaction can be couched in the form of a threat: "If you don't give me that newspaper," says the buyer, "I won't give you this 50 cents." The vendor replies: "Oh, yeah? If you don't give me that 50 cents, I will not give you this newspaper." What is this but a rather convoluted way of saying, "Hey, let's trade the paper for the four bits."

When I threaten that unless you pay me I won't give you this newspaper, what else am I doing but attempting to transfer wealth from you to me? To be sure, I will give you something in return for your money, but still, at least from my own point of view, I will register a wealth improvement, since I prefer the money to the daily paper.

All we have said about the newspaper sale "threat" applies also to blackmail (as distinct from extortion). This is because in both the newspaper and blackmail case, what is threatened is *per se* legal. In contrast, I may not properly turn off your TV (nor, therefore, threaten to do so) since it is your property, and for me to take this extortionate action would be a criminal act.

Posner dismisses this distinction between coercive and non-coercive threats on the ground that all threats constitute a sterile redistribution activity, like (simple) theft.[9] Even conceding for the sake of argument that the blackmail threat "diminishes social wealth by the sum of the resources employed by the threatener to make his threat credible and of the victim to resist the threat,"[10] should that render it fit for legal prohibition? There are lots of idle, time wasting, "sterile" activities which presumably no one would wish to make into a criminal offense: watching soap operas, reading poetry, listening to non-baroque music, gardening, and camping.

Or consider voluntary charity, birthday gifts, and other forms of altruism. Here, too, resources are used by the donor (to set up criteria for gifts, to find the recipient) as well as the recipient (to adopt the behavior set for him in the criteria, to make an application). Surely, if threats are a drain on society, then charity also "diminishes social wealth." But neither allegation is true. On the contrary, both the donor and the recipient voluntarily take on these costs. Consequently, then, this behavior is *not* a drain on society, since neither would do so did he not expect to be more than compensated for his initial investment. That is, the philanthropist expects more pleasure from his donation than the attendant costs, and the recipient expects a greater transfer of money than the costs of obtaining it, complying with the applicable conditions, etc.

The same argument applies in blackmail cases, but *not* with extortion. In the latter, there is no voluntary exchange. The extortionist might well gain, but the victim's rights are violated, in that he must give up something to which he was legally entitled. When someone extorts you with the statement "your money or your life!" and you give up the former, you are wronged since you own both. In sharp contrast, when someone threatens "Give me money or I reveal your secret," you are *not* wronged since you do *not* have title to both, any more than you may fairly claim both the money and the newspaper in the previous example.

---

9 *Id.* at 1820
10 *Id.*

III. POSNER'S TAXONOMY OF BLACKMAIL DISSECTED

Posner carefully delineates seven different circumstantial categories across which the term blackmail applies. He proceeds to argue that legal prohibition is efficient across these various categories. We now turn to a detailed examination of this taxonomy.

1. Criminal acts for which the blackmailer's victim has been duly punished.[11]

Which agency is more likely to maximize wealth or optimally allocate resources to the punishment of criminals—the market or the political system? If, in your opinion, it is the latter, then you will favor disallowing the blackmail of, for example, ex-convicts (a form of private punishment). You will be content to substitute the wisdom of politicians in "a legislature mulling over the question whether to forbid blackmail"[12] as to whether this should be allowed to occur or not.

Consider how Posner handles the case of the employer who refuses to hire a person with a criminal record, vis-à-vis the blackmailer. He states:

> The difference is that the employer benefits from imposing this additional sanction; presumably it is a cost-minimizing policy. A blackmail transaction does not confer an equivalent social benefit, once its deterrent effect is discounted because of concern with over deterrence. It merely transfers wealth to the blackmailer.[13]

But blackmail does not "merely" transfer wealth to the blackmailer; it *also* provides a service for the blackmailee, namely silence. Thus the two cases are on a par, as holds true for all commercial activity; it benefits *all* traders. Posner attempts to deny this on the ground that just because information garnered by blackmailers increases, it will not necessarily be more widely disseminated: "the information gathered by the blackmailer may be suppressed."[14] Yes, it will (likely) be disseminated if the blackmail contract is not consummated, and suppressed if it is. But wealth will increase *either* way.

In the former case, Posner concedes as much.[15] But in the latter, he complains, the stock of *suppressed* information will increase. But what is wrong

---

[11] *Id.* at 1821
[12] *Id.* at 1822
[13] *Id.*
[14] *Id.*
[15] *Id.*

with attaining knowledge for its own sake, without spreading it around? Every scholar who does research but does not publish is guilty of that which Posner charges the blackmailer. Are we to jail all of those who learn simply for their own pleasure without sharing it with others? Nor can we even claim that quiet study and deliberation, without "dissemination" is contrary to wealth creation. From the fact that a man chooses to spend his time in this way, whether in the library, the laboratory, or as a blackmailer, we are entitled to deduce that this was a productive use of his time, of greater value to him than his opportunity costs.

Posner claims it will be "rare"[16] that information unearthed by the blackmailer will be publicized: "often the benefits of the information will be highly diffuse, being spread across a variety of actual and potential transactors with the blackmail victim, some of whom may not even be identifiable."[17] He gives as an example blackmailing a person with AIDS who deceives his sex partners about his condition. But there are all sorts of ways to internalize such externalities. One could publish this information in a free society; potential customers include all those contemplating sexual relations with *anyone*.

2. Criminal acts that were not detected, hence not punished.

The gist of Posner's critique is that government protection will tend to "optimize law enforcement,"[18] and that the activities of private police, such as blackmail, will move us away from this optimal point and hence reduce wealth.

Posner relies on a model of crime and punishment which is itself flawed. Here, "within some range, increasing the fine for an illegal activity by another dollar is essentially costless and enables a reduction in the resources devoted to catching and prosecuting offenders (and hence the costs incurred in these activities) without any impairment of deterrence."[19] But why should this essentially unjust, lawless approach be accepted as the basis for optimization? It is unjust because, in principle, it allows for *any* punishment for *any* crime, and judges the results solely on the basis of "cost minimization." If the death penalty would stop petty theft most efficiently, then, suggests this view, it should be imposed—unasked is the question of whether someone who steals bubble gum *deserves* to be executed.

Another flaw is that this is essentially a central planning model of law enforcement. The police are assumed to be governmental. When Posner states

---

[16] *Id.* at 1820.
[17] *Id.* at 1822–23.
[18] *Id.* at 1823.
[19] *Id.* at 1823–24.

"Private enforcers, however, may treat an increase in the fine as an induce-ment to invest more resources in enforcement rather than, as intended, as a signal to invest fewer resources,"[20] he sees the "private enforcers," i.e., the blackmailers, as interlopers, interfering with the privileged intentions of the monopoly state police. Contrary to Posner, if a private policeman, who must withstand the market test of profit and loss, [something avoided by his public sector counterpart][21] decides to invest more resources in enforcement, then this is prima facie proof that such expenditures are *efficient*, not the reverse.

Posner's critique of private enterprise police continues:

> Private enforcement can be disruptive in another way as well. Sup-pose police obtain valuable information by paying informers. The price they pay will be lower if blackmail is forbidden, since compe-tition between police and blackmailers for information concerning guilt would drive up the price of the information. [22]

On this ground, *all* private enterprise should be forbidden, if it is in any way in competition with the state. If the government owns a steel mill, for instance, then private producers bid up the price of factors, such as labor, coal, and iron, against it. Government—horrors!—would then have to pay more! Happily, Posner pulls back from this precipice with the concession that "private enforcers might have so much lower costs of operation than public enforcers as to make private enforcement more efficient on balance than pub-lic enforcement."[23]

Unfortunately, he does not place the burden of proof on the public sphere; for Posner,[24] it is the *private* sector which must prove its usefulness. He states this in the context of his mirror image problem: "we wanted to re-duce rather than increase the severity of criminal punishments and, corre-spondingly, increase rather than reduce the investment of resources in catch-ing criminals."[25] (The "we" here clearly refers to government.) "But this is an-other reason not to rely on blackmailers, viewed as private law enforcers (which in a functional sense they are), as part of our criminal law enforce-ment system."[26] If Posner placed the burden the other way around (that is, correctly), he would have instead said that "this is another reason not to rely

---

[20] *Id.* at 1824.
[21] See on this Patrick Tinsley, *Private Police: A Note*, 14 J. LIBERTARIAN STUD., 95–100 (1998); MURRAY N. ROTHBARD, FOR A NEW LIBERTY, ch. 11 (1973).
[22] Posner, *supra* note 1, at 1824.
[23] *Id.* at 1825.
[24] Strange, in a supposed friend of free enterprise.
[25] Posner, *supra* note 1, at 1824.
[26] *Id.* at 1825.

on [*government justice*], viewed as [*public*] law enforcers, as part of our (*private*) law enforcement system."

3. Acts that are wrongful but not criminal, such as acts that the common law classifies as torts.

Posner objects to blackmail in this case on the ground that "the law has given the exclusive right of enforcement to the victim (which) would be undermined by allowing a third party to blackmail the injurer-defendant. Blackmail would deplete the wrongdoer's resources and thus make it more difficult for the victim of the wrong to enforce his right to damages."[27] One problem with this answer is that it is an instance of legal positivism. The law says X, therefore X is correct. Go tell that to the victims of Nazism or Communism, many of whom were unjustly but *legally* punished. The law may have given the exclusive right to obtain money from the tortfeasor to the victim, but that arrangement may not be *just*. If no one has a right to obtain money from a tort violator, then anyone who sells him anything , e.g. a meal, can be found guilty of a crime, and, presumably, punished to the same extent as the blackmailer. This is because what the blackmailer is guilty of in this instance, according to Posner, is not blackmail itself, but rather "depleting the wrong doer's resources." The same result occurs when the restaurant sells a meal to the criminal and charges him a price.

It is true that the criminal has less money after the blackmailer or restaurateur is through with him. But this simple observation is misleading. *Both* of these things—being blackmailed and buying food—are consensual acts. As such, they *increase* wealth. This is obvious in the case of the meal: If the criminal didn't purchase it, he would be worse off. Perhaps he would even die. Then, surely, this purchase would not "deplete the wrong doer's (total, real) resources." Presumably "the victim of the wrong" could obtain more compensation from a live criminal than a dead one. However, the identical analysis applies to blackmail. This act, too, increases the criminal's total resources, even though his stock of money declines.

4. Acts, whether civilly or criminally wrongful, of which the blackmailer (or his principal) was the victim.

Posner claims "no one seems to object to a person's collecting information about his or her spouse's adulterous activities, and threatening to disclose that information in a divorce proceeding or other forum, in order to extract

---

[27] *Id.* at 1827.

maximum compensation for the offending spouse's breach of the marital obligations."[28]

Posner's inconsistency here is particularly glaring, since there is no difference in principle between this and any other instance of blackmail. In all such cases, this one specifically included, there is a "threat" to do something completely licit, unless one is paid to refrain. Why does the spouse who "threatens to disclose that information in a divorce proceeding or other forum, in order to extract maximum compensation" not fit that bill? Blackmail is blackmail is blackmail. Why should "a threat *merely* to litigate a civil suit" (emphasis added), or "confidentiality clauses" which are paid for, not be considered blackmail?

5. Disreputable, immoral, or otherwise censurable acts that do not, however, violate any law, or at least any commonly enforced law.

Consider this statement from Landes and Posner cited herein:

> The social decision not to regulate a particular activity is a judgement that the expenditure of resources on trying to discover and punish it would be socially wasted. That judgement is undermined if blackmailers are encouraged to expend substantial resources on attempting to apprehend and punish people engaged in the activity.[29]

This suggests a remarkable confidence in our political institutions, one seemingly not shaken even by the entire edifice of the Public Choice school.

Second, just because something is legal does not mean it is "encouraged." Eating lima beans is, at least so far, a protected activity. But the state does not thereby *encourage* this practice, it only *allows* it. We reject the notion that which is not prohibited is somehow *subsidized*.

Posner explains his reasoning in the course of discussing the hypothetical example of a secret, non-practicing homosexual. He writes:

> [A]ssume that the blackmailer's victim is a homosexual and confided this to a friend but refrains from homosexual acts, and in fact is married. The friend threatens to tell the victim's wife about his homosexuality unless the victim will pay him to keep silent. This is

---

[28] *Id.* at 1828.
[29] *Id.* at 1829 (quoting William Landes and Richard A. Posner, *The Private Enforcement of Law,* 4 J. LEGAL STUD. 1 (1975)).

a classic blackmail threat, yet it is difficult to see what the benefits would be of allowing it to be made.[30]

First, the notion that unless "benefits" can be shown, an act should be prohibited, is a dubious proposition. Secondly, the act of blackmail will encourage the blackmailee to pick his "friends" more carefully. Third, there is the usual "benefit" in the case of blackmail: the homosexual values the silence of his "friend" more than the money he must part with. The difference between these two is a *net gain*; it must be positive, or he would not have agreed to pay.

Posner replies by listing three costs:

> One would be to raise the cost of having a homosexual preference—of being a homosexual. Another would be to increase the resources expended on discovering homosexual preference and on negotiating contracts to prevent the discovery from being revealed. A third would be to increase the resources devoted to concealing homosexuality and to other defensive measures against the threat of blackmail.[31]

But why is it unjust to raise the costs of being gay—higher, that is, than they would have been had injustice been perpetrated on blackmailers? The point is, the only way to lower costs for homosexuals in this way is to raise them for blackmailers. Why is the former group more deserving than the latter?

In any case, gays are hardly the only non-typical group which pays extra costs. Adults above 6'5" and below 4'11" are forced to pay extra costs for clothing: ditto for those too fat or thin to wear off-the-rack products. The sick pay extra for medicine, as do those born without limbs or kidneys. More is paid for food by those who have a penchant for caviar instead of burgers. Diamonds cost more than costume jewelry. Is that fair? Would not wealth increase if these things were cheaper? Should the government subsidize all of these things to this end, the implication of Posner's analysis, in order to maximize wealth?

Admittedly, legalizing blackmail might increase resources devoted to defining sexual preference, but if all such investments are made voluntarily, the presumption must be that the benefits will outweigh these costs and that profit will be earned, at least *ex ante*.

---

[30] *Id.* at 1830.
[31] *Id.* at 1830–31.

Posner claims that "homosexuality is an involuntary and unalterable condition."[32] On this basis, he argues that legalizing blackmail would bring "about a pure redistribution of wealth from the homosexual to the blackmailer."[33] But why should this occurrence, if true, be rejected? Why should we believe that the allocation of wealth between the blackmail and homosexual communities is ideal under prohibition of the former? Why not of the latter? Since *neither per se* commits an invasion of person or property, *both* should be allowed by law—and let wealth distribution between them fall where it may.

And why is "entrapping"[34] people so wrong that it should be prohibited by law? For the libertarian, the test is "does an act *per se* involve the use of initiatory violence?" Although pimping, prostitution, alcohol, gambling, pornography[35] and entrapment sometimes do just that, they need not do so, and therefore, should be legal. Posner cites *State v. Harrington* etc., "Where the defendant, a lawyer, procured a woman to entice his client's husband to commit adultery with her, and then threatened to expose the husband's adultery in order to obtain better divorce terms for the wife."[36] No coercion was practiced by either party in this example. However, "entrapment" of a sort (morally but not economically distinguishable from this scenario) occurs in everyday commercial and social life. What are lipstick, perfume and stockings but an attempt to "entrap" a man, perhaps eventually into marriage? What are bargains, cut rate prices, specials and other such arrows in the quiver of a retailer but attempts to "entrap" purchasers into buying things they otherwise might have gone without? All advertising, whether or not it is of the beautiful blond sitting on the hood of a car variety, is an attempt to "entrap" people into opening their wallets.[37]

Posner finally declares that "blackmail really is the economic equivalent of theft," and observes that "the blackmailer is unlikely to pay tax on his blackmail income."[38] Certainly, when blackmail is illegal, the blackmailer is no more likely to pay taxes than distillers were when whisky was illegal. But now that booze is legal, firms in this industry pay taxes. Why should it be any dif-

---

[32] *Id.* at 1831.
[33] *Id.*
[34] *Id.* at 1832.
[35] WALTER BLOCK, DEFENDING THE UNDEFENDABLE (1976).
[36] Posner, *supra* note 1, at 1832 fn. 33.
[37] For a critique of advertising which is consistent with Posner's views on entrapment, *see* JOHN KENNETH GALBRAITH, THE AFFLUENT SOCIETY, (1958); for a definitive rejoinder *see* Friedrich A. Hayek, *The Non Sequitur of the 'Dependence Effect,'* in STUDIES IN PHILOSOPHY, POLITICS AND ECONOMICS (1967); ISRAEL M. KIRZNER, COMPETITION AND ENTREPRENEURSHIP (1973).
[38] Posner, *supra* note 1, at 1834.

ferent for the blackmailer? But, for the sake of argument, suppose it is. Assume, that is, that the blackmailer, under legalization, still refuses to pay taxes. In other words, he keeps his own money, protecting it from the predation of the state, which attempts to steal it from him. The only way this could amount to theft is if refusing to turn over (a portion of) your own hard earned money to the government is considered stealing.

Consider Posner's treatment of gossip, which he describes as "an informal and very cheap system of deterring the lesser forms of wrongdoing."[39] He goes so far as to complain that gossip's "efficacy would be undermined by blackmail because the gossip would sell his information to the blackmailer and thence to the wrongdoer and thereafter his lips would be sealed."[40] This is particularly difficult to understand in view of the fact that Posner continually takes the side of the person who is blackmailed. From this perspective, the target of blackmail would vastly prefer to have his secret controlled by the *blackmailer* rather than the gossip. In the latter case, the jig is up, and the information is revealed, no matter how great a value is placed upon it by the blackmailee. In contrast, at least the blackmailer allows the blackmailed to buy his way out of such a predicament, should he value privacy more than its cost.

Ultimately we must consider the starting point of the analysis. Posner, whether purposefully or inadvertently, adopts that of the *status quo*. The burden of proof, for him, rests on those who would change the law from prohibition to legalization. In contrast, the initial premise for the libertarian implies that blackmail is simply the "threat" to engage in gossip. In a free enterprise private property regime, to do so does not constitute an invasion. Posner, curiously, defends gossip; contradictorily, he sees as the starting point of his analysis the *status quo* which criminalizes "threats" or warnings of impending gossip.

Posner sees blackmail as a "form of extortion." Nothing could be further from the truth. In the former case, the threat consists of doing no more than one unarguably has a right to do: exercise his vocal chords in an act of free speech. In the latter, in sharp contrast, one can threaten to "beat up"[41] one's victim. Is the distinction between violating and not violating person and property one not worth making? This seems to be the implication of the Posnerian world view.

---

[39] *Id.* at 1835.
[40] *Id.*
[41] *Id.*

6. Any of the acts in the previous categories, but the blackmailer's victim did not in fact commit the act for which he is being blackmailed. [42]

According to Posner,

> A blackmailer could attempt to blackmail someone with a threat to accuse him falsely, but we should expect such cases to be rare because the victim has a good remedy: sue the blackmailer for defamation. The remedy is not perfect, however, because the blackmailer may not have the resources to pay a legal judgment. Criminalizing this form of blackmail can thus be viewed as backing up the law against defamation. [43]

The clear implication is that the law prohibiting defamation is itself a legitimate one. Let us test this contention by asking if defamation is a *per se* violation of person or property rights. At first glance it would appear to be an unequivocal interference with others, in that it ruins their reputations. Upon further reflection, however, reputations, even though they are self-referential, paradoxically consist of the possessions of others. [44] That is, A's reputation consists of and of nothing but, the thoughts of other people B, C, D … What A does tends to determine his reputation, and he can capitalize on it by selling the goodwill derived thereby. However, since A cannot own the thoughts of B, C, D, and his reputation consists of their thoughts and *only* their thoughts, [45] then he, paradoxically (logically), *cannot* own his reputation. Therefore, when we the present authors defame A, we are not doing anything akin to stealing something from him, A. This being the case, it would be improper to criminalize our behavior. Thus, the case for prohibiting blackmail on the ground that it "backs up the law against defamation" is not a very convincing one.

Suppose, somehow, that reputations are indeed legitimately owned by the people to whom they refer. Then, defamation, as per Posner, should indeed be a criminal act. But this position is open to various reductios. Critical book, movie, and play reviews all, if successful, tend to denigrate the reputations of writers, producers, directors, actors and playwrights. That is, all such critiques, have negative effects similar to defamation. If it is appropriate to le-

---

[42] *Id.* at 1836.
[43] *Id.*
[44] Block, *supra* note 35.
[45] What *A* thinks of *himself* has much to do with his self esteem, but nothing at all with his reputation. For a critique of this concept *see* MICHAEL R. EDELSTEIN & DAVID RAMSEY STEELE, THREE-MINUTE THERAPY: CHANGE YOUR THINKING, CHANGE YOUR LIFE (1997).

gally proscribe defamation on this ground, this must apply to negative reviews of all other kinds as well.

Let us grant that defamation is lying, while negative critiques express differences of opinion. To be sure, there are important differences between these two concepts. But in any given real world situation, the two shade uncomfortably into one another. Is it a false accusation, or a mere matter of opinion, for example, to say that Jay Leno is a lousy comedian, or Robin Williams a poor actor? If lying is the telling of an untruth, then anyone who asserts that 2+2=5, or that the world is flat, should be clapped into prison. But what about "a chicken in every pot?" Should lying politicians be imprisoned? How about the claim that God exists? Is this a lie? Should all religious people be jailed? Do we really want to entrust such decisions to the tender mercies of the state apparatus? The weather man, surely, lies roughly half the time. So do husbands who invariably tell their wives their dress is attractive. Home owners often lie to criminals requesting the whereabouts of their valuables. Under Posner, prison crowding would dramatically and unwarrantedly escalate.

IV. BLACKMAIL, GOSSIP, SILENCE, AND THEFT

Consider Posner's explanation of

> why it is not blackmail for a person who gets wind that another is about to disclose damaging information about him to approach that person and pay him to keep mum. Allowing such transactions is unlikely to give rise to an industry of dirt-seekers, with all the squandered resources thereby implied, since the dirt-seekers could not advertise for or otherwise seek out customers (which would be blackmail) but would have to wait for the latter to come upon them by chance.[46]

Of course, the mere approach to the blackmailer by the blackmailee would not be considered criminal blackmail. The crime of blackmail applies to the blackmailer, not the blackmailee who is widely seen as the "victim" of the piece. The real question, then, is, when the blackmailee approaches the blackmailer and the latter *accepts* the former's offer of money for silence, is the latter guilty of a crime? Posner says not, due to the unlikeliness of squandered resources. A contrary opinion is offered by Katz,[47] who states that this

---

[46] Posner, *supra* note 1, at 1836.
[47] Katz, *supra* note 3, at 1572.

is one of "a line of cases that has regularly plagued German criminal courts." That is to say, at least in the minds of German judges, it is by no means as clear as Posner seems to think that his case is *not* one of blackmail.

But suppose, if only for argument's sake, that Posner is correct in his view that this is not blackmail. Could his unlikeliness of squandered resources be the correct explanation? There are reasons to reject this hypothesis. What is to prevent a wealth "wasting" Blackmail, Inc.[48] from trolling in an attempt to encourage potential blackmailees to approach him? That is, this business firm knows that husband A has been unfaithful to his wife. He cannot, of course, approach A directly, and offer to maintain silence, in return for money. That would be a no-no for Posner. However, the blackmailer *can* approach A, or write him a letter, informing him of an intention to tell all to Mrs. A. Then, he can sit back and wait for A to approach him, the blackmailer. Strangely, Posner himself mentions this scenario[49] without realizing it undercuts his own case. This may not constitute blackmail in Posner's view, but it has all the earmarks of it. As well, it is as resource "wasting" as the ordinary, traditional, more direct blackmail.

Posner asks why blackmail is "regarded with great distaste and punished severely in comparison with other nonviolent thefts?"[50] But as we have argued above, blackmail is *not* theft. In theft, someone steals your money, under the threat of inflicting violence on you or yours. Clearly, he has no right to initiate such violence. In blackmail, someone threatens to *gossip* about you unless paid off.

Posner offers several explanations for the relative severity of legal sanctions in the case of blackmail. First, he argues that blackmail involves advance planning as opposed to being impulsive. [51] (We note in passing that this argument provides only weak support of blackmail prohibitionism since just because something is premeditated—canned speeches, marriage proposals, etc.—does not necessarily render it fit to legally ban. [52])

Another argument offered by Posner is that it will be difficult to capture blackmailers; after all, the blackmailee will scarcely complain, fearing the loss of his secret. According to Posner, "Because the probability of punishment is very low, the punishment must be set high to deter, and so blackmail will have the appearance of being a serious crime."[53]

There is yet another eminently reasonable explanation offered by Posner.

---

[48] Richard Epstein, *Blackmail, Inc.*, 50 U. CHI. L. REV. 553 (1983).
[49] Posner, *supra* note 1, at 1838.
[50] *Id.* at 1836.
[51] *Id.* at 1836–37.
[52] A synonym for "premeditated" is "purposeful."
[53] Posner, *supra* note 1, at 1837.

> Rational blackmailers will not approach people who are likely either to defy them or to bargain them down, but will concentrate on the psychologically or otherwise vulnerable. This selection bias will make the blackmailer seem especially vicious and predatory, and will thus create pressure for severe punishment."[54]

For who are the "vulnerable?" Surely, among other things, they have the lowest productivity. That is, there is a positive correlation between "vulnerability" in this sense and "squandering" resources. So, if we want to increase per capita GDP, and no advocate of the "economic approach"[55] worthy of his econometric equations could reject that, any phenomenon which particularly disconcerts, brings down, and in the extreme, drives to suicide those with low earnings capacity, is only to be *applauded*. Blackmail, according to Posner, fits that bill to a "T," preying on those who are "psychologically or otherwise vulnerable." Therefore, blackmail will maximize wealth by eliminating, or at lease reducing the control over resources, of those with less ability in this regard.

Posner claims as an "effect of the criminalization of blackmail, that of eliminating property rights in the blackmailer's information."[56] But this is not so. When blackmail is criminalized, the blackmailer still owns the information. The real effect is that of placing a price ceiling of zero on it. He still owns it and can still dispose of it, but only for free, that is, as a *gossip*. Criminalization merely means that he cannot *sell* it. This must be something of an anomaly for a member in good standing of the Chicago school, who can usually be counted upon to *oppose* price controls. Every empirical generalization, it would appear, can have exceptions.

V. CONCLUSION

Blackmail has sinister connotations in everyday discourse, suggesting shady dealing and ill-gotten gain. But blackmail *per se*, the exchange of silence for cash, is an uncomplicated voluntary act between consenting adults. It would seem to constitute a simple example of mutually beneficial exchange.

Richard Posner is on record as holding to an ethic of wealth maximization, which justifies institutions based on consent. Logically, then, Posner should favor the legalization of blackmail insofar as it is a voluntary trade (of

---

[54] *Id.* at 1839.
[55] To call this the "economic" approach is to imply, falsely, that all economists must adhere to it. Nothing could be further from the truth. Less tendentious nomenclature might be "the Chicago School" approach.
[56] Posner, *supra* note 1, at 1840.

money for silence), and consequently net wealth enhancing. But he does not; instead, he supports the legal *status quo* of prohibition.

We have argued that voluntary blackmail becomes easily confused with coercive extortion, and that this fact accounts for some of Posner's objection to legalization. But legal positivism also plays a role; to Posner, laws against blackmail are assumed to be efficient, and hence justified, because they *exist*. Thus the anomaly of a leading Chicago school economist favoring the continued prohibition of this particular "capitalist act between consenting adults"[57] becomes understandable, if not justifiable.

When blackmail is criminalized, the real effect is that of placing a price ceiling of zero on it; the prospective blackmailer still owns the (damaging) information and can still dispose of it, but only for *free*, that is, in the form of *gossip*. Criminalization, in other words, merely means that he cannot *sell* it.

Consider some other examples of activities subject to social opprobrium which also happen to be currently illegal: buying and selling heroin; prostitution; baby selling; pornography; and commerce in used body parts (e.g., kidneys).[58] All of these things have one thing in common with blackmail: not a one of them violates the libertarian axiom of non-aggression against non-aggressors. Our contention is that blackmail is blamed for the same reasons as all these others: there is an insufficient appreciation for the virtue and value of laissez-faire capitalism and individual sovereignty. Blackmail prohibition is merely one more instance of the violation of these principles.

---

[57] ROBERT NOZICK, ANARCHY, STATE AND UTOPIA 163 (1974).
[58] Curiously, Posner favors free markets in all of these goods and services. RICHARD A. POSNER, ECONOMIC ANALYSIS OF LAW (1992).

Chapter 9.

Blackmail and Economic Analysis:

Critique of Ginsburg and Shechtman

Blackmail consists of two things, each indisputably legal on their own; yet, when combined in a single act, the result is considered a crime. First, one may gossip, and, provided that what is said is true, there is nothing illegal about it. Truth is an absolute defense. Second, if one may speak the truth, one may also threaten to speak the truth. Yet if someone requests money in exchange for silence—money in exchange for giving up the right of free speech—it is a crime.

The law and economics literature takes the position that blackmail should be illegal on efficiency grounds. The present authors reject this law and economics analysis. They maintain that since it is legal to gossip, it should therefore not be against the law to threaten to gossip, unless paid off not to do so. In a word, blackmail is a victimless crime, and must be legalized, if justice is to be attained. The authors criticize several authors who take the efficiency position, but focus their argument on a paper written by Douglas Ginsburg and Paul Shechtman.

I. INTRODUCTION

Under libertarian law, no one may threaten, or initiate violence against, a person or his justly acquired property. All else is open, however. That is, a man can do anything else he wishes, provided only that he respect this one axiom of liberty.

Certainly he may ask for or demand money. Certainly he may engage in his free speech rights to gossip. Certainly he may refrain from the exercise of these rights, for a fee. That is to say, blackmail would be legal in a libertarian society, for it consists of no more than this. Of course, no one may engage in extortion, which is to be sharply distinguished from blackmail. For here the threat is not to gossip about other people's embarrassing secrets, or to do any other licit act, but rather to visit mayhem upon the victim; e.g., the threat is to kill or in other ways violate his personal or property rights.

If blackmail law is "enigmatic,"[1] this is not intrinsic; it is not due to the issues themselves. Rather, it is because there are many authors, including the two now under review,[2] who very clearly see this difference between black-mail and extortion, and yet advocate not only prohibiting the latter, but, contrary to libertarianism, the former as well. It will be worthwhile citing G&S at some length to show just how fully, clearly and accurately, they understand this distinction:

> The legal literature especially suffers from an inability to define blackmail in a way that meaningfully distinguishes it from threats of unquestioned legality made in the course of economic bargaining. All agree that a key employee may lawfully threaten to quit unless his wages are raised, and that if his threat comes at a time when his employer is particularly vulnerable, he may have engaged in sharp practices but not criminal conduct. [3] Many threats, such as those of a customer to take his custom elsewhere if a price is not lowered, or to enter production for his own use if suppliers are not more obliging, are actually relied upon in a competitive exchange economy to discipline the market. But despite our general ability to agree on the lawfulness of particular threats, drafting a general law that separates blackmail from bargaining has proved an elusive task.

> Related to this problem of definition is an apparent paradox embedded in the law of blackmail. Consider this paradigmatic blackmail transaction: B has taken a photograph of A, a temperance advocate, drinking a whiskey; he approaches A with an offer to sell him the photographic negative, threatening disclosure to the newspapers if A fails to pay. Again, all would agree: B is guilty of blackmail. *The point to notice, however, is that B has threatened to do only what he had an undoubted right to do, namely to facilitate the publication of the photograph.* Had B not approached A but sent the photograph directly to the publishers, no liability would have attached. The paradox, then, is that of a legal system that gives B the right to

---

[1] As claimed by Douglas H. Ginsburg and Paul Shechtman, *Blackmail: An Economic Analysis of the Law*, 141 U. PA. L. REV. 1849 (1993), hereinafter referred to as "G&S."
[2] G&S, *supra* note 1.
[3] A friendly amendment: presumably, he is not already under an employment contract incompatible with this action.

reveal information, but prevents him from seeking remuneration in exchange for his forbearance.[4]

Not only are G&S crystal clear on the concept of blackmail, they are equally so when it comes to extortion, which they call robbery, and offer the common law definition: "taking of money or goods of any value from the person of another or in his presence and against his will by violence or putting him in fear."[5]

II. A. ENGLISH ORIGINS

In their historical exegesis of this law, our authors trenchantly take cognizance of the fact that

> one could not lawfully threaten another with death, arson or accusation of an infamous crime in order to gain money. ... Thus the blackmailer ... either threatened or offered to commit a crime, and the law rather unremarkably treated him like the blackmailer menacing death or arson. *What one could not lawfully do, one could not lawfully threaten to do in order to be paid for refraining.*[6]

So far, so good. Apart from G&S characterizing what we call blackmail and what we call extortion with the same appellation, "blackmail," there are no differences between us. For they agree that the "blackmail" which threatens "death or arson" should be illegal, and, at least thus far, call it a "paradox" that the blackmail which threatens no more than that which is indubitably legal should be outlawed. However, although they agree that "What one could not lawfully do, one could not lawfully threaten to do in order to be paid for refraining," they do not embrace the obverse: What one *could* lawfully do, one

---

[4] G&S, *supra* note 1, at 1849–50 (emphasis added).

[5] *Id.* at 1850 fn. 2. Note, however, that the common law ordinarily made one exception to the rule that the robber (extortionist) had to place the victim in fear of "immediate personal violence." And this was the accusation of "unnatural acts" or "sodomical practices." Nowadays, this accusation would be unexceptionable. Indeed, what with advent of the gay rights movement, the accusee would wear, as it were, a badge of honor. But in the days of yore this was a serious accusation indeed. The modern equivalent might be to be accused of racism, discrimination, sexual harassment or heterosexism.

Libertarians, then, face the question of whether a (false) accusation of criminal behavior (whether or not coupled with a demand for money to forbear) is licit blackmail or illicit extortion. For no one else does this question even arise.

[6] G&S, *supra* note 1, at 1852 (emphasis added).

could lawfully threaten to do in order to be paid for refraining. Were they to have taken this logical step, they would have totally embraced the libertarian perspective on blackmail, and this present article would have been unnecessary.

Instead, our authors take the opposite tack. Toward this end they analyze the English Motor Association (EMA) cases.[7] This EMA alliance had the legal right to fix prices for its member firms; it published a "Stop List" of automobile dealers who did not conform to these mandates, to facilitate a boycott by the Association. In 1926, Shop List Superintendent Percy Denyer offered not to include Read's Garage on its enemies list, if he would pay £250 to the EMA. Instead of complying, Read sued, successfully, accusing Denyer of blackmail.[8] State G&S: "On appeal, Denyer's counsel argued that '(a) menace implies an improper motive,' so that '(w)hen a person has a lawful right to do an act for the protection of his own trade interest, he is not using menaces if he demands money as an alternative to doing such an act.'"[9]

With one slight difference, this is precisely the libertarian viewpoint. The only thing to be changed to conform with this philosophy is to forthrightly admit that Denyer had "menaced" Read, but that this "menace," or threat, was an entirely legitimate one, since, if one has the right to do X, then one must have the right to threaten to do X. And obversely, if one has no right to do X, then one has no right to threaten, or to menace, to do X.

Report G&S: "Lord Hewart, C.J., in response to this argument wrote … 'In the opinion of the Court, that proposition is not merely untrue; it is precisely the reverse of the truth. It is an excuse which might be offered by blackmailers.'"[10]

Hewart is undoubtedly correct. Find in favor of Denyer vis-à-vis Read, and allow this to serve as a precedent, and blackmail could not be punished. But in his jihad against this activity, Hewart is precluded from agreeing with the obverse of G&S's statement: "What one *could* lawfully do, one *could* lawfully threaten to do in order to be paid for refraining."

Scrutton, L.J., criticized Hewart as follows:

> I cannot understand this. The blackmailer is demanding money in return for a promise to abstain from making public an accusation of crime. The very agreement is illegal, even if the crime of a certain class has been committed. A man has no right to suppress his knowledge of a felony. How can this be analogous to proposing not

---

[7] *Id.* at 1853–55.
[8] *The King v. Denyer*, 2 K.B. 258, 260 (Eng. Crim. App. 1926), cited in *Id.* at 1853 fn. 13.
[9] G&S, *supra* note 1, at 1853.
[10] *Id.*

to do a thing which you have the legal right to do, if money is paid you, there being no public mischief in the agreement. ...

A. has land facing a new house of B's. A. proposes to build on that land a house which will spoil the view from or light to B's house and depreciate the value of his property. B implores A not to build. A says: 'I will not build if you pay me £1,000, but I shall build if you do not.' B pays the money and A does not build. Could it be seriously argued that B could recover the money back as obtained by threats? [11]

G&S interpret Scrutton as saying that "there could be no instance in which the law of threats and the substantive law concerning the thing threatened would be out of step with each other: if it would be lawful to carry out the threat, then it is lawful so to threaten, and the converse."[12]

We claim this is a misreading of Scrutton; it is a fair summary of the Hewart position, but that is very opposite of Scrutton's; rather, it is the one against which Scrutton was reacting. Both judges, along with G&S, mistakenly wish to ban blackmail. Hewart was at least logically consistent; given that blackmail should be illegal, it should also be impermissible to threaten that which one has a right to do (since that is all that blackmail consists of). But Scrutton, with G&S backing, wishes to have it both ways: to say that it is *legitimate* to threaten that which one has a right to do, and that blackmail, which consists of precisely that, no more and no less, should nonetheless be forbidden.

G&S are of the opinion that Scrutton protected the "ordinary blackmailer [who] normally threatens to do what he has a perfect right to do—namely, communicate some compromising conduct to a person whose knowledge is likely to affect the person threatened."[13] But Scrutton specifically (and illogically) rejected this eminently reasonable conclusion; he spuriously distinguished this case from ordinarily doing what one has a right to do on the ground that in the case of blackmail "the very agreement is illegal." Why is it

---

[11] In *Hardie & Lane, Ltd. v. Chilton*, 2 K.B. 306, 320, 331 (Eng. Crim. App. 1928), cited in *Id.* at 1854.
[12] G&S, *supra* note 1, at 1854.
[13] *Id.*

illegal if both parties to the contract, the blackmailer and the blackmailee, *agree* to it?[14]

Further, Scrutton is on shaky ground, at least in terms of the libertarian axiom, in claiming that it should be against the law to "abstain from making public an accusation of crime."[15] Under libertarianism, there are no positive obligations apart from those which a man brings upon himself, for example contractually. There are only negative responsibilities, preeminently to refrain from invading other persons or their property. The philosophical difficulty with non-contractual positive obligations is that they are open ended. For surely it is "abstaining from making public an accusation of crime" if I shut my eyes to crime when it occurs under my very nose. That is, if I take no interest in ferreting out criminal behavior. But there is a lot of crime going on, especially if we contemplate that which occurs in the whole world, not just in one's own (entire) country, and why should we not be so inclusive? If so, we are all always and ever guilty of this "crime." We should all, with no exceptions, be in jail right now, if cognizance be given to this specious doctrine.

G&S cite Atkin, L.J., as follows:

> [I]f a man may lawfully, in the furtherance of business interests, do acts which will seriously injure another in his business he may also lawfully, if he is still acting in the furtherance of his business interests, offer that other to accept a sum of money as an alternative to doing the injurious acts. He must no doubt be acting not for the mere purpose of putting money in his pocket, but for some legitimate purpose other than the mere acquisition of money.[16]

Now this is more than just passing curious. What other purpose of business *is* there for a person, pray tell, other than to "put ... money in his

---

[14] Make no mistake. The blackmailee is no "victim," as is commonly charged. On the contrary, he values the blackmailer's silence more than the money he must pay. Therefore, he is a *beneficiary* of the blackmailer. This can be clearly seen by answering the following question: suppose you were an adulterer, and someone found out about your secret. Would you rather that person be a blackmailer, who would keep quiet for a fee, or a gossip, who would spill the beans no matter how much you were willing to pay for silence? Obviously, the adulterer would be far better off in the former case.

[15] Yes, it should be unlawful to "*suppress* ... knowledge of a felony," but that is an entirely different matter. There is all the world of difference between *refraining* from doing something, which is an intra personal decision, that is, one decides for oneself what to do without invading anyone else, and *suppressing* it, which implies *inter* personal relations, that is, one man stops another from telling the police of a crime.

[16] G&S, *supra* note 1, at 1855.

pocket?" There *is* no legitimate purpose of business other than the "mere" acquisition of money.[17] Why this gratuitous attack on earning a living?[18]

Perhaps even more seriously, this judge fails to come to grips with the idea that if it is legal to do something for no money, it should be legal to do it for money as well. For the legal rightness or wrongness of an act, at least under the libertarian code, can be found in the act itself, not in the extraneous fact of whether it was done for money. Murder and rape are wrong because they constitute invasions. Doing them for free, or at a low price, cannot alter that elemental legal fact.

G&S see very clearly what is involved in blackmail. It is, for them as well as for us, a voluntary trade between consenting adults which will necessarily increase economic welfare, at least in the *ex ante* sense. Why, then, do they advocate the prohibition of such contracts? It is due, it would appear, to their (partial) support for socialism. Before explicitly making their case, they give two hints of this. First, "our claim is that an *economic planner*, shaping the laws to achieve economic efficiency, would include a law of blackmail in the criminal code."[19] And second, they favor "the rule that a *rational economic planner* would prescribe for distinguishing socially useful from socially wasteful threat activity."[20]

It might be objected, at the outset, that this is not really socialism; that even under free enterprise, we must each engage in rational economic planning on our own accounts. This cannot be denied. But it is one thing to plan for ourselves; it is quite another to enact legislation with the express purpose, and effect, of planning for the entire society.[21] And this, we claim, is not only precisely what the prohibition of blackmail does, but also what G&S explicitly want it to do.

A second objection is that communism was typically conducted by means of directives, mandates, and economic goals, not laws such as the prohibition of blackmail. But this is a superficial distinction. Laws, directives, mandates

---

[17] To be sure, people have many purposes for the money they earn from business pursuits: feeding their families, engaging in charity, saving the world, etc., but none of them are possible *unless* they acquire money.

[18] According to a VANCOUVER SUN newspaper headline (22 July 1997, p. B1), "Police turn blind eye to marijuana for the sick; officers would only act if people were supplying children or selling drugs for a profit." Selling to children we can understand. But earning a profit? And this is <u>Canada</u>, for goodness sake, not Cuba or North Viet Nam.

[19] G&S, *supra* note 1, at 1850 (emphasis added).

[20] *Id.* (emphasis added).

[21] F.A. HAYEK, THE FATAL CONCEIT: THE ERRORS OF SOCIALISM (1989); F. A. HAYEK, NEW STUDIES IN PHILOSOPHY, POLITICS, ECONOMICS AND THE HISTORY OF IDEAS (1978). For a critique of Hayek for being insufficiently thorough in his rejection of socialism, *see* Walter Block, *Hayek's Road to Serfdom*, 12 J. LIBERTARIAN STUD. 327 (1996).

and goals are merely different names for the same thing. What they all have in common is that those in the know determine how the rest of us shall act, with penalties for disobedience; this is typically couched in the rhetoric of being for our own good, or in the public interest, or for wealth maximization as in the present case, or some such.

A third objection is that what G&S are advocating is economic efficiency, not central planning. But the two are not as unrelated as might appear at first glance. Yes, economic efficiency and socialism are polar opposites. If there is one thing we have learned from recent events in Eastern Europe, Korea, Cuba, etc., it is that economic growth, wealth, well-being and central planning are incompatible.[22] However, hope springs eternal in the hearts of some. Even though it is an unreachable quest, there would appear to be an unremitting hope that economic efficiency might one day be attained through planning from the top. This was the implicit and oft-times explicit goal of the socialists of the 19th century, and it seems that not much has changed for those of the 20th century writing under the banner of Law and Economics.

III. THE ECONOMICS OF BLACKMAIL

What are the specifics of G&S's "rational planning" as regards blackmail? We are asked to contemplate the case where A will pay $300 in blackmail to B to keep silent about A's secret, and it will cost B $200 to unearth the requisite information. State G&S:

> If blackmail were not a crime, B presumably would proceed to research, to threaten, and to collect. On the other hand, if blackmail is a crime, B will be encouraged to seek alternative employment for his time and money. And that is precisely the point. Without a blackmail law, $200 of real resources would have been invested in order to produce nil output. No *rational economic planner*[23] *would tolerate the existence of an industry dedicated to digging up dirt, at real resource cost, and then reburying it.*[24]

First, even on the assumption that there are no other flaws in this argument, why should the law be constructed so as to maximize wealth in this

---

[22] JAMES GWARTNEY, ROBERT LAWSON AND WALTER BLOCK, ECONOMIC FREEDOM OF THE WORLD 1975-1995 (1996).
[23] This is the third time (and counting) G&S have used this phrase; too many to be merely accidental.
[24] G&S, *supra* note 1, at 1860 (emphasis added).

way? Why should a man be prevented from engaging in activities that have "nil output?" Shouldn't the majesty of the law be above such pedestrian concerns? For the clear implication is that all sorts of "goofing off" would have to be declared illegal: sunning oneself, playing solitaire, watching soap operas on t.v., engaging in sports (other than handball, an addiction of one of the present authors), going on nature walks, sleeping more than necessary, etc.

Second, as it happens, there are defects in this contention. Thus, even if it can somehow be shown that the purpose of the law is to maximize wealth, we cannot conclude that blackmail should be banned in order to achieve this end.

Why is this? Sometimes secrets come for free, by accident, with no research expenditure. G&S furnish us with no reasons to suppose that blackmail would "produce nil output" under these circumstances.[25] Therefore, according to their own argument, blackmail should be legalized in such cases. But it is extremely difficult to determine whether or not "research" has taken place. Or, to put this in words G&S would appreciate, it is very expensive and resource wasting to do so. Therefore, based on their own reasoning, it would appear that blackmail should again be legalized.

But let us assume away this possibility. That is, we will now suppose that embarrassing secrets can only be unearthed with the expenditure of real resources. Are there any reasons to suppose that such actions would still produce a positive output?

There are. For one thing, there is truth seeking for its own sake. Scientific research is only the tip of the iceberg in this regard, perhaps the most well known case where men seek knowledge, with no implication that it will ever be worthwhile in a strict monetary sense. There are numerous cases where people expend real resources on information gathering that others deem of "nil" productivity. These range from gathering gossip to reading escape literature to perusing the newspaper comics to daydreaming. Presumably, all of this will be outlawed by the G&S's benevolent dictator.[26]

If we take G&S at their literal word, we would have to outlaw all businesses which go bankrupt, and even those that post losses. This does not mean, merely, that those whose firms go belly up will be subject, as they now

---

[25] *See* more detailed discussion of this point below, when we consider Lindgren's objections to G&S.

[26] G&S, *supra* note 1, at 1860 have stated that our rational economic planner would *tolerate* the existence of an industry dedicated to digging up dirt, at real resource cost, and then reburying it. If this does not imply economic czardom, we are not sure what does. Who are the economic planners to "tolerate," or to not "tolerate" the actions of free men? Who appointed them to their exalted status? By what right do they impose on us, the great unwashed, their version of the good society?

are, to chapter 11 proceedings. Not at all. It means that such people will additionally be penalized by the same *criminal* code with which we punish blackmailers. And why is this? It is because both of them, the bankrupt and the blackmailer, are guilty in G&S eyes of the *crime* of "produc[ing] nil output," that is, of *criminally* wasting resources. If incarceration is sauce for the blackmailing goose because he wastes resources, it ought to be sauce as well for the bankrupt businessman, guilty of the same offense.

G&S might object to this *reductio ad absurdum* on the following grounds: yes, business failure is a waste of resources, but no one sets up shop with the *intention* of failing.[27] In contrast, the blackmailer has as his goal the use of money (for research) in ways that at least G&S regard as wasteful.

Our reply is that "If wishes were horses, then beggars would ride." Reality is more important than mere intentions. So what if the rich heir who is also a blithering idiot in commerce *wants* to prosper? The sad fact is that he will, in all reasonable likelihood, squander his fortune. Shouldn't the "rational economic planner" beloved of G&S step in and stop this foolishness? The problem with the rational central planner is that he is never around when you need him.

This objection that we are manufacturing on behalf of G&S suffers from another difficulty: it is vulnerable to the following *reductio*. Suppose it is determined that women, or teenagers, or blacks, are poorer entrepreneurs than males, or adults, or whites.[28] Then, using insights provided by G&S, it would appear to follow that the central planner would be well advised to set up a

---

[27] *But see* the fictional but realistic case of Francisco D'Anconia in AYN RAND, ATLAS SHRUGGED (1957). He deliberately sets out to lose money. Of course, to be fair to G&S, Francisco does so for the ultimate purpose of what they might consider wealth enhancement, namely the opposition to socialism. On the other hand, since G&S seem to favor the latter system (at least in part), they can take scant comfort from this complication.

To return to nonfiction, there are numerous cases on record where people purposefully wreck their businesses for psychological reasons of their own: depression, manic depressiveness, and, closer to the case of the "spite fence," (of which more below) in order to irritate someone.

[28] We do not advocate any such policy. Our only point is that if G&S remain loyal to their socialist thesis that wealth can best be maximized by a rational economic planner, then *they* must be wedded to it; that is, *G&S* must favor a law not allowing people to waste resources in this way. Declarations of incompetence for elderly people would be merely the tip of the iceberg in this regard. If the "rational economic planner" is serious, he must put a stop to the criminal waste of resources on the part of all of those, for example, who do not have good collateral and would not receive bank loans. If a bank will not lend someone money, why should that person be allowed to spend his *own* money on the venture?

program of business licenses. No one who is not a white male adult[29] may set up or run a firm.[30]

Nor can G&S coherently maintain that one learns from past business failures; there are many cases on record where a person went bankrupt two, three or even more times before striking it rich. This is undoubtedly true, but the best statistical estimators of success (remember, we are talking about a *rational* central planner) is hardly previous failure. In any case, people also learn from "investigative journalism" of the sort that ends up in supermarket tabloids. If G&S are to be consistent with their wealth maximization denigration of blackmail, they must carry through with these other activities.

G&S place themselves on the record as opposing on wealth maximization grounds the digging up of dirt and then reburying it. Are there ever cases where such an act can have positive economic value? To be sure, there are. One example is for purposes of exercise. Digging dirt is one of the most physically intensive athletic endeavors possible to imagine. Who knows, perhaps one day this will become an Olympic sporting event.

More generally, apart from information seeking, it is an everyday occurrence for men to act in a way that others think not worthwhile.[31] People do this all the time: they exercise to lose weight, and then eat heavily and gain it all back. As well, they play cards, gamble, drink alcohol, watch football, etc., all of which is obviously self-defeating. If the goal of the law is to ban all activities that "produce nil output" in the views of some people, the grand inquisitors will have a lot of grist for their mill.

---

[29] Or whichever groups are determined to be best at making profits.

[30] Under socialism, of course, people are investing and risking *society's* resources. As such, they should not be given the go ahead without the imprimatur of the "rational central planner." It is only under capitalism, and private property rights, the most efficient wealth producing mechanism known to man, that people are free to invest on their own, without a by your leave from a central Authority. But this is the only system fully compatible with blackmail *legalization*.

[31] According to Ludwig von MIses,

> [T]he ultimate ends of human action are not open to examination from any absolute standard. Ultimate ends are ultimately given, they are purely subjective, they differ with various people. ... Praxeology and economics deal with the means for the attainment of ends chosen by the acting individuals. They do not express any opinion with regard to such problems as whether or not sybaritism is better than asceticism.
>
> The notions of abnormality and perversity therefore have no place in economics. It does not say that a man is perverse because he prefers the disagreeable, the detrimental, and the painful to the agreeable, the beneficial and the pleasant.

LUDWIG VON MISES, HUMAN ACTION 95 (1966)

But perhaps the most basic mistake of G&S is to fail to reckon with subjectivity in economics. According to folk wisdom, "One man's meat is another man's poison." What is "nil output" to the central planner need not be a zero to all. To act as if it is, is to be guilty of what Hayek called the "fatal conceit."[32]
States Mises:

> Some economists believe that it is the task of economics to establish how in the whole of society the greatest possible satisfaction of all people or of the greatest number could be attained. They do not realize that there is no method which would allow us to measure the state of satisfaction attained by various individuals.[33]

On the other hand, when objectivity does not suit our authors, they are quick to jettison it. They explicitly take note of, and reject, yet another critique of their position. It is that legalizing blackmail will enhance the power of the blackmailers of the world to act so as to reduce the behavior of which the blackmailees are ashamed. The presumption is that even if this behavior is legal, it cannot have been too good, or they would not have consented to pay to keep it secret. The implication is, then, that the less of such activity, the better for society. However, in the view of G&S, who suddenly turn subjectivist, "avoidance of [this] conduct ... cannot be presumed to be a gain."[34]

Next, correctly noting that blackmail need not involve the threat to convey information, G&S turn to the example of the spite fence. This is an edifice built not to enhance the privacy of the owner, but rather to serve as a threat to the neighbor whose view is thereby disrupted, in an attempt to annoy him, or make him pay the former to forbear.

G&S[35] claim that an "omniscient lawgiver"[36] would set the maximum legal fence height at the point at which the two neighbors' marginal utilities were equal, but that "in the real world of less than omniscient lawgivers" he would do no such thing. This sounds reasonable, but it is not. First, what about property rights? Given that owners have a basic right to build as high as they wish, the "omniscient lawgiver" will be acting the part of the thief, relieving the owner of his rights against his will. Second, this determination ignores the fact that markets have alternatives to "wise" central planners; namely, the internalization of such externalities through restrictive covenants[37] and con-

---

[32] *See* F.A. HAYEK, THE FATAL CONCEIT: THE ERRORS OF SOCIALISM (1989).
[33] Mises, *supra* note 31, at 242.
[34] G&S, *supra* note 1, at 1860 fn. 41.
[35] *Id.* at 1862.
[36] First cousin, presumably, to the rational economic central planner.
[37] BERNARD SIEGAN, LAND USE WITHOUT ZONING (1972); Bernard H. Siegan, *Non-Zoning in Houston,* 13 J. L. & ECON. (1970).

dominiums. If there is a problem of fence heights, and views of distant mountains foregone, the builder of a large tract of land can sell subdivisions subject to his own best estimates of where the respective marginal utilities will equate. He will succeed or fail in earning a profit (in part) on the basis of these decisions concerning fence heights. Here, there is no socialistic violation of property rights, as each parcel of land is sold subject to these prior conditions.

At least, however, G&S are to be congratulated for realizing that the real world does not boast of omniscient lawgivers. What are we to make, then, of their claim[38] that the *non*-omniscient lawgiver should be empowered not to pick the optimal fence height (x, in their diagram), but rather the height at which the marginal utility of the builder approaches zero (z, in their diagram)? The only possible interpretation is that they have somehow very quickly forgotten all about the limitations to their analysis which they themselves had previously adumbrated just a few lines of print before. The point is, without omniscience, the socialist judge is no more able to determine the one fence height than the other.

Notwithstanding these considerations, G&S worry that "solely in order to convince A of the seriousness of his threat, B may have to put up the unwanted footage only to take it down again later. Real resources are thus expended to establish the credibility of B's threat, but in the end there is nothing to show for the effort ... A rational economic planner (lawgiver) would simply prohibit the threat at the outset."[39]

God forbid that real resources should ever be wasted. Let us move heaven and earth to make sure that no such horror ever comes to pass. Let us pervert the law to this end. Perhaps, conceivably, this sentiment would make (economic but not legal) sense in a world of perfect competition, full information, homogeneous goods, zero profits, continuous equilibrium and all the rest. But in the *real* world, there is no such thing. Rather, there is a process which, while continually nudging the economy in this direction, never achieves this goal. Bargaining, even wasteful bargaining from the *ex post* perspective, is necessarily part and parcel of this market groping.

Suppose that Cletus's marginal revenue product in his present position is $100,000. His boss, mistakenly, pays him only $70,000. Cletus leaves for greener pastures. Cletus's boss hires a replacement, who soon has to be fired for incompetence. Cletus's boss hires him back for the higher salary. Resources, horrors!, are wasted in this scenario. "Real resources are thus expended to establish the credibility of [Cletus's] threat." Worse, "there is noth-

---

[38] G&S, *supra* note 1, at 1862–63.

[39] *Id.* at 1863.

ing to show for the effort." With G&S in charge, the rational economic planner (wage controller, in this case) would have forced Cletus's boss immediately to pay him what he is worth. This is not serious analysis. This is argument from the *deus ex machina*.

On the other hand, very much to the credit of G&S, they do admit that "[o]ur rational (not omniscient) economic planner ... does not have access to the appropriate graph for each A and B."[40] That is to say, presumably, that the judge's decision cannot be trusted to ensure resources are not wasted. If so, then, it would appear, we are back to laissez-faire capitalism and private property rights, where people may do whatever they wish, provided only that they refrain from invasions of the persons and property rights of other men.

However salutary, this is not at all, unfortunately, the direction in which they are heading. For G&S[41] reveal themselves to be Coaseans, e.g., opponents of any fixed private property rights at all. In the specific case under discussion, there is no reason to assume that the man had a right to build a fence as high as he wished. For the true Coasean, this is only true so long as, in the opinion of the (non-omniscient) judge, resources will be more valuable under this system of law than under the one where the man whose view will be interrupted has the right to determine fence height.[42]

G&S concede that "spite" can have an independent value to the fence builder.[43] This means, presumably, that on the assumption that the law favors

---

[40] *Id.* at 1864.
[41] *Id.* at 1862.
[42] For critiques of the Coasean version of socialism, see Walter Block, *Coase and Demsetz on Private Property Rights*, 1 J. LIBERTARIAN STUD. 111 (1977); Walter Block, *Ethics, Efficiency, Coasean Property Rights and Psychic Income: A Reply to Demsetz*, 8 REV. AUSTRIAN ECON. 61 (1995); Walter Block, *O.J.'s Defense: A Reductio Ad Absurdum of the Economics of Ronald Coase and Richard Posner*, 3 EUR. J. L. & ECON. 265 (1996); Roy E. Cordato, *Subjective Value, Time Passage, and the Economics of Harmful Effects*, 12 HAMLINE L. REV. 229 (1989); Roy E. Cordato, *Knowledge Problems and the Problem of Social Cost*, 14 J. HIST. ECON. THOUGHT 14 (1992); ROY E. CORDATO, WELFARE ECONOMICS AND EXTERNALITIES IN AN OPEN-ENDED UNIVERSE: A MODERN AUSTRIAN PERSPECTIVE (1992); Elisabeth Krecke, *Law and the Market Order: An Austrian Critique of the Economic Analysis of Law*, paper presented at the Ludwig von Mises Institute's Austrian Scholar's Conference, New York City, October 9-11, 1992, forthcoming in 1 COMMENTARIES L. & ECON. (1998); GARY NORTH, THE COASE THEOREM (1992); GARY NORTH, TOOLS OF DOMINION: THE CASE LAWS OF EXODUS (1990).
[43] G&S, *supra* note 1, at 1864.

privacy vis-à-vis view "rights,"[44] that is, the right of the builder to construct a fence reaching to the heavens if he wishes, that there is no danger of the dreaded "nil output." For "there would be no reason in economic theory to dishonor his preference for making A suffer."[45]

However, in returning to more traditional blackmail of the embarrassing secret exposing variety, these authors[46] are back at the same old "nil output" lemonade stand. Why the difference? This is because one can always tear down or reduce the size of the fence, which was only needed to establish to A that B really would go ahead and build it—in order to be paid off not to do so. But in the case of threatening to gossip (e.g., blackmail), in contrast, how can the threatener establish his credibility apart from going ahead and revealing the secret? However, once he does that he will have nothing further to hold over the blackmailee.

One's first reaction to this concern might well be to dismiss it cavalierly. After all, every occupation has its problems. Why should we worry about the plight of the poor misunderstood blackmailer? Let him solve these problems for himself, or get out of the business. But for G&S this is important. For credibility

---

[44] Under libertarian law, there can be no such things as "view" rights. If there were, I would be able to sue you for "getting in my face," even if you were 10 miles away, since you would be disturbing my "view." But there is no such thing as "privacy" rights either. States Rothbard:

> But is there really such a right to privacy? How can there be? How can there be a right to prevent Smith by force from disseminating knowledge which he possesses? Surely there can be no such right. Smith owns his own body, and therefore has the property right to own the knowledge he has inside his head, including his knowledge about Jones. And therefore he has the corollary right to print and disseminate that knowledge. In short, ... *there is no such thing as a right to privacy except the right to protect one's property from invasion.* The *only* right 'to privacy' is the right to protect one's property from being invaded by someone else. In brief, no one has the right to burgle someone else's home, or to wiretap someone's phone lines. Wiretapping is properly a crime <u>not</u> because of some vague and wooly 'invasion of a "right to privacy"', but because it is an invasion of the *property right* of the person being wiretapped.

Murray N. Rothbard, The Ethics of Liberty 121–22.

What, then, of the dispute between B, the fence builder, and A, his neighbor whose view will be truncated? In the absence of any restrictive covenant between them, B can build as high as he wishes; as long as he does so on his own property, he is not guilty of an invasion of A's legitimate property, which does not include an uninterrupted view.

[45] G&S, *supra* note 1, at 1864.

[46] *Id.* at 1865.

is an asset only insofar as B is an entrepreneur of blackmail, i.e., someone who expects to engage in similar future transactions from which to realize a return on the investment in credibility. Should B succeed in his efforts first to make himself credible and then to acquire information that he can threaten to disclose, the result will be an *industry the output of which is nil*, although resources are consumed in its operation, viz. for information gathering and threatening.[47]

But why would credibility be important only to a blackmailer continuing in business? Why not, also, for reasons of self-respect, or psychological well-being? How can you hold your head up in the neighborhood if a blackmailee doesn't knuckle under to a threat—even apart from future monetary considerations?

G&S conclude this section as follows:

> In short, therefore, a legal system designed to maximize allocative efficiency would penalize not only (1) threats to do an act that the threatener has no *right* to do, i.e., that would occasion criminal or civil liability, but also (2) threats to do something that the threatener does have a *right* to do but that would (a) consume real resources, and (b) yield no product other than the enjoyment of spite or of an enhanced reputation as a credible issuer of threats. Reciprocally, it would not penalize the utterance of a threat to take an action that is (1) lawful in itself, i.e., neither tortious nor criminal, and (2) would confer some material benefit on the party making the threat.[48]

We have underlined G&S's use of the word "right" in this quote for a reason. They use it in the traditional way, as if there were such things as "rights" apart from wealth maximization considerations. But they are not entitled to do so. In their own philosophy, "rights" mean no more than legal mandates designed (by central planners and judges) to maximize wealth. For them, there are no such things *as* rights apart from this. Thus, the (valid) distinction they are attempting to draw here, between blackmail and extortion, is one they are (logically) forbidden to draw.

A second problem is that this statement is incompatible with their previous one to the effect that "there would be no reason in economic theory to

---

[47] *Id.* at 1865.
[48] *Id.* at 1865 (emphasis added).

dishonor his preference for making A suffer."[49] If there is nothing in economic theory which can distinguish between the psychic income of spite enjoyment and "material benefit," G&S are logically precluded from drawing the conclusion they do. Again, because of subjectivist considerations, there is simply no way to objectively define "material benefits." One man's material benefits are another person's "nil outputs."

Let us try to make this point in another way. Suppose there were a farmer who wanted to leave some acreage idle.[50] G&S, naturally, upon pain of contradiction, would have to object to this on the ground that it did not "confer some material benefit on" anyone. They would have to condemn it as a "nil output." Presumably they would do to this waster of resources what they would do to the blackmailer (whose crime in their eyes is precisely this, wasting resources), namely, throw him into prison. Just as they have rejected "spite" as a valuable contribution to the economy,[51] they would presumably refuse to consider the joy of contemplation of idle land as an economic benefit. Similarly with workers enjoying leisure, say, at their annual vacation. This, too, would have to be denounced out of hand as "wasteful."[52] Nor can G&S object to the foregoing on the ground that neither the farmer nor the worker "consumes resources."[53] On the contrary, both do so. The worker, obviously, will still eat food; worse, most vacationers significantly use resources for their nefarious deeds. But even the farmer utilizes scarce resources. As long as leaving the land fallow does not increase its productivity (this would be the analogue of the optimal vacation), there is an alternative cost in terms of the foodstuffs that could have been grown there which are foregone. And this is to ignore interest payments that might be due to the bank for the mortgage on the land.[54]

---

[49] *Id.* at 1864.

[50] Or a worker who wished to take a vacation. Or a person who wished to leave some clothes in his closet, unworn.

[51] Well, strictly speaking, they did and then they didn't. That is, as we have seen, they have contradicted themselves on this point.

[52] A case could conceivably be made by those of the G&S persuasion that a certain small amount of leisure is necessary for laborers in order to make them more efficient. If so, then these authors would only incarcerate those taking holidays for longer than this optimal period. On the other hand, slave owners worked their property the entire year around, giving leisure only during the evenings and on Sundays. This would imply that all those who slacken off for more than this amount of time are guilty of the non-maximization of wealth, and should be jailed.

[53] G&S, *supra* note 1, at 1866.

[54] Russell Hardin, *Blackmailing for Mutual Good*, 141 U. PA. L. REV. 1787, 1806 (1993) states: "Richard Posner (1986) says blackmail ... has no social product and should therefore be criminalized. This is a very odd conclusion. Much of what I do has no social product (for instance, I consume, I waste time), but surely it should not be criminalized

IV. GREENMAIL

Why, then, is there a widespread revulsion toward blackmail, given that G&S's explanation must be rejected? Goodhart explains this on the basis of "unexamined moral norms;"[55] naturally, G&S repudiate so reasonable an exegesis. Instead, our authors rely upon Campbell,[56] who interprets blackmail law in terms of refraining from earning profits in business. He worries about "the powerful man who announces his intention of starting operations in a field in which he has hitherto shown no interest, unless those already established in that field pay him to stay out."[57] Instead of giving the back of the hand to this argument, G&S liken it to their own concern with their "test of material advantage."[58]

A moment's consideration will show, even on this rigidly narrow ground, that Campbell's greenmail has a positive productivity. Not, of course, to those mired, as are G&S, in the perfectly competitive model, where, paradoxically, no competition at all in its rivalristic sense takes place. But to those who appreciate the market process,[59] it is easy to see that this threat from an outside interloper might pay large dividends in terms of economic efficiency. Certainly, if we have learned anything from the life and times of Michael Milken,[60] it is that the possibility of such threats can keep firms lean and mean.

G&S discuss "the general principle of the Model Penal Code, which makes it unlawful to threaten a lawful act if carrying out the threat would not benefit the actor."[61] The question to be posed, in response, is, Why would the actor carry it out if it would not in some way benefit him? Indeed, can we not deduce from the fact that the actor did carry it out that it *did,* at least in some way, benefit him?

States Mises in this regard:

---

[55] G&S, *supra* note 1, at 1867.
[56] Campbell, *The Anomalies of Blackmail,* 55 LEGAL Q. REV. 382 (1939).
[57] *Id.* at 390, cited in G&S, *supra* note 1, at 1867.
[58] G&S, *supra* note 1, at 1868.
[59] Mises, *supra* note 31; ISRAEL M. KIRZNER, COMPETITION AND ENTREPRENEURSHIP (1973); JOSEPH A. SCHUMPETER, CAPITALISM, SOCIALISM AND DEMOCRACY (1942).
[60] Berle and Means warned of the power of entrenched corporate boards, but called for government control as a solution. They didn't appreciate the role of corporate raiding as a way of promoting competition in the board room. *See* A.A. BERLE, JR. AND GARDNER C. MEANS, THE MODERN CORPORATION AND PRIVATE PROPERTY (1932). For a discussion of the economics of acquisitions and mergers, and the effect it has on getting rid of deadwood at the top, *see* Robert W. McGee, *Mergers and Acquisitions: An Economic and Legal Analysis,* 22 CREIGHTON L. REV. 665 (1988–89).
[61] G&S, *supra* note 1, at 1868.

The ultimate end of action is always the satisfaction of some desires of the acting man. Since nobody is in a position to substitute his own value judgments for those of the acting individual, it is vain to pass judgment on other people's aims and volitions. No man is qualified to declare what would make another man happier or less discontented. The critic either tells us what he believes he would aim at if he were in the place of his fellow; or, in dictatorial arrogance blithely disposing of his fellow's will and aspirations, declares what condition of this other man would better suit himself, the critic.[62]

And according to Rothbard: "All (human) action aims at rendering conditions at some time in the future more satisfactory for the actor than they would have been without the intervention of the action."[63]

V. THE BENEFITS OF BLACKMAIL

In this section G&S comment upon the blackmail theory of Landes and Posner.[64] They do so for two reasons. One, in order to make good on their promise[65] to show that there are no beneficial effects to blackmailees which can offset the research and other costs of the blackmailer.[66] And two, to further defend their view that "self-interest," which is "the general principle of the Model Penal Code," is and should be "the touchstone of a lawful threat."[67] That is, unless the blackmailer gains a value recognized by G&S, he should be jailed.

G&S[68] offer the case of the "lawful bookmaker, who cannot sue to enforce a gambling debt, (who) threatens to tell the client's 'aged and pious parents who consider betting sinful about their son's activities.'"[69] Our authors favor

---

[62] Mises, *supra* note 31, at 19.
[63] MURRAY N. ROTHBARD, MAN, ECONOMY AND STATE 3 (1993).
[64] William Landes and Richard A. Posner, *The Private Enforcement of Law*, 4 J. LEGAL STUD. 1 (1975).
[65] G&S, *supra* note 1, at 1860 fn. 41.
[66] We again reiterate our objection to the whole G&S "Law and Economics" premise. Central planning cannot create wealth, let alone maximize it. *See* LUDWIG VON MISES, SOCIALISM (1969). Even if it could, it is not the function of law to penny pinch and cut costs; rather, its purpose is to protect rights and thereby promote justice. Happily, however, there is no incompatibility between the two goals. The central plan of G&S is as unable to attain wealth as it is to foster legal legitimacy.
[67] G&S, *supra* note 1, at 1870.
[68] *Id.*
[69] G&S cite Campbell, *The Anomalies of Blackmail*, 55 LEGAL Q. REV. 382, 395 (1939).

legalizing what would otherwise be a blackmail threat "as lawful economic bargaining"[70] on the assumption that it is intended to get the parents to pay off the bookmaker. On the other hand, if the bookmaker is making the threat not out of any benefit for himself, but, presumably, out of sheer cussedness, then G&S are ready to pounce on him, and declare his act to be illegal blackmail.

This is difficult to understand. Even passing over the point that actions are not in effect uncaused, that in the mind of the actor *ex ante* every human action is an attempt to better his welfare, we have in this case a benefit for the actor which one would have thought would have satisfied even G&S. Namely, the bookmaker is resorting to blackmail *in order to be paid the money rightfully due him.* Of course, as a blackmailer, he doesn't expect the *parents* to pay the son's gambling debts. For them to do so, it would have meant the failure of the blackmail threat. Rather, he expects the *son* to fork over the money he owes, out of concern that his parents never hear of his dissolute ways.

But what of G&S's first concern in this section, to denigrate the claim that the blackmailer will have some beneficial (e.g., wealth enhancing) effects in reducing improper behavior? In order to make this point, they introduce another example: "Suppose that A desires to engage in an activity, such as chewing tobacco in public, but that a B's report of his behavior to C would cause her to lose respect for A's character; indeed, C might lose affection for A as a result."[71]

For G&S, the question of whether blackmail is wealth enhancing comes down to the issue of whether C gains from knowing A's secret. In the view of these authors,

> If C is concerned with A's welfare (e.g., tobacco stains A's teeth) and not with her own (e.g., it will be unpleasant to kiss A), then it is not at all clear that C is any better off when A conforms his conduct to her desires, nor that C is any worse off when A fails to do so. But it is certainly difficult to see how the welfare of an altruistic C is affected by A's behavior when that behavior is unknown to her.[72]

This is highly problematic.[73] Surely a C is better off knowing that her husband or boyfriend engages in bisexual activity with multiple partners and indulges in unprotected sex or is an intravenous drug user, because the chances of his contracting AIDS is much enhanced by such behavior. She most cer-

---

[70] G&S, *supra* note 1, at 1870.
[71] *Id.* at 1871.
[72] *Id.* at 1872.
[73] *Id.* at 1872 text, and fn. 71.

tainly *is* "affected by A's behavior (even, if anything, *especially*) when that be-havior is unknown to her." G&S maintain that "Sometimes what we don't know can't hurt us."[74] To this we say, which of us would *not* like to know if our spouse were acting in a way contrary to our interests? Would G&S them-selves step forward in this regard?

And what about A? Why leave him out of the economic calculation? He will presumably[75] benefit given the assumption that the tobacco chewing habit is harmful to himself, and that legalized blackmail is more likely to deter him from such self-inflicted mischief.

G&S adopt a similar stance with regard to the aged pious parents of the gambler. They, too, it appears, are better off not knowing, given that "the blackmail victim was bound by ties of affection"[76] to the respective A, as op-posed to self-interest. But if you don't know of your son's weakness, how can you help him overcome it? Surely, this would be an important motivation for altruistic parents.

In concluding this section, G&S state the following about blackmail:

> If such threats were lawful, there would be an incentive for people
> to expend resources to develop embarrassing information about
> others in the hope of then selling their silence. In that case, some
> people would be deterred from engaging in embarrassing (but law-
> ful) conduct, while some others who were undeterred would find
> that their business or social acquaintances or family were informed
> of their activity.[77]

Two sentences, and two errors. First, G&S have it backwards. Legalization would only give incentive for people to expend these resources compared to prohibition. But assume a system of natural liberty, where the libertarian ax-iom of non-invasion is followed. Here, there would be no particular incentive to invest resources in this calling compared to any other legal one. It is only under prohibition that *less* than the optimal amount of resources will be spent on ferreting out such information. One might as well say that under legaliza-tion of alcohol, "there would be an incentive for people to expend resources" in this industry, implying an over optimal expenditure. On the contrary, the

---

74 *Id.* at 1872 fn. 72.
75 We speak here as advocates, for argument's sake, of the G&S philosophy which admits of interpersonal comparisons of utility, paternalism, socialism, central planning and all the rest. Based on the Austrian welfare insights this whole discussion is invalid. *See* Mises, *supra* note 31; Murray N. Rothbard, *Toward a Reconstruction of Utility and Welfare Economics*, Center for Libertarian Studies, Occasional paper No. 3 (1977); Rothbard, *supra* note 63.
76. G&S, *supra* note 1, at 1873.
77 *Id.* at 1873.

presumption[78] is that the correct amount of investment is now being made there. And the same applies to blackmail, at least when the bench mark applied is the voluntary choices of people free to do whatever they please, as long as they do not invade the persons or property of others. This is in sharp contrast to the central planning criterion employed by G&S.

Second mistake. It is not true, under legalization, that people's choices would be limited to the two mentioned by G&S. There is a third option to being "deterred from engaging in embarrassing (but lawful) conduct, or suffering when one's business or social acquaintances or family were informed of their activity." It is to pay off the blackmailer for his silence. Then, albeit for a fee (e.g., this payment), one can have his cake and eat it too. Namely, a man can engage in shameful behavior, without any acquaintance or family member coming to know of it.

VI. POSTSCRIPT

In this section G&S attempt to refute the theories of Lindgren and Boyle,[79] who, in our own opinion, are equally mistaken in their analysis of blackmail.

The general rule for all such debates between blackmail prohibitionists is that the critic is always right. That is, there are numerous scholars who oppose legalization. Each of them, with but few exceptions, offers his own separate theories. As a direct implication, each of them is critical of the views of all the others. As a result, whenever there is an intra prohibitionist debate, the critic is invariably correct. This follows from the fact that they are all wrong in their explanations, as the truth of the matter is that the case for legalization is the only correct and logically coherent one.

One instance of this general rule occurred earlier in the paper now under review, where G&S successfully, in our view, criticize Landes-Posner.[80] The latter authors attempt to account for opposition to blackmail on the ground that it is a private attempt at law enforcement; and, as there are good and sufficient reasons for leaving such efforts totally in the hands of the government, private interferences such as blackmail will typically lead to an over investment in resources allotted for this purpose. State G&S:

---

[78] At least in equilibrium.
[79] James Boyle, *A Theory of Law and Information: Copyright, Spleens, Blackmail and Insider Trading,* 80 CAL. L. REV. 1413 (1992).
[80] *Supra* note 64.

> [I]nformation may be humiliating, but not incriminating, for any number of very particularized reasons (G&S mention Campbell's (1939) example of the gambler with aged pious parents). These may be quite unrelated to any 'social decisions' about the economics of enforcement, and yet the prohibition upon blackmail will apply; more than concern for optimal norm enforcement is needed, therefore, to explain the law against blackmail.[81]

Another instance is furnished by DeLong who dismisses all "economic" justifications of prohibition,[82] as follows:

> Why does blackmail strike us as so wrongful? So wrongful that even in the midst of a transaction cost analysis, the economist Ronald Coase would refer to it as 'moral murder?' None of the foregoing (economic) theories seems to touch the nerve that the blackmailer rubs; none explains the societal abhorrence of the blackmailer's craft. *Purely economic explanations of the criminal law often produce bizarre conclusions, such as that blackmail rules are intended to reduce expenditures by blackmailers.* Such provocations are part of the charm of economic analysis. We all know that blackmail laws are meant to do more than prevent waste.[83]

And now, in conclusion, let us illustrate this principle once again. Lindgren, whose own defense of prohibitionism has been subjected to withering attack, now has the better of G&S, despite the replies of the latter.

G&S's main point is of course that blackmail requires the improper allocation to it of scarce resources, mainly in order to ferret out secrets. Lindgren remarks, quite reasonably in our view, that this theory is "unable to explain

---

[81] G&S, *supra* note 1, at 1870.

[82] E.g., Steven Shavell, *An Economic Analysis of Threats and Their legality: Blackmail, Extortion and Robbery*, 141 U. Pa. L. Rev. 1877 (1993); Richard Posner, *Blackmail, Privacy and Freedom of Contract*, 141 U. Pa. L. Rev. 1817 (1993); and G&S, *supra* note 1.

[83] Sidney W. DeLong, *Blackmailers, Bribe Takers, and the Second Paradox*, 141 U. Pa. L. Rev. 1663, 1689 (1993). We have only one slight demur to this magnificent evisceration of the "economic" approach. As economists, we do not at all find this to be "charming." We see it rather as a tragic misallocation of scholarly economic time and effort, and as no less than an academic perversion. We especially resent that these economists, in calling their approach one of "economics," willy nilly include people such as ourselves. They ought to come up with another appellation. Suggestions: Chicago economics, Chicago law and economics, utilitarian economics, pragmatic economics, legal positivism.

why it is blackmail[84] to sell information that is not purposefully acquired."[85] G&S, in Lindgren's view, may thus be able to explain "commercial research blackmail" and "entrepreneurial blackmail" but not "participant or opportunistic blackmail."

G&S reject this criticism on the ground that the gain to the blackmailer who carries through on his threat is only as "an entrepreneur of blackmail, i.e., someone who expects to engage in similar future transactions from which to realize a return on the investment in credibility."[86] Even if this were true, however, it still does not obviate Lindgren's point. Let us focus, at least for the moment, on *this* case of blackmail, the one for which the information was obtained for free. Forget about future implications, at least for the sake of argument. Or, assume that the world will abruptly end right after *this present instance* of blackmail occurs. Now is it or is it not true, G&S, that *this* case of blackmail, where the information was acquired by accident, required no expenditure, at least for information gathering purposes? We cannot see how G&S can rationally deny this Lindgren point.

The G&S contention is not necessarily true. Of course it cannot be denied that establishing credibility as a blackmailer will tend to enhance future reputational capital. On the other hand, if a person gets a reputation as a blackmailer, people with secrets to hide will certainly tend to steer clear of him. This will be a loss, not a gain, to his future career. Further, there are other "rational" motivations apart from enhancing future entrepreneurial blackmail that might explain why the blackmailer "B stands to gain ... by actually carrying through his threat to send compromising information to the newspapers."[87] For one thing, he might have an "anal" personality, and be unable to bear not carrying out something to its conclusion. For another, there is always the psychic income of a job well done.

Nor do G&S emerge unscathed from their tangle with Boyle,[88] who offers yet another reason, apart from future entrepreneurial blackmail, to carry through on the threat: enhanced status as a gossip. G&S try much the same reply with Boyle as they did with Lindgren, but with equal ineffectual results. Yes, G&S[89] cannot be denied when they assert that "the lesson of his experience is that the acquisition of damaging information is a profitable enterprise," but this does not necessarily mean that the accidental acquirer will

---

[84] That is, improper. In our view, it is blackmail alright, but even so it should be lawful. In contrast, according to usage in the anti-blackmail literature, to prove that something is blackmail is per se to have succeeded in showing it to be illicit.

[85] James Lindgren, *Unraveling the Paradox of Blackmail*, 84 COLUM. L. REV. 670, 695 (1984).

[86] G&S, *supra* note 1, at 1865, 1875.

[87] *Id.*

[88] *Supra* note 79.

[89] G&S, *supra* note 1, at 1876 fn. 92.

carry through and enter this profession. And one must agree with G&S when they claim: "The prohibition of blackmail thus serves a prophylactic purpose by discouraging even the accidental acquirer of damaging information from acquiring an incentive to seek out information for use in a future blackmail attempt."[90]

But one must still insist that this is irrelevant to the issue under debate: whether *this, present non-entrepreneurial* blackmail attempt cost any money for information retrieval. And the undeniable answer is that it did not.

VII. CONCLUSION

At the outset of their piece, G&S stated that "drafting a general law that separates blackmail from bargaining has proved an elusive task."[91] As far as we are concerned, this is just as elusive as it ever was, despite the Herculean efforts of these authors. It is an elusive task because it simply cannot be done. It is and always will be, we suggest, just as elusive as finding a square circle or parallel lines that meet. If it is lawful to do X, it must necessarily be lawful to *threaten* to do X. If it is not lawful to do X, only then is it not lawful to threaten to do it. Wealth maximization is simply irrelevant to this basic legal premise.[92]

---

[90] *Id.* at 1876 fn. 92.
[91] G&S, *supra* note 1, at 1849.
[92] States Rips of the Bill Cosby case,

> Ms. Autumn Jackson was entitled, consistent with her constitutional rights, to sell her story to the press. Moreover, she, along with anyone else, was legally entitled to request money from Mr. Cosby or any other person.
>
> Why then it is unlawful for her to threaten to sell her story if she does not receive the money?"
>
> The prosecution of Ms. Jackson is particularly difficult to justify because the legal community commonly practices the same kind of 'extortion' she is accused of.
>
> A lawyer representing a client who has been injured by the conduct of an opposing party will threaten to file a complaint. Fearing public exposure from a suit, the opposing party settles the case before the filing, with the agreement promising confidentiality.

See Michael D. Rips, *To Ask is Not Always to Extort*, NEW YORK TIMES, July 18, 1997. There is nothing in G&S, *supra* note 1, that will satisfy this plaintive cry for elemental justice.

Chapter 10.

Shavell on Threats, Blackmail, Extortion and Robbery And Other Bad Things

In his article on threats, Steven Shavell starts off his analysis of threats reasonably enough, by defining and distinguishing between four different varieties.[1] To put this into table form, they are as follows:

Case	Threat—Give me valuable consideration or I will:
1. Robbery	physically injure you or your property right now
2. Extortion	physically injure you or your property in future
3. Blackmail	reveal your secrets
4. Business	withdraw business (refuse to buy from you)

In the first three cases, the demand is that the target of the threat give the threatener money, or perhaps some other valuable consideration such as sexual services. In the latter case, typically, the demand is for a lower price, quicker delivery, or some such.

These four cases divide naturally into two subsets. In the first category, extortion and robbery, the threat is to do something that no one would deny is illegal, and should indeed be prohibited by law. Namely, the threat is to engage in a physical invasion of person or property, whether now (case 1) or in the future (case 2); it matters not which. If the first two comprise a matched set, so, too, do the last. For in this pair, what is being threatened, or offered, is patently legal. Gossiping about secrets constitutes no more and no less than a paradigm right of free speech. Similarly, at least in a free society, one may refuse to patronize a supplier for any reason at all, or for no reason. This holds, that is, as long as people are free to boycott while motivated by considerations of race, sex, religion, or nationality; since we are not, we as a society do not, to that extent, constitute a free society, one based on contractual rights.

States Epstein:

> The refusal to deal for any reason lies at the root of a system of
> freedom of contract, itself the centerpiece of any common law or-
> der based on the autonomy principle. The employment discrimina-

---

[1] *See* Steven Shavell, *An Economic Analysis of Threats and their illegality: Blackmail, Extortion and Robbery*, 141 U. PA. L. REV. 1877, 1877 (1993).

tion laws represent the antitheses of freedom of contract. ... [They are] an unjustified limitation on the principle of freedom of contract, notwithstanding the overwhelming social consensus in their favor.[2]

And in Rothbard's view: "Discrimination, in the sense of choosing favorably or unfavorably in accordance with whatever criteria a person may employ, is an integral part of freedom of choice, and hence of a free society."[3]

One would expect that the four cases would break naturally along this fault line (e.g., the first pair vs. the second) for the authors who deal with them. If so, one would be disappointed. Shavell, for example, applies his version of economic analysis to these threats.[4] For him, the philosophical dividing line amongst the four threats separates off the last one from the first three; that is, for this author, the main distinction is between extortion, robbery and blackmail on the one hand, and business threats on the other.[5] It does not, as in my view, break them up into two pairs (e.g., extortion and robbery vs. blackmail and business threats). Unfortunately, we are given no account of how this division came to be made, nor any explicit defense of it.

Another anomaly is that, for Shavell, the usual line of demarcation between the normative and the positive seems almost not to exist.[6] Although he tells us his analysis will focus on the costs and benefits of establishing a credible threat, he talks in the same breath of the social undesirability of threats, of the social advantage of laws punishing them, and of the virtues of punishing preparatory behavior versus punishing the making of threats.[7] Further, he sees the threatenee as a victim.[8] This is easy to understand in the case of extortion and robbery. After all, these are not at all mutually agreed upon contracts. But in blackmail and refusal to engage in commercial interaction, it is not clear there is or can be a victim. Shavell, in any case, sees the blackmailee[9] and boycottee as "victims" without giving any reasons for this choice of descriptive appellation.

---

[2] RICHARD EPSTEIN, FORBIDDEN GROUNDS, xii. (1992).

[3] MURRAY N. ROTHBARD, FOR A NEW LIBERTY, 206 (1973).

[4] *See* Shavell, *supra* note 1, at 1878.

[5] *See Id.*

[6] *See, generally, Id.*

[7] *See Id.*, at 1878.

[8] *See Id.*

[9] *See* Russell Hardin, *Blackmailing for Mutual Good*, 141 U. PA. L. REV. 1798 (1993). Hardin uses the more neutral, and hence more welcome word "target." For a criticism of this article, although not on that ground, *see* chapter 7 of this volume.

I. DESCRIPTIVE ANALYSIS OF THREATS

A. Preparatory Behavior

Shavell treats robbery and blackmail as legal equals.[10] However, to carry out blackmail, a person must merely obtain information about the intended target that the latter does not want revealed. To commit robbery, an individual must find a potential victim in circumstances where he could not defend himself or secure help; then, the perpetrator must threaten or commit violence against the victim. Interestingly, a commercial threat, his fourth category, continues to occupy the historical memory hole. Let us resuscitate it. The parallel statement, here, would be: To engage in demanding a lower price, the commercial threatener must seek out a low price offerer. But it is not only threateners who undertake preparatory activity. Victims do too. According to Shavell, the blackmailee can, for example, reduce the number of unfaithful acts in which he engages, and the person fearful of robbery can stay home at night more often.[11] To continue our parallel constructed case, the businessman worried about the threat of customers who refuse to purchase can lower his price. As should by now be clear, it is unimportant whether threats are made or preparatory behavior is undertaken. The key element is whether or not the various actors have the right to do these things. Certainly, a businessman has the right to threaten to go elsewhere unless his demands are met. So too does the gossip (or blackmailer) have the right to engage in free speech, at his own discretion. But it is equally clear that the robber or extortionist has no right whatsoever to threaten bodily harm if his demands are not met. How a scholarly commentator could overlook this basic point must continue to be a puzzle.

B. The Making of Threats

Shavell quite reasonably asserts that for the victim to accede to the threat, "it must be that T's threat will be carried out if, but only if, V rejects the demand; for then V will profit by meeting the demand."[12] This state of affairs will obtain if T has zero cost in carrying out the threat, or gets angry when refused, or has paid a third party to act in this way, or wishes to establish a reputation as one who carries out threats when not paid off to hold back. Based on these considerations, Shavell correctly concludes, "Rules that penal-

---

[10] *See* Shavell, *supra* note 1, at 1879.

[11] *See Id.*

[12] *Id.* at 1881.

ize the making of threats and their execution will generally increase the expected cost of making threats, and thus reduce the number of occasions in which a threatener will decide to make a threat."[13]

But now comes the puzzler. States our author: "A complication with regard to a discovery that T is accepting payments is that this in itself may well not be illegal. If it is not illegal, then T's acceptance of payments must be combined with other evidence for it to help in convicting T of making threats. Similarly, V's execution of a threat may not be illegal (suppose the threat is to expose information) and thus must be combined with other evidence to assist in convicting T."[14]

The difficulty is that it is hard to see why our author would be so intent upon convicting T, given that he is engaged in what would otherwise be construed, even by Shavell, as "not ... illegal."[15] Since when does the law, in all its majesty, seek to punish *legal* behavior?

C. Application to Different Types of Threat.

Shavell's treatment of robbery and extortion is, given his logical positivist outlook, a reasonable one, except that he seems to have only private robbers and extortionists in mind. However, as is well known, governments, also, may contain bands of extortionists and thieves, and of course far worse. It would have been of great interest to see how Shavell would have incorporated this phenomenon into his analysis. The difficulty is that his remarks do not apply in a straightforward manner to a criminal sovereign. For example, Shavell states, "Legal rules against robbery undoubtedly reduce the amount of robbery substantially, despite the incidence of this crime."[16] But the leaders of government make the legal rules and, presumably, do not enact any that would ensnare themselves. Similarly, our author mentions "the legal rules against extortion are probably effective in deterring a tremendous amount of that activity; in the absence of the enforcement of legal rules against extortion, we would likely be overrun by extortionate enterprise."[17] But when governments threaten to jail us if we refuse to pay unjustified taxes, they engage in extortion and no "legal rules" prevent them from so doing.

Two types of extortion come readily to mind, one engaged in by government itself, the other permitted by it. The first is the practice, on the part of

[13] *Id.* at 1883.

[14] *Id.* at 1881 fn. 13.

[15] *Id.*

[16] *Id.* at 1888.

[17] *Id.* at 1889.

numerous District Attorneys, of prosecuting non-criminals for offenses, which would not otherwise attract their attention, when their ultimate goal is to induce them to provide evidence against major criminals.

How often, for example, have we seen in television cop shows a tableau where the police threaten to harass an innocent businessman unless he turns on a malefactor. But this is no less than extortion. The threat is to prosecute this innocent person (an illegal act) unless he does their bidding.

The second example comes from the arena of labor relations. According to union legislation such as the Wagner Act, it is illegal to refuse to "bargain fairly" with organized labor. But shunning, boycott, or refusal to deal with, is part and parcel of the right of free association. To be forced to "deal with" someone against your will is to be extorted. Prohibitionists of blackmail such as Shavell never protest such extortion, even though, unlike blackmail, here the threat is to use violence, and government makes it.

For a third source of cases illustrating this point Russell Madden states:

> Extortion has always been a favorite activity of governmental agencies. Ordinarily, threatening someone with harm unless he accedes to another's demands is rightfully a crime. Whether the perpetrator is a neighbor seeking to use your lawn mower or an organized crime thug reminding you to pay your monthly 'protection fee,' such behavior is condemned and prosecuted rigorously. ...
>
> Unfortunately, in today's political reality, *legal* extortion is the guiding principle that authorities at all levels of government practice with enthusiasm. ... Typically, a property owner is required to comply with government demands in return for being permitted to engage in some activity.[18]

Examples given include building codes, zoning, payments for new building, the IRS, constraints on tobacco and alcohol producers, etc.

This, it cannot be over emphasized, is truly a puzzle. Extortion, which is the threat of violence, and clearly incompatible with rights, is intellectually justified by most scholars. On the other hand these scholars denigrate blackmail, which is merely the threat to take advantage of free speech rights.

In this analysis of Bolivia and Colombia, Shavell comes close to recognizing this point, but not close enough.[19] He shows evidence of realizing that the duly constituted governments, especially in this region of the world, are

---

[18] Russell Madden, *Or Else...*, 47 THE FREEMAN 749 (1997).

[19] *See* Shavell, *supra* note 1, at 1888.

themselves robbers and thieves.[20] However, he contents himself with a glance at "certain guerrilla and bandit groups,"[21] which would appear not to be these officially in power.

Now consider his treatment of blackmail. Shavell certainly sees this behavior in a different light than extortion or robbery since he declares that when he "reveal[s] his information ... this is not a crime" unlike the other two cases. Indeed, as he avers, "it might be difficult to successfully prosecute the blackmailer in the absence of independent evidence that he had made a threat."[22] But how can making a threat to do something (reveal information), which is itself licit, be a crime? And what are we to make of this statement? "[T]he blackmailer can sometimes phrase the threats in a nuanced way to avoid crossing the line of criminality, even though the meaning of the threats will be clear to victims."[23] How can it be a crime if it avoids crossing the line of "criminality?" Yet our author characterizes such behavior, which even he believes has not crossed this line, as "blackmail" (by this term he denotes that a crime has been committed).[24] It is hard to avoid the conclusion that this statement constitutes a contradiction in terms.

However there is at least the seeming concession that "Unlike the victim of an extortion or robbery threat, the blackmail victim may suffer more if the threatener is brought to justice than if he is not."[25] If this is so, in what sense, then, can it be that the blackmailee is a "victim?" We know he is not—certainly not when compared to the situation in which his secret is in the hands of a gossip, who will spill the beans no matter how valuable silence is to the secret holder. If we are going to incarcerate the blackmailee because he is a "victim," and his position is far worse when the gossip has power over him, then we must not only jail the gossip, we must do so for an even longer length of time. Since no one advocates criminalizing gossip, it is hard to understand why anyone would entertain this notion for blackmail, particularly if victimization is the concern.

Following Epstein,[26] Shavell worries that legalization would "vastly increase ... the scope of blackmail."[27] But if this activity should be legalized,

---

[20] *See Id.*

[21] *Id.* at 1889 fn. 21.

[22] *Id.* at 1889.

[23] *Id.* at 1890.

[24] *See Id.*

[25] *See Id.* at 1891.

[26] *See* Richard Epstein, *Blackmail, Inc.*, 50 U. CHI. L. REV. 553 (1983). *But see* chapter 13, this volume.

[27] Shavell, *supra* note 1, at 1891.

why should we worry about it as a matter of law, any more than we are concerned about the expansion of bowling, television, or gossip, for that matter? Shavell is unhappy at the prospect that Epstein's "Blackmail, Inc." would "entice people into embarrassing situations"[28] and then blackmail them for so acting.[29] But there is already quite a bit of enticement going on, with virtually none of it emanating from the private sector. The prime examples are furnished by the government so favored by Shavell, with its unwise and improper prohibition of drugs. If he were seriously concerned about enticement,[30] he could do worse to set his sights on that arena instead of the one at hand.

Our author probes the relationship between the legal status of blackmail and the rate of capture and degree of punishment for criminals, real criminals that is, ones with real victims, who actually suffer from the threats and invasions made upon them.[31] He correctly notes that prohibition of blackmail will tend to reduce the probability that criminals are punished "because people will generally have less incentive to obtain information about the commission of crimes when blackmail is illegal."[32] As against that, Shavell claims that people who already have information on criminal behavior will be more likely to report it to the state authorities under blackmail criminalization, which is true enough, and that "under plausible assumptions the state's punishment will be more severe than a blackmailer's."[33]

This doesn't seem all that plausible. First, blackmail is not the only victimless crime. Also included under this rubric must be drugs, pornography, prostitution, gambling and cigarettes. To the extent that government allocates scarce police and court manpower to such exercises of personal freedom, it incapacitates itself from retarding real crime. Second, the public sector "jus-

---

[28] *Id.*

[29] *See Id.*

[30] Or is the proper word here, "entrapment?" After all, there is quite a lot of enticement that goes on in the market place, e.g., advertising, without anyone calling for its total elimination (apart from cigarettes). Perhaps this is next on this wish list for the would-be regulators of our society.

[31] *See* Shavell, *supra* note 1, at 1891.

[32] *Id.* For this insight, Shavell credits Richard Epstein, *Blackmail, Inc.*, 50 U. CHI. L. REV. 553 (1983); Richard Posner, *Blackmail, Privacy and Freedom of Contract*, 141 U. PA.L. REV. 1817 (1993); James Lindgren, *Unraveling the Paradox of Blackmail*, 84 COLUM. L. REV. 670 (1984); Ronald Coase, *The 1987 McCorkle Lecture: Blackmail*, 74 VA. L. REV. 655 (1988); Daniel Ellsberg, *The Theory and Practice of Blackmail, in* BARGAINING: FORMAL THEORIES OF NEGOTIATION (1975); William Landes & Richard Posner, *The Private Enforcement of Law*, 41. J. LEGAL STUD. 1, 43 (1975).

[33] Shavell, *supra* note 1, at 1892.

tice" system includes plea bargaining, "turn-em-loose-Bruce" judges, Miranda warnings, search technicalities and other ACLU-inspired interferences with the just punishment of criminals. Inmates are paroled before serving sentences by boards composed of social workers, psychologists and "criminologists," none of whom bear any responsibility[34] for the recidivism they engender.[35] It is difficult to believe that private enterprise blackmailers could not do a better job of quelling crimes than the self-enfeebled state.

On the other hand, there is a sense in which our author may be correct, although he cannot be expected to derive much comfort from it. I refer to the extra legal punishment to which prisoners (many of them guilty of only minor, or, worse, victimless crimes) are subjected in statist jails: homosexual gang rapes.[36] Here, the state, unable to promote justice even in its own jails, truly comes into its own as a savage agent of punishment, in a manner way beyond the scope of any mere blackmailer. However, this, of course, is highly illegal, and should presumably be stopped. It is remarkable, however, that Shavell can place such great faith in a public institution, which has so far proven unable to stop these occurrences, to say nothing of its failure to keep its own prisons drug free. He complains of the lack of "public humiliation"[37] for the criminal who is made to pay for his crime by a blackmailer. This cannot be denied. However, a spell in the "pokey" is almost a rite of passage in the strata of society from which criminal behavior is most highly over represented. Far from a "public humiliation," it is almost a badge of honor. Even if, somehow, Shavell were correct in this contention, he would still have to come to grips with those who liken blackmail to a living death or hell on earth. For example, Coase[38] refers to it as "moral murder."[39]

---

[34] See, generally, THOMAS SOWELL, THE VISION OF THE ANOINTED (1995); THOMAS SOWELL, A CONFLICT OF VISIONS: IDEOLOGICAL ORIGIN OF POLITICAL STRUGGLES (1987); THOMAS SOWELL, INSIDE AMERICAN EDUCATION: THE DECLINE, THE DECEPTION, THE DOGMAS (1993).

[35] In a just society, surely, one dedicated to the diminution of crimes with victims, these who determine as professionals that the people they return to the street will not commit further outrages should bear responsibility for these acts when they do occur. That is, these parole officers should be made to pay the penalty for these additional crimes their parolees unleash upon the new innocent victims.

[36] This was depicted most dramatically in the recent movie *The Shawshank Redemption*.

[37] Shavell, *supra* note 1, at 1892.

[38] See Ronald Coase, *The 1987 McCorkle Lecture: Blackmail*, 74 VA. L. REV. 655 (1988).

[39] See Sidney W. Delong, *Blackmailers, Bribe Takers, and the Second Paradox*, 141 U. PA.L.REV., 1689 (1993). For a critique of this article, *see* chapter 2, this volume.

Our author focuses attention on three "commonly made threats and other legally permissible threats. The first is to withdraw business unless price ... is favorably adjusted." The second is to threaten a lawsuit unless paid damages, and the third is to build a fence on your own property blocking your neighbor's view unless he pays you or "constrains his bothersome dog."[40] But the question facing Shavell, and others who advocate prohibition, is why should these threats be legal but not those made by the blackmailer? Curiously, our author seems unaware that such a question might reasonably be posed. Certainly, he does not even so much as attempt to answer it.

II. NORMATIVE ANALYSIS OF THREATS

A. Commentary on the General Effect of Threats on Social Welfare

"[E]fforts expended by threateners putting themselves in a position to carry out threats is a social waste; such effort is not producing anything of value for final consumption. Similarly, precautions taken by potential victims avoiding threats reduce social welfare."[41]

There are several problems here. First, it is by no means obvious that nothing in threats is productive of final consumption value. What about psychic enjoyment? Suppose a person enjoys the making of the threat *per se*, the sheer value of not only seeing people squirm, but of actually having caused this discomfort. For such misanthropy to be ruled out of court, Shavell will need far more than the value-free economics he inconsistently brings to the table. Namely, he would need an ethical theory to attain this goal—one which he valiantly, but not successfully, attempts to eschew.

Second, even accepting the "nice guys don't do that" value judgment implicit in his analysis, Shavell's general theory applies only to robbery and extortion, not to blackmail, and, even by his own admission, not to the three threats he discusses in his section D.[42] That is to say, given that we have agreed not to count malevolence as a value, we can now definitely state that robbery and extortion are wealth destroying. There is only loss, no gain (as we are now refusing to count the improved condition of the sadist as a social benefit.) Certainly, these two activities cannot pass muster under Pareto conditions, as there is at least one person, the victim of robbery or extortion, who must count himself worse off. (If the robbery victim did not consider his util-

---

[40] *See* Shavell, *supra* note 1, at 1893–94.

[41] *Id.* at 1894.

[42] *See Id.*

ity to be reduced by this event, it must be something of the sort that he was just on the point of giving the robber the money anyway, and he doesn't mind the robber jumping the gun, so to speak. In other words, it wasn't really a robbery.)

But this does not at all apply to blackmail nor Shavell's three other cases. Here, there is no need to preclude sadism from counting as a benefit—because there need not be any such motivation involved. These examples, moreover, satisfy the Pareto criterion; there is at least one person benefited by the contract in question, and no one who is worse off. Of course, it cannot be denied that the blackmailee, the seller, the injured party and the neighbor with a view would be better off if the blackmailer had not unearthed the secret, the buyer had not found a better offer, the injured party was not contemplating a lawsuit and the properly owner had no desire to build a fence. But all this is beside the point. The real issue is, given that these four have done what they have done (all of which should be considered perfectly legal) will they *now* worsen the well-being of their contractual partners by making an agreement with them? And the unavoidable answer is that they will not. How could it be otherwise? For if the blackmailee, (etc.,) felt that the payment for silence (etc.,) could reduce his wealth, he would simply have refused the offer (or threat.) All voluntary contracts between consenting adults (specifically including these four) must, by definition, fulfill Pareto conditions. If one partner felt the contract put him in an inferior position, he would simply have refused to sign it.

So much for Shavell's first category, preparatory behavior. The second is "the making of threats independently of whether they are eventually expected."[43] These will reduce welfare, he tells us, in that they "can create fear and anxiety in victims." While there may be some psychologists who would agree with Shavell in this, there are others who disagree.[44] The latter group reasons that fear and anxiety are products of irrational thoughts people feed themselves, not of actual events which might come about. Suppose, for the sake of argument, that our author is correct in his foray into the field of psychology, and that Ellis and Edelstein are wrong in their conclusions. This still does not save his contention that since threats create fear and anxiety, they reduce economic welfare.

For again, we must set beside the minus of fear and anxiety and the plus of imposing such emotions on other people, and of enjoying their discomfort. And this, again, applies to only the best of the examples Shavell can marshal,

---

[43] *See Id.*

[44] See *generally* MICHAEL R. EDELSTEIN & DAVID RAMSEY STEELE, THREE MINUTE THERAPY (1997); ALBERT ELLIS & ROBERT A. HARPER, A GUIDE TO RATIONAL LIVING (1961).

namely, robbery and extortion. When we come to blackmail, the threat to buy elsewhere, to bring suit, or to build a fence, the fear and anxiety created in the victim if any does result (remember, we are still only supposing this to be so, contrary to Ellis and Edelstein, for the sake of argument),[45] can be more than offset by the contracted gains to be made: the silence, freedom from a lawsuit, the uninterrupted view, etc.

Still less does it save Shavell's claim that things which reduce economic welfare ought to be banned by law; for this, as we have seen, is an ethical conclusion, which needs support from an ethical premise—something our author refuses to vouchsafe us. Contends Rothbard in this regard: "it is the responsibility of any scientist, indeed any intellectual, to refrain from any value judgment whatever unless he can support it on the basis of a coherent and defensible ethical system. This means, of course, that those economists who, on whatever grounds, are not prepared to think about and advance an ethical system should strictly refrain from any value pronouncements or policy conclusions at all."[46]

Shavell's perspective on the matter is problematic. When I open up a competitive grocery store across the street from yours, we do not decide the legality of my action on the basis of whether or not the benefits to me and to my new customers outweigh the losses to you. Rather, we allow me to do this action because it is done with my own private property, and does not conflict with any of your rights. Why should we analyze blackmail, or any other law for that matter, differently?

Shavell seems most concerned with "repeated threats," presumably made by the blackmailer.[47] These are "potentially a significant detriment to social welfare." But this applies with just as much force as the buyer's threat to take his business elsewhere unless price is lowered. This too, can be done repeatedly. Curiously, our author seems not at all concerned with the deleterious effect of these ongoing threats. Why this irrational prejudice against the ancient practice of blackmail?

---

[45] *See, generally, Id.*

[46] Murray Rothbard, *Praxeology, Value Judgements and Public Policy*, in THE FOUNDATIONS OF MODERN AUSTRIAN ECONOMICS (1976); *see also* Walter Block, *On Value Freedom in Economics*, 17 AM. ECONOMISTS 38 (1973); Murray N. Rothbard, *Value Implications of Economic Theory*, AM. ECONOMISTS (Spring 1973).

[47] *See* Shavell, *supra* note 1, at 1894.

B. Optimal Use of the Law Against Undesirable Threat

Having established, at least to his own satisfaction, his claim that threats are undesirable, Shavell now moves to a consideration of how the law can optimally deal with them.[48] Interventions can be made at any of the four stages: preparatory behavior, the making of the threat, collection of payment and the carrying out of the threat.[49] Since he thinks we have already reached the limits of the "magnitudes of punishment," he advocates government action on all four margins.[50]

As far as preparatory behavior is concerned, such as setting eavesdropping devices in order to obtain secrets with which to blackmail people, Shavell makes an important and relevant distinction. Regarding government intervention, he sees a "difficulty in differentiating innocent behavior from that which is preparatory to the making of threats. If, for instance, a person is prowling the halls of a motel with a camera, it will be hard to demonstrate from this alone that he was planning to take photographs for blackmail."[51]

This is somewhat unusual for our author since his self-styled economics approach does not readily lend itself to distinguishing innocent behavior from the guilty variety.[52] In any case, if the prowling photographer may be "innocent" of blackmail, why may not this apply to the blackmailer himself? The difficulty is that Shavell nowhere clarifies the distinction between guilt and innocence. He holds the blackmailer guilty of criminal behavior for making threats, but not the fence builder, the price shopper (gouger?) and the lawsuit launcher, who are equally "guilty" of making threats. Seemingly, he does this for no other reason than that the latter are not widely considered legally objectionable, while the former is.[53]

He also rejects government intervention at the level of threat-making on the ground that "all three types of threat," e.g., robbery, extortion and black-

---

[48] *See Id.* at 1895.

[49] *See Id.* Shavell claims three, but I count four.

[50] *See Id.*

[51] *Id.* at 1895–96.

[52] First of all, as we have seen above, these are normative terms, and the "economic approach" is presumably a positive one. Second, did Shavell really make this distinction, he would have taken the diametric opposite stance of the one he did on the legalization of blackmail, for, as has been shown, it consists of nothing more than the juxtaposition of two acts, each of which, when carried out alone, would be deemed by all (including himself) to be innocent.

[53] On the other hand, there are laws against price "gouging" if not shopping around for better bargains, although no one has ever explained the difference between these two economic acts (apart from the fact that one occurs on the demand side, the other on the side of supply).

mail, tend to keep their behavior hidden from the eyes of the law.[54] This cannot be denied. But why the linkage between "all three" of these threats? Why do the lawsuit launcher, the bargain hunter and the fence builder keep slipping down the memory hole?

In like manner, Shavell does not advocate capture of the presumably evil blackmailer for receiving payment or carrying out the threat. Why? Again, the malefactor will tend to avoid the light of day for his "evil" doings. Since none of the four is likely to yield results, the plan appears to be to utilize all of them. But then our author states: "[I]f proof of threat-making had been sufficient, a conviction would already have been obtained."[55] This, however, is incorrect. For blackmail consists of two legal whites, each of which, were they to occur in isolation, would be totally licit. Namely, the threat to reveal a secret and a demand for money. The peculiarity (not to say logical contradiction) of blackmail prohibitionism is that when these two take place as part of one larger act, the two legal whites somehow turn black. Thus, Shavell is incorrect in asserting that the threat, alone, when not coupled with a demand for money, is either illegal or constitutes an act of blackmail, which should be prohibited. No "conviction" could be obtained merely on the strength of a threat alone. This, standing on its own, would not be blackmail but rather the issuance of a warning that a person intends to engage in malicious gossip.

C. Applications

Shavell considers a socially harmless act such as taking a shower or engaging in sexual intercourse with one's own wife in private. Nevertheless, due to considerations of modesty, a man might be willing to pay to prevent circulation of pictures of such events.

It is for this reason, apparently, that he states: "In such cases blackmail is almost, but not entirely analogous to robbery or extortion and thus seems socially undesirable."[56] Remarkably, no further reason for this claim is given. This is difficult to understand, given that the law allows for the circulation of such pictures. Suppose a paparazzi with a long distance camera took a picture through an open window of a married couple engaged in sexual relations. Licit, so far. If a man can see it, the photographer can record it. And his viewing of this act violates no rational law. Next, this worthy shows the picture to a few friends, perhaps even to an editor. Again, no law worthy of the name has yet been broken. Nor will it be when a newspaper publishes it. For if the pho-

---

[54] *See* Shavell, *supra* note 1, at 1896.

[55] *Id.*

[56] *Id.* at 1897.

tographer owns his view of the naked people, he owns the pictured representation of that vista—e.g., the art work in question—and may do with it precisely as he wishes. But, if, (horrors!), the photographer has the common decency to approach the subjects of his photograph, to give them the option of regaining their privacy then, at long last for Shavell, his act finally becomes illegitimate. That this is precisely the point at which the blackmailer becomes the benefactor of the victim, whereas before he was not, matters not one whit to our author.

As long as they can be seen with the naked eye, and or with the help of technological enhancement, they have no right of privacy. According to some primitive societies, in sharp contrast, to take someone's picture is to (somehow) steal his soul. We in the west, presumably, reject such claims as arrant superstition. However, blackmail law as presently construed would appear to be in keeping with such uncivilized understandings of causation.

Shavell gives as the reason for his stance the claim that "the efforts to undertake blackmail and the efforts to guard against it are social wastes."[57] He says this, but we are not required to take it at face value, since he does not apply this to the plaintiff, the fence builder, or the bargain hunter. Our author also states, "if people take showers less frequently (for example, when they are in hotel rooms), they experience a loss in utility for no socially good reason."[58] This, too, is problematic. Any hotel, which makes available to outsiders views of its showering guests who wish to retain their privacy (e.g., are willing to go to the effort of lowering blinds, closing bathroom doors, shower curtains) is a hotel, which will soon have no customers. If Shavell were correct, it would be a "social waste" for hotels to install doors, blinds, shower curtains, and for guests to be "forced" to avail themselves of these accommodations if they wish privacy. Is taking and circulating pictures of people against their will conducive of "social welfare?" Shavell is an agnostic on this question:

> Consider the case of photographs of a person taking a shower being sent to the person's co-workers. It could be that those who see the photographs would not enjoy viewing them in any sense; rather, they would feel awkward, especially when in the presence of the blackmail victim. Another possibility, though, is that people might enjoy seeing photographs of a person taking a shower. For example, the blackmail victim may be an extremely attractive young woman and her male co-workers may take a prurient interest in the photo-

---

[57] *Id.*

[58] *Id.* at 1898.

graphs. Thus, in theory, it is not apparent how revelation of information would affect social welfare.[59]

This is a particularly troublesome way to do public policy analysis. The
issue necessarily turns on a weighing of the utilities of one person against
those of another (or others). But it is impossible to interpersonally compare
utility.[60] This agnosticism would appear to be the inevitable conclusion of any
such analysis. Judges may indeed try to rule so as to maximize wealth, but this
attempt is fatally compromised by the fatal methodology of interpersonal
comparisons of utility.

Much more reasonable, and conducive to definitive conclusion, is to determine such matters on the basis of private property rights. That is, it is up to
the plaintiffs "to close the doors shutters and blinds, etc." If they do so, no one
can even see them in embarrassing circumstances, let alone capture their im-
ages forevermore. But if they fail to take these elementary precautions, it is
open season on looking at and photographing them. And if a busybody with
"prurient interests" can view those engaged in sex or showering, he can share
these visions with others of like mind. As well, he can refrain from so doing,
for a fee! That is one of the implications of a free society.

Shavell considers cases of blackmail where the information concerns non-
criminal but socially harmful activity, for example "the wasteful but not illegal
spending of church funds by a minister."[61] For our author, the case for blackmail under this assumption is "ambiguous."[62] On the one hand there will be a
reduction in undesirable "wasteful" activities.[63] On the other blackmail comes
in a package deal: there are also search costs, and perhaps expensive efforts to
guard against being uncovered. But it is more than just passing curious that
this author should see "ambiguity" in so simple a scenario. After all, it is no
more than a commonplace for there to be costs and benefits attached to economic activity. Markets solve such problems every day. For example, I am
now sitting on a chair. It has benefits, but also costs. Is there any "ambiguity"
about the transaction that brought this item into my possession? Not a bit of
it. In my subjective estimation, I placed the chair higher than the price I had
to pay for it. At least in the *ex ante* sense, all such choices must always be

---

[59] *Id.*

[60] *See* Murray Rothbard, *Toward a Reconstruction of Utility and Welfare Economics*, Center for
Libertarian Studies, Occasional Paper #3 (1977).

[61] Shavell, *supra* note 1, at 1898.

[62] *Id.*

[63] *Id.*

beneficial—as there is no other criterion on the basis of which to judge such matters.

A similar analysis applies in the present case. If the minister values secrecy more than the money demanded of him by the blackmailer, he will pay and we must judge that social welfare, at least from this one transaction, has increased, again in the *ex ante* sense. If the minister ranks these goods the other way around, he will not pay, and again social welfare will be enhanced (or at least not decreased) as the man of the cloth refuses to pay a greater value to achieve a lesser. In these circumstances, it will be up to the blackmailer as to whether or not to carry through in revealing the secret. Again there will be certain costs (postage, money for a telephone call, the risks of being associated with an immoral clergymen, perhaps) and benefits (an enhanced reputation for carrying through, practically required for the professional practice of blackmail.) Here, too, welfare will be promoted *ex ante*, as the blackmailer takes that course of action, which seems most likely to benefit him.

Suppose "Mrs. Grundy" objects, on the ground that, for her, the occurrence of blackmail is a negative externality. Would we then have to renounce the claim that blackmail is wealth enhancing? Not at all! This third party simply has no way to demonstrate her preference.[64] She could be lying, or exaggerating. In any case, if we allow improvable and unsupportable "neighborhood effects" into the analysis, we must, to be logical, carry through in all cases. If so, there is no warrant, then, to assume that my purchase of the chair was wealth creating. For surely, there is, somewhere, an obscure group of people who object to anyone sitting on chairs.

Shavell will undoubtedly have an objection to the foregoing. He might even agree, on the micro level, that each of these decisions will be welfare maximizing in the narrow—individual sense. His concern, however, will be with the macro: will the value to the entire society of putting a crimp hi the plans of all wastrel ministers be more, equally or less offset by the attendant costs? If this is truly his concern, he is doomed to disappointment. "Ambiguous" doesn't begin to describe this situation. To put it that way is to make it appear as if this were a mere empirical issue, one amenable to solution, at least in principle. But this is impossible to solve, depending as it does on interpersonal comparisons of utility. Another way to put the matter is to hark back to the diamonds–water paradox that so vexed Adam Smith. There is simply no economic way of telling whether all of one commodity is worth more than all of another since we never make such macro choices. (Although

---

[64] *See* Murray N. Rothbard, *Toward a Reconstruction of Utility and Welfare Economics*, San Francisco: Center for Libertarian Studies, Occasional Paper #3 (1977).

if we ever did, the better choice would not be too onerous a one, at least for diamonds vs. water.)

Shavell might have another objection: allowing blackmail may not sufficiently reduce ministerial wastefulness with church money. Two points need to be made in this context. First, blackmail cannot be expected to root out all incidence of such behavior; as long as it better attains this goal than the prohibition of blackmail, whether or not coupled with state activity to this end, it is salutary from a utilitarian point of view. Second, it seems an improper burden to place on the pro legalization side that blackmail has to root out such clergy misconduct, let alone do it more efficiently than governmental efforts. It is sufficient for the libertarian criterion that blackmail does not involve an initiation of violence against an innocent person. And it should be sufficient on utilitarian grounds that the two parties to the contract, the blackmailer and the blackmailee, both benefit from it. If it has salutary effects on third parties such as the minister, well and good. But this is hardly a requirement.

Shavell's third concern is with blackmail where the secret information concerns the commitment of a crime (e.g., a real one, that is. replete with a victim whose person or property is actually invaded). Previously he had concluded indeterminacy in criminal incentives in that, with blackmail, more thieves would be punished but some would receive lower monetary rather than imprisonment penalties. Now, he adds a new twist, the better and more clearly to show the social uselessness of legalized blackmail: rewards for providing information to the authorities leading to arrest and convictions. He states: "Rather than inducing individuals to obtain information by allowing them to blackmail someone, like a thief, these individuals could be equivalently induced, were that desired, by offering them a reward equal to the amount they could obtain through blackmail—and by making blackmail illegal at the same time."[65]

Our author puts forth three reasons in behalf of this legal state of affairs. One, he thinks, "the state can impose higher penalties."[66] We have already cast aspersions on this claim. Two, "presuming the judicial process has been designed to guard against errors, it is better to have this mechanism determine punishment than blackmailers."[67] Yes, and if horses were wishes, beggars would ride. If you pack enough heroic assumptions into your premise, you can validly conclude almost anything. By all means, let us assume into existence an all powerful, totally efficient and omni-benevolent government; then,

---

[65] Shavell, *supra* note 1, at 1899–1900.

[66] *Id.* at 1900.

[67] *Id.*

surely, it can outperform private enterprise.[68] And three, that old saw, the wastage (cost) of resources devoted to blackmail. There is a basic problem with Shavell's argument from reward: it violates *ceteris paribus* conditions. Here we are debating two kinds of sanctions against criminals, public and private (blackmail) ones. Things may not be evenly balanced, but at least it is a horse race. Along comes our author pressing his thumb down on one of the sides of the scale with wads of money. Why not try an infinite amount of money as a bounty that would really highlight the inadequacy of blackmail?

Two can play this game. I hereby propose a government subsidy for blackmailers, and a tax on all those who keep themselves aloof from this activity. That ought to win the race for this type of private crime fighting, hands down.

It may be unfair to characterize Shavell as never having met a public sector program he didn't like, but this comes perilously close to the truth where we consider penology. Coercive socialism doesn't work in *any* human endeavor, and the one under consideration is no exception.

Shavell worries that if law enforcement officers themselves are allowed to blackmail criminals, this will set up misallocations of effort away from apprehending poor and toward rich criminals, and will create conflicts of interest with their day jobs.[69] In this he seems correct. But to ban blackmail on these grounds is unjustified. We can coherently legalize blackmail for everyone else apart from state employees in the penal system (and then continue to anxiously await the day the entire industry is privatized).

III. COMMONLY MADE THREATS

With this section, the penultimate one, Shavell has his last chance to explain the philosophical difference between blackmail and other non-invasive

---

[68] To say the least, this sentiment of Shavell's runs counter to everything with which the Public Choice School has become associated. See JAMES M. BUCHANAN & GORDON TULLOCK, THE CALCULUS OF CONSENT: LOGICAL FOUNDATIONS OF CONSTITUTIONAL DEMOCRAC (1971); JAMES M. BUCHANAN & GEOFFREY BRENNAN, THE POWER OF TAX: ANALYTICAL FOUNDATION OF A FISCAL CONSTITUTION (1980); TOWARDS A THEORY OF THE RENT-SEEKING SOCIETY (James M. Buchanan, Robert D. Tollison, & Gordon. Tullock eds.) (1980); Robert Lloyd & Joseph P. McGarrity, *A Probit Analysis of the Senate Vote on Gramm-Rudman*, PUBLIC CHOICE, 81–90 (1995); Kevin B. Grier & Joseph P. McGarrity, *The Effect of Macroeconomic Fluctuations on the Electoral Fortunes of House Incumbents*, 16 J.L. & ECON., 143 (1998).

[69] *See* Shavell, *supra* note 1, at 1901.

threats (suit launching, price shopping, fence building, etc.). As before, he doesn't seem to realize this as lacunae. Instead, he resorts to claiming, "threats to withdraw business unless price or some other term is altered are usually good things."[70] So, for that matter, are warnings about impending gossip, and being willing to refrain from revealing secrets. A constant refrain, here, is the claim that such threats are "socially desirable."[71] Forgotten in the entire hyperbola are the attendant costs, something never far from central stage when it comes to robbery and extortion, Shavell maintains that the threat to bring a civil suit does not compromise deterrence. Yes. But how can it be denied that it sets up fear in the heart of the defendant?[72] Why are these 'social costs' lost sight of only here, but not in the cases of blackmail, robbery, and extortion? Our author claims that these other threats are part of the "normal bargaining process,"[73] and to be sure, they are. But if blackmail were legalized, it too, would become normalized. Come to think of it, murder rape and theft are also "normal" in a statistical sense. What this has to do with what should be legal, and what not, is at best obscure. Shavell even goes so far as to admit that these other situations (e.g., fence building, etc.) can result in "social waste" without drawing the conclusion he would in the context of blackmail.[74]

IV. CONCLUSION

Shavell claims that blackmail prohibition is not paradoxical. It is thought to be so by many commentators because "it makes punishable the threat to reveal information even though revealing information itself is not punishable."[75] However, thanks to the "lens of economics,"[76] the paradox vanishes. That is to say: "We know that permitting blackmail will lead potential victims to curtail innocent behavior and take other steps to avoid blackmail, and also will induce potential blackmailers to invest efforts in obtaining embarrassing information. These effects are undesirable, and warrant making blackmail illegal."[77]

---

[70] *Id.*

[71] *Id.*

[72] Given, of course, that they do not avail themselves of the techniques of Edelstein and Steele or Ellis and Harper. *See, supra* note 44.

[73] Shavell, *supra* note 1, at 1901.

[74] *Id.* at 1902.

[75] *Id.*

[76] *Id.*

[77] *Id.*

The point seems to be that all "undesirable" things should be outlawed. I wonder what his position is on fattening foods, tobacco, hang gliding, homosexuality, and interracial marriages—all of which have been deemed "undesirable" by numerous people all throughout history and some even at the present time.

Paradoxically, and I use that word advisedly, I agree with Shavell's conclusion, if not his reasoning. Blackmail does not constitute a paradox because it ought to be decriminalized, and there is nothing remarkable about two separate acts, each of which alone is licit, remaining legal even when they are taken together.

As for our author's "economic lens," it seems opaque to me. There are many things, which are not conducive to economic well-being, apart from those mentioned above as being considered "undesirable." For example, watching too much TV, reading junk novels, gossip papers such as the National Enquirer, following soap operas, etc. Why narrow considerations of GDP should determine the law is hard to see.

Shavell does score a point against Lindgren[78] in pointing out that the adventitiously acquired embarrassing information (the workman goes up a ladder and accidentally sees someone in "awkward" circumstances) is costless. However, Shavell fails to reckon with the fact that the incentive to evade blackmail would result in precisely the same act as is required to avoid embarrassment: namely, closing the blinds or curtains. Thus, it is not clear that there is any extra incentive for doing the one over and above the other.

Nor does my own value free economic lens "suggest"[79] any public policy conclusion (e.g., prohibiting blackmail, offering rewards for information on criminals) whatsoever. Perhaps his lens has an admixture of normative presuppositions ground into the glass.

---

[78] *See* James Lindgren, *Unraveling the Paradox of Blackmail*, 84 COLUM. L. REV. 670 (1984).
[79] Shavell, *supra* note 1, at 1903.

Chapter 11.

Blackmail from A to Z: A Reply to Joseph Isenbergh's "Blackmail from A to C"

The long and the short of blackmail is that it consists of two acts, each of which, were they to occur alone, would be considered legal by everyone. Yet somehow, when these elements occur together, virtually all commentators who have ever written on the subject consider the complex act consisting of both elements to be unlawful. There is only a corporal's guard that demurs. Is the mainstream view due perhaps to some sort of alchemy? How else can two legal "rights" be rendered a "wrong" when they take place in tandem?

Let us consider the specifics. Which two acts together constitute blackmail? First, there is a threat or an offer, depending upon your point of view.[1] Whatever it is called, it states that some act, which in and of itself is perfectly legal, will be done.[2] The proposition typically is to engage in free speech rights and gossip about the secrets of the blackmailee or target.[3] However, the topic could be almost anything. The proposition could be to build a fence on my own land that blocks your view. It could be to write a negative review of your recently published book. It could even be to withhold selling you a piece of my property.

Second, there is a demand or a request. This again depends upon your point of view. Characteristically in the case of blackmail, the proposal concerns money or other valuable considerations.

Now put the two acts together. For example, the proposition is that unless you give me money, I will tell the newspapers that you patronize prostitutes. Unless you grant me special privileges, I will build a tall fence. Unless you do some service for me, I will give your book a negative review. Unless you pay me my price, I will not sell you my motorcycle.

What each of these scenarios has in common is that it is legal to ask for money, services, or privileges. Also, it is not a crime to gossip about one's sexual practices, erect a structure on my own land, cast aspersions on your literary skills, or keep my motorcycle for myself.

Blackmail must be sharply distinguished from extortion. Extortion also combines a request for money with a threat. Only here the threat is to do

---

[1] *See* Chapter 13, this volume

[2] *Id.*

[3] *Id.*

something clearly unlawful, such as kill someone, burn down a house, or kidnap children. Blackmail and extortion are commonly confused, perhaps because they both combine a threat and a demand. However, these two acts resemble each other only superficially. They are as distinct as rape and seduction[4] or trade and robbery.

Isenbergh attempts to rationalize the present outlawry of blackmail.[5] His "concern ... is limited to 'pure' or 'informational' blackmail: the sale of silence by someone who is otherwise free to disclose what he knows."[6] He proposes a nomenclature to deal with this issue.[7] A is the blackmailee or target; B is the blackmailer, the man who solicits money or other valuable consideration in order to keep silent; and C is the person to whom B threatens to make available this information.[8]

Isenbergh fully accepts our characterization of blackmail as the amalgamation of two otherwise licit acts and correctly distinguishes it from extortion: "Blackmail, as addressed here, does not include threats of disclosure barred by statute or contract, such as a doctor's threat to reveal a patient's loathsome disease, which belong to the broader class of 'extortion.'"[9]

---

[4] *See* Walter E. Williams, *The Legitimate Role of Government in a Free Society*, THE FRANK M. ENGEL LECTURES 1978–1997, 633, 640 (Roger C. Bird ed., 1998).

[5] Joseph Isenbergh, *Blackmail from A to C*, 141 U. PA. L. REV. 1905 (1993).

[6] *Id.* at 1905.

[7] *Id.*

[8] *Id.*

[9] *Id.* at 1905–06. This is just a first approximation. In our view, contrary to Isenbergh's legal positivism, some statutes (e.g., the prohibition of victimless crimes, such as prostitution or drugs) are themselves improper. Therefore, his statement, in order to be correct, implicitly assumes legitimacy of the statute barring disclosure. The second, and illicit one, is to prevent others (e.g., "scabs") from taking these positions. For this distinction, *see* Walter Block, *Labor Relations, Unions and Collective Bargaining: A Political Economic Analysis*, 16 SOC. POL. &: ECON. STUD. 477 (1991); Bill Kauffman, *The Child Labor Amendment Debate of the 1920s; or, Catholics and Mugwumps and Farmers*, 10 J. LIBERTARIAN STUD. 139 (1992); SYLVESTER PETRO, THE LABOR POLICY OF THE FREE SOCIETY (1957); Barry W. Poulson, *Substantive Due Process and Labor Law*, 6 J. LIBERTARIAN STUD. 267 (1982); MORGAN O. REYNOLDS, POWER AND PRIVILEGE: LABOR UNIONS IN AMERICA (1984); MORGAN O. REYNOLDS, MAKING AMERICA POORER: THE COST OF LABOR LAW (1987); Morgan O. Reynolds, *An Economic Analysis of the Norris-LaGuardia Act, the Wagner Act and the Labor Representation Industry*, 6 J. LIBERTARIAN STUD. 227 (1982).

Nevertheless, Isenbergh distinguishes between some threats coupled with a demand for money from other seemingly identical threats.[10] One he labels "permissible threats."[11] The other he labels "blackmail."[12] He states:

> "Pay me higher wages or I will go on strike or quit," "pay me the price I am asking for this good or I will sell it to someone else," and "marry me or I will shave my head and join the Foreign Legion" are, I think, *permissible threats* almost anywhere, while "paint my house or I will tell your boyfriend about your sex change operation" and "if you fire me I'll tell the IRS about your secret Swiss bank account" are *blackmail.*[13]

Our author continues, "[t]hreats of the latter type often elicit a strong aesthetic reaction," while, presumably, those of the former type do not.[14] But aesthetic tastes surely cannot be the bedrock of the law. They are far too subjective. On what legal principle can we justify making "permissible threats" legal while outlawing blackmail?[15]

Isenbergh answers that "[t]he justification for the prohibition of blackmail, if there is one, must therefore lie in the particular nature of information."[16] Why is this? It is because

> [i]n a frictionless world (one in which it were costless to bargain over the value of information), prohibition of blackmail would surely not be correct. For most rights in property other than information, even in our world of significant transactional costs, prohi-

---

[10] *Id.* at 1906.

[11] *Id.*

[12] *Id.*

[13] *Id.* (emphasis added). One small caveat. To quit a job, assuming no labor contract is in effect, must be legitimate. To not be allowed to quit is slavery. Going on strike is another matter. Despite being legal, a strike—just like extortion—actually consists of two acts, one of which should be legal, the other not. The first, and licit one, is to quit the job.

[14] Isenbergh, *supra* note 5, at 1906.

[15] It is precisely our contention that there *is* no justification for the prohibition of blackmail.

[16] Isenbergh, *supra* note 5, at 1907

bition of bargaining is likely to impede the appropriate allocation of those rights.[17]

Isenbergh's theory can thus be seen as an instance of the fallacious argument of "market failure."[18] If markets were perfect, i.e., there were no transactional costs, then we could have laissez-faire capitalism. Unfortunately, however, they are not. On the contrary, there are "frictions." Therefore, we must have government intervention, regulation, and prohibition.

Isenbergh, however, does not fit neatly into either the total prohibitionist or the total legalization model. Instead, he wants to

> retain the prohibition of blackmail for: 1) information, however acquired, held by B concerning a prosecutable crime or tort committed by A against C; and 2) information acquired by B outside a prior course of dealing with A ... [and] make B's agreement with A not to disclose information unenforceable and to treat B's receipt of compensation for silence as a form of complicity in whatever is kept silent.[19]

At the outset, one can see that none of this follows any precept of justice. Instead it is an attempt to tailor the law to reach certain specific economic goals. This is akin to "fine tuning," or centrally planning, the economy.

---

[17] *Id.* Isenbergh, as it shall later become apparent, is a devotee of the "economics" approach to law and economics. In his view, the sole desideratum of the law is to maximize wealth. *Id.* at 1912. Thus, when Isenbergh uses the word "correct" in the present context, he does not mean what ordinary mortals do—that it is in accord with principles of justice. He denotes simply that, in his opinion, a given law will or will not maximize wealth.

[18] Though popular, this is an invalid line of reasoning. It is certainly possible, even if "imperfections" (e.g., the real world, compared to the artificial one of "perfect competition") exist, for markets to outperform bureaucrats, no matter what the criterion of success. For critiques of this market failure argument, *see* THE THEORY OF MARKET FAILURE (Tyler Cowen ed., 1988); HANS-HERMANN HOPPE, THE ECONOMICS AND ETHICS OF PRIVATE PROPERTY: STUDIES IN POLITICAL ECONOMY AND PHILOSOPHY (1993); MURRAY N. ROTHBARD, MAN, ECONOMY AND STATE (1993); and Walter Block, *The Justification for Taxation in the Public Finance Literature: An Unorthodox View*, 3 J. PUB. FIN. & PUB. CHOICE 141 (1989).

[19] Isenbergh, *supra* note 5, at 1908.

I. BLACKMAIL AS PROHIBITED BARGAINING

According to Isenbergh:

> What is prohibited under the law of blackmail is a certain type of bargaining over the disclosure of information, rather than the bare result, which is some sort of compensation given for silence. It is B's threat of disclosure that is barred, not any and all reward from A for B's discretion. Thus if A spontaneously offers to reward B's discretion regarding private information, or simply does so without bargaining, there is no prohibited blackmail, even if it is likely that B's discretion would end with the withdrawal of the reward. The law of blackmail is in this respect like that of prostitution, which usually bars specific bargaining over the sale of sex rather than all transfers of wealth in consideration of sex.[20]

Why should bargaining be singled out for special concern in blackmail? There is nothing intrinsically invasive about negotiating. If we are to be logically consistent and ban discussions over contracts in blackmail, why not prohibit all occupations and professions whose main function is to arrange the details of commerce? This includes, for example, lawyers, auctioneers, real estate agents, stockbrokers, middlemen, and intermediaries of all types and varieties functioning in the business world. And what about people and groups who reduce transactional costs in the social world—personal columns in newspapers, matchmakers, organizers of singles dances, and church clubs for the unmarried?

There is far more bargaining in a modem society than just these examples. In order to be inclusive, why not ban bargaining entirely and insist upon sales at retail or sticker prices? That is, if I advertise to sell my car for five thousand dollars and someone were to offer me four thousand dollars, he should be incarcerated for that crime. We should be dealt with in a similar summary manner if we were to accept his offer. Thus, Isenbergh's view of the law can be interpreted as racist and discriminatory because certain nations and ethnic groups make more of a virtue out of bargaining than others.[21]

Isenberg might object that he is limiting his crusade against bargaining to commercial interactions concerning information. However, two objections immediately arise. First, if bargaining is so bad, why limit its prohibition to

---

[20] *Id.* at 1908–09.

[21] In certain cultures, it is almost an insult to offer to pay the sticker price. It is a mark of good breeding for buyers and sellers to haggle with one another.

just information? Why not broaden the prohibition as outlined above? Second, Isenbergh homes in on the informational aspects of blackmail. But many of the cases he mentions focus, at least partially and often almost completely, on information availability, or the lack thereof.[22] Surely, most middlemen and intermediaries function as information providers. Bargaining between the retailer and customer of consumer durables, houses, cars, and similar goods also serves as an information-creating institution.

Another problem is if the blackmail contract is initiated by the blackmailee, then Isenbergh will give him a free ride, legally speaking. But if inaugurated by the blackmailer, Isenberg will throw the book at him. Why? Is it not the same identical contract in either case? It seems unreasonable for its legality to turn on so superficial a fact.

In the view of Murray Rothbard:

> Suppose that, in the above case, instead of Smith [the blackmailer] going to Jones [the blackmailee with an offer of silence, Jones had heard of Smith's knowledge and his intent to print it, and went to Smith to offer to purchase the latter's silence? Should that contract be illegal? And if so, why? But if Jones' offer should be legal while Smith's is illegal, should it be illegal for Smith to turn down Jones' offer, and then ask for more money as the price of his silence? And, furthermore, should it be illegal for Smith to subtly let Jones know that Smith has the information and intends to publish, and then allow Jones to make the actual offer? But how could this simple letting Jones know in advance be considered as illegal? Could it not be rather construed as a simple act of courtesy to Jones? The shoals get muddier and muddier, and the support for outlawry of blackmail contracts—especially by libertarians who believe in property rights—becomes ever more flimsy.[23]

Then there is the gratuitous and unwarranted attack on the practice of issuing warnings. Isenbergh characterizes the blackmailer's initial statement to the blackmailee as a threat, but he might as well have called it a warning (or even an offer).[24] If I may legally do X to you, why should it be illegal to warn you that I may or will do X should you see fit not to accede to my demands? Warnings themselves are not, *per se*, an invasion of person or property. On that ground alone they should be allowed. To resort to mere pragmatism,

[22] *See* Isenbergh, *supra* note 7, at 1906.

[23] MURRAY N. ROTHBARD, THE ETHICS OF LIBERTY 125 (1982).

[24] Isenbergh, *supra* note 5, at 1905.

surely it will be a better world when people are allowed to warn each other of intended actions, than one when they are legally constrained to launch (legal) attacks on one another totally without warning.[25]

And what are we to say of Isenbergh's contention that laws prohibiting prostitution should be allowed to serve as the model for those on blackmail? At the very least, this is unacceptable, barring reasons adduced in its defense. Why should "capitalist acts between consenting adults" be banned?[26] Are these not quintessentially victimless crimes, as even Isenbergh himself acknowledges?[27] This applies also to "gambling" and "trade in narcotics," both of which he also mentions.[28]

Moreover, Isenbergh is factually incorrect when he maintains that it is illegal to engage only in "specific bargaining over the sale of sex rather than all transfers of wealth in consideration of sex."[29] Marriage is legal in our society. And what is the prenuptial agreement, part and parcel of many marital relationships, but a bargain over at least some transfers of wealth in consideration, to some degree, for sexual favors?

In any case, it is the height of hypocrisy to "legalize" prostitution but to arrest people for bargaining over the price of sexual services. This restricts entry into the "oldest profession" by poor women who are led by their poverty to become "street walkers."[30] The reason this law should serve as the model for any other, including blackmail, is never clearly articulated by Isenbergh.

---

[25] Epstein states of the inability to give warnings: "This ... will work to the disadvantage of the other party, who is now deprived of the choice that the threat would have otherwise given him." Richard A. Epstein, *Blackmail, Inc.*, 50 U. CHI. L. REV. 553, 558 (1983).

[26] *See* ROBERT NOZICK, ANARCY, STATE AND UTOPIA (1974)

[27] *See* Isenbergh, *supra* note 5, at 1908.

[28] *Id.* at 1909.

[29] *Id.* at 1908–09.

[30] For arguments in favor of legalizing victimless crimes, *see* WALTER BLOCK, DEFENDING THE UNDEFENDABLE (1991); THE CRISIS IN DRUG PROHIBITION (David Boaz ed., 1991); JOEL FEINBERG, HARMLESS WRONGDOING: THE MORAL LIMITS OF THE CRIMINAL LAW (1990); DEALING WITH DRUGS: CONSEQUENCES OF GOVERNMENT CONTROL (Ronald Hamowy ed., 1987); THOMAS SUSZ, CEREMONIAL CHEMISTRY: THE RITUAL PERSECUTION OF DRUGS, ADDICTS AND PUSHERS (1985); and MARK. THORNTON, THE ECONOMICS OF PROHIBITION (1991).

II. THE EXTENT OF BLACKMAIL

Isenbergh states that while the incidence of blackmail in popular fiction, television, and movies is very high, it must be less in real life.[31] But he then gives examples that are everyday occurrences: "A parent's threat to tell a child's playmates that he sleeps with a nightlight unless he cleans his room;" the threat of a disgruntled worker to snitch to the IRS about an employer's tax evasion unless promoted; and divorce settlements enlarged by the implicit threat to reveal concealed income to the IRS.[32]

Then there is emotional blackmail: "You'll break your mother's heart if you...." Given that the installation of this guilt practically comes with mother's milk, it must be very frequent. Similarly, the threat, "If you don't do your homework, your father will hear of it when he gets home" is an everyday occurrence.

Another difficulty is that Isenbergh considers "determining the point at which [such] ubiquitous minor threats molt into prohibited blackmail" at the same time he admits that just this sort of thing "falls literally within the Model Penal Code's definition of criminal coercion."[33] How can it be a "minor threat" if it is a criminal matter? To swoop down on all parents who violate this code would render any jurisdiction that did so far more totalitarian than anything the Soviet Union's Stalin or China's Mao ever dreamed. If we are not to descend to this level of barbarism and make a dead letter out of blackmail law, we must legalize the practice. It would be hard to manufacture better *reductios ad absurdum* of blackmail law than the scenarios offered by Isenbergh. The puzzle is that he is not convinced by them, certainly not to the point of total decriminalization.

III. BLACKMAIL AND PROPERTY RIGHTS

There are two ways to establish property rights: intrinsically and instrumentally. In the former case, a man owns himself and his justly acquired property as a matter of right, regardless of any other consideration.[34] It is a

---

[31] *See* Isenbergh, *supra* note 5, at 1909.

[32] *Id.* at 1909–10.

[33] *Id.*

[34] JOHN LOCKE, THE SECOND TREATISE OF CIVIL GOVERNMENT 14–26 (1946 ed.).

matter of logic[35] or natural law.[36] In the latter case, we prohibit slavery, theft, assault, and battery to serve a higher purpose, not because these actions are necessarily illicit.

Isenbergh is an instrumentalist, and his higher purpose is to enhance wealth or economic value, or reduce costs, most notably transactional costs. That is: "[t]he assignment of property rights to those who value them most reduces the necessity of exchanges or other transactions to bring them to higher valued uses. An important function of a legal regime is, therefore, to maintain property rights in the hands of owners who value them most."[37]

Isenbergh never examines why this goal is worthy of being the basic premise of law, its very foundation. Nor does he face the question whether Law X is just, even though it will maximize value, or increase wealth the most, or reduce transactional costs to their lowest possible level. By the very fact that Law X does indeed have these properties, it is thereby known to be just. For him, to say that a law is just, appropriate, or proper is to say no more than that it most efficiently promotes affluence. There is no more to just law than that. This is the basis upon which Isenbergh analyzes blackmail.

That being the case, it behooves him to show that laws against murder, theft, rape, and assault actually have these effects. He proceeds:

> The prohibition of murder accords an individual the property right in his own life; the prohibition of battery frames an individual's rights in his body; the prohibition of theft sets the contours of other property rights. That life is worth more a priori to its owner than to any other person is revealed by the rarity of exchanges in which someone consents to being killed for a payment from another who would enjoy doing it. That people value their bodies more than batterers can similarly be inferred from the infrequency of their consenting to being beaten for a fee.[38]

This will not do. Isenbergh has given the game away before he even really gets going. He admits at the outset that, upon occasion, a man indeed "consents to being killed for a payment."[39] Men sometimes, albeit rarely, do "con-

---

[35] HANS-HERMANN HOPPE, THE ECONOMICS AND ETHICS OF PRIVATE PROPERTY:STUDIES IN POLITICAL ECONOMY AND PHILOSOPHY (1993).

[36] MURRAY N. ROTHBARD, FOR A NEW LIBERTY (1978); MURRAY N. ROTHBARD, THE ETHICS OF LIBERTY (1982).

[37] *See* Isenbergh, *supra* note 7, at 1910.

[38] *Id.* at 1910–11.

[39] *Id.* at 1911.

sent [] to being beaten for a fee."[40] If so, then logic implies that, in the majority of cases when people will not voluntarily undergo this treatment, we should have laws against murder and battery. But in the minority of cases, when they will undergo this treatment, we should not. It is hard to see any way around this difficulty.

Further, it is presently illegal to consent to being "killed for a payment from another who would enjoy doing it."[41] Why do we have to prohibit these contracts with the force of law if the goal is to maximize wealth, and virtually no one would do this act anyway? On the other hand, what else can we conclude from the few times this occurs, other than that it maximizes value in these cases?

Another difficulty is that the number of people who "consent[] to being beaten for a fee" is not really as rare as Isenbergh seems to think.[42] Certainly, this describes every athlete who ever stepped into the ring to compete for prizes. This includes professional boxers, kick boxers, wrestlers, and sumo wrestlers. All of these athletes, even world champions with perfect records of victories get pummeled, pushed, and punched. In a word, these athletes are treated approximately how we would describe assault and battery if it were to have occurred outside the ring. This is only the tip of the iceberg. There are many others who voluntarily submit to being, in effect, beaten, and are paid for their pains. This includes all contact sports such as football, hockey, soccer, rugby, and basketball, when crashing into other men often results in bruises and injuries.

Isenbergh also errs when he states: "If homicide ... [was] legal, ... [r]elations between people in such a world would have the character of blackmail."[43] On the contrary, they would have the character of extortion. For in the latter case, there is a threat of an intrinsically illegal act: murder; in the former, the threat must be one that is legal.

These are just the beginnings of the problems. On a practical level, Isenbergh's legal advice would open up a whole can of worms in criminal law. For example, murderers would have a defense hitherto not available to them: my victim would have been willing to have me murder him because he knew I valued his death more than he valued his life. Similarly for rapists: my victim would have consented to my attack, given that she had low self-esteem and my need for her body was so great. They could even use Isenbergh as an expert witness. According to him, there are some cases, admittedly rare, when

---

[40] *Id.*

[41] *Id.*

[42] *Id.*

[43] *Id.*

the murder victim would value the money he is paid for being killed more than his own life.[44]

Isenbergh utilizes his philosophy of property rights to shed light on blackmail outlawry. True to his premises he asserts:

> If we could determine the flow of information costlessly from some sort of meta-vantage point, we would want the information held by B to be disclosed to C when its value to C was greater than its value to A, but to be kept private when it was worth more to A. There being no omniscient traffic controller, we generally leave it to private bargaining to steer property rights to owners who value them most.[45]

This is where Isenbergh's focus on "market failure" plays a role. Ordinarily, this is precisely what markets, competition, and economic freedom accomplish; buying and selling, "bartering and trucking," in Adam Smith's famous phraseology, are organized in order to attain expressly that. I buy a newspaper from you for one dollar. I value the item more than that amount; you value it less. Therefore, when the money and the paper exchange hands, each of them migrates from a man who values it less to one who values it more. Total wealth is thus enhanced.

Presumably, this would work as well in the market for secrets and information, e.g., blackmail. B has the choice to tell A's story to C or to be paid off by A to desist. Supposedly, B will go in whichever direction that will earn him the greatest returns. This will maximize overall wealth in that B will cooperate with the one who values the information most. In contrast, the usual "market failure" argument is that C cannot place full value on this information when he does not yet know what it is. If B starts to tell C about it, then and to the degree he succeeds, B will have lowered the payment he could otherwise have obtained. Why? Because C already has some of the information; why should he pay what he otherwise would have?

One answer to this is that it relies on the vantage point of the "omniscient traffic controller," one which Isenbergh has explicitly eschewed.[46] There is no way for any of us mere mortals to know, in any specific case, that information

[44] For an elaboration of these arguments, *see* Walter Block, *O.J. 's Defense: A Reductio Ad Absurdum of the Economics of Coase and Posner*, 3 EUR. J. L. & ECON. 265 (1996). *See also* Murray N. Rothbard, *Toward A Reconstruction Of Utility And Welfare Economics*, Center for Libertarian Studies Occasional Paper No. 3 (1977).

[45] Isenbergh, *supra* note 5, at 1912.

[46] *Id.*

which C would have considered more valuable went to A (he purchased silence from B for a fee and thus preserved his privacy) instead. But it is the
same in the ordinary case of a newspaper sale. The presumption, again, is that
this increased wealth, at least in the *ex ante* sense, because I valued the newspaper more highly than the one dollar, and you valued the money more than
the periodical. However, did this maximize wealth? No one, apart from the
"omniscient traffic controller," or a socialistic central planner with the temer-
ity to think he knows our interests better than we do ourselves, and thus, can
overturn our freely contracted choices for our own good, could make such a
statement.[47] There is always the possibility that there is a third person who
values this particular newspaper more than I do, or values this particular dollar bill more than you.[48] Our point is that if there is a "market failure" in
blackmail that justifies outlawry on economic grounds, this applies to every
trade in the market without exception. The "market failure" argument, then,
proves far too much.[49]

Isenbergh ends this section with a query of blackmail: "1) whether the
prohibition thereby prevents the flow of information to those who value it
most; and 2) if it does, what is gained."[50] Instead of directly answering it, he
turns to an examination of five theories of blackmail for answers.

IV. ESTABLISHED THEORIES OF BLACKMAIL

A. Prohibition of Blackmail as Protection of Privacy

As indicated by the subheading, Isenbergh considers under this rubric
theories of blackmail outlawry that rely upon the protection of privacy as
their goal. One problem with Isenbergh's treatment is that he accepts, without
quibble, that people do indeed have a right to privacy.[51] In the libertarian
view, however, there is no such thing as a right to privacy, apart from that af-

---

[47] *Id.*

[48] There never has been a successful demonstration of "market failure." For further elaboration, *see* note 18, *supra*.

[49] This tacitly assumes that the purpose of the law is to maximize wealth, as opposed to promoting justice. Isenbergh shows no evidence of having recognized this as a challenge to be addressed.

[50] Isenbergh, *supra* note 5, at 1912.

[51] *Id.* at 1912–15.

forded by private property rights.[52] If there were, such things as investigative reporting, detective agencies, and gossip would all have to be banned.

For the sake of argument, let us accept Isenbergh's approach on this matter. Given the legitimacy of protecting privacy, Isenbergh asks which will better safeguard this "right:" blackmail outlawry, which hurts A now, but lowers the probability that future Bs will act "predatorily" with regard to future As; or blackmail legalization, which has the exact opposite effect? It will help the As of the world at present, but will put more of them at risk in the future because it increases incentives to ferret out secrets with which still other people can be blackmailed.

This conundrum is similar to that regarding the legal prohibition of paying off the kidnapper. Such a law would hurt A now, the parent of a kidnapped child who is willing to compensate the kidnapper for a release, but is prevented from so doing. However, it would help future As, who are less likely to be victimized by future kidnappers who, at the margin, will turn to other pursuits.

For Isenbergh, this is strictly a cost benefit economic analysis. It is doomed to failure, given the intellectual illegitimacy of interpersonal comparisons of utility. Unless we have a rate of transformation with which to compare the present misery of the parent of a kidnapped child with the future happiness of other parents who, thanks to this law, will not suffer the same consequences, we can make no rational determination of this question. It is clear that there exists no yardstick based on which these feelings can be scientifically compared. To presume there is one, as is implicitly done by Isenbergh, is thus to remove our analysis from the realm of rationality.[53]

How would a principled philosophy address this issue? It would ask, does paying off a kidnapper constitute a *per se* invasive act; does asking for a fee to keep silent constitute a *per se* invasive act? The latter, at least, is clear. Even Isenbergh admits, as long as the blackmailee initiates the contract, blackmail is legally unobjectionable. "[I]f A spontaneously offers to reward B's discre-

---

[52] Rothbard, *supra* note 23, at 122–22.

[53] This question is reminiscent of the one concerning the well-being of cows. Are they better off because human beings eat them? The answer is obvious. No cow victimized by Wendy's, Burger King, or McDonald's can be considered to have had its welfare enhanced. But there is also a pro side. Were we as a race not enamored by beef, we would not care for, or bring into existence, quite so many cows.

How can this query possibly be answered? Any rational response would have to assume some rate of exchange (utility comparison) between being killed and eaten on a massive scale and more of the species being born and raised. There is no such rate of exchange. This question cannot be answered in any meaningful nonequivocal way.

tion regarding private information, or simply does so without bargaining, there is no prohibited blackmail."[54] If there is a case for either of these prohibitions, it does not apply to blackmail; rather, it pertains to the victim paying off the kidnapper. For at least there is the claim that in making such a payment, the victim is aiding and abetting the criminal. Isenbergh wishes "to treat B's receipt of compensation for silence as a form of complicity in whatever is kept silent."[55] This is a gratuitous and contrived attack. In contrast, a reasonable case can be made that the parents of the kidnapped child are really complicit with the criminal gang when they make a payment for safe release. For this only encourages them to continue their nefarious behavior; to add insult to injury, the payment gives the kidnappers the means through which they can rent a safe house, buy a car, and engage in the investment of other kidnapping capital.

Ultimately, however, this argument fails. The victim of kidnapping, unlike the blackmailee, has endured an uninvited border crossing, or a violation of the libertarian axiom of nonaggression.[56] In making the disbursement, he is acting defensively, trying merely to secure what is really his: the right to raise his child.[57]

Other difficulties in this section concern the fact that Isenbergh allows to pass without objection the characterization of blackmailers as "predatory" and "predators."[58] From the point of view of a blackmailee with a desire for privacy, any sniffing around for compromising secrets will be resented.[59] We all sometimes resent the perfectly legal activities of others. For example, I might be indignant if you make overtures to an attractive woman I desire for myself; yet, this is certainly your right in a free society. On the other hand, from the perspective of a blackmailee whose secret is already known, the blackmailer is

---

[54] See Isenbergh, *supra* note 5, at 1908.

[55] *Id.*

[56] Rothbard states:

> The libertarian creed rests upon one central axiom: that no man or group of men may aggress against the person or property of anyone else. This may be called the "nonaggression axiom." "Aggression" is defined as the initiation of the use or threat of physical violence against the person or property of anyone else. Aggression is therefore synonymous with invasion.

Rothbard, supra note 36, at 23.

[57] LYSANDER SPOONER, NO TREASON: THE CONSTITUTION OF NO AUTHORITY (Ralph Myles ed., 1966).

[58] See Isenbergh, *supra* note 5, at 1914.

[59] *Id.*

hardly guilty of predation, at least compared to the situation where the gossip has the requisite information. In this case, all is lost. In comparison, at least the blackmailer has the decency to allow you to purchase his silence.

Then, too, why should we heavily weigh, or even weigh at all, the welfare of those with embarrassing pasts? Did they not do something immoral, shameful, or criminal? Why encourage this immoral behavior in the future by reducing the incentive of blackmailers to ferret out this information, and thereby decrease the incidence of blackmail in the future?

B. Prohibition of Blackmail as an Instrument of Disclosure

In these theories, A, the holder of the secret, and B, the blackmailer, are in cahoots, and the victim is C, the real victim, the person who would gain if the information was publicized. Outlawry is interpreted as an impetus toward disclosure. But "not ... a very powerful one,"[60] according to Isenbergh, because no law "prohibits B from bargaining with C,"[61] and "it is often difficult for B to communicate to C the value of the information without communicating the information itself."[62]

None of this can be denied. However, Isenbergh's discussion continues to be marred by a spurious comparative weighing of interpersonal utilities. Consider the following: "The pecuniary value to the public of information on A's tax evasion is at least equal to A's pecuniary benefit from concealment. Knowledge of A's tax fraud would gain the Treasury A's delinquent taxes, plus penalties, along with the value of future deterrence of A and others."[63]

If "pecuniary" means that one simply adds up the dollars concerned, then of course Isenbergh is correct, but only tautologically so. This, in any case, is insufficient to establish his goal of maximizing wealth unless we may directly infer economic well-being from severity of taxation. But there is no warrant to do any such thing.

This statement implicitly assumes that the government can spend the money as wisely on behalf of the citizens as they can on their own account. Particularly in this epoch when the taxpayers are forced to work for their government a greater proportion of the year than applied to the Medieval serfs on behalf of their masters, it takes great courage to assert that a dollar spent

---

[60] *Id.* at 1916.

[61] *Id.* fn. 29.

[62] *Id.* at 1916.

[63] *Id.* at 1915, n. 28.

by the state will create as much value as that allowed to remain in the private sector.[64]

C. The Blackmailer as a Rogue Agent

In the view of the latter, the wrongness of blackmail is that B bargains with "leverage" or "chips" which properly belong to C. Prohibition, then, is merely a special case of the law against theft. But if this were so, then Isenbergh asks, "isn't it also at least wrongish [sic] to deny to C (by total silence) the leverage that more properly belongs to him?"[65] Isenbergh trenchantly maintains that Lindgren's "theory of blackmail starts by finding existing leverage in C, but does not account for how or why it is there. What, beyond the prohibition of blackmail itself, gives C leverage that C would not otherwise have with respect to information concerning A?"[66]

The only problem with this insightful critique of Lindgren is that Isenbergh, based on his own theory, is logically precluded from making it. Or, at the very least, Isenbergh's views open up to Lindgren a defense he would not otherwise have (one from which the libertarian theory, for example, would be immune). The reason C properly owns these "chips" is because allowing him to do so maximizes wealth. This response even safeguards Lindgren from Isenbergh's otherwise scathing "practical aspect" *reductios* of his perspective:

Suppose B recognizes A as a fellow death camp guard and seeks money to keep it quiet. Is the C to whom that leverage properly belongs an immigration official or prosecutor? What if A no longer has any exposure to legal sanction and faces only loss of reputation? Does the leverage belong to no one? To Jews and Gypsies because they have some strands of DNA in common with A's victims? Or perhaps to historians?[67]

---

[64] It would remain unproven, and unprovable, in any case. Suppose, for example, that taxes were only one percent of the G.D.P., but that they were compulsory. How can it be shown then, that even a dollar forcibly taken from a man will garner more for him than had he been able to spend it himself? And if this somehow could be shown, then we would furnish all robbers with a new and startling defense: "I would have spent this money I stole from my victim on wine, women and song. This would have benefitted the previous owner of these funds to a greater degree than had he been allowed to spend it himself." How could we say nay to the criminal, once we allow into court Isenbergh's perspective? There is, of course, the vast literature of "market failure" in support of this. For critiques, *see* Rothbard and Hoppe, *supra* note 18.

[65] Isenbergh, *supra* note 5, at 1917 fn. 35.

[66] *Id.* at 1917.

[67] *Id.* at 1918.

The answer available to Lindgren, thanks to the opening afforded him by Isenbergh, is that the leverage properly belongs to whichever of these people whose ownership would maximize wealth. The beauty of this response is that Lindgren is not even compelled to pick out one of these alternatives himself. He can always demand that of Isenbergh, the holder of this curious theory.

D. Blackmail as Private Enforcement of Criminal and Moral Rules

Isenbergh opens this section with: "The only theory of blackmail surfacing in academic writing that would not prohibit the transaction finds in the blackmail bargain a mechanism of private enforcement—through the agency of B—of criminal laws or moral standards."[68] This is false. While the libertarian theory of blackmail in support of legalization certainly includes this point in its arsenal of arguments, it is by no means limited to this contention.

Even worse is Isenbergh's declaration: "No published writing that I know of embraces this view."[69] It is not bizarre that Isenbergh has failed to do his homework. Perhaps he can use as an excuse that some of this literature (but certainly not all!) was published in obscure journals. But this seems to be the only accurate description of Lindgren's reason to allow this statement into print. For Lindgren is Isenbergh's (co)editor, and one of the articles adumbrating this line of thought, and said not to exist, has singled Lindgren out (among others) for special critique.[70] To add insult to injury, Lindgren himself even replied to this article.[71] Most of this took place, needless to say, long before the publication of Isenbergh.[72]

Why does Isenbergh reject this eminently reasonable thesis?

Unfortunately, he devotes but a single paragraph to criticism. His main objection would appear to be that "[a]ny benefit from blackmail in the form of an incentive for good conduct by A, however, is likely to be marginal."[73]

---

[68] *Id.*

[69] *Id.* at 1918 fn. 35.

[70] *See* chapter 11, this volume.

[71] James Lindgren, *In Defense of Keeping Blackmail a Crime: Responding to Block and Gordon*, 20 LOY. LA L. REV. 35 (1986).

[72] *See* Isenbergh, *supra* note 5. Perhaps we are being too harsh on Isenbergh. He did, after all, have the decency to at least mention the possibility that blackmail may be worthy of legalization, and indeed, argues partially on behalf of this contention. The same cannot be said for virtually any other scholar who has written on the side of prohibition. With regard to these other writers, it is as if they were to argue for prohibition of alcohol, cigarettes, and addictive drugs without even considering that there is another side to the issue.

[73] *Id.* at 1919.

The reply to this is straightforward: every bit helps. With crime as rampant as it is, if the legalization of blackmail can help reduce its incidence even a tiny bit, this is all to the good. In any case, crime and immorality reduction is hardly the main reason for legalization.

Isenbergh objects that "the most that can be expected from exposing private conduct to blackmail may only be somewhat greater discretion in people's private conduct."[74] Well, what is wrong with that? Surely discretion, rather than blatancy, better oils the social wheels of civilization.

Isenbergh's second objection is that "B is not going to get rich tracking down bank robbers and shaking them down for blackmail. B is far more likely to get dead in this line of work."[75] True enough, perhaps, but totally irrelevant. Just because an occupation is dangerous is no reason to legally proscribe or even denigrate it. The jobs of policeman, fireman, and test pilot are all hazardous, yet they each contribute in their own way to human well-being. The blackmailer, too, could add his mite to the pot. Would Isenbergh ban these other professions on this ground? Hardly.

E. Blackmail as Deadweight Loss

Although wedded to a version of the "economic approach" to blackmail,[76] Isenbergh casts a critical eye on other versions of this theory.[77] The view under attack is that blackmail wastes resources and should be banned on that basis because it would "leave the same distribution of information as before [A and B had] bargained. B and A would therefore have invested time and effort in a transaction that brought nothing new. It would be as though they had dug a hole and filled it up again."[78]

Isenbergh rejects this on the grounds that it "proves too much," is over-inclusive, and would prohibit the purchase of a "scenic easement."[79] He might have also objected that if people wish to dig holes and fill them up again, that should be their own business and should be beyond the scope of the law. In

---

[74] *Id.*

[75] *Id.*

[76] This misnomer implies that all economists would subscribe to the view that law should be the handmaiden of enhancing a very narrow and erroneous understanding of economic well-being. There is a wealth of literature both for and against this "economic" approach.

[77] *See* Isenbergh, *supra* note 5, at 1919–20.

[78] *Id.* at 1919.

[79] *Id.* at 1920.

any case, only a very superficial perspective on human well-being would reject the possibility that there might be joy in such activities for some people.[80]

And it is the same with his view that "[t]o be sure, one ought not to encourage pointless bargaining."[81] But some people like "pointless bargaining." Others, in contrast, like Chicago economics. We say, pay your money and take your choice. *Non gustibus disputandum*. It is unclear why either of the above pair should be banned by law, but not the other. This suggests that Isenbergh has ignored the economics of leisure: it is not productive in the sense of wealth creation, but it certainly, at least for those who are not totally driven workaholics, is conducive to the good life.

Nor am I convinced by Isenbergh's citation of "Ronald Coase, the acknowledged godfather of legal analysis based on transaction costs"[82] in order to reject Nozick's doctrine[83] of "unproductive exchanges." Yes, "Nozick's landowner is better off than if the neighbor had sold his lot to someone else who wanted to build on it, a possibility that is now permanently foreclosed," but he would have been better off in the *ex ante* sense even apart from this consideration.[84] We can deduce that a person is better off whenever he makes a trade, merely by the fact that he made it.[85] This includes digging holes and filling them up, soap operas, "pointless" bargaining, and all the rest. Rothbard states:

> actual choice reveals, or demonstrates, a man's preferences; i.e., ... his preferences are deducible from what he has chosen in action. Thus, if a man chooses to spend an hour at a concert rather than a movie, we deduce that the former was preferred, or ranked higher on his value scale.[86]

---

[80] In our subjective evaluation of human action, there are things from which people derive great joy which seem to us to be even sillier than digging holes and filling them up again. At least that act constitutes physical exercise, and we are big fans of athletic endeavors. But what are we to make of watching soap operas, playing checkers, gardening, and mowing the grass? Surely these are far more wasteful! Were we advocates of the "economic approach," and if we had a taste for dictatorship, we would recommend forthwith that all these be rendered unlawful. If Isenbergh can do this for digging holes and filling them up again, why cannot we call for a ban on everything we deem worthless?

[81] Isenbergh, *supra* note 5, at 1920.

[82] *Id.* at 1921.

[83] ROBERT NOZICK, ANARCHY, STATE AND UTOPIA (1974)

[84] Isenbergh, *supra* note 5, at 1921 fn. 43.

[85] This is always limited to the *ex ante* sense.

[86] Rothbard, *supra* note 44, at 2.

V. BARGAINING OVER BUILDING ON CONTIGUOUS LOTS

Isenbergh advocates blackmail legalization except for actions pertaining to information. To establish his credentials in this regard, he states:

> If B has the right to build on his lot in a way that would impair A's view, B might seek compensation from A for not building. This transaction falls into the formal pattern of blackmail. Indeed, if B has no interest in building for its own sake and wants only to profit from selling an easement to A, B's announced intention to build is blackmail as defined in the Model Penal Code. B's bargaining with A ought, nonetheless, not be prohibited, no matter what the intrinsic value B attaches to building.[87]

I welcome Isenbergh to the ranks of blackmail legalizers, even though his adherence to this position is limited to non-informational cases. There are so few of us, it would be impracticable to turn away even partial adherents. However, even his limited agreement is problematic.

First, it is improper for the law to even take cognizance of motivations in determining what is legal. Acts, not intentions, are the *sine qua non* of rational law. This does not mean that purposes may not perhaps decide the severity of an offense, but to have guilt or innocence turn solely on motive is entirely another matter.

Isenbergh reports without criticism, that in the eyes of the law, the same act can either be a violation or not, depending only on intention. We do this for no other law, and we ought not for blackmail either. For example, killing someone by accident (e.g., in a highway fatality) and on purpose (e.g., first degree murder) are both still violations of the law, even though we may deal with the perpetrators in vastly different ways. In contrast, if B, the builder of the fence that will spoil A's view, intends to do this solely because of the benefits to him of this edifice, then he is innocent of blackmail. However, if he undertakes the same action, only this time he builds the fence not because he gains from it directly, but solely in the hope that A will pay him to rip it down, he is guilty of this offense.

---

[87] Isenbergh, *supra* note 5, at 1921–22.

Second, it is always possible for B to plead in his defense that he really enjoys the fence for its own sake (e.g., privacy) and had not even realized that his neighbor, A, would lose scenic value. How can we say to him nay in the absence of firm evidence (e.g., a diary to which he committed his innermost thoughts)?[88]

Third, Isenbergh reveals himself as an agnostic with regard to the initial assignment of property rights.[89] For him, this is a moot point. He contents himself with noting that "[a]s long as the opportunity and difficulty of bargaining are symmetrical, the transactional burden in cases where B sells A an easement under one regime is no greater than the burden under the other regime of sales by A to B of the right to build."[90]

But this will not do at all. The "transactional burden" is far from the only consideration of the matter. What Isenbergh is doing, in following Coase, is maintaining that it really does not matter whether owners or non-owners of property determine what shall be built there.[91] Instead, the alternative "property rights" scheme would be a recipe for disaster. If non-owners can make such determinations, this would place a premium on non-ownership. This would spell the doom of property rights as an economic institution. On a practical level, there are many non-owners of each piece of property; which of them would have the privilege of determining building patterns on their neighbor's holdings?

VI. BARGAINING OVER INFORMATION

If Isenbergh's views were at least in weak conformity with libertarianism on non-informational blackmail, the same, alas, cannot be said for blackmail with regard to information. According to Isenbergh:

> B's information should be controlled by A or disclosed to C according to whether A or C values the information more. Unlike the case of contiguous lots, however, the regime of free bargaining between

---

[88] That we as a society do precisely that in thousands of other cases is of no moment. The question is, should we perpetrate such injustice?

[89] *See* Isenbergh, *supra* note 7, at 1922.

[90] *Id.* at 1923.

[91] Ronald H. Coase, *The Problem of Social Cost*, 3 J. L. &. ECON. 1 (1960). This new right of non-owners to determine building patterns need not be limited to neighbors. Destruction of scenic views is hardly limited to contiguous plots of land.

B and A does not clearly tend toward that result. ... Information is less susceptible to exclusive ownership than other property. ...

Regardless of who ultimately values the information the most, at the time of a potential blackmail bargain, B stands to gain more from the effort of bargaining with A, who already knows the value of the information. B cannot bargain with C over the value of the information without revealing some part of it, thereby reducing the amount still undisclosed."[92]

There are difficulties here. Why should information go to those who value it more, as opposed to those who own it? Suppose you, a millionaire, value my dog Lil more than I do. That is, you would be willing to pay far more for this animal than I can afford. Should you be allowed to seize him against my will? That would seem to be the implication of Isenbergh's view. But it is difficult to reconcile this with his avowed desire to maximize wealth. If you, the millionaire can seize my dog on this ground, what about me, should you take a liking to having me as a slave? Down this garden path lay *reductios* galore, but not a bit of wealth maximization.

How can we even know that anyone values anything more than anyone else other than by an act of purchase? I know that you value this newspaper more than I do because I just sold it to you for one dollar. I infer that you place a greater value on it than this amount, and you can deduce that I rank the newspaper at a lower level than that. In the absence of a voluntary sale, however, no such conclusion can be drawn. Rothbard speaks of the fallacy of "treatment of preference-scales as if they existed as separate entities apart from real action."[93] The only way that Isenbergh can make any claim about C's preferences is to use his own imagination. By stipulation, there is no way in which C can register his evaluation of the information which he does not (yet) have, apart from the artificial efforts taken on his supposed behalf by Isenbergh.[94]

From whence do we derive the conclusion that when a seller reveals some part of the information to be departed, he reduces the value of the remainder?

---

[92] Isenbergh, *supra* note 5, at 1923.

[93] Rothbard, *supra* note 44, at 7.

[94] This applies as well to Isenbergh's claim that "it is difficult in any event for B to get *full value* for information in dealings with C." Isenberg, *supra* note 5, at 1925 (emphasis added). There can be no value, let alone "full value," that C places on anything, in the absence of a demonstrated preference on his part. And this, even Isenbergh would presumably agree, is ruled out by the nature of the situation.

This will come as shocking news to all those in the advertising business. Book flyers and movie previews give part of the plot away, but this is in an effort to increase sales, not decrease them. Auto retailers commonly invite prospective purchasers to test drive their vehicles; taking them up on this offer constitutes the "revealing [of] some part of ... [the] information," but this is part and parcel of a sales ploy.[95] True, these efforts are sometimes unsuccessful; sometimes they boomerang. But if the advertising industry makes a positive contribution to the G.D.P., the presumption is that more often than not they are successful.

Were the Isenberghs of the world to accept this interpretation of advertising, they would presumably want to make blackmail compulsory, instead of illegal. Then the "market failure" would be the other way around; instead of having too much blackmail in the free, unregulated market, we would have too little. But this is merely part of the interventionistic mindset, which finds it difficult to rest easy because nothing is neither prohibited nor mandatory.

VII. AN ALTERNATIVE REGIME FOR BARGAINING OVER PRIVATE INFORMATION

Isenbergh proposes three underpinnings for blackmail legislation. It should: "enhance the likelihood that [private information] will be controlled by the one who values it most;" reduce "the incentives to invest resources in discovering information and bargaining over it;" and reduce "the incentives for those whom the information concerns (A ...) to leave it exposed to discovery by B in the first place."[96]

Based on these three considerations, Isenbergh proposes, in effect, a utilitarian calculus, where the benefits of one of these is compared to the others when there is any conflict between them. For example, "Any gains from A's greater control over private information must therefore be *weighed against* the possible cost of B's increased efforts to unearth information and A's own cost of preserving privacy."[97] An important objection is that there are no measures of utility (e.g., "utils"), and that even if there were, it would still be illegitimate to compare them across people. If, somehow, this were possible, it would, in any case, leave utilitarians such as Isenbergh open to the objection of the "utility monster," a person or a creature who just happens to enjoy eating warm human flesh but who derives more pleasure from this than the negative

---

[95] Isenbergh, *supra* note 5, at 1923.

[96] *Id.* at 1925.

[97] *Id.* at 1926 (emphasis added).

utility suffered from the tortures of being eaten alive. Would Isenbergh advocate a law giving full rein (or reign) to such an individual? And if not, what reasons can he offer for employing utility, "social cost," happiness calculations, and all the rest to our relatively more pedestrian concerns?

As part of his "weighing" of costs, Isenbergh states: "Journalists, for example, might be somewhat more inclined to uncover stories for the sole purpose of covering them up again, while it would be better for them to pursue stories that can be more profitably sold to the public."[98] "[W]ould be better for them" according to what criteria?[99]

What seems to rankle Isenbergh is that blackmail should lead to a withholding of information from the public. This suggests a kinship between his views on blackmail and those of the neoclassical economists on monopoly. In the latter case, advocates of antitrust incessantly complain of the fact that the "imperfect competitor" is withholding, not information, but goods or resources that would better be utilized by consumers. In our view, these critics of the market share with Isenbergh a remarkable faith, again, in interpersonal comparisons of utility.

It is at this point in his essay that Isenbergh reveals himself as an outlier on blackmail law. The overwhelming majority of commentators on this issue favor a complete ban. There is a corporal's guard that endorses total legalization. Isenbergh, in sharp contrast to both camps, maintains uniquely that "[i]t is not necessary ... to take free bargaining absolutely or not at all."[100] Instead, he advocates outlawry in certain circumstances and decriminalization in others. Which is which?

His first candidate for outlawry is blackmail over "prosecutable crimes." This is because "[i]f the public benefits from the prohibition of a crime—and generally it does—it follows that the public gains more from the discovery of the crime than the criminal gains from concealing it."[101]

One problem with this is that it is simply impermissible to make such interpersonal comparisons of utility. Isenbergh, paradoxically, furnishes us with yet another reason for rejecting this claim:

> It is true that if a given criminal prohibition is inefficient, to prohibit blackmail against those who have committed the underlying crime makes things worse. A devotee of freedom who thinks, for example, that gambling and prostitution ought not to be illegal

---

[98] *Id.* at 1926 fn. 49.

[99] *Id.*

[100] Isenbergh, *supra* note 5, at 1926.

[101] *Id.* at 1927.

would be likely also to think that gamblers and prostitutes ought to be able to buy their privacy.[102]

But this is only a small sample of illegitimate laws, for the libertarian. In this era when law books come not in the hundreds or even thousands, but tens of thousands of pages, the presumption is that virtually all law is illegitimate. It is concerned with improperly transferring wealth from its rightful owners to, in effect, recipients of stolen property; or with inappropriately regulating business; or with tariffs; or with stultifying taxes.[103]

But we need not resort to such peripheral matters. We can do so, also, with regard to legislation that even libertarians favor; for example, laws against murder or rape.

Consider the following. B knows that A committed such a crime. Is B guilty of complicity yet? No. This knowledge is merely information that B has attained, either inadvertently or through purposeful research. It matters not which. As long as there are no obligations to turn in criminals to law enforcement authorities, B is so far an innocent man.[104] Again there are two legal whites, which, even when combined, do not constitute a legal black. There is knowledge of A's crime and B's silence. Neither of them alone, nor together, establish B's guilt for any crime, including complicity.

We now introduce blackmail into the analytic framework. Here, B agrees to continue his silence about A's crime for a fee, and this deal is initiated either by A or B. According to Isenbergh, B is now guilty of complicity, whereas before (with no blackmail, just knowledge of A's crime), B was innocent. But B did no more in this second scenario than he did before. That is, B kept silent in both cases, in the first instance for no compensation, and in the second for a monetary reward. Why should the mere exchange of money (with no other act occurring except the agreement to keep silent for money), coupled, of course, with the threat to tell all if not paid, render B, an innocent man, complicit in A's crime? B, conceivably, may be guilty of making threats of exposure or issuing warnings thereof, but it is a reach to consider him complicit in A's original crime because he was not so complicit based on his mere silence before the blackmail contract was consummated.

Why should he now be considered complicit? It is difficult to avoid the explanation that this conclusion is solely a function of Isenbergh's central

---

[102] *Id.* at 1927 fn. 50.

[103] It is also concerned with protecting person and property.

[104] There can be no such duty in a free society. If there were, we would all be drafted, in effect, into the police department. Under libertarianism, the only obligations are to not aggress against person or property and to uphold contractual commitments.

planning notions about the economic efficiency of knowledge dispersal. But to accept this would be to agree to the triumph of "economics" over justice.[105]

These convolutions in law seem contrived for the sole purpose of preventing (or reducing incentives toward) B's deliberate search for information about A's secrets. This is already done by thousands of journalists for periodicals of the National Enquirer stripe. As a practical matter, therefore, it is unlikely to have much of an effect.

Isenbergh defends his position as follows: "The idea would be to impose on blackmailers part of the social cost of the concealment of information in cases where the information was more valuable disclosed."[106]

We have already called into question how any such determination could be made. But suppose, somehow, that it could. That is, we now posit that the information on a (real, not victimless) criminal occurrence is more valuable disclosed than concealed. Why single out the poor, misunderstood blackmailer for special (negative) attention? If we stipulate that disclosure is more utilitarian than concealment, and further that the name of the game is to attain the most utils, then why is it not incumbent on everyone, not just the blackmailer, to ferret out this information? Why not, that is, commandeer the labor of all citizens to this end? And if not, what did the inoffensive blackmailer ever do to deserve being singled out?[107]

Isenbergh next attempts to subvert justice in order to promote his pet economic scheme of wealth maximization concerns by making blackmail contracts not illegal, but unenforceable.[108] However, the presumption underlying democratic rule is that we all pay taxes to the government, preeminently, for two services: protection of person and property and enforcement of contracts. If the state refuses to uphold its basic obligations, why should it be paid taxes? Further, once we let this cloven hoof into the door, there is no logical stopping point. If we can increase utility by abrogating these contracts, how

---

[105] Isenbergh's contentions about social cost are no more restricted by economics than the polar opposite. That is, one need not be an economist to buy into Isenbergh's legal conclusions, nor are all economists, because they are economists, logically required to agree.

[106] Isenbergh, *supra* note 5, at 1929.

[107] One of the arguments against rent control is that it singles out a small minority of people, landlords, for special responsibilities regarding the poor. Leaving aside the issue of whether these laws succeed in their announced aims, they do so in a way that does not apply to clothing, food, medical services, and other goods and services used by the poor. For example, the entire community is called upon to help clothe, feed, and cure the poor, but only the landlord is expected to shelter them. There seems to be a similar bias operating in the present case vis-á-vis the blackmailer.

[108] *See* Isenbergh, *supra* note 5, at 1928.

about in all other cases when people waste valuable resources, as in the case of soap operas, digging holes for the sheer pleasure of filling them up again, checkers, etc? We might well conclude that contracts concerning all these matters should be rendered unenforceable.

Hardin states: "Richard Posner says blackmail ... has no social product and should therefore be criminalized. This is a very odd conclusion. Much of what I do has no social product (for instance, I consume, I waste time), but surely it should not be criminalized."[109]

Isenbergh's answer to Hardin, it would appear, would be, "No, we won't put you in jail. But any contracts concerning your time wastage will now be considered unenforceable." How, then, will poor Hardin be able to purchase the resources that help him waste time enjoyably? The answer is that he would not. Assume that Hardin likes to waste time by lollygagging around in his swimming pool. No contractor would have built this amenity for him, had he known that the Isenbergh forces would have rendered unenforceable any such contract with Hardin. The latter, presumably, could still waste time to his heart's content, but would be unable to do so by combining his time with resources. Surely, this would take much of the fun out of it.

Isenbergh goes so far as to "want to distinguish, if possible, between information already held by B (or obtained fortuitously) and information generated by B's special efforts for the purpose of blackmail."[110] As a practical legal matter, this would appear doomed to failure.[111] As a matter of justice, there would appear to be no distinction worth making in this regard. Why should "special efforts" to obtain information attract the attention of a law whose aim is to promote justice, given that it is legal to gossip about it, and that it is legal to accept a blackmail contract to keep silent about it? True, it is presently illegal to initiate such a contract, but this is a mistake in the law as now constituted.

---

[109] Russell Hardin, *Blackmail for Mutual Good*, 141 U. PA. L. REV. 1787 1806 (1993).

[110] Isenbergh, *supra* note 5, at 1929.

[111] In the course of explicating this view, Isenbergh states: "If, for example, A has written B a compromising letter, A can offer to buy it back, while B cannot offer to sell it," *Id.* at 1929, n. 55. There are undoubtedly "economic" considerations underlying this assertion, but certainly not ones pertaining to justice. This claim resembles Ellen Fein's advice to the effect that boys may ask girls for dates, but never the other way around. *See* ELLEN FEIN, THE RULES: TIME TESTED SECRETS FOR CAPTURING THE HEART OF MR. RIGHT (1995). One can perhaps see sound (sociobiological) reasons for the latter; not so, unfortunately, for the former. *See* EDWARD O. WILSON, SOCIOBIOLOGY (1980).

Consider Isenbergh's analysis of Judge Posner's support of *United States v. Lallemand*[112] in the light of his own

> new legal regime for bargaining over private information ... :
>
> 1. Contracts not to disclose knowledge of prosecutable crimes and torts would be invalid and unenforceable. To enter into such a contract would in addition imply a measure of complicity in the underlying crime or tort.
>
> 2. Contracts not to disclose private information entered into between persons with no prior course of dealing would also be invalid and unenforceable.
>
> 3. Other contracts not to disclose private information would be valid.[113]

In this case, B, a male homosexual, blackmailed A, a married male homosexual, with a videotape of the two of them, A and B, having sex. B was convicted and jailed when A's wife accidentally found the tape.

Isenbergh states:

> *Lallemand* is not a case of blackmail for an involuntary condition (homosexuality). A's exposure to blackmail did not flow simply from his homosexuality. A chose to marry someone from whom he concealed his sexual orientation, and to seek out other sexual partners. ... It is not immediately obvious why the law should have protected A from an ill-considered, or even unlucky, choice of extramarital lover.
>
> Because A and B had a voluntary course of dealing (even though B in fact deliberately set out to acquire compromising information about B [sic]).[114] B's demands on A here would be permissible under the regime proposed in this Article. ... [T]o permit the blackmail in *Lallemand* would quite possibly be the right result on balance, measured by social cost. B's acquisition of information entailed little more cost or effort than the activity that A might other-

---

[112] 989 F.2d 936 (5th Cir. 1993).

[113] *See* Isenbergh, *supra* note 5, at 1930.

[114] Presumably, Isenbergh meant "A" here.

wise have carried on with a different companion not bent on blackmail. ... B's opportunism hardly inspires admiration, to be sure, but it entailed little net social cost.[115]

In Isenbergh's reply we have an indication of all that is wrong in his approach. Most basically, to make the law of blackmail (or anything else, for that matter) turn on such an irrelevant issue as cost suggests a perversion of justice.

DeLong dismisses all "economic" justifications of prohibition as follows:

> Why does blackmail strike us as so wrongful? So wrongful that even in the midst of a transaction cost analysis, the economist Ronald Coase would refer to it as "moral murder?" None of the foregoing [economic] theories seems to touch the nerve that the blackmailer rubs; none explains the societal abhorrence of the blackmailer's craft. *Purely economic explanations of the criminal law often produce bizarre conclusions, such as that blackmail rules are intended to reduce expenditures by blackmailers.* Such provocations are part of the charm of economic analysis. We all know that blackmail laws are meant to do more than prevent waste.[116]

Our only objection is that we do not at all regard this as "charming." If the law is to be predicated on cost, that is bad enough; but to base it on "social cost," a term fatally compromised by interpersonal comparisons of utility, is far worse.

Then there is the issue of the involuntariness of homosexuality. Why is this even relevant? If murder were one day found to be caused by inner compulsion, we would scarcely allow murderers to roam free. Surely the defense of homosexuality as a legal act has to do with the fact that it is a victimless "crime," a matter of consent between two adults. Even if homosexuality was attributable to an inner compulsion, as possibly it is in the case of addictive drugs, as long as the sexual act is not the result of an "outer" compulsion, namely rape, it should be legal.

Nor need we accept Isenbergh's contention that "B's opportunism hardly inspires admiration. "[117] It did, after all, help A's wife learn of her predicament

---

[115] Isenbergh, *supra* note 5, at 1931–32 fn. 57.

[116] Sidney W. DeLong, *Blackmailers, Bribe Takers, and the Second Paradox*, 141 U.PA. L. REV. 1663, 1689 (1993) (emphasis added).

[117] Isenbergh, *supra* note 5, at 1932, n.57.

in this specific case and, in general, serves as an impediment to such acts of infidelity.

But the most problematic matter in this case is that Isenbergh, by his own admission, is precluded from criticizing Posner in this manner. If he is to be consistent with his own analysis, he must take one more fact into account: the legality of homosexuality. In certain epochs, and in certain jurisdictions (e.g., Massachusetts in 1997), it has been legal. Here, Isenbergh may logically take the view he does. But in other eras and other geographical locations (e.g., Saudi Arabia in 1997 or Alabama in 1902), homosexuality has been a "prosecutable crime." Isenbergh must then, upon pain of self-contradiction, subscribe to Posner's view of the matter. For Isenbergh is on record as maintaining that under such circumstances, blackmail contracts should be "invalid and unenforceable."[118] Moreover, blackmailers would be complicit in the "underlying crime."[119] This is not exactly Posner's position, to be sure, but it is consistent in that both would punish the blackmailer, albeit for different reasons.

VIII. CONCLUSION

Let us consider one last argument against basing legal regimes on narrowly construed economic considerations. Relative prices change. That is their very nature. They do so incessantly, continuously. If law is based on calculations of cost, let alone social cost, it too will vary, along with the underlying prices from which it is derived. This fact applies to information as well. Does anyone doubt that the fax, telephone, e-mail, computers, videotape, VCRs, and camcorders have radically shifted, and shifted yet again, the costs of information gathering? And, although any predictions on the matter are fraught with danger, the burgeoning computer field, with new innovations and discoveries piling up every month, indicates more of the same in the future.

If we tie the tail of law onto the dog of economics, our legal system will be in a continual state of flux. It will not even approach the rule of law, which is a necessary condition of reasonable legal institutions.[120]

Isenbergh speaks of "information" being "worth more to A ... than to C" and therefore blackmail being "productive."[121] He discusses "A, B, and C in

---

[118] *Id.* at 1930.

[119] *Id.* at 1927 fn.50.

[120] Friedrich A. Hayek, Constitution of Liberty 397–411 (1971); Randy E. Barnett, The Structure of Liberty: Justice And the Rule of Law (1998).

[121] Isenbergh, *supra* note 5, at 1932.

the aggregate [being better or] worse off," depending upon the legal status of blackmail.[122] He even concedes that "[t]he balance of advantage between these two regimes is not self-evident."[123] He shows no evidence of realizing that continual price changes will render all of these calculations obsolete. Isenbergh reaches his "conclusion even though it may well be that the gains from improved allocation of rights in information would be roughly balanced by a possible increase in costly transacting."[124] He even discusses "[w]hat tips the scales in [his] mind" in his evaluation of the two systems.[125] But if the social costs on each side are roughly equal,[126] such that even Isenbergh can be tipped in one direction or the other, then once price changes are incorporated into the analysis, even the appearance of legal rigor will be converted into shifting sands and, ultimately, quicksand.[127]

Even worse, this affliction occurs at a point in time, not merely over time. Suppose, for example, that information-intensive relative prices in Hawaii and Vermont are different. Courts in these two places, both faithfully following Isenbergh's "principles," can and will reach opposite judicial findings.

We conclude, very much contrary to Isenbergh, that if justice is to be served, blackmail should be legalized totally, with no exceptions whatsoever.

---

[122] *Id.*

[123] *Id.*

[124] *Id.* at 1933.

[125] *Id.*

[126] We persevere in maintaining that this is equivalent to betting on which of two pins more angels can dance.

[127] For contrasting points of view, *see* Steven Shavell, *An Economic Analysis of Threats and Their Illegality: Blackmail, Extortion, and Robbery*, 141 U. PA. L. REV. 1877 (1983). On adherence to the "economic" underpinning of law concerning the relevant cost calculations, see James Lindgren, *Blackmail: An Afterword*, 141 U. PA. L. REV. 1975, 1983 (1993).

Chapter 12

Blackmail *is* Private Justice: A Reply to Jennifer Gerarda Brown

Libertarianism is a political theory. It asks only one question, "under what conditions is the use of force justified?," and responds with only one answer: "in retaliation against the prior use or threat of force or fraud against persons and justly owned property." Property may be legitimately acquired through a process of homesteading of virgin territory, trade, gifts, inheritance and any other peaceful and voluntary means. Initiatory force against an innocent person or his rightfully owned property, or its threat, is strictly prohibited by law. The libertarian axiom is "Thou shalt not aggress against non-aggressors."

What is the libertarian perspective on blackmail? The key issue for this political philosophy is whether or not the blackmailer threatens or initiates violence against people who themselves are innocent of these violations of the libertarian code. If blackmail necessarily involves such uninvited border crossings, it should be prohibited; if not, it should be legalized.

Superficially, it would appear that blackmail should be illegal under the libertarian code of law. For the blackmailer threatens to do something not in the interests of the threatened party, and this sounds like the initiation of aggression. However, upon further consideration it is apparent that this is not the case. For the blackmailer threatens not to violate the rights of the person or property of the blackmailee, but only to engage in his own free speech rights to gossip about the latter's secret. If it is licit to actually reveal another person's hidden information, it cannot be rights violative to threaten to do so for a fee, nor to refrain from so doing on this basis.

Brown focuses on "incriminating information" blackmail;[1] this is a special case where the secret consists of knowledge concerning the commission of a crime.[2] She considers the argument that it can "confer social benefits" in

---

[1] Jennifer Gerarda Brown, *Blackmail as Private Justice*, 141 U.PA. L. REV. 1935, 1936 (1993).

[2] For the sake of argument, I shall assume we are talking about real crime, that is, the kind that constitutes a physical invasion. The libertarian analysis of blackmail with regard to other kind of "crime," victimless crimes, would be somewhat different. Consider such activities as homosexuality, gambling, prostitution, pornography, addictive drug use. In these cases, the libertarian would advocate legalization of these acts; he would certainly not support turning it to the police people who engage in them on a consenting adult basis. This is to be distinguished from blackmailing such people, which would still be legitimate, even in these cases, since engaging in it is not rights violative.

terms of crime reduction. How? If incriminating blackmail were legalized people would have more of an incentive to seek out information about outlaw activity. This would reduce crime since the culprits would now have to share their booty with blackmailers.[3] If the blackmailee refused to knuckle under to these demands, the blackmailer would have a greater incentive to "report crimes to the police, if only to make blackmail threats credible in the future."

While this appears to be an honest attempt to portray the argument for the legalization of blackmail, her presentation is marred in several ways.

First, as "Devil's Advocate," she favors only "incriminating" blackmail, not any other kind. It would take us too far afield to defend the libertarian case in behalf of legalization for cases other than incriminating blackmail. All that can be said at this point is that *no* type of blackmail violates the libertarian axiom against non-aggression. But blackmail, of whatever stripe, must be sharply distinguished from extortion. Here, the threat is not the licit one of gossiping about secrets unless paid off, but rather to initiate violence, such as murder, rape, arson, kidnapping, etc.

Second, this author concedes too much to the other side of the debate; according to Brown: "Granted, blackmail might also benefit criminals by allowing them to postpone detection by public officials."[4] Yes, of course, this applies to a blackmailee-criminal who pays off the blackmailer, where the latter keeps his part of the bargain. But where is the justification for Brown's implicit assumption that in the absence of blackmail legalization the blackmailer would have spilled the beans to the police? This appears unwarranted.

Third, Brown[5] couches her tongue in cheek support not on the basis of principle, but rather cost benefit analysis: "But this potential benefit to some criminals would not necessarily exceed the additional costs imposed by blackmail ... even if blackmail caused the probability of *public* detection to fall in some cases, this loss could be more than compensated by increased use of both casually and deliberately acquired information by private blackmailers."[6]

---

[3] WALTER BLOCK, DEFENDING THE UNDEFENDABLE at 47–48 (1976) makes a similar point.

[4] Brown, *supra* note 1, at 1936.

[5] Brown, *supra* note 1, at 1936–37.

[6] Another difficulty with her presentation is that she doesn't seem aware that she is treading on already occupied ground. Brown states: "[T]he literature about blackmail has given short shrift to the ways blackmail might generally deter crime." Brown, *supra* note 1, at 1937 fn. 6. No truer words could be said. However, the weak implication is that no other commentators have made similar points in behalf of blackmail legalization. If this is true, she would appear to have overlooked Leo Katz, *Blackmail and Other Forms of Arm-Twisting*, 141 U. PA. L. REV. 1567 (1993).

But if Brown's implicit assumption is incorrect, there is no need for any balancing, or cost benefit analysis, or empirical study thereof. Blackmail legalization unambiguously leads to less crime, on the assumption that offenders are rational,[7] and will reduce their participation in acts as they become less profitable, *ceteris paribus*.

Despite these shortcomings, I appreciate Brown's attempt to "set out the *best* case for blackmail before concluding that it should be illegal."[8] One accomplishes little by knocking down straw men, after all. She continues: "Even in the 'best case' scenario, this arguably productive form of blackmail remains unappealing." There are several reasons for this, according to the author. First, it is part and parcel of the deterrence theory of punishment, and this, in addition to being too limited (e.g., it ignores "retribution, incapacitation and rehabilitation"[9]) has flaws of its own. Second, "blackmail might achieve deterrence at the expense of other goals of the criminal justice system," such as "education of the public."[10] However, these cannot occur to the extent that criminal justice is, not privatized, as Brown would have it, but rather kept secret.

But as far as libertarianism is concerned, all this is much beside the point. For scholars in this tradition, it matters not whether blackmail is or is not inconsistent with other goals, such as deterrence or public education. The only question is, Does blackmail consist of a *per se* rights violation. Since it clearly does not, these other issues are at best irrelevant, and at worst sow the seeds of confusion.

As it happens, Brown seems unduly pessimistic about these practical (albeit irrelevant) issues. Were blackmail legalized (even if only for incriminating information), while "*all* law enforcement activity" by definition could no longer remain "in the light of public scrutiny and involvement,"[11] there would still be a goodly bit that would still be widely known. To the extent that the public needs to be educated, this could be achieved via the remaining non-secret elements. For example, there will be at least some cases where the blackmail contract will not be made, and the blackmailee's secret will be made available to the public. Probably, the blackmailer will let it be known that the secret is being made available precisely because the blackmailee refused to purchase his service of keeping silent. Why? Because such occasional lapses, will enable the blackmailer to convince future clients of his seriousness. This,

---

[7] *See* ISAAC EHRLICH and GARY BECKER, THE ECONOMICS OF CRIME.

[8] Brown, *supra* note 1, at 1937.

[9] *Id.* at 1938.

[10] *Id.* at 1937–38.

[11] *Id.* at 1938.

of course, is not Brown's paradigm central case blackmail, in which, by defini-tion, secrecy is maintained. But this certainly serves the role of public education.[12]

Further, not all of these other goals are worthy of pursuing. For example, Brown's own nomination, educating the public, would itself appear to be in-compatible with the democratic philosophy she presumably embraces. For according to this doctrine, the voters are supreme. In Brown's opinion, how-ever, they are much in need of "education." If the latter is correct, how can we justify allowing the great unwashed the right to vote in elections?

I. THE BEST CASE FOR INCRIMINATING BLACKMAIL

In this section Brown continues her avoidance of legal principle in behalf of expediency. That she does so in order to adumbrate the best case she can for decriminalizing blackmail suggests that she is skirting dangerously close to employing a straw man strategy. She goes so far as to intimate that black-mail might be legalized in certain neighborhoods, but not others, depending upon the cooperativeness of the local people with the authorities. This author states:

> For example, the legislature might determine that in some neigh-borhoods or communities, people readily and frequently tip off the police about certain crimes, while in other communities, people try to minimize interaction with law enforcement officials and might require additional economic incentives to use incriminating infor-mation they might have. Thus, empirical data about the culture and reporting behaviors of an identified community could help guide a legislature in defining the range of crimes covered by the statute.[13]

She is willing, moreover, to tailor the law to conform to the likely re-sponses of the blackmailees. She assumes, reasonably enough, that drug deal-ers, but not embezzlers, are likely to react with great violence to blackmail offers.[14] Therefore, the law should allow the latter, but not the former.

---

[12] Brown herself, *Id.* 1946, states: "future blackmail threats will be more credible if blackmailers report crimes when blackmailee refuse to pay. Blackmailers might also turn in the criminals they unsuccessfully blackmail more readily if they have no fear of facing criminal charges themselves."

[13] *Id.* at 1939 fn. 12.

[14] *Id.* at 1940.

The difficulty here, at least for the libertarian, is that while embezzlement is a real crime, drug trafficking is not. The embezzler engages in fraud, which amounts to the theft of property. According to Rothbard:

> Fraud as implicit theft stems from the right of free contract, derived in turn from the rights of private property. Thus, suppose that Smith and Jones agree on a contractual exchange of property titles: Smith will pay $1,000 in return for Jones' car. If Smith appropriates the car and then refuses to turn over $1,000 to Jones, then Smith has in effect stolen the $1,000; Smith is an aggressor against $1,000 now properly belonging to Jones. Thus, failure to keep a contract of this type is tantamount to theft, and therefore to a physical appropriation of another's property fully as 'violent' as trespass or simple burglary without armed assault.[15]

In sharp contrast, the purchase and sale of addictive drugs is or at least can be a "capitalist act between consenting adults."[16] Here, no violence at all takes place, *per se.* That there is brutality and ferocity associated with drug trafficking is solely a function of its present tragic legal prohibition. When there is a dispute over commercial arrangements in this industry the parties may not avail themselves of police or courts. Instead, they are left with no option but to fight it out amongst themselves. But it is (and was) the same with alcohol. Nowadays, if I have a conflict with my wine merchant, I peacefully sue him in small claims court. During alcohol prohibition in the early part of this century, this alternative was not available to me. Had I gone to sought justice, then, I would have been imprisoned.

If anything, then, the legal prescription on blackmail as private law enforcement would be the very opposite: crime fighting resources, whether public or private, ought be aimed at the embezzler, not the drug dealer.

II. THE DETERRENCE VALUE OF BLACKMAIL

A. An Economic Model of Deterrence

Having set the stage with a rather weak case for blackmail legalization in the case of incriminating information, Brown is now ready to show it is not a productive activity. In this section she very sensibly notes that crime tends to

---

[15] MURRAY ROTHBARD, THE ETHICS OF LIBERTY at 78 (1982).
[16] ROBERT NOZICK, ANARCHY, STATE AND UTOPIA (1974).

be reduced by increasing both the penalties associated with being caught, and the probability of this occurring; and that the former is typically more economical in terms of crime fighting expenditures than the latter.

As is her wont, however, her discussion ignores issues of justice.[17] Suppose, for example, it were possible to reduce crime greatly by imposing the death penalty for stealing one stick of bubble gum, a sort of super Singapore punishment regime. This might well be "efficient" from the perspective of at least some version of this term, but it would scarcely make the punishment commensurate with the crime.

B. Blackmail as a Mechanism of Criminal Law Enforcement

Brown[18] offers four different types of jurisdictions for our consideration, according to whether or not blackmail is legal, and if the government imposes the obligation on the citizenry to report crimes. [19]

	Blackmail Legal	Blackmail Illegal
Duty to report crime	A	B
No duty to report crime	C	D

That is, under A, government imposes a duty to report criminal activity, and blackmail is allowed; B, government imposes a duty to report criminal activity, and blackmail is prohibited; C, government imposes no duty to report criminal activity, and blackmail is allowed; and D, government imposes no duty to report criminal activity, and blackmail is prohibited. The latter case, D, describes the actual legal situation in the U.S., while C is the only one consistent with libertarianism.

Libertarians must reject selections A and B because of the positive obligations imposed therein. The difficulty with positive obligations is that they are inherently a theft of services. Why should a person who has committed no crime go to prison for failure to report the misconduct of another; unless he

---

[17] See ASSESSING THE CRIMINAL: RESTITUTION, RETRIBUTION AND THE LEGAL PROCESS (Randy E. Barnett & John Hagel III, eds.) (1977); MURRAY ROTHBARD, THE ETHICS OF LIBERTY (1982); MURRAY ROTHBARD, FOR A NEW LIBERTY (1978).

[18] Brown, *supra* note 1, at 1944.

[19] See *Id.* at 1947, figure 1.

has agreed to do so, this amounts to a draft, in effect forced enslavement, of police personnel.[20]

While still upholding what she considers the "best case" for blackmail, Brown[21] rejects the argument that bounties for tips on criminals would be even more efficient than blackmail, due to the additional "transaction costs when the state serves as a middle person [sic] — paying a bounty to the informant and collecting a fine from the criminal once convicted." This point could be strengthened by noting that the government, in virtually all cases, runs its prisons at a loss. Therefore, there is no possibility of collecting any fines net of its costs.

III. THE DANGERS OF BLACKMAIL

Now, at long last, Brown attempts to show that, despite all the good efforts she has made in its behalf as devil's advocate, blackmail should not really be legalized after all. She organizes her reasons into two categories, questions of efficiency and moral principles.

A. Economic Inefficiency of Blackmail

Our author is to be congratulated for rejecting the argument that "Blackmail ... involves coercion of the blackmailee."[22] She repudiates this claim on

---

[20] Some might argue that this obligation is a part of citizenship; that the person who lives in a certain jurisdiction thereby in effect agrees to take on this responsibility. However, the "in effect" or implicit contract argument is a very dangerous one. Almost anything can be proven in this way. (E.g., you have an implicit contract to give me money, since you are now reading this article.) The fallacy can clearly be seen in two ways. First, empirically: there never has been, in all the history of the world, a constitution signed by all, or even virtually all of the inhabitants at any time; at most, such agreements are signed by a mere handful of people, as in the case of our own Declaration of Independence. Second, rationally: let us assume that there were people who owned land *before* the advent of this supposed contract, and passed it down, through the years, to their descendants who are now alive. Certainly, there can be no contract, implicit or otherwise, binding these people to any such obligation, since they can trace their land ownership to a time before its existence. And if not for them, then not for anyone who bought or rented land from them. For further elaboration on this point, *see* LYSANDER SPOONER, NO TREASON (1870); HANS-HERMANN HOPPE, THE ECONOMICS AND ETHICS OF PRIVATE PROPERTY: STUDIES IN POLITICAL ECONOMY AND PHILOSOPHY (1993); MURRAY ROTHBARD, THE ETHICS OF LIBERTY (1982).

[21] Brown, *supra* note 1, 1948.

[22] *Id.* at 1950 tn. 32.

the ground that "the blackmailee may be faced with a hard choice between the consequences of disclosure and paying the blackmailer does not necessarily make the blackmail any more coercive than the choice facing many parties to wholly legitimate economic transactions."[23] As an example she might have used Fletcher's case where the blackmailer offers to sell to the supposed victim a baseball autographed by Babe Ruth with the knowledge that the "victim's" child, who is dying, would receive great solace from having the ball.[24] The blackmailer demands an inordinately high price for this sports equipment memorabilia, based on his knowledge of the "victim's" special need. This is as apt an example of "hard bargaining" as one is likely to confront, but it hardly involves coercion, since the baseball is the legitimate property of the seller, and he can surely place any value on it he wishes, and for whatever reason. Let us now consider Brown's [25] views on the Coase [26] v. Lindgren [27] debate. Coase had argued that blackmail was economically inefficient in that resources were being devoted to a solely redistributional task where no new net wealth was being created. That is, the blackmailer spent time and effort to uncover the secrets of the blackmailee, and then more of the same in order to negotiate with him over the terms of the contract. If successful, the agreement would then suppress the information; the only thing that would have been accomplished would be a transfer of funds from the blackmailee to the blackmailer. Lindgren had agreed with this, but only for information purposefully sought for this purpose, at a cost. But he disagreed with Coase when it came to knowledge accidentally obtained with no resource investment involved. Coase's reply to this is that even for casually acquired information there would still be bargaining costs.

The proper answer to this debate from my point of view is "a pox on both your houses." Coase and Lindgren agree that in effect digging up dirt and

---

[23] Her insight is slightly marred, however, by her citation of Lindgren to the effect that "Even highly coercive threats are present in many types of legitimate economic bargaining." James Lindgren, *Unraveling the Paradox of Blackmail*, 84 COLUM. L. REV. 670, 701 (1984). This is almost self-contradictory in that Brown is here presumably engaged in arguing that blackmail does not involve coercion. How can it help her to cite the diametric opposite stance in support of this contention? Another difficulty is that it is hard to imagine a legitimate economic interaction that involves coercion. One would have thought that if an act, economic or otherwise, is coercive, it is to that extent illegitimate.

[24] George P. Fletcher, *Blackmail: The Paradigmatic Case*, 141 U. PA. L. REV. 1617, 1618 (1993).

[25] Brown, *supra* note1, at 1951–53.

[26] Ronald Coase, *The 1987 McCorkle Lecture: Blackmail*, 74 VA. L. REV. at 655–76. (1988).

[27] James Lindgren, *Blackmail: On Waste, Morals and Ronald Coase*, 36 UCLA L. REV. 597 (1989).

then burying it again serves no socially useful purpose. In this they are both wrong. Why would anyone do it if there were no benefit to be derived therefrom? According to "folk wisdom" the question was asked, "Why climb Mount Everest?" And the answer given was "Because it is there." The translation into economic jargon of this reply is as follows: even apart from the fame and adulation given to those who have successfully reached its peak, the psychic benefits are greater than the costs. How else to explain that men would want to engage in such acts of derring do, even in private?

But precisely the same insight applies in the present context. Why dig up a dirty bit of information that people would rather keep secret, whether or not it has to do with criminal behavior? Although there are to be sure other possible explanations, one reason is because it is there! Now tastes are of course such that adulation is heaped upon those who can scale mountains, and we tend to sneer at men who delve into other's secrets, and morality may well incline us in the same direction. But for all that the economic analysis is exactly the same. It simply will not do for Coase and Lindgren, and Brown as well, to denigrate as non-productive, at least in the *ex ante* sense, the voluntary acts of other people. The gambling industry has as its main result the (not so) arbitrary transfer of funds from one person to another. Would any of these three authors contend it is therefore non-productive? Hardly.

They are each arguing in effect over how many angels can dance at the tip of a pin. What determines economic efficiency is not whether resources are used, and new wealth is created in some objective sense, but rather whether, in the minds of the actors themselves who are involved in the situation, their efforts are more than repaid by the results attained, at least in the *ex ante* sense. The only time we as outsiders can determine if an act is economically efficient in this sense is if there are two willing partners to the exchange. (Or, as in the case of climbing the mountain, the man involved undertakes it on a voluntary basis.) The point is, costs are essentially subjective.[28] They consist of alternatives foregone, or, strictly speaking, the second best option not undertaken whenever a choice is made. But this next best opportunity, is a hypothetical. No other person can witness it. By its very nature it can only be known to the economic actor himself. Specifically, there is simply no way to determine whether or not the costs of bargaining alone are greater, smaller, or equal to the expenditures.

Brown[29] insists that deterrence must be included in any such calculations, and that this must be entered on the side of blackmail legalization. After all, "When the blackmail is based on incriminating information, it may aug-

---

[28] *See, generally,* LUDWIG VON MISES, HUMAN ACTION.

[29] Brown, *supra* note 1, at 1952.

ment the potential costs of criminal activity and deter crime, thereby increasing social welfare."

There are problems here as well. The concept of "social welfare" is fatally flawed by invalid interpersonal comparisons of utility.[30] Nor is it even necessary. Surely, criminal activity not only harms but violates the rights of each victim. Is that not enough of a reason to oppose it? Her insight is further impaired by an exception she offers to this general rule: "Some crime may benefit the criminal more than it harms anyone else. Reduction of such crime would not necessarily increase social welfare."[31] If by this she means victimless crimes such as those prohibiting prostitution or drug trafficking or homosexuality or pornography, all limited to consenting adults, well and good. But then, from her own perspective, she ought to oppose incriminating blackmail, not favor it. On the other hand, her other remarks about drug prohibition,[32] lend little credence to this interpretation. But if this is not the explanation for this remarkable comment, then she opens herself up to the rejoinder concerning the "utility monster." This is a person who derives a gigantic amount of joy, happiness, utility, from cannibalism, much more, we calculate, than the negative amount suffered by those being eaten. Brown's remarks suggest that she would have to defend this creature's right to murder people since this would enhance "social welfare."[33] And that if she refuses to do so, then she may not logically make the point that "some crime may benefit the criminal more than it harms anyone else."

Another difficulty is that deterrence itself is less important, philosophically, than it is cracked up to be. States Rothbard:

---

[30] Murray N. Rothbard, *Toward a Reconstruction of Utility and Welfare Economics*, San Francisco Center for Libertarian Studies, Occasional Paper #3 at 21 (1977); LIONEL ROBBINS, AN ESSAY ON THE NATURE AND SIGNIFICANCE OF ECONOMIC SCIENCE (2nd ed. 1935); Lionel Robbins, *Interpersonal Comparison of Utility*, ECONOMIC JOURNAL at 635–41 (December 1938).

[31] Brown, *supra* note 1, at 1952, fn. 40.

[32] *Id.* at 1940; *Id.* at 1956, fn. 47.

[33] Brown believes that privacy invasions also impose "social costs." *Id.* at 1953, fn. 41 An alternative and I believe more correct way of looking at this matter is that some people strive to promote privacy (locksmiths, guards, the purveyors of gated communities) while others attempt to reduce it (detectives, investigators, reporters, photographers). *Each* of them promotes social welfare in the sense of increasing *ex ante* utility. For example, when I buy a 12 foot high fence for $1,000, I value it at more than that amount and the seller at less; therefore, we both gain. Similarly, when you hire a detective for $500 you place a greater value on his time than that, and he, a lesser value. This may well pose insuperable problems for GDP calculations, given that both of these expenditures are to some extent at cross purposes, but not for social welfare theory.

this criterion of deterrence implies schemas of punishment which almost everyone would consider grossly unjust. For example: if there were no punishment for crime at all, a great number of people would commit petty theft, such as stealing fruit from a fruit stand. On the other hand, most people have a far greater built-in inner objection to themselves committing murder than they have to petty shoplifting, and would be far less apt to commit the grosser crime. Therefore, if the object of punishment is to deter from crime, then a far greater punishment would be required for preventing shoplifting than for preventing murder, a system that goes against most people's ethical standards. As a result, with deterrence as the criterion there would have to be stringent capital punishment for petty thievery—for the theft of bubblegum—while murderers might only incur the penalty of a few months in jail.

Similarly, a classic critique of the deterrence principle is that, if deterrence were our sole criterion, it would be perfectly proper for the police or courts to execute publicly for a crime someone whom *they* know to be innocent, but whom they had convinced the public was guilty. The knowing execution of an innocent man—provided, of course, that the knowledge can be kept secret—would exert a deterrence effect just as fully as the execution of the guilty. And yet, of course, such a policy, too, goes violently against almost everyone's standards of justice. … In short, the deterrence principle implies a gross violation of the intuitive sense that justice connotes some form of fitting and proportionate punishment of the guilty party and to him alone.[34]

Brown next considers the Landes–Posner critique of private law enforcement,[35] based on the claim that this would lead to both under- and over-investment in crime fighting. The argument of these two authors for the first of these positions is that the private policeman, e.g., the blackmailer, would lower the penalties imposed on the criminal, since they would now be limited to money, not jail time. However, as Brown trenchantly notes, such private acts would "simply supplement public enforcement. The state can still incarcerate the offender if he is apprehended."[36]

---

[34] MURRAY N. ROTHBARD, THE ETHICS OF LIBERTY at 91 (1982).

[35] William Landes and Richard A. Posner, *The Private Enforcement of Law*, 4 J. LEGAL STUD. 1, 43 (1975).

[36] Brown, *supra* note 1, at 1954.

As well, Landes-Posner maintain that only public prosecutors, but not private blackmailers could be expected to engage in discretionary non-enforcement of bad laws.[37] But there is an obvious answer here, for Brown as well as these two authors, and for all other scholars who rely on the apparatus of the state to achieve justice: let them repeal the unjust laws for which the government is itself responsible. Why blame the poor innocent blackmailer who is merely acting in a way which in effect supports the law as written?

Then there is the Landes-Posner claim that blackmail will also lead to excessive crime reduction. This is difficult to understand on the face of it, even apart from the fact that if blackmail leads to *both* over and under optimal allocation of resources, there is a distinct possibility that the two will balance one another, leading to no misallocation at all. The main error is that, again on the assumption of real crimes against person and property such as rape and murder, and not victimless "crimes," there cannot possibly *be* extraneous crime prevention. Yes, it would be silly to spend the entire GDP, or any amount approaching that, on protection against murder, for then we would all die of starvation.[38] But consider this from a marginal perspective, not a total one. X% is now spent on crime prevention. Mr. Smith, based on his own utility maximization considerations, now wishes to spend and additional $1 on this goal. On what basis can Landes and Posner possibly object? Certainly not because welfare will thereby be reduced; not, that is, if they take Smith's preferences into account.

Next, Brown[39] takes issue with Epstein.[40] The latter author sees in legalization the debauchery of the blackmailee, who would be forced to engage in (real) crimes in order to make his payments to the blackmailer. Brown,[41] with a little help from her friend Lindgren,[42] points out, unobjectionably, that "we do not generally criminalize activities simply because they are paid for with

---

[37] What are "bad laws?" For the libertarian, this is an easy question. Bad laws include those which punish victimless "criminals." But Brown eschews this answer, at least with regard to drug laws. What, then, is her definition of a "bad law?" The fear, here, is that prosecutors of the Brown variety would be free to indulge their arbitrary opinion as to what comprises good and bad law.

[38] On the other hand, if this were the freely chosen decision of all the people, then there is nothing in economic analysis that can say them nay. I characterize this as "silly" in that such a decision is likely to come only from the political process, not the economic.

[39] Brown, *supra* note 1, at 1958–1962.

[40] Richard Epstein, *Blackmail, Inc.*, 50 U. CHI. L. REV. 553 (1983).

[41] Brown, *supra* note 1, at 1960–61.

[42] *See* James Lindgren, *More Blackmail Ink: a Critique of 'Blackmail, Inc.,' Epstein's Theory of Blackmail*, 16 CONN. L. REV. 909 at 920–21 (1984).

illegal gains. People often commit crimes to pay for legitimate goods and services, but that is not a rationale for criminalizing the production of those items." The point here being, presumably, the libertarian one that we monomaniacally focus on the propriety of blackmail itself, and ignore all irrelevant considerations.

If this practice passes muster under the non-aggression axiom, then it should be legalized no matter what its ancillary or externalities effects. If blackmail is legitimate, and the blackmailee goes out a commits a crime[43] to finance his payments, so be it; blackmail stays legal, and we strive mightily to quell these other villainies. The alternative, that we prohibit blackmail, would force us to do the same with regard to gambling, beautiful women, luxury autos, etc., because men upon occasion commit crimes in order to attain these values. Too bad, then, that Brown doesn't follow through with this magnificent insight of hers when it comes to the dangers of blackmail.[44] In the event, she says,

> In our zeal to deter one set of crimes, we might create incentives to commit others. The blackmailer could turn out to be as dangerous as the criminal with whom he transacts business. Because actual or potential physical force is part of many crimes, many blackmailers will have to be prepared to deal with violent blackmailees. It might prove difficult to know when blackmailers are merely prepared for violence and when they initiate it.

> Monitoring blackmailers' activities would be difficult, and they might use criminal methods to operate an otherwise legitimate business. For example, a blackmailer might approach a criminal and threaten not only to disclose incriminating information to the authorities unless paid, but also to harm the criminal's person or property. The criminal is unlikely to report the illegal threat, because she will fear detection of her criminal activity is she goes to the authorities.

Had Brown kept faith with her earlier vision, she would have said something very different. For example: "Too bad that blackmail might become associated with the initiation of violence, or with real crime. But that is no reason to ban it. Butchers, bakers and candle stick makers also, sometimes, murder and rape, but no rational person ever advocated the banning of these pro-

---

[43] A real one, that is, not a victimless one like blackmail.

[44] Brown, *supra* note 1, at 1961.

fessions. If the blackmailer commits crimes, well and good, we will stop him. But we will respect his law abiding (purely blackmail) activities." Instead, she contents herself with the quite sound but far less satisfying claim that "The possibility that the blackmailer will commit crimes may not be as great a problem as initially appears."[45]

B. Lindgren's Structural Theory of Blackmail: Equity and Externalities

In this section Brown[46] distinguishes her views from those of Lindgren.[47] While of all the scholars she criticizes Brown is perhaps most sympathetic to Lindgren, there is no perfect congruity between their perspectives. Brown attributes to this author the opinion that blackmail should be outlawed "because it harms third parties by compromising their rights."[48] She does not appear to realize that these are two very different reasons, one of them valid, the other not. If we were to ban all acts which merely *harmed* others, there would be no one left outside of prison. You date a woman in whom I was interested, and you have harmed me. You open a store in competition with mine, and again you have harmed me. You buy a loaf of bread, thus raising its price by a minuscule amount; when I later make a similar purchase, you are once again exposed as having harmed me.

Compromising my rights is of course, at least for the libertarian, an entirely different matter. If Brown had looked into this charge, she might have come to grips with the real fallacy underlying Lindgren's theory. Instead, she focuses on the irrelevant charge of harm. And her response to this? Yes, blackmail harms other people (negative externalities) but it also helps them (positive externalities).[49] Thus, the legal statutes of blackmail should turn on the issue of whether the positive or negative harm predominates.

Even on the face of it, assuming for the moment that these entities *could* be meaningfully compared, the whole idea seems preposterous. We do not apply such an empirical externalities test to any other act to determine its legality. Consider broccoli, for example. Its benefits in terms of vitamins, roughage, good health, etc., are undoubted. This alone has both positive and negative externalities, as some people benefit from the good health of the broccoli eaters, and others lose out, thereby (e.g., misanthropes).

---

[45] *Id.*

[46] *Id.* at 1963–66.

[47] Lindgren, *supra* note 41.

[48] Brown, *supra* note 1, at 1963.

[49] *Id.*

On the other hand, this vegetable has proved to be an implement of torture for generations of youngsters, although a few weird kids take to it like a duck to water. Is the reason broccoli is still legal because its positive effects outweigh the negatives? Hardly. Were this utilitarian calculation[50] to be reversed, and broccoli found to be harmful on balance (it is still healthy, say, but the hatred of it on the part of the young people of the country comes to more than offset this factor), would the law automatically be changed? *Should* it be, under such circumstances? Merely to ask these nonsensical questions is to answer them. We *can't* compare the joy and displeasure associated with broccoli (or of anything else, for that matter, such as blackmail). Even if we could, somehow, this still would be beside the point. For acts should be outlawed if and only if they violate the libertarian strictures against uninvited border crossings, not because of any alleged preponderance of incomparable external costs over external benefits.

What of part II of the Lindgren case, the claim that the blackmailer has in effect stolen the leverage or "chips" of third parties (information which properly belongs to them) and thus necessarily engages in "unjust enrichment?"[51] The proper way to refute this claim is to show that it is the blackmailer, not any third party, who is the legitimate owner of the knowledge in question. But Brown does not take this tack. On the contrary, she again resorts to "externalities (which) can be both negative and positive. If the activity is otherwise beneficial, we should not assume that its costs—including effect on third parties—necessarily outweigh these benefits."[52] This is all well and good, insofar as it goes. It is, after all, a criticism of Lindgren, and his is a theory much in need of correction. And it does wound Lindgren's thesis, based upon his own premises that negative and positive externalities can be compared, one with the other. But they cannot, and thus Brown's criticism of Lindgren is ultimately unsatisfying.

Consider in this regard Brown's[53] analysis of Lindgren's[54] "hypothetical case of blackmail in which a woman threatens to disclose that a company is criminally violating pollution standards by using a smoke stack without pollution control equipment. She may live near the smokestack and suffer some damage from the pollution, for which she can seek some compensation. But if she asks for $1,000,000 to keep quiet about the pollution and 'seeks nothing for the public's benefit,' Lindgren says, she has 'clearly' committed blackmail.

---

[50] Again, assuming that interpersonal comparisons do not render it totally meaningless.

[51] Brown, *supra* note 1, at 1963.

[52] *Id.* at 1964.

[53] *Id.* at 1965.

[54] James Lindgren, *Unraveling the Paradox of Blackmail*, 84 COLUM. L. REV. 670, 714 (1984).

This is because '(t)here is an almost total disjunction between the advantage sought and the leverage used.'"

There are several difficulties here. First, pollution, contrary to practically the universal received opinion, is not an external diseconomy, akin, for example, to competition. On the contrary, at least under libertarian law, it is an invasion, similar to trespass. It is the encroachment of soot particles into the bodies (stomachs, lungs) and property of other people. Pollution is (falsely) considered a negative externality because for more than a 100 years (roughly, 1835–1960) it was allowed, even protected, by the law of the land. Secondly, the information that this crime (now that, at long last, the state correctly looks at it in this manner) has occurred properly belongs to the woman in question. Who else could appropriately be the owner of that knowledge, apart from the person who saw it with her own eyes? Does this woman have a right to disclose information about this occurrence to other people? Of this we can be sure, at least as long as free speech rights obtain in this country. No one, not even Lindgren, would object were she to make the authorities aware of the pollution. Does she, in contrast, have an obligation to do so? Not even Brown maintains this. If one may legally do something, may one refrain (given no obligation to do it) for a fee? This seems to follow from the very logic of the case. This, then, is the proper answer to Lindgren: the woman owns this knowledge "chip," and may do whatever she wishes with it, as long as what she does, does not constitute a physical invasion. As the offer to keep silent for a fee (the amount is immaterial) does not constitute aggression against non-aggressors, the woman is totally within her rights to blackmail the polluting firm.

But none of this for Brown. In lieu, she [55] claims that "Lindgren's mistake is to see 'public benefit' only in the short term. By failing to recognize that this woman's blackmail imposes costs on a wrongdoer that, if allowed, might deter other polluters because they fear similar treatment, Lindgren creates a greater 'disjunction' between the interests of the blackmailer and the public than may actually exist. Particularly when the blackmail may confer some social benefits of deterrence, the exchange seems fair: the blackmailer 'appropriates' the state's leverage but also creates some deterrence value that inures to the benefit of the general public." To this I say, "benefits, schmenefits." It matters for

---

[55] Brown, *supra* note 1, at 1965.

legal analysis not one whit whether we look at matters in the short or long run.[56]

Brown's, in other words, is a superficial analysis. She agrees with Lindgren on theoretical or basic grounds, and only quarrels with him on the most cursory of issues. Did I have to choose between them, I would side with Lindgren. For Brown concedes to him that the state really owns the knowledge of the pollution (which, so far, only this woman, and of course the polluter himself, possess). Brown maintains that the woman is using this "chip" for the public good. But that is not for Brown or this woman to determine. If the government really owns the information, it is for *it* to determine how best it is to be used. Suppose I stole Brown's pen from her, and then used it to edit her next article. The point is not whether or not my actions actually help Brown or not; the issue is that I have no right to this pen *even if* I use it to help Brown. In like manner, once Brown concedes to Lindgren that the state is the proper owner of the information inside this woman's head, it is entirely irrelevant if she uses it for what Brown sees as the state's purpose. It is for the *state* to make any such determination.[57]

What of the issue that, but for the blackmailer, the blackmailee (who is, in this case, a criminal polluter-trespasser) would have more money with which to make restitution to the victim? Yes, if we wish to indulge in a bit of interpersonal comparing of utilities, we should indeed, along with Brown "consider the possibility that those benefits will outweigh the losses to individual victims who are unable to collect restitution from a criminal defendant who, but for the blackmail payments, would have been able to make restitution." On the other hand, we should do so, also, for *everyone* from whom the blackmailee-criminal purchased *anything*. If we followed Brown's advice on this, we should have to punish the polluter's grocer or shoe shine boy, not only his blackmailer, for reducing the amount of money this polluter would have with which to compensate his victims. This, however, would be in behalf of the victim of the real crime (not of blackmail), for, in justice, he is due compensation. But we should no more properly incarcerate the grocer or the shoe shine boy for selling goods or services to the blackmailee-criminal than we should the blackmailer himself, for providing yet another service to the

---

[56] In any case, there is no "social rate" of time discount which can be used to compute a present discounted value for the "public good." Without a time preference rate, there is no way in which short and long run values can be compared. There is no doubt that in the make believe world occupied by Lindgren (and most commentators) the long run scores heavily against the short run. Brown's mistake is to join Lindgren's world in the first place.

[57] I here assume, only for the sake of argument, that the state has a right to make such a determination.

blackmailee-criminal, this time, silence. The point is, the blackmailer occupies exactly the same legal position as do the grocer and shoe shine boy. Since no one, not even Brown or Lindgren advocates incarcerating the latter, they should leave off holding this position with regard to the former.

IV. MORALITY ON A SYSTEMIC SCALE: AGAINST BLACKMAIL

Here, Brown for the first time gives her own views, having left off playing the role of either devil's advocate or critic.[58] She grounds her own defense of the illegality of blackmail in "the community's collective interest in the administration of justice as a public event that binds and defines us. We are intuitively suspicious of private justice, and private justice is the essence of incriminating blackmail."[59]

Before we go any further, a few more critical remarks. There is no such thing as a "community," apart from the individuals who comprise it.[60] Thus, there can be no "collective interest" in the administration of justice or of anything else for that matter. There are only the individual interests of many people. For there to be a "community" or a "collective interest" over and above that which applies to individual human beings, there must be some such thing as a "group mind," or a "collective conscience," or "mass consciousness." Needless to say, no such entity has ever been captured or held in captivity.

While we are indeed "defined" by many things, and a search for justice may well be one of them, we are only bound by the libertarian axiom of non-aggression, and by any obligations over and above that which we voluntarily take upon ourselves. If there is something else that should be (not morally but) legally binding on us, it has never been justified.[61]

Yes, there is indeed great revulsion against blackmail;[62] however, we are not at all commonly "suspicious of private justice." The American Arbitration Association, the Hague, the International Court of World Settlements, the administrators of Canon Law, the rabbis who execute Talmudic Law, the

---

[58] See Brown, *supra* note 1, 1966–73.

[59] *Id.* at 1967.

[60] For more on the methodological individualism which underlies this statement, *see* Walter Block, *On Robert Nozick's 'On Austrian Methodology'*, INQUIRY, Vol. 23, No.4 pp. 397–444 (Fall 1980).

[61] For a devastating critique of this notion, *see, generally,* Nozick, *supra* note 16.

[62] Much but not all of it is in reaction to extortion, with which blackmail is commonly confused.

World Court, the punishment circles of many Indian tribes, while not as well known or revered as government courts, are certainly highly respected amongst people aware of them. They are certainly institutions of non-governmental justice. If "The Godfather" movies are to be believed, even the Mafia employs private courts.

A case can be made that the same applies to the United Nations. It, too, is not itself a government, although its membership is of course composed of such entities. That is, the U.N. has no power to tax, nor to preclude other governments (that is, other world wide treaty organizations such as ITO) from competing with it. These two are the criterion for government: ability to use legitimate force, and a monopoly power thereof. As the U.N. has neither one nor the other,[63] it cannot be considered a government. That being the case, all of its judicial, mediation and arbitration services might conceivably be considered instances of "private justice."

Brown doesn't seem to appreciate that her theory implies nothing less than that the U.N be turned into a world government, where Americans will of necessity be outvoted by Chinese, Indians, and others. For if there is something untoward about a non-public authority, say, justice is determined by a contract between Smith and Jones, then there must be something improper, too, and equally so, about a contract (e.g., treaty) between any two U.N. member countries, such as Finland and Bolivia.

Brown continues her screed against privatization: "To say that a public authority enforces the criminal law is to state a near tautology. Many define criminal prohibitions not just by the severity of their associated penalty, but also by the state's exclusive entitlement to enforce them."[64] She buttresses the latter by citing Blackstone as follows: "Whatever power, therefore, individuals had of punishing offenses against the law of nature, that is now vested in the magistrate alone, who bears the sword of justice by the consent of the whole community."[65]

The German government under the Nazis was a legitimate one, at least in terms of the niceties of democracy.[66] Although Hitler won the election which

---

[63] It certainly has no monopoly power. Nor does it have the ability to compel its member nations, certainly not the stronger ones, to do its bidding. It does have soldiers under its ostensible command, but these serve, mainly as "human fences" and cannot be demanded of member nations, only requested.

[64] Brown, *supra* note 1, at 1967.

[65] *Id.* at 1967 fn. 93.

[66] As much cannot be said for the Russia of Lenin or Stalin, the China of Mao, the Cambodia of Pol Pot, the Uganda of Idi Amin. These were dictatorships, not democracies.

brought him to power by a plurality, not a majority, this was much in the same way as Clinton came to office for his first term. Would Brown go so far as to assert as a "near tautology" that criminal prohibitions are defined by the *Nazi* "state's exclusive entitlement to enforce them?" Hardly. Therefore, she needs to revise her statement. What are the options? Certainly, we cannot say that government involvement is *sufficient* for criminal justice? Is it, then, *necessary*? This, too, is difficult to accept, given the splendid records of the private justice associations mentioned above, which in the minds of at least some commentators, compare favorably with government institutions.

Then there is the issue of "consent of the whole community." The German Jews, the Ibos, the Soviet kulaks by no stretch of the imagination can be said to have consented to anything at all, much less to the judicial power of those who abused them. But even here in the United States this concept is not exactly in conformity with the facts. Yes, "consent" is celebrated on stage and screen and in popular songs and jingles, but where is the evidence for it? How many people signed the Constitution, the Declaration of Independence or the Articles of Confederation? How many people signed the constitutions of the thirteen states which together began this country? Let it not be objected that signatures are not needed. They are, at law, for even the most unimportant of commercial contracts. Should anything less be required for the momentous justification of the state upon which all else, at least for Brown, rests? Can we infer consent from voting in elections? From payment of taxes? From failure to leave the country in protest? None of these arguments will suffice.[67]

Yes, "[t]he criminal action belongs not to the victim, but to the state,"[68] but only if the former has first *relinquished* this basic human right to the latter. In the absence of any evidence for this contention, it is far from a "truism about the nature of criminal law [that it] seem[s] to lead inexorably to the conclusion that it should be enforced publicly rather than privately;"[69] in fact, the very opposite seems more nearly to be true. Namely, that if (criminal) justice is to be done, it *cannot* be done by a government which does not rest upon the consent of the governed, no matter how much scholars such as Brown would like to believe that this is the case.

Happily, our author recognizes at least some small vestigial traces of private rights which have somehow withstood the onslaught of the modern state. She mentions[70] in this context the victim's rights movement, restorative jus-

---

[67] LYSANDER SPOONER, NO TREASON (1870).

[68] Brown, *supra* note 1, at 1967–68.

[69] *Id.* at 1968.

[70] *Id.* at 1968–69.

tice, reconciliation,[71] victim-offender mediation and alternative dispute resolution; she might also have included under this rubric the move to force
criminals to compensate victims, and the one to privatize jails. But she only
acknowledges such phenomena the better to give the back of her hand to
them.[72] To this end she cites Mnookin and Kornhouser to the effect that governmental law really underlies all such findings, which are, in any case,
merely (less expensive) attempts to forecast those of the state,[73] and also the
socialist Fiss who is hostile to the private sector because it does not stamp out
all wealth disparity.[74]

At last we arrive at the very source of Brown's hostility to blackmail legalization, even for what she is pleased to believe is the only rational case for
it, when used with regard to the criminal-blackmailee. She states:

> Resource disparities will affect outcomes in blackmail powerfully.
> Legalized blackmail allows wealthy criminals to prevent (or at least
> postpone) disclosure of their crime by purchasing the blackmailer's
> silence. Poorer criminals lack this purchasing power, and are thus
> more likely to be reported, apprehended, and imprisoned.[75]

In other words, but for unfair income disparity, presumably, Brown would
favor blackmail legalization, at least as regards incriminating facts. But given
that not all people have the same amount of money, all bets are off.

This is highly problematic. First of all, if this author is correct in maintaining that inequality in wealth logically implies changing the law of blackmail from what it would otherwise be (legalized, that is, in the case of incriminating information), much, much more follows as well. If she is willing

---

[71] But why does she mention them in quotation marks? As her further comments, below, perhaps indicate, it would appear that she doubts their very legitimacy.

[72] Brown, *supra* note 1, at 1969, fns. 98, 99.

[73] *Id.* at 1958, fn. 54.

[74] Fiss unwittingly gives the "consent by the governed" game away when he says, "These (government) officials ... possess a power that has been defined and conferred by public law, *not by
private agreement.*" Owen M. Fiss, *Against Settlement,* 93 YALE L.J. 1073 (1984). Undoubtedly,
what Fiss meant to say by this was not that the public law could not trace itself back, if we went
far enough into the past, to private agreement, e.g., that the governed indeed had once consented to being ruled under democratic procedures. Rather, he intended to denote that *this
particular* private settlement owed its genesis to private, not public agreement. But for all of
that his original statement, taken quite literally, is precisely correct: There never was any original agreement under which public sector law operates.

[75] Brown, *supra* note 1, at 1970.

to pervert what even she considers as justice in this one case, why not else-where? For example, suppose a poor man rapes a rich woman. Ordinarily, the wealth status of neither of them would be at all relevant. But we live and we learn. Under the Brown dispensation, perhaps he shouldn't be imprisoned. Perhaps he should even get a medal, if he is poor enough to warrant one. Who knows? Brown's egalitarian principles do not indicate any specific con-clusion, only that we tip the scales of justice in favor of the poor and against the rich to some degree or other. Perhaps there should be a sort of Handicap-per General for the administration of justice, who would right the imbalance imposed on the law by income inequality by precisely the right amount. All these things seem to be in keeping with Brown's legal philosophy. It is impos-sible to further specify, since she only vouchsafes us with the view that things are unfair as they are, but provides us with no numerical program to right these wrongs.

Further, Brown's quarrel is really not so much (at all?) with blackmail leg-islation, but with all of jurisprudence. Were she writing about divorce, or con-tracts, or constitutional law, or any other aspect of the criminal code, and did so in a manner logically consistent with her remarkable egalitarian complaint as set out here, she would have to favor a wholesale revamping of them as well in favor of the poverty stricken and against the wealthy.

In justification of her position on educating the public, Brown [76] cites a host of authorities attesting to the benefits of the spotlight of publicity being placed on the doings of the courts, whether in "accusation, trial, vindication through acquittal, or condemnation through conviction and punishment." But this is entirely irrelevant to the main point at issue: whether or not there is room for private justice. Surely the American Arbitration Association, or any of the other private court institutions mentioned above, *need not* close its doors to outsiders, nor to the press. And on the other hand, closed door trials in government courts are not exactly unknown. To be sure blackmailers and blackmailees are not at all publicity hounds. But our author is here discussing matters of relevance to *all* of private justice, not just to blackmail; thus, she cannot make use of any such objection.

Brown[77] argues that "[p]ublic enforcement of the criminal law also helps to insure that criminals receive the protection of constitutional limitations on law enforcement." But this is by no means necessarily a benefit. The specter of obviously guilty felons let loose under technicalities nowhere mentioned in the Constitution,[78] while victims and their families look on helplessly, is not

---

[76] *Id.* at 971.

[77] *Id.* at 1972.

[78] Perhaps found in one of its many "penumbras."

one which inspires much confidence.[79] Even if it were stipulated to be a bene-fit, it scarcely follows that private courts are, in effect, lawless. Brown is of course worried that "Blackmailers would not feel these (constitutional) con-straints, for criminals might pay blackmail to conceal their crimes even when the blackmailer gains evidence in a manner which would be unconstitutional if the government were the actor."[80] But here our author is really objecting to how the information was attained, not to the actual blackmail. If this is so, there is no need to outlaw blackmail, *per se*. All the law need do is set out how such knowledge may be acquired. Specifically, it should stipulate that infor-mation may be gained in any way at all, as long as it does not violate the liber-tarian prohibition against aggression against non-aggressors.

Another Brown criticism of legalization concerns the fact that the black-mailee need not be guilty of a crime and may be in need of procedural protec-tions against the blackmailer.[81] But there is a simple answer: if you are ac-cused by a blackmailer of a crime you didn't commit, simply refuse the serv-ices of the blackmailer, even if you have no iron clad alibi. Tell him to "Publish and be damned."[82] A mere unsubstantiated accusation will not suffice even to discomfort you, if the blackmailer carries through on his threat to "expose" you as the criminal. If it would, every criminal would send anonymous letters accusing hundreds of innocent people of the crime he himself committed, in order to lay down a smokescreen to reduce the probability of his own appre-hension.

---

[79] The interpretation of these "protections" seems almost purposefully perverse. If the police commit some technical violation of the Miranda precedent, or of search and seizure laws, why is it necessary to throw out evidence derived thereby, and thus free the obviously guilty crimi-nal? Cannot the guilty parties, the cops, be made to pay for their transgressions, perhaps with the loss of pay. To allow the perpetrator to escape justice due to procedural error is to subscribe to the view that two wrongs make a right. This is particularly infuriating in that in the black-mail case, as we have seen, opponents of legalization such as Brown claim on one side of their mouths that two rights can make a wrong, and on the other side that two wrongs can make a right. Are we to be spared nothing?

[80] Brown, *supra* note 1, at 1972.

[81] *Id.*

[82] Statement of the Duke of Wellington. ELIZABETH LONGFORD, WELLINGTON: THE YEARS OF THE SWORD, 166–67 (1969).

V. CONCLUSION

I entirely agree with Brown that "[e]ven if the crime were very rare, the basis for blackmail's illegality would not be a trivial matter. Blackmail captures the imagination of many legal scholars because more than most crimes, it treads so closely to legitimate, even encouraged, economic activity."[83] Certainly, lawyers themselves are practically every day guilty of blackmail, at the very least whenever they threaten to sue unless their client is given certain moneys.

All the more important, then, not to lose sight of the libertarian axiom of non-aggression, and the fact that the basis of law is and must always be only the protection of persons and legitimately held property rights. Since blackmail of whatever stripe or variety is not in conflict with this dicta, e.g., does not constitute an uninvited border crossing, it should be legalized.

---

[83] Brown, *supra* note 1, at 1973.

Part III.
Critiques of Other Scholars' Views on Blackmail

Chapter 13.

Blackmail, Extortion and Free Speech: A Reply to Posner, Epstein, Nozick and Lindgren

At one time in the history of the law, "blackmail" and "extortion" were used synonymously to denote the demand for money or other valuable consideration upon the threat of force or violence.[1] Such acts were proscribed by law; very properly so, since the bedrock of civilized order is that people refrain from initiating force or fraud or the threat thereof against each other.

But while "extortion" has continued to be used in this restricted manner, the concept of "blackmail" has been expanded enormously.[2] Nowadays, blackmail is used to denote practically any commercial practice strongly disapproved of by the speaker, such as the OPEC price increase[3] as well as what is still meant by extortion. This is unfortunate, if only on semantic grounds. But it is even more problematic since there is now no concept in the English language which unambiguously refers to a demand for money or other valuable consideration under the threat of exercising one's right of free speech by publicizing someone else's secret without use of the threat of force or violence.

For the purposes of this Article, we shall define blackmail in precisely that way. In Section I, we make and defend the claim that the prohibition of blackmail is incompatible with the philosophy underlying our criminal law. In Sections II, III, IV and V, we consider and reject objections to this thesis made by, respectively, Richard Posner,[4] Richard Epstein,[5] Robert Nozick[6] and James Lindgren.[7]

---

[1] W.H.D. Winder, *The Development of Blackmail*, 5 MODERN L. REV. 21, 21–24 (1941).

[2] According to the Oxford English Dictionary, blackmail was first used in its modern sense in 1840. OXFORD ENGLISH DICTIONARY at 895 (1971).

[3] *See, e.g.*, P. JOHNSON, MODERN TIMES: THE WORLD FROM THE TWENTIES TO THE EIGHTIES at 667 (1983).

[4] RICHARD POSNER, ECONOMIC ANALYSIS OF LAW (2d ed. 1977).

[5] Richard Epstein, *Blackmail, Inc.*, 50 U. CHI. L. REV. 553 (1983).

[6] ROBERT NOZICK, ANARCHY, STATE, & UTOPIA (1974).

[7] James Lindgren, *Unraveling the Paradox of Blackmail*, 84 COLUM. L. REV. 670 (1984).

I. IN DEFENSE OF LEGALIZING BLACKMAIL

As defined, blackmail should not be accorded the legal sanctions usually meted out in response to criminal behavior since it does not entail the violation of rights.[8] Rather, it consists of the offer of a commercial trade. The blackmailer will remain silent about the humiliating, embarrassing or even criminal secret of the blackmailee,[9] accepting payment in return. If the offer to trade money for silence is rejected, the blackmailer will publicize the secret, which is part of his rights of free speech. In these terms the distinction between extortion and blackmail may be made as follows: extortion utilizes a threat to do something illicit, such as commit murder, arson or kidnapping. The threat of blackmail is limited to what would otherwise be illicit-commit an act of free speech. If a person has the right to do X, he necessarily has the right to give warning of the fact that he will do or may do X—that is, to threaten to do X. Blackmail is thus a non-criminal act.

Blackmail, then, is a "capitalist act between consenting adults," to use the felicitous phrase introduced by Robert Nozick.[10] As such, according to the laws of economics, it must benefit both parties.[11] It is easy to see how the blackmailer gains from the trade. He is paid merely for holding his tongue. But the "victim" also gains. Both parties gain from a voluntary trade, and this is as true of the exchange of money for silence as it is for any other case. The payment extracted must be worth less to the victim than the costs of having his secret uncovered. Otherwise he or she would reject the deal, stating in effect, "Publish and be damned!"[12] In contrast to the gossip, who tells the se-

---

[8] Let nothing said above be interpreted as affirming the propriety or morality of blackmail. This practice has not been claimed to be ethical. Our only claim is that blackmail is not akin to theft, not an invasive act, nor threat thereof, nor an initiation of violence, nor a violation of rights-and that therefore it should not be prohibited by force of law. Our present blackmail statutes are violations of the free speech rights of blackmailers. They do not protect the persons or property of the so-called victims of blackmail. Society would be better off, and human rights more secure, if our blackmail legislation were terminated.

[9] Just as the law cannot properly compel the individual to be a good Samaritan, so can it not compel him to acquaint the legal authorities with the facts concerning crimes he knows to have taken place. Turning in the criminal may thus be an act over and above the call of duty, but it is not an act of duty itself.

[10] Nozick, *supra* note 6.

[11] *Id.* at 84–87.

[12] This quote is attributed to Arthur Wellesley, Duke of Wellington, when his mistress threatened to publish her diary and his letters. J. BARTLETT, FAMILIAR QUOTATIONS 506a (E. Beck 14th ed. 1968).

cret without even affording the victim the opportunity of purchasing silence, the blackmailer can be seen as a benefactor.

Also, blackmail has social, or spillover, benefits. Were it legalized, the presumption is that more people would engage in this activity. If this occurred, real criminal activity would be retarded. The miscreants would now have to share their ill-gotten gains with the blackmailer. This would reduce the expected gain from criminal activity,[13] since the apprehended perpetrator would not only have to give up his booty, but would also be penalized up to the value he places on not going to jail, which may well be higher than the proceeds of any specific crime.

II. POSNER: THE EFFICIENCY OBJECTION TO BLACK-MAIL

One objection to our account of blackmail has been put forth by Richard Posner.[14] He begins by confining himself to cases where the threat of the blackmailer is to expose a crime committed by the blackmailee. In Posner's view, "[o]verenforcement of the law would result if the blackmailer were able to extract the full fine from the offender."[15] His reasoning seems to be that if the state subjects the criminal to the optimal fine, and the blackmailer extracts his own pound of flesh, then the total amount of enforcement will be too high. But this is, at best, highly conjectural. It can hardly be assumed that government has in its infinite wisdom hit upon precisely the optimal fine, nor does Posner put forth any evidence to back up such a claim. As Epstein trenchantly remarks, this "explanation ... presupposes that we have reason to believe that the current level of public enforcement is optimal by some standard. Standing alone, it cannot explain why blackmail is considered criminal without regard to mode or levels of public enforcement."[16]

The Posnerian objection could be couched in terms of resources allocated toward the apprehension of criminals instead of in terms of optimal levels of fines or payments imposed by the blackmailer. Given that the blackmailer works as a sort of private enterprise policeman—discouraging crime by threatening to capture its fruits for himself—the resources he expends, added to the public resources devoted to this task, might result in an overallocation

---

[13] WALTER BLOCK, DEFENDING THE UNDEFENDABLE at 53–58 (1976).

[14] Posner, *supra* note 4.

[15] *Id.* at 473. *See, also,* William Landes and Richard A. Posner, *The Private Enforcement of Law,* 4 J. LEGAL STUD. 1, 42–43 (1975).

[16] Epstein, *supra* note 5, at 561–62, fn 15.

of resources. But this would be true if and only if the public investment in this activity is optimal. The overallocation claim also founders on the unproven assumption that governmental activity in this area is perfectly allocated.

Posner fails to show that a public monopoly of law enforcement is optimal. He argues that "an efficient criminal sanction will ordinarily involve combining a severe penalty with a relatively low probability of apprehension and conviction."[17] That is to say, instead of attempting to capture each and every criminal in order to maximize profits, as a private agency might, a public monopoly of law enforcement can take a more efficient path. It can devote relatively few resources to catching criminals and deal harshly with those it does catch, without any loss in deterrent effect. Why is this? Deterrence, Posner correctly maintains, is a function of the severity of the sentence multiplied by the probability of enforcement.[18] The state can compensate for decreases in one variable by increasing the other. Hence, Posner concluded that a public monopoly of law enforcement could spend less on catching criminals than private agencies, and not necessarily reduce deterrence.[19] With a public monopoly, as the probability of having a sentence enforced is decreased, the severity of the sentence could be increased.

But this ingenious argument, even if correct, fails as a reason not to legalize blackmail. At best it shows that a monopoly of law enforcement is more efficient than a system of private agencies. It does not show that a combination of public and private enforcement is less efficient than a public monopoly alone. Perhaps the augmented deterrence which blackmail would add to public enforcement is optimal, even if one concedes to Posner that a public agency is needed. Posner's reply here is obvious. Wouldn't it be more efficient, if private deterrence augments a public agency, to provide the augmented deterrence simply by increasing the severity of the sentences? But this need not be the case. It may turn out that beyond a certain point people will be so unwilling to enforce a sentence that the product of the sentence multiplied by the probability of application will be insufficient to secure much deterrence. Presumably this is why sentencing parking violators to death would not be efficient. It does not automatically follow that the higher the sentence the less that can be spent on enforcement, and still keep the level of deterrence constant.

One might wonder whether the argument can be carried a stage further. How do we know—given that a public agency is not necessarily more efficient than a private one—that a public agency is more efficient in overall deterrence

---

[17] Posner, *supra* note 4, at 463.

[18] *Id.* at 465.

[19] *Id.* at 463.

than a system of private agencies? We do not know this; however, it does seem plausible that the effect Posner describes operates at some level. To the extent that it does, an agency aimed at providing deterrence most efficiently is in a position, by taking advantage of Posner's effect, to spend fewer resources on enforcement than an agency interested in maximizing revenue from criminals. This, however, introduces a further qualification to Posner's argument. An agency interested in providing deterrence most efficiently need not be a public agency, much less a monopoly. Why can't a private protection agency aim at providing deterrence efficiently? For all Posner has shown, a private agency can do so as long as it aims at maximizing its revenue by fees from consumers rather than from fines, or at least not exclusively from fines.

There is, however, a more basic reason for dismissing Posner's objection to our analysis of blackmail. Let us assume that government crime prevention activity, whether in terms of fines specified or resources expended, is optimal. Under such an assumption, of course, it would be true that both public and private efforts, added together, are over-optimal. Still, it does not follow that private initiatives such as blackmail must be reduced, let alone prohibited. For there is an alternative—diminish or eliminate the public sector! There are several reasons for preferring this option.

First, the *raison d'etre* for state action is that private efforts will not be forthcoming, or will be insufficient (e.g., the free rider problem and external neighborhood effects). However, such a situation does not prevail in this case. Far from there being insufficient or no private activity, Posner's complaint is that the blackmailer, in conjunction with the government, will over-allocate resources to crime prevention. Therefore, if public plus private efforts are superfluous, and if the argument for government activity is based on the absence of individual initiatives, then it is the former which should be cut back, not the latter.

There is a second reason for curtailing the public rather than the private sector. This has to do with the concept of an optimal amount of investment in crime prevention. This may be paradoxical to some. At a time of rampant criminality, at a time when numerous public opinion polls have shown that this is an issue of great if not prime importance to an outraged citizenry, it may appear grotesque to think of too many resources being devoted to prevention of crime. Nevertheless, the concept does make sense. As more funds are devoted to this task, there is a point where each dollar buys less additional crime reduction. Eventually, the utility of an extra dollar spent in this way will fall below its value in alternative pursuits. We could, in the extreme case, spend the entire Gross National Product on dealing with crime while starving to death.

But this level of expenditure depends solely on the preference of the individual (as does the rate, extent and even existence of the declining utility of money spent in retarding crime). Some people may be passionately devoted to this enterprise; others may be pacifists on the crime question; and most will occupy a middle ground.

Consider the analogy to charity. Assume that both private and public charitable efforts, taken together, are excessive. Under our first line of argument, the latter, not the former, should be reined in since the *raison d'etre* for welfare is the insufficiency or nonexistence of private charity. According to our second line of argument, private charity, at whatever level, simply cannot be excessive, since it depends entirely on the subjective value preferences of the individuals concerned.[20]

What of cases where the blackmailer's threat is not to expose a crime of his "victim," but to make known an embarrassing, but not illegal, episode in his life? Here, too, Posner favors the prohibition of blackmail. In his view blackmail should be forbidden in areas where there are no legal prohibitions at all—where the information would humiliate, but not incriminate, the blackmailer's victim. The social decision not to regulate a particular activity is a judgment that the expenditure of resources on trying to discover and punish it would be socially wasted. That judgment is undermined if blackmailers are encouraged to expend substantial resources on investigating people engaged in the activity.[21]

This argument seems to be a complete *non sequitur*. The decision not to regulate a particular activity is based, at most, only on the view that it would not be efficient to spend public resources to enforce public regulations. This provides no insight into the efficiency of also spending private resources that will partly deter the activity. Posner contents himself with deducing that such an activity is "socially wasteful" from the fact that blackmail of noncriminals is prohibited.[22] But this circular tack proves far too much. If mere legal prohibition of X proves X to be "socially wasteful," how can we analyze, for example, the prohibition of alcohol in the U.S. during the 1930's? Must we say that alcohol consumption was "socially useful" before and after Prohibition, while

---

[20] In making this claim, we must of course, consider the possibility of external economies. Obviously, if person A contributes to charity, or squelches crime by blackmailing, person B can reduce his own efforts and "free ride" on A. But this is an explanation for the possible underallocation of resources in these activities, not overallocation as feared by Posner. Also, this phenomenon can take place in either the public or private sector. Since here we are concerned with distinguishing between these alternatives, possible positive externalities can be safely ignored.

[21] Posner, *supra* note 4, at 473.

[22] *Id.*

"socially wasteful" only during this era? If we do, our only "evidence" will be the law of the land. Posner's circular opposition to the legalization of blackmail is not based on any theory of law; it is merely an *ad hoc* expression of Posner's own subjective tastes on the matter. Perhaps Posner's argument is that since enforcement is inefficient, private enforcement would be inefficient as well. But we have already seen a reason to reject this premise. Posner has not demonstrated the superior efficiency, in all cases, of public enforcement.

Even if one grants Posner all his arguments about the inefficiency of blackmail, it does not follow that he has made a case for its prohibition. Perhaps trying to prohibit blackmail is also inefficient. If it is, putting up with the inefficiencies Posner discusses may be worthwhile. If the inefficiencies of prohibiting blackmail outweigh the inefficiencies of blackmail itself, this needs to be shown by argument. Nonetheless Posner says nothing about the inefficiency of prohibiting blackmail.

Finally, there is one further weakness in Posner's treatment of blackmail. Suppose that all he says is correct. Then, blackmail must be a wasteful and inefficient means of deterring crime and of interfering with noncriminal customs. Does it follow from this that blackmail should be prohibited? Is it a crime to be an inefficient enforcer of law? Should our analysis be focused on the effect of blackmail as a deterrent of certain types of behavior? While its effects in this area are extremely important, the primary aim of the activity is to secure certain gains to those engaged in it. To make a case for the prohibition of blackmail on the grounds of efficiency, one must show that there is something "wrong" with transactions of this kind. That blackmail is not the best means to achieve some other purpose (i.e., law enforcement) is of secondary significance. This holds true, of course, unless blackmail's effect on law enforcement is socially more important than the direct gains and losses of the transaction. But this would need to be shown by argument.

III. EPSTEIN: MORALITY AND BLACKMAIL, INC.

We now turn to the case made by Richard Epstein in support of prohibiting blackmail.[23] At first blush, this is a rather unlikely statement, since the first two sections of Blackmail, Inc. constitute perhaps the most magnificent, comprehensive, insightful, articulate, careful and well-reasoned defense of the legalization of blackmail ever penned.

Epstein begins by resisting Posner's claim that the matter is settled merely because a legislature holds an activity to be illegal.

---

[23] Epstein, *supra* note 5.

It is a grave mistake to confuse the necessary conditions of notice and codification with the sufficient substantive conditions for criminal responsibility. If the legislature sought to declare marriage, schooling, or gardening criminal offenses, in all likelihood it could define their content with sufficient precision to avoid any procedural challenges based upon the want of notice. But even in a system that placed no constitutional limitations upon the legislative power (as is still the case in England, where much of this debate has originated) to declare a certain activity criminal, we should still demand some explanation of why this particular activity, but not others, should be classified as illegal.[24]

Epstein continues with a moral theory of criminal responsibility that is nothing less than superlative in its focus on force or fraud, or the threat thereof, as the essence of criminal activity.[25] He also recognizes the *sine qua non* of blackmail analysis: that the blackmailer threatens to do that which he otherwise has a complete right to do, that is, to exercise his rights of free speech. As stated by Epstein, "where a person *has* the right to do a certain act—for example, not to sell at a particular price—he has the right to threaten to do that act."[26] Going over and above the call of duty, Epstein even recognizes that the only exception to the legitimacy of blackmail is when the information utilized is discovered improperly through force or fraud.[27]

Epstein then attempts "to account for the powerful sentiment that blackmail should be criminal."[28] Given the airtight defense of the case for legalization he has just rendered, this is no easy task. He begins by leaving off the micro discussion of the blackmailer and the blackmailee, and takes up the macro level of the larger social framework. Epstein asks: "[W]hat would the world look like if blackmail were legalized to the extent that seems to be required by our general moral theory?"[29] His answer is Blackmail, Inc., a large corporation in the "open and public" blackmail market, which would offer to acquire information leading to the degradation or humiliation of people-so that silence about these secrets could be sold to them.[30] He forecasts, quite reasonably, that the contracts Blackmail, Inc. would draw between itself and its suppliers

---

[24] *Id.* at 554.

[25] *Id.* at 555–56. For a fully developed legal philosophy, *see, generally,* MURRAY N. ROTHBARD, THE ETHICS OF LIBERTY.

[26] Epstein, *supra* note 5, at 557 (emphasis in original).

[27] *Id.* at 558–60.

[28] *Id.* at 562.

[29] *Id.* (emphasis omitted).

[30] *Id.* at 563.

of information would be quite complex.[31] Maybe so. But this complexity hardly justifies his claim that he has borne "limited fruit" in his quest to justify the prohibition of blackmail.[32] For one thing, he has not demonstrated that if blackmail were legalized, large firms engaging in blackmail would arise on the market. Blackmail, Inc. is a possibility; but for all Epstein has shown, it is no more than a possibility. Yet his argument in part turns on the existence of such firms.

Next, Epstein considers the commercial relationship between Blackmail, Inc. and the blackmailee. Here he believes that he has uncovered the essential evil of blackmail. First, not only may Blackmail, Inc. demand money of the blackmailee, but if the latter does not have the prerequisite funds, the corporation may hint, "ever so slightly, that it thinks strenuous efforts to obtain the necessary cash should be undertaken."[33] Continues Epstein, "[d]o we believe that [the blackmailee] would never resort to fraud or theft given this kind of pressure, when the very nature of the transaction cuts off his access to the usual financial sources, such as banks or friends, who would want to know the purpose of the loan?"[34] Secondly, not only can Blackmail, Inc. engage in blackmail, but as a "full service firm" it can help the blackmailee uphold the fraud and deceit he perpetrates on the people from whom he hides his guilty secret.[35]

Here we arrive at the rub of the matter, Epstein's reason why blackmail should be prohibited by law. "We now see the critical difference between blackmail and kindred transactions, such as the protection of trade secrets. Only blackmail breeds fraud and deceit."[36] But this will not do. For one thing, it proves far too much. Yes, the legalization of blackmail may well encourage and cause the "victim" to make "strenuous efforts" to engage in fraud or theft to pay off his tormentor. But people steal for so many other reasons: impressing their friends, "buying baby a new pair of shoes," poverty, alcoholism, addiction, jealousy, dares, and for various and sundry political ideals. If blackmail should be prohibited because it may encourage crime, so should these other activities. This is surely unacceptable. What should be legally proscribed

---

[31] *Id.*

[32] *Id.* at 563–64.

[33] *Id.* at 564.

[34] *Id.*

[35] *Id.*

[36] *Id.* at 564–65.

is crime itself, not phenomena which may or may not[37] lead to criminal behavior.

Epstein's second criticism, on the grounds of supporting fraud,[38] fails on the same ground. Yes, Blackmail, Inc. may better enable the bed wetter, the communist or the homosexual to keep his secret, perpetuating the "fraud" he practices on those who would do him ill, if they only knew. However, since these activities are not prohibited, how can it be a punishable offense to help these potential blackmailers keep their guilt secrets? If X is a legal, non-prohibited act, and A helps B carry it out Epstein's attempt to justify the criminalization of blackmail is equivalent to urging the incarceration of A but not B!

In the first sections of his article, Epstein was quite clear that threats of force or fraud were the necessary and sufficient conditions for categorizing an activity as criminal. But in his sociological Section III although he still maintains this distinction,[39] he appears to have lost sight of vital importance.

Perhaps this arises out of a confusion between morality (the study of what is or is not immoral) and legal philosophy (the study of what should or should not be prohibited by force of law). Epstein holds that "[a]s a *moral* matter ... blackmail is criminal because of its necessary tendency to induce deception and other wrongs."[40] He claims that blackmail "breeds fraud and deceit,"[41] and characterizes it as "sneaky and dirty."[42] Blackmail may well be underhanded, evil, vicious, reprehensible and immoral. But this is entirely beside the point. Our concern here is solely with the question of the criminal, not moral, status of blackmail.[43] Unless Epstein advocates that all immoral people be incarcerated, he must relinquish his opposition to the legalization of blackmail. He may have successfully explained why blackmail is abhorrent in popular sentiment, but he has not justified its legal prohibition.

---

[37] States Epstein: "Blackmail is made a crime not only because of what it is, but because of what it necessarily leads to." *Id.* at 566. But this is surely incorrect. Is it really necessary that the "victim" of blackmail give in to his baser instincts and engage in real crime? Cannot even one blackmailee resist the temptation? Surely there is no logical contradiction in supposing that a blackmailee could overcome the temptation to commit the crime.

[38] *Id.* at 564.

[39] The blackmailee "is subject only to blackmail, not the threats of force of fraud." *Id.* at 565.

[40] *Id.* (emphasis added).

[41] *Id.*

[42] *Id.* at 566. Epstein also argues against blackmail on the grounds that it leads to the concealment of information. His argument is effectively criticized in Lindgren, *supra* note 7, at 684–87.

[43] *See, supra* note 8.

IV. NOZICK: BLACKMAIL AS AN UNPRODUCTIVE EXCHANGE

A third objection, developed by Robert Nozick, arises in the realm of philosophy.[44] Nozick begins his critique of the position staked out in this article by distinguishing between productive and nonproductive activities. If a set of exchanges were impossible or forcibly prohibited so that everyone knew they couldn't be done, one of the parties to the potential exchange would be no worse off. A strange kind of productive exchange it would be whose forbidding leaves one party no worse off! (The party who does not give up anything for the abstention, or need not because the neighbor has no other motive to proceed with the action, is left better off). Though people value a blackmailer's silence, and pay for it, his being silent is not a productive activity. His victims would be as well off if the blackmailer did not exist at all, and so wasn't threatening them. And they would be no worse off if the exchange were known to be absolutely impossible.[45]

On the basis of this distinction, Nozick would allow, as a productive exchange, a person to purchase your neighbor's abstention, from building a "monstrosity" on his land, which "he has a right to do."[46] However, suppose that the neighbor has no desire to erect the structure on the land; he formulates his plan and informs you of it solely in order to sell you his abstention from it. Such an exchange would not be a productive one; it merely gives you relief from something that would not threaten if not for the possibility of an exchange to get relief from it.[47]

In other words, it is acceptable for the neighbor who honestly wants to build the "monstrosity" to be bought out of this notion, since it is a productive exchange; but, for the bluffer to attempt such a trade, it would be an unproductive imposition. Applying this example to our subject, many cases of blackmail seem allowable.

---

[44] Nozick, *supra* note 6.

[45] *Id.* at 85.

[46] *Id.* at 84–85. Lord Wright in *Thorne v. Motor Trade Ass'n*, 1937 A.C. 797, would agree: "[A man] may offer not to build on his plot of land if he is compensated for abstaining. He is entitled to bargain as a consideration for agreeing not to use his own and as he lawfully may. and the other man may think it worthwhile to pay hint rather than have the amenities of his house destroyed by an eyesore."

[47] *Id.* at 820. But according to A. H. Campbell, although "a man may doubtless ask a price n from his neighbor for refraining from building and spoiling the neighbor's view, "the land must be 'building land,'" and does "not necessarily cover a threat to erect a 'spite fence.'" A.H. Campbell, *The Anomalies of Blackmail*, 15 LAW Q. REV. 382, 382 & fn.13 (1939).

Imagine that the neighbor builds the monstrosity just because he dislikes you and knows that building it will anger you. Suppose instead that he constructs the monstrosity for the same reason but knows that one response of yours will be to offer him money to desist. Neither of these cases seems to be one of impermissible conduct, and the latter is not, by Nozick's criterion, an unproductive exchange.[48] If so, isn't a case of blackmail where the collection of information is motivated by dislike of the victim a productive exchange? Only if the blackmailer would not collect the information unless he could threaten the victim with exposure would we have a case of unproductive exchange.[49]

There are problems, however, with this view. Based on the given criteria, which distinguish the productive (both parties benefit and both lose if prohibited) from the unproductive (if it were prohibited one party—the "victim"—would be no worse off), the shenanigans of *both* the "honest" builder and the bluffer would be unproductive. Both harm the "victim." Both, therefore, should be banned by law. For in each case the victim would be no worse off if the activity was thought to be impossible. The honest Dr. Frankenstein should be allowed to proceed, and to be bought off; this is conceded. But so should the bluffing Dr. Frankenstein, for Nozick has failed to maintain a relevant difference between them. It is difficult to see, moreover, why "unproductive" exchanges, in this sense, ought to be prohibited or singled out for special regulations.

Nozick also fails to distinguish between the idea of the activity thought to be impossible and the idea of the activity which is forcibly prohibited. In his explanation he uses the two activities interchangeably. Yes, the "victim" would be better off if the blackmailer did not exist, or did not realize it was possible for him to act in such a way. But if the blackmailer did exist, and did realize this, the "victim" would be made worse off by forcibly prohibiting his activity. In such a scenario the blackmailer would be able to exercise his option of free speech and gossip about the "victim's" secret, says Rothbard, outlawing a blackmail contract means that the blackmailer has no further incentive not to disseminate the unwelcome, hitherto secret information about the blackmailed party.[50]

Nozick then launches into a defense of the medieval just-price theory in an attempt to determine precisely how much consideration a blackmailer deserves for his services. "[A] seller of such silence could legitimately charge

---

[48] Nozick, *supra* note 6, at 84–85.

[49] *Id.* at 84.

[50] David Gordon wishes to thank Robert Nozick for very helpful suggestions, and wishes to deny responsibility for the material which appears in Section IV after this point.

only for what he forgoes by silence."[51] On the face of it, this seems a quixotic argument. Nozick further complicates matters by asserting that a person ... who delights in revealing secrets[ ] may charge differently."[52] Presumably, this amount would be greater than that charged by the blackmailer only interested in pecuniary gains. But this unearths more difficulties than it solves. Asks Rothbard:

> *Why* is it only licit to charge the payment foregone? Why *not* charge whatever the blackmailee is willing to pay? In the first place, both transactions are voluntary, and within the purview of both parties' property rights. Secondly, *no one knows*, either conceptually or in practice, what price the blackmailer could have gotten for his secret on the market. No one can predict a market price in advance of the actual exchange. [W]hat outside legal enforcement agency will ever be able to discover *to what extent* the blackmailer delights in revealing secrets and therefore what price he may legally charge to the 'victim'? More broadly, it is conceptually impossible ever to discover the existence or the extent of this subjective delight or of any other psychic factors that may enter into his value-scale and therefore into his exchange.[53]

Nozick's last contribution to the dialogue consists of this assertion: "Protective services are productive and benefit their recipient whereas the 'protection racket' is not productive. Being sold the racketeers' mere abstention from harming you makes your situation no better than if they had nothing to do with you at all."[54]

This is true enough. But it is not even relevant to our discussion of blackmail, which we have defined as demanding money under the threat of doing something legal. Rather, it is an attack on extortion, as we have defined it, which is the demand for money upon a threat of what one does not have the right to do. In a protection racket, the threat is to murder, rape or pillage unless tribute is granted. Nothing said above should be construed as a defense

---

[51] Nozick appears to equivocate between utilizing this criterion and another one called felicitously by Rothbard the "drop dead." Rothbard, *supra* note 25, at 240–43, wherein an exchange is nonproductive if the "victim" would be better off if the blackmailer didn't exist at all. At one point, Nozick claims that this second criterion is a necessary condition for unproductive activity, Nozick, *supra* note 6, at 84, but later seems to regard it as sufficient. *Id.* at 85–86.

[52] Rothbard, *supra* note 25, at 242.

[53] Rothbard, *supra* note 26, at 242-43 (emphasis in original).

[54] Nozick, *supra* note 6, at 86.

of such an activity. Indeed, we have been at some pain to distinguish extortion, whether or not of the protection racket variety, from legitimate blackmail.[55]

V. LINDGREN: BLACKMAIL AND THE IMPROPER USE OF INFORMATION

Another attempt to justify the illegality of blackmail is offered by James Lindgren.[56] His theory stresses the "triangular nature of the transaction," or "third-party leverage."[57] In this view, there are really three main actors in the blackmail drama, not two: A is the blackmail victim; B is the blackmailer; and C is the "forgotten man." C is the individual ignored in the typical analysis of blackmail, the person who, but for the willingness of B to keep a secret, would react negatively to the interests of A. In the case of the threat to expose a bed wetter, for example, C represents those people who would shun A; in the case of the threat to expose a crime, C represents the state who would prosecute and incarcerate.

---

[55] Another person who fails to distinguish between extortion and blackmail is the best-selling author Dick Francis. In his book, *The Danger*, the hero, a person whose firm specialized in helping kidnap victims, speaks as follows:

> We sometimes did, as a firm, work for no pay; it depended on circumstances. All the partners agreed that a family in need should get help regardless, and none of us begrudged it. We never charged enough anyway to make ourselves rich, being in existence on the whole to defeat extortion, not to practice it. A flat fee, plus expenses: no percentages. Our clients knew for sure that the size of the ransom in no way affected our own reward. D. FRANCIS, THE DANGER 147 (1983).

Francis, in other words, like Nozick, fails to see the crucial difference between, in this case, what the kidnapper does (extortion) and what the hero's firm does (stop extortionate kidnappers). The point is that it does not really matter what the firm charges for its services. It could charge an arm and a leg; it could charge the sun the moon and the stars; it could even charge more than the ransom demanded by the kidnappers themselves! The firm would still not be guilty of extortion, since it would be threatening only that which it has every right to threaten- to withhold its services unless its very high prices were met. Unless this crucial distinction is maintained, we are in danger of incarcerating innocents who refuse to be good Samaritans (by providing kidnap-rescue services for "high" prices) along with the really guilty parties, the kidnappers.

[56] Lindgren, *supra* note 7.

[57] *Id.* at 702.

Why, then in Lindgren's analysis, is blackmail a crime? Because in all cases, B is trading in on information to which he has no legitimate title. Says Lindgren:

> At the heart of blackmail, then, is the triangular nature of the transaction, and particularly this disjunction between the blackmailer's personal benefit and the interests of the third parties whose leverage he uses. In effect, the blackmailer attempts to gain an advantage in return for suppressing someone else's actual or potential interest. The blackmailer is negotiating for his own gain with someone else's leverage or bargaining chips. …

> Under my theory, blackmail is the seeking of an advantage by threatening to press an actual or potential dispute that is primarily between the blackmail victim and someone else. The blackmailer threatens to bring others into the dispute but typically asks for something for himself he turns someone else's power, usually group power, to personal benefit. The bargaining is unfair in that the threatener uses leverage that is less his than someone else's.[58]

Perhaps an example would be useful here. Suppose you discover that a married woman is having an affair. You threaten to tell her husband unless she agrees to commence an affair with you. In Lindgren's view you have intervened in a matter—the status of the couple's marriage—that does not directly concern you. You are attempting to benefit from information that properly belongs to the couple, or perhaps to the husband.

Lindgren's theory of blackmail cannot be sustained. Why should it be illegal to use information about matters that involve someone else's interests more than one's own? Offhand, this seems a perfectly normal, permissible activity. Suppose, for example, that someone accidentally overhears information about a business deal to which he is not a party. As a result of this information he is able to make a "killing" in the market. Should this be illegal? Or suppose someone, such as a detective, learns of an extramarital affair and sells this information to the spouse of the person involved in the affair. This transaction is clearly legal, yet the seller benefits from information that concerns others more than himself. Lindgren's theory would prohibit this transaction.

Professor Lindgren has anticipated cases of this kind and thinks that he can escape unscathed. He remarks:

---

[58] *Id.* at 702–03.

> [S]ome sales of private information are legitimate. For instance, a police informer may learn damaging information about a criminal and release it to the police in return for money. ... Under my theory ... the informer has merely promoted the resolution of the dispute between the government and the criminal on its merits by releasing information to one of the principles. He did not suppress, appropriate or settle the government's interest. The result: no blackmail.[59]

Lindgren is quite right in saying that there is no blackmail in this ease. But this misses the point. Shouldn't this conduct, even though it is not blackmail, also be prohibited? Under Lindgren's principle the person is using information that involves the interests of others more than it involves his interests for his own benefit. It will not do to say that the information-seller has merely added to the available data rather than engaged in suppression as does the blackmailer. Why is one form of interference better or worse than the other? On what grounds is it being claimed, if indeed it is, that the more information available to the parties the more legal the situation? It is not, at any rate, immediately evident why it is alright to assist a party to a dispute who would benefit by increased knowledge, while one may not help a person who wishes to conceal information.

Lindgren may reply that this criticism ignores the aim of his argument. "[A] core principle of our legal system," he notes, "is the assignment of enforcement rights to the victim: an individual enforces a private wrong and the state enforces a public wrong."[60] Blackmail, Lindgren thinks, "suppresses" this fundamental right. In point of fact it does not do so. The victim is as free as before to pursue all his legal remedies. In our example, the husband is not deprived of any of his legal rights by not being told of his wife's adultery. The fact that he might take a certain course of action if he knew about the adultery, which he would not do otherwise, generates no duty in others to assist him to acquire that information. There is, in general, no "right to information;" otherwise, someone who acquired knowledge of an affair, for example, would be under a duty to disclose it. If there were such a "right to information," it would be illegal for attorneys, doctors, economists, and others whose main stock in trade is the sense of providing information.

The fundamental flaw in Lindgren's method of analysis, we suggest, is his loose talk about "leverage" and using "chips" that belong to someone else. While the reader gets some idea of what Lindgren means, his vivid expres-

---

[59] *Id.* at 706.

[60] *Id* at 704 (footnotes omitted).

sions dissolve into unclarity on closer analysis. Exactly what constitutes someone's "chips?" If Lindgren had explicitly stated precisely which rights the blackmailer is allegedly violating, instead of placing crucial reliance on metaphor, he would have seen that his theory depends upon an insupportable claim that one has a duty to provide information to certain persons, whom he terms "victims." The sense in which he uses the word "victim" is also left largely a matter of mystery.[61]

VI. CONCLUSION

We must conclude, and hope that we have demonstrated, that the efforts of Professors Richard Posner, Richard Epstein, Robert Nozick and James Lindgren have not been successful in demonstrating that blackmail, as opposed to extortion, should remain illegal. Their efforts, of course, have been nothing short of brilliant. Given that one is assigned the task of defending the prohibition of blackmail, it would be hard to see how they could have been more resourceful, creative or insightful.

The authors of the present Article, in contrast, did not start out with any particular position on this issue. This is because, perhaps, we strongly resisted the notion that denigrated, despised and immoral actions necessarily need to be prohibited by law. As a result, in our view, we were able to maintain the distinction between extortion (threatening an act which is in and of itself illegal), which should remain prohibited, and blackmail (threatening an act which apart from the demand for valuable consideration is legal), which should be legalized.

[61] We do not mean to suggest by these remarks that Lindgren's article is of no value. On the contrary, its criticisms of other theories of blackmail are highly penetrating.

Chapter 14.

Berman on Blackmail: Taking Motives Fervently

I. INTRODUCTION

Should blackmail be legalized?

In the view of most people, this is a no-brainer. Of course blackmail should not be made licit. It is a vicious crime.

Berman has his finger on the pulse of the man in the street when he says: "It is a safe bet that blackmail's criminalization does not appear puzzling to the casual observer. Not only does it resemble other varieties of theft, the criminalization of which rarely raises eyebrows, but blackmail just smells likes [sic] a nasty practice."[1]

And if there were any question about this, we can call upon the support of a very popular novelist; in the view of Arthur Conan Doyle:

> "But who is he?"

> "I'll tell you, Watson. He is the king of all the blackmailers. Heaven help the man, and still more the woman, whose secret and reputation come into the power of Milverton! With a smiling face and a heart of marble, he will squeeze and squeeze until he has drained them dry. ... I have said that he is the worst man in London, and I would ask you how could one compare the ruffian, who in hot blood bludgeons his mate, with this man, who methodically and at his leisure tortures the soul and wrings the nerves in order to add to his already swollen money-bags?" ...

> "But surely," said I, "the fellow must be within the grasp of the law?"

> "Technically, no doubt, but practically not. What would it profit a woman, for example, to get him a few month's imprisonment if her own ruin must immediately follow? His victims dare not hit back."[2]

---

[1] Mitchell N. Berman, *The Evidentiary Theory of Blackmail: Taking Motives Seriously*, 65 U. CHI. L. REV. 795 (1998).

[2] ARTHUR CONAN DOYLE, *The Adventures of Charles Augustus Milverton*, in THE RETURN OF SHERLOCK HOLMES, reprinted in THE COMPLETE SHERLOCK HOLMES pp. 481, 572–73 (1960).

One last bit of evidence on this matter, not that any is needed. While No-bel Prize winning economist Ronald Coase cannot by any stretch of the imagination be considered an intellectual common man, he shows his affinity for the popular abhorrence of blackmail by castigating it as "moral murder."[3]

Nor is it the case that this view is shared only by unlearned people. As it happens, virtually all legal theorists who have written about this subject have agreed that blackmail ought to maintain its present status as a prohibited act.

There are some commentators, however, who have taken the opposite point of view, and, in my own view, show that the case for prohibition of blackmail is weak or nonexistent.[4] How can the view that blackmail ought to be legalized possibly be defended?

We start off, first, with the distinction between blackmail and extortion. In both cases, there is a threat, coupled with a demand for money.[5] But in the former case, the threat consists of doing no more than one has a legal right to do in any case. For example, to blab the secret, or to gossip about the adultery. In the latter case, the threat consists of doing something that is patently ille-gal, and ought to be considered in this light. For instance, initiating violence against the victim, such as is involved in murder, arson or rape.

By no stretch of the imagination can it ever be said that the extortionist does his victim a favor. If I come to you, gun in hand, and demand your money with the threat of killing you if you resist, to think that I am your benefactor would be a cruel joke. However, precisely this claim can indeed be made with regard to blackmail. After all, if you are an adulterer, desperate to keep your secret hidden, in whose hands would you rather your secret be? A gossip, in which case the jig is up, or a blackmailer, who at least has the de-cency to offer you a monetary way out of your predicament? Obviously, the

---

[3] Ronald Coase, *The 1987 McCorkle Lecture: Blackmail*, 74 VA. L. REV. at 655–76 (1988). Cited by Sidney W. DeLong, *Blackmailers, Bribe Takers, and the Second Paradox*, 141 U. PA. L. REV., at 1689. For a critique of this article, *see* Chapter 5, this volume.

[4] *See* Ronald Joseph Scalise, Jr., *Blackmail, Legality, and Liberalism*, 74 TUL.L. REV. 1483 (2000). I wish to single out this article because it has numerous parallels with my own treatment. I did not heavily cite it, as it deserved, since it came across my desk only after I had written the pre-sent article. Nevertheless, I acknowledge its precedence, in many ways, in my critique of Ber-man.

5 Or other valuable consideration, such as sexual favors.

latter is vastly preferable.[6] Were it not, you would always be free to utter, in reply to a demand for money from a blackmailer, "Publish and be damned."[7]

One would think, then, that the discussion on this matter in the law reviews and scholarly academic journals would largely consist of a debate between these two schools of thought; the first, the mainstream perspective, which holds that blackmail is properly criminalized, and ought to remain so, and second, the critics, or libertarian,[8] which takes the position that as blackmail threatens only that which the blackmailer has a right to do, it should be legalized. If one thought this, however, one would be almost entirely mistaken.

In actual point of fact, with but only a few exceptions, there has been no debate at all between these two views. While the libertarians have indeed criticized the mainstream view, there have been only four rejoinders in the other direction. More typically, the response of those who counsel continued blackmail prohibition is to ignore them entirely, or to dismiss them without any serious discussion.[9]

Virtually all of the publications on this topic have been devoted not to the debate between these two schools of thought, but rather have occurred within

---

[6] Can it reasonably be objected that the extortionist, too, does you a favor by not shooting you, and instead taking your money? This is of course true. However, there is a disanalogy between the two cases. The blackmailer has every right to spill the beans (we assume he came by his information about you in a licit manner to abstract from that problem) while the extortionist has no right whatever to do to you what he threatens.

[7] Duke of Wellington. ELIZABETH LONGFORD, WELLINGTON: THE YEARS OF THE SWORD, 1661–67 (1969), cited in Richard Posner, *Blackmail, Privacy and Freedom of Contract*, U. PA. L. REV. at 1839, fn. 43 (1993).

[8] Libertarianism is a theory of the proper use of physical force. Its basis is private property rights based on homesteading, and the non-aggression axiom: it is improper to threaten or use violence against a person or his legitimately owned property.

[9] One very fragmentary "response" is by Posner, *supra* note 7, at 1817–47, who dismisses the case for legalized blackmail very succinctly indeed, in but one word, as "remarkable." *Id.* at 1832 fn. 32. For a rejoinder to Posner, *see* chapter 8. Another occurs in the present paper under discussion, where Berman notes that Rothbard is "one exception" in that he disputes the claim that "blackmail is properly made criminal." It is more than passing curious that in a paper devoted to a detailed examination of the views of dozens of theorists, all of whom maintain that "blackmail is properly made criminal," Berman would dismiss these views to the contrary as follows: "Because Rothbard's conclusion stands or falls upon familiar libertarian premises ... it need not be addressed here." Further, Berman, *supra* note 1, at 814, characterizes as "radical" but does not criticize Isenbergh's proposal to decriminalize some but not all types of blackmail. Evidently, this is as far as Berman can go in his treatment of heterodox views. The case for complete decriminalization of this practice presumably goes too far to be even considered.

the mainstream consensus. Namely, the range of opinion has been for the most part limited to the view that blackmail must indeed remain criminalized but the various participants diverge as to their reasons for this contention. Some take a consequentialist or utilitarian stance, and others a principled or deontological perspective.[10]

To characterize this intra mainstream debate from the perspective of one who takes the position of "a pox on both your houses," it would be that each of these views is extremely effective in criticizing the other, but totally unable to withstand the denunciations offered by the other against its own stance. It is as if there were some sort of intellectual schizophrenia going on: When on the attack, the mainstream commentators on blackmail legalization speak in a very sharp and incisive voice; when they give their own views on the subject, the very opposite occurs: they open themselves to the equally devastating responses of their fellows.[11] Several years ago there was a National Basketball Association player by the name of Ernie DiGregorio. His reputation as an offensive player was a good one. But his defensive skills were greatly wanting, so much so that he earned the nickname, "Ernie No-D."[12] In my view, the mainstream commentators are all offense (against the theories of their fellows), no defense (of their own analyses).

How does Berman's[13] contribution fit in with the blackmail literature? This author can be found within the mainstream analysis of blackmail, in that he favors its status quo legal prohibition.

He begins by "arguing that no current theory adequately unravels the paradox"[14] of blackmail.[15] By paradox, he means, uncontroversially, How can two acts, when engaged in together be illegal, given that when they are undertaken in isolation, they are both legal? He states: "I am legally free to reveal embarrassing information about you. Generally speaking, I am also free to

---

[10] The symposium put out by the University of Pennsylvania Law Review, Vol. 141, No. 5, May, 1993, for example, contained 12 articles which all agreed with the conclusion that blackmail is properly illegal, and only differed as to the underlying justifications.

[11] As well, the criticisms of the libertarians who favor legalization have in my opinion been crushing albeit for the most part ignored.

[12] For those who are uninitiated in the niceties of the world of the NBA, "no-D" indicates a lack of defensive abilities.

[13] Berman, *supra* note 1.

[14] *Id.* at 798.

[15] By this he announces that he is rejecting both sides of the mainstream perspective, which, for him, is the only game in town. That is, although he mentions that Rothbard rejects both sides of the mainstream view, Berman does not condescend to criticize this libertarian position.

negotiate payment to refrain from exercising a legal right. But if I combine the two—offering to remain silent for a fee—I am guilty of a felony: blackmail."[16]

He notes that the advocates of the present law prohibiting blackmail contracts fall into two camps: those who justify the *status quo* on utilitarian or consequentialist grounds, and those who defend it for deontological or principled reasons.[17] And where does he, himself, fit in, in terms of this distinction, in his own view? He rejects both, stating: "both ... will ... always prove unable to distinguish blackmail from such behavior which is, and should remain, free from criminal sanction."[18] In this I am in entire accord with Berman.

In what he sees as sharp contrast to the mainstream position, Berman announces that his own view is "the evidentiary theory of blackmail,"[19] about which more below. He interprets this theory as free of the criticisms he will level against the mainstream view, both the consequentialist and deontological versions. To anticipate my criticism of Berman, I shall claim that far from his theory being distinct from these others, it is part and parcel of (both of) them; that his own theory is subject to the same objections he so well levels at consequentialist and deontological defenses of blackmail prohibition, plus additional ones, to be mentioned.

II. CRITIQUE

With this introduction, we are now ready to consider Berman's[20] critique of mainstream views on blackmail, other than his own. He begins with a critique of those I consider to be his fellow travelers in this regard, and, as is

---

[16] Berman, *supra* note 1,. at 797.

[17] *Id.* at 798.

[18] *Id.* at 798.

[19] *Id.* at 798.

[20] Berman, *supra* note 1.

typical of this genre, his "offense" is for the most part no less than devastating, as shall be seen.[21]

First, Berman sets up the barrier over which any theory of blackmail must pass:

> Any satisfactory theory must account for both parts of the black-mail puzzle. First, it must explain whether and why blackmail should be made criminal. Second, if it supports criminalization of blackmail, it must explain whether and why unconditional performance of the acts a blackmailer might threaten should remain lawful. ... By and large, the theories in the first group (adverse so-cial consequences) passably perform the second task of distinguish-ing the threat from the act. But they fail to accomplish the first task—showing why blackmail should be criminal. In contrast, sev-eral theories in the second group (blackmail is wrong in and of it-self) provide seemingly persuasive explanations for blackmail's criminalization, but fail to account adequately for the difference between the threat and the act. No prior theory performs both jobs satisfactorily.[22]

This is a reasonable enough criterion. The question remains as to whether Berman's own theory will survive such a test, and, also, how well does the libertarian legalization thesis do in this regard (in showing why there is no such thing as a blackmail puzzle, or paradox.)

A. Consequentialists

Berman begins his analysis with theories which defend blackmail prohi-bition on grounds of reducing harm, or negative social consequences. He con-siders the views of economists who believe that blackmail contracts are eco-nomically inefficient, and should be prohibited on that basis. We shall con-

---

[21] Berman mentions in passing that "Professor James Lindgren (is) the most intensely commit-ted contributor to the debate" (over blackmail). *Id*. at 798. If the degree of "intense commit-ment" to this debate can be measured by numbers of pages published on the topic, Berman was correct in his assessment at the time he published in1998. The total number of pages published by Lindgren up until and including 1997 was 152.5; by Block, as of that date, 58 pages (correc-tions were made in this calculation for number of co authors, but not for size of page). As of the present date of this writing (2001) these positions have been reversed; Block, now stands at 252 pages, Lindgren, remains at 152.5.

[22] Berman, *supra* note 1, at 800–801. I entirely agree with Berman's last statement.

sider his views in some detail, not because he refutes them well,[23] nor yet because the theories he deals with are not in any great need of refutation,[24] but mainly as a means of using his refutations of other mainstream legal philosophers, against his own views.

Berman distinguishes[25] "four types of blackmail based on the manner in which the damaging information is obtained: in 'opportunistic blackmail,' the blackmailer innocently stumbles upon information he subsequently realizes will serve as useful blackmail fodder; in 'participant blackmail,' he was a participant in the conduct about which he later blackmails the victim; in 'commercial research blackmail,' the blackmailer consciously seeks information in order to blackmail his victim; and in 'entrepreneurial blackmail,' the blackmailer entices a victim into a compromising situation for the specific purpose of producing the material with which he can blackmail."[26]

Berman quite correctly points out, against the claims of Ginsberg and Schectman,[27] that at least insofar as the first two types of blackmail are concerned, there can be no question of any economic costs, since there are none. Hence, these, at least, even in the view of Ginsberg and Schectman, ought to be legalized. Since these two authors advocate no such thing, this is a flaw in their view, sees Berman, to his credit. We might add that even if it can somehow be shown that blackmail does involve costs, it still does not follow that it ought to be prohibited. For surely there are numerous "inefficient" activities we pursue, all of which "waste" resources. For example, lying around in a hammock on a lazy summer's day; watching soap operas; goofing off; day dreaming; floating mindlessly in a swimming pool; etc. Yet, it would be a very courageous legal philosopher who would acquiesce in the notion that since these acts are all improvident, they ought to be outlawed, the basic premise of the so-called economic point of view on blackmail.[28]

---

[23] Which he does, for the most part.

[24] This has been done not only by the libertarian literature on blackmail, but also by the mainstream writings on this subject, which is self-refutational, taken as a whole, in that no attempt to explain the so-called paradox survives without fatal objections. However, "you can never have too much of the truth," and thus even more piling on is always welcome.

[25] Following MIKE HEPWORTH, BLACKMAIL: PUBLICITY AND SECRECY IN EVERYDAY LIFE AT 73–77 (1976).

[26] Berman, *supra* note 1, at 804.

[27] *See* Douglas N. Ginsburg & Paul Shechtman, *Blackmail: An Economic Analysis of the Law*, 141 U. PA. L. REV. 849 (1993). For another rejoinder to Ginsberg and Schectman, *see* chapter 9, this volume.

[28] Economics is a positive, not a normative, science. Therefore, there cannot *be* any such thing as an economic point of view on whether or not blackmail should be legalized.

Consider now Berman's criticism of Shavell. The latter argues that "'potential victims will exercise excessive precautions or reduce their level of innocent, yet embarrassing, activities' to prevent being blackmailed by persons who chance upon damaging information."[29] Berman points out "Such an assumption is an economic reason for making blackmail illegal only if the costs of these consequences outweigh their social benefits." But Berman overlooks the insight that *even if* the cost benefit analysis could somehow be made to indicate this,[30] that the normative positive distinction would still vitiate against any such conclusion.

Then, too, this omission on Berman's part mars his otherwise splendid rejection of Posner's argument for the *status quo* on blackmail legislation. In the words of the former, the latter: "concedes that the social welfare arguments against ... blackmail threats to reveal that a victim has engaged either in a criminal act for which he was not caught and punished or in disreputable or immoral acts that do not violate any commonly enforced law are inconclusive."[31] And what artillery does Berman launch at Posner's refusal to embrace blackmail legalization, even though, by his own admission, he cannot make the case that all such acts are wealth reducing, the be-all and end-all of his philosophy? Berman states:

> [T]he economic case against blackmail cannot survive without more rigorous empirical work and predictive modeling [sic]. Unless and until the law and economics scholars can demonstrate more persuasively that blackmail reduces social wealth, it will remain difficult to reconcile their defense of blackmail's criminalization with their methodology's scientific and positivist aspirations."

---

[29] Berman, *supra* note 1, at 807.

[30] It cannot be. The problem run in to by all such attempts to measure benefits and costs between one person and another is known in economics as the insoluble problem of interpersonal comparisons of utility, and the impossibility of cardinal utility. All we can know is that one person, for example, prefers an apple to an orange. This is the valid notion of ordinal utility. Cardinal utility would imply that the person in question derives, say, 10 "utils" (measures of happiness) from the apple, and only 5 from the orange. In addition to this illicit concept, cost benefit analysis requires the additional step of interpersonal comparisons: John obtains 20 utils from an apple, Bill only 10; therefore the former likes apples twice as much as the latter.

[31] *Id.* at 810.

But all the "empirical work" in the world cannot demonstrate that one party disvalues an act more or less than another party values it.[32]

Here is how Berman dismisses the utilitarian argument for blackmail prohibition:

> The foregoing analysis supports three conclusions about the law and economics argument on blackmail. First, the economic approach fails to justify prohibitions against adventitious blackmail. Second, whether other major forms of blackmail are truly disadvantageous on law and economics principles is far from certain once one takes externalities into proper account. Third, it is unlikely that the economic argument warrants resort to the criminal law.[33]

In the view of Epstein,[34] decriminalization will lead to "Blackmail, Inc." a firm specializing in this practice on a commercial basis. For Epstein, quoted by Berman, "blackmail is criminal because it has a necessary tendency to induce other acts of theft and deception, the criminalization of which is wholly unpuzzling."[35]

Berman has three reasons for rejecting this contention of Epstein's. His first is as follows: "Consider, for example, a blackmail proposal in which the blackmailer demands sexual favors for the nondisclosure of embarrassing information that the victim has no moral obligation to divulge (such as her own illegitimate birth). This form of blackmail would neither induce the victim to engage in theft or fraud nor encourage any 'deception' that society has a legitimate interest in deterring. Under Epstein's reasoning, it should not be criminalized."[36]

Although a clever attempt to undermine Epstein, this example cannot withstand scrutiny. First of all, if Blackmail, Inc. got wind of the illegitimate

---

[32] A puzzle in nomenclature. Berman, *Id.* at 811, discusses "why blackmail is not merely discouraged or even prohibited, but criminalized." Berman states: "assuming that the blackmail deal is unproductive, the question remains why it should be illegal, let alone criminal." *Id.* at 829. Both of these statements appear to maintain a distinction between that which is prohibited, or illegal, on the one hand, and criminal, on the other. But surely each implies the other. That is, if an act is illegal, then to undertake it is criminal. Alternatively, is something is criminal, then to do it is to engage in a prohibited, or illegal, act.

[33] *Id.* at 814.

[34] Richard Epstein, *Blackmail, Inc.*, 50 U. CHI. L. REV. 553 (1983).

[35] Berman, *supra* note 1, at 814, quoting Epstein, *supra* note 34, at 553.

[36] Berman, *supra* note 1, at 816.

birth of this woman, and she were so ashamed of it that she would rather dispense sexual favors than be exposed, then her own economic condition would be reduced from what it would have been had this whole episode not arisen.[37] But if we believe that crime arises due to poverty, and she is poorer in a very meaningful manner, then she is more apt to engage in criminal behavior than otherwise. Not only does this premise follow based on a reduction in her general wealth level, it also may be derived, more specifically, from the fact that she now has less time available to earn an honest living. The dispensing of sexual favors, after all, takes time. Time is money, according to the old aphorism. With more of her daily routine taken up in satisfying her blackmailer, there is just that much less time available to her to earn an honest living. This might well, further, incline her to a life of crime.

Let me elaborate. Whether or not it is true that the blackmailed woman will more likely turn to crime as a result of the "ravages" of Blackmail, Inc., Berman, at least, is in no position to object to this contention. This is because Berman is attempting a *reductio* on Epstein; that is, Berman is implicitly accepting, for the sake of argument, Epstein's premise that if the girl were to turn to a life of crime due her becoming a blackmailee,[38] then Epstein would be correct. The power of Berman's example, I take it, is that he has seemingly found a *bona fide* case of blackmail with no impetus for the blackmailee to turn to crime, as Epstein avers. Berman has not unearthed such a case.

Berman then maintains that the "second problem with Epstein's theory is that the claim upon which it rests—that force and fraud demarcate the criminal law's proper reach—is extremely dubious. Even aside from "victimless" offenses such as gambling, prostitution, and drug use, criminalization of which is notoriously suspect on liberal principles, the state makes numerous activities criminal that appear not to involve either force or fraud. These offenses cover a wide range of conduct from statutory rape to indecent exposure to larceny by stealth."[39]

---

[37] Of course, it is always better, from her point of view, that her secret be in the hands of Blackmail, Inc., rather than a gossip, but that is another matter. Right now, we are attempting to establish that her wealth position would be worsened once her secret gets out, it matters not to whom.

[38] I refuse to characterize this woman as a "victim" of blackmail, for several reasons. One, because "victim" implies a perpetrator, or a victimizer, and this is akin to conceding that the blackmailer is a criminal. Two, because it is not even a matter of contention that gossip should be proscribed by law. But gossip worsens the position of a person with a secret to keep far more than does blackmail. If we as a society are not going to incarcerate the gossip, the issue of doing so for the blackmailer should not even arise.

[39] Berman, *supra* note 1, at 817.

But this, too, is problematic. First of all, Berman treads dangerously close to legal positivism, the doctrine that all laws are necessarily just.[40] He does this in implying that just because "gambling, prostitution, and drug use" are illegal, they somehow serve as a counter weight to Epstein's libertarian claim that force and fraud are necessary and sufficient for outlawry.[41] He does crawl back from this position by conceding that these laws are "notoriously suspect on liberal principles,"[42] but this is not the half of it. These laws are a moral monstrosity in the free society, precisely because of Epstein's well founded concern with force and fraud. And why the quotation marks around the word "victimless?" These acts are indubitably victimless, not of course in the sense that the dependents of the gambler, or drug user, will not be worse off from these practices,[43] but because they are volitional on the part of the prostitute or addict.

More serious is Berman's claim that statutory rape, indecent exposure or larceny by stealth are all both properly criminal and do not violate Epstein's strictures against force and fraud. Let us consider each in turn. Laws prohibiting statutory rape, provided that they deal with underage children, are certainly compatible with Epsteinian notions. Children, in the absence of appropriate adult supervision, are in effect defined as people with whom fraud is necessarily perpetrated upon. One simply cannot treat youngsters as adults, and the refusal to do so hardly counts as a violation of the libertarian axiom proscribing violence against non-aggressors or their property.

Indecent exposure, contrary to Berman, should not be a crime at all. True, it does not at all involve initiatory aggression, but, as their are no "victims," it should not be legally prohibited. Nudism cannot be a *per se* violation of law, lest there would be no legal nudist camps. Were going about *sans* clothes necessarily invasive, it could not be allowed, period.[44] But what of the rending of the social fabric, if naked people are able to cavort entirely upon

---

[40] The mention of Nazi law, or, for that matter, Communist law, ought to put paid to that notion.

[41] As it happens, although Epstein does indeed take the libertarian position on this one issue, his own views are not totally compatible with that philosophy. *See* on this, David Gordon, review of RICHARD A. EPSTEIN, SIMPLE RULES FOR A COMPLEX WORLD, in MISES REVIEW (Fall 1995).

[42] Berman, *supra* note 1, at 817.

[43] Which would occur, in any case, with regard to the dependents of real victims of real crimes, such as murder, theft, rape, etc.

[44] Compare nudity, or exposure of the unclothed human body (there is nothing "indecent" about this), with murder, or rape or kidnap, which are intrinsically unlawful, at least under the libertarian legal code.

their own recognizance, with no consideration given to others who might be offended, even outraged, by such goings on? The solution to this problem does not lie in the criminalization of nudity; rather, it may be found in the institution of private property. How would this work? How, without a law to the contrary, could people be prevented from, say, fornicating on their front porches, in plain view of sundry passers by? This could be accomplished via private street ownership.

The road owner, for much the same reasons as the condominium developer, would find it in his best interests to preclude public nudity. Did he not, the value of his lands would suffer, and he would become a candidate for bankruptcy. Conceivably, there might be some few streets in the nation where nakedness would not be obviated through contractual arrangements; there are, after all, some plots of land devoted to nudist colonies. But virtually all road owners would substitute contract for legal prohibition. And this is just as it should be, for, while no one wants rampant nudity, everywhere, it simply is not a crime, akin to murder or rape, Berman to the contrary notwithstanding.

Third, is "larceny by stealth." Presumably, by this Berman alludes to pick pocketing, bad check writing, mislabeling products, selling underweight, counterfeiting credit cards,[45] or some such. Now it must be admitted at the outset, these are crimes, but not of violence. Superficially, then, Berman seems to have Epstein over a barrel. Here are acts which clearly ought to be proscribed by law, and yet they do not utilize "force." But Epstein mentions both force and fraud, and surely the latter four mentioned above are fraudulent. What about pickpocketing? If it is done well, it can hardly be done "forcefully." And, say what you will about it, it is not fraud. Has Berman finally come up with an example that embarrasses Epstein's libertarian insight? Not a bit of it. Berman's mistake is that he interprets force, or violence, far too narrowly. He sees it, almost, as a term in physics, not law. That is, for him, the criterion is implicitly in terms of foot pounds of energy expended, or "work" in the sense of force multiplied by distance. But for Epstein, and all libertarians, this is not at all the meaning of the term. Rather, for him, it is understood strictly in legal terminology: as doing "violence," that is, violating, the rights of person or property.[46] And while pickpocketing certainly contains no vio-

---

[45] Notice, I do not say "counterfeiting fiat currency." This is because dollars, lira, pounds, marks, yen, etc., are already counterfeited (of gold), and far from counterfeiting counterfeit money being a crime, it should be seen as a legal act. See WALTER BLOCK, DEFENDING THE UNDEFENDABLE at 109–20.

[46] We sometimes speak in terms of "doing violence to the facts." We hardly mean bashing the facts on the head with a baseball bat, whatever that would mean. This elocution is rather a somewhat poetic synonym for lying, or at least being mistaken.

lence known to the student of physics,[47] it cannot be denied that it is in violation of private property rights to wallets.

Having refuted Berman's critique of Epstein on blackmail is certainly not to say that the views of the latter are warranted. Just because Berman fails to lay a glove on Epstein does not ensure the validity of his scare model of Blackmail, Inc. This is not the time or the place for a full scale critique of Epstein on blackmail. Suffice it to say that many actions "lead to" crime. But there is many a slip between cup and lip. "Leading" to crime, a tendency for crime to occur in the wake of something or other, is not the same as crime, *per se*. Only the latter should be prohibited by law. Which entirely innocent acts, for example, are correlated with criminal behavior? Soccer games, for one thing; the "soccer hoodlums" of Europe seem almost brought to a frenzy by the advent of this game. Nor are such occurrences by any means a monopoly of under developed civilizations in other parts of the world. When the Chicago Bulls won their last NBA championship, their fans celebrated by rioting and looting. Movies depicting gang violence are often followed up by such acts in real life. Were we to take Epstein seriously, the soccer and basketball athletes, and the movie actors, producers and writers who "lead to" these crimes would all be incarcerated, a manifest injustice.[48] Let blackmail be ever so much strongly associated with crime, real crime, that is, it does not follow in the slightest that the act of offering to keep silent for a fee should be criminalized.

B. Deontologists

So much for the consequentialists. What of the deontologists? The first commentator considered by Berman who dismisses blackmail legalization not for its supposed bad effects but for its presumed intrinsically evil nature is Gorr.[49] Berman introduces this author as a corrective for the views of Feinberg.[50] The latter commentator arouses Berman's ire since he actually has the audacity to maintain that at least one kind of blackmail, that exposing adultery, should be legalized.[51] Instead of directly confronting Feinberg on

---

[47] Delicacy is all

[48] Berman offers a magnificent example of the sneaker manufacturers who justifiably persist in providing these products to the public despite their knowledge that inner city youth target wearers of them. Berman, *supra* note 1, fn 67.

[49] Michael Gorr, *Nozick's Argument Against Blackmail*, 58 PERSONALIST 187 (1977); Michael Gorr, *Liberalism and the Paradox of Blackmail*, 21 PHIL. & PUB. AFF. 43 (1992)

[50] JOEL FEINBERG, HARMLESS WRONGDOING.

[51] Feinberg's work favors the legalization of blackmail at least in part.

this apostasy, he dismisses him on the ground that his "conclusion is startling."[52]

It is here that Berman indicates the glimmerings of a philosophy which will undermine his own perspective. He states: "Because it is clearly wrongful not to report the identity of someone who has committed a felony, there would be nothing puzzling or problematic about criminalizing the conditional offer not to report a crime."[53] The difficulty, here, is with "clearly wrongful." By use of this phrase, without any supporting documentation whatsoever, Berman reveals himself as a scholar who is willing to use imprecise language as the premise of his conclusions. What is clearly wrongful? Is it immoral?[54] Should it be punished by law? Does it merely mean that the speaker opposes such action? Is it "clearly wrongful" to smoke cigarettes, or for a fat person to eat chocolate, and is there "nothing puzzling or problematic about criminalizing" these activities also?

The problem, here, apart from lack of clarity concerning crucial terminology, is that Berman is implicitly extolling a "Good Samaritan" concept of the law. Not satisfied with prohibiting the invasion of other people's persons or their property, this author is here calling for criminalization for *failure* to perform deeds which are essentially supererogatory. To turn in a criminal to the authorities, or to give charity to the poor, *is over and above the call* of legal duty. It simply cannot be a requirement of law, since if it were, we would *all* be in jail. For if it is a legal obligation to "report the identity of someone who has committed a felony,"[55] then it is a requirement that one go out and *look* for felons to inform on. This is essentially an open ended requirement, or a positive obligation in philosophical parlance, which, by its very nature, can have no limit. Even sleep, apart from that amount required to maximize the turning in of criminals to the authorities, would be proscribed. It will do no good to contend that the obligation is satisfied by merely notifying the police of crimes one happens to witness, by accident.[56] For if it is really an obligation, then it is a positive one: one must devote one's entire life to this process. Similarly with charity. If it, too, is a positive commitment, then one must give away

---

[52] Berman, *supra* note 1, at 822.

[53] *Id.* at 821.

[54] Berman on numerous occasions uses the concepts of "immorality," "unnecessary misery" and "harm causing" as a stick with which to beat his opponents, without condescending to define these terms.

[55] *Id.* at 821.

[56] If this were all there were to the obligation, then people would go around with blinders on, lest they witness anything untoward.

all of one's worldly possessions,[57] until one's wealth level has reached that of the poorest members of society.

Another philosophical difficulty arises when Berman states, in his refutation of Gorr: "And if we do not believe that an actor knows where her moral duty lies, it makes no sense to hold her morally culpable for risking violation of that duty." If this were all there were to it, it would be unobjectionable. After all, it would appear to logically follow that we cannot hold anyone morally blameworthy[58] if he does not know his moral duty. However, Berman means to imply more than this; specifically, that if a person is not morally blameworthy, that he should not be punished by law for committing a crime, and this is indeed a difficulty.

Take the following case. A person who clearly cannot be blameworthy (a baby,[59] a sleeping or an insane person) somehow fires a pistol and kills an innocent passerby. Traditional law, of the sort advocated by Berman, would hold the perpetrator of this crime morally blameless, and therefore nonindictable for the crime of murder.

But suppose there were available a machine[60] which could switch the life from a live murder into the body of his dead victim. E.g., into one compartment of this machine we could (forcibly) place the baby, sleeping or insane person who discharged the pistol, and into the other, the body of the victim of this shooting. Then, we could pull the switch, and out would emerge a newly enlivened ex dead victim, along with a now newly dead baby[61], sleeping or insane person. The question is, should we pull that switch? That is, will justice be served if we do, and not if we as a society decline to do so? Clearly, the interests of justice would be served if we undertook this transfer operation, for of all the people in our little tableau, the dead victim is the most innocent. It will not do to merely look at the shooter and ask if he is morally culpable or not, the practice of most legal theorists, including Berman. This is very much beside the point. The real issue is, there is only one life available, and there are two competitors for that life; the murdered man, on the one hand, and the baby, sleeping or insane person on the other. Whatever the moral merits or demerits of the perpetrator of this crime, the *best* that can be said about him is that there were extenuating or ameliorating circumstances involved. What

---

57 And if we take this to its logical conclusion, why should we not, then, also enslave ourselves to the poor?

58 Whatever that means, and Berman vouchsafes us no answer.

59 I owe this example to Matthew Block

60 Inspired by ROBERT NOZICK, ANARCHY, STATE, AND UTOPIA (1974).

61 If the idea of taking the baby's life away from it is hard to contemplate, substitute for its parent for it, or whoever left the gun in its grasp.

can be said in behalf of the victim, in contrast, is that he is totally, completely and fully innocent of *any* wrongdoing whatsoever, and if anyone deserves this one life available, it is he.[62] Motives, culpability, blameworthiness, immorality are all very much beside the point.

But Berman is having none of this. In his view, "Whereas victims are concerned solely with harm, the law is concerned with the defendant's culpability, of which harm is but a minor ingredient."[63] It doesn't seem to be able to permeate Berman's view that there is another competing theory of punishment available for consideration. In this the libertarian view, the victim, not the perpetrator, takes center stage. It is the plight of the latter, not the situation of the former, that is of immense concern. In Berman's opinion, in contrast, can we but find the criminal blameless, or come up with an excuse for him, then all attempts to render the victim whole again—surely the essence of punishment theory—will have to go by the boards.

Let us look at Katz's[64] case of Smithy vs Louie through the eyes of Berman. Both of these worthies break into Bartleby's home on successive nights, to steal his valuables. Smithy beats him up and does not take his treasure, while Louie does the latter not the former. Bartleby prefers his treatment at Smithy's hands to Louie's, since he values his property more than his physical integrity.

> Berman sums up as follows: The law, of course, would punish Smithy the batterer more severely than Louie the thief, and Katz approves. The criminal law, he argues, should not take account of a victim's idiosyncratic preferences. Whereas victims are concerned solely with harm, the law is concerned with the defendant's culpability. ... Smithy is punished more severely than Louie because battery is morally worse than theft. For the same reason, the law rightly views blackmail in light of what the blackmailer intends to take money from one who does not want to part with it.[65]

Although it is Berman citing Katz in this paragraph, the former does not disagree with the latter in any of these contentions. Berman confines his criti-

---

[62] Unfortunately, for Berman, his theory, to be discussed below, depends intimately upon moral blameworthiness.

[63] Berman, *supra* note 1, at 828.

[64] *See* Leo Katz, *Blackmail and Other Forms of Arm-Twisting*, 141 U. PA. L. REV. at 1582–83 (1993).

[65] *Id.* at 828.

cism to Katz's mere assertion, without discussion or argument, as to which acts are immoral, and why.[66]

This refusal of Berman's to elucidate his own concept of immorality—a lynchpin of his perspective on blackmail, and on much else in criminal law—comes with particular ill grace given his castigation of Katz that he "simply asserts that the act the blackmailer threatens is immoral." And again: "whether the act threatened is a moral right or a moral wrong (or something else) cannot be simply assumed without argument.[67]

As well, it is patently false that the blackmailer takes "money from one who does not want to part with it." Very much to the contrary, the holder of a secret will give his eye teeth to the blackmailer to ensure he does not spill the beans. The blackmailee is deliriously happy to fall into the clutches of someone who will keep silent, for a fee, rather than someone who will blab no matter what he does.

Further, what are we to make of the claim that "battery is morally worse than theft?" How can Katz make such a statement, and Berman acquiesce in it, without a shred of discussion of what morality is? The trouble with mainstream punishment theory is that there is no deontological connection between what the perpetrator does, and what he suffers in return. In contrast, libertarian punishment theory is predicated on the notion that the punishment should be proportionate to the crime. Specifically, this translates into the formula that whatever the miscreant does to his victim is done to him, only twice over. Sometimes called "two teeth for a tooth" theory,[68] this mandates that whatever the perpetrator does to the victim, he be repaid two fold, with cognizance taken of the costs of capturing him, and with a premium for endangering the latter.

How would this work with the pedestrian theft of a television set? First off, the criminal must be made to disgorge the TV he stole, giving it back to the victim. Second, what the burglar tried to do to the victim must be done to him; that is, in this case, a second TV must be seized from the brigand, and given over the to the robbery victim.[69] Assuming that the crook turns himself over to the police immediately after the dastardly act, there is no further pen-

---

[66] *Id.* This criticism, in my view, applies to Berman as well.

[67] *Id.*

[68] MURRAY N. ROTHBARD, THE ETHICS OF LIBERTY at 88, fn. 6. (1998).

[69] If the wrongdoer does not have a tv set of his own with which to make recompense, its value will be in effect taken out of his hide. That is, he will be forcibly enslaved, until he earns the requisite funds. In the libertarian society, only slavery and kidnapping of innocent people, not criminals, is proscribed by law.

alty for the costs of searching for him, convicting him, etc.[70] However, if the miscreant came to the victim's domicile with a gun, while the occupant was at home, this is far worse, in terms of endangerment, than if he came unarmed, to an empty house. He will be in any case forced to play Russian roulette, but in the latter case there will be many more chambers, and many fewer bullets, than in the former. Monetary payment may be negotiated between victim and perpetrator at any stage in the negotiations.[71] For example, if the crime is sexual battery, and the punishment includes the use of a broomstick on the rapist,[72] the latter with the permission of the former, may be able to come to an agreement as to the monetary payment in lieu of this punishment.

Contrast this type of punishment with the mainstream view on the matter. Under present law, the victim is an afterthought. The main emphasis is on rehabilitating, re-educating, the criminal. Naturally, all of this is done at taxpayer (e.g., victim) expense. This is to add insult to injury. First, the citizen is mulcted by the criminal stealing his TV set. Then, he is made to cough up a second time, to keep the criminal in a nice cozy jail, with air conditioning, color TV,[73] a gymnasium, weight lifting room, hot and cold running social workers, public defender lawyers, etc.

To return to the case in point. In the libertarian perspective, there is no need to make any essentially arbitrary assessments of which is "worse," battery or theft. In *each* case, what was done to the victim is carried out twice fold upon the person and or property of the evil doer, with due allowances for peripheral punishments as outlined above.[74]

---

[70] This would be the "transactions costs" so beloved in the University of Chicago Law and Economics tradition. *See,* on this, Ronald H. Coase, *The Problem of Social Cost,* J. L. & ECON. 3:1-44 (1960).

[71] The victim may, before the criminal is even caught, contractually give over these rights to an agent (a private police force or insurance company) so as to forestall any retaliation.

[72] This would be done twice, according to our formula.

[73] A poetic injustice in the case of tv theft, for the bad guy might benefit from viewing the idiot box while the previous owner is forced to do without.

[74] The main competitor with libertarian punishment theory is put forth by the University of Chicago School. Based on utilitarianism, this perspective posits that punishment be set so as to minimize the costs of crime, or to maximize some measure of social welfare, such as GDP. The difficulty here, can be seen by assuming that the "best," e.g., most "economical" or "efficient" punishment for petty theft was the death penalty. Even if this deed indeed maximize GDP, it would still be unjust, e.g., disproportionate to the crime. For the utilitarian viewpoint on crime and punishment, *see* DAVID FRIEDMAN, THE MACHINERY OF FREEDOM: GUIDE TO A RADICAL CAPITALISM (1989).

In contrast to the libertarian theory, Berman asks, stipulating for argument's sake that compensation to the victim of crime is justified: "[H]ow does one set the proper compensation level? Ideally, the state should replicate the market price for the boundary crossing that is, the price upon which the persons threatened by the conduct and the person who wishes to engage in it would agree in a voluntary transaction."[75]

This, however, seems tongue in cheek, for no sooner does Berman raise this issue but he discards it:

> [T]he likely existence of a transactional surplus (where the minimum price acceptable to the seller is less than the maximum price acceptable to the buyer) makes it impossible to ascertain the hypothetical market price. And it would be unfair to allow the boundary crosser to appropriate all the benefits of the exchange by compensating the 'seller' of the right in an amount (less than the market price) necessary to keep him on the same indifference curve."[76]

True, setting up quasi market shadow prices is not a rational way to go about compensating the victim, but this leaves untouched the libertarian approach.[77]

In his treatment of Nozick,[78] Berman seems to buy into the notion[79] that the rights of two different people can clash. He describes Nozick's position as follows: "when the state does prohibit conduct that risks crossing the moral boundary of another, it should usually compensate the party whose liberty is thus infringed."[80] But if rights are properly specified, they can never be incompatible with one another. To say that I have a right to do X, and that you have a right to prevent me from doing X. To support the infringement of liberty, in a book dedicated to articulating the implications of liberty, is rather problematic. It is even possible to describe this line of reasoning as descending to the depths of self contradiction.

---

[75] Berman, *supra* note 1, at 830–31.

[76] *Id.* at 831.

[77] For a critique of indifference curves on the ground that all of human action consists of preference and ranking, see Murray N. Rothbard, "Toward a Reconstruction of Utility and Welfare Economics," in THE LOGIC OF ACTION: METHOD, MONEY AND THE AUSTRIAN SCHOOL, VOL. I (1997).

[78] Nozick, *supra* note 60.

[79] I infer this from the fact that Berman scathingly dismisses all the other of Nozick's contentions he deals with, except for this one. *See* Berman, *supra* note 1, at 829–32.

[80] *Id.* at 831.

Berman's treatment of Nozick's theory of unproductive exchange also leaves something to be desired. Berman[81] approvingly cites Nozick[82] to the effect that "If your next door neighbor plans to erect a certain structure on his land, which he has a right to do, you might be better off if he didn't exist at all. Yet purchasing his abstention from proceeding with his plans will be a productive exchange. Suppose, however, that the neighbor has no desire to erect the structure on the land; he formulates his plan and informs you of it solely in order to sell you his abstention from it. Such an exchange would not be a productive one; it merely gives you relief from something that would not threaten if not for the possibility of an exchange to get relief from it."

States Berman: "As Nozick's last sentence suggests, the proposal leading up to the hypothesized unproductive exchange is a threat because it is coercive, not an offer."

But this is a particularly perverse way of distinguishing between a threat and an offer. The point is, the neighbor has every right to erect this structure on his land, as even Nozick, and thus Berman, acknowledge. But if he has a right to do this, he also has a right to refrain. And if he has a right to refrain, he has a right to be paid for so doing, if he can find a willing customer. And he can!: you, his neighbor.

Rothbard provides the definitive critique to Nozick, explicitly, and by extension, to Berman:

> For his criterion of a 'productive' exchange is one where each party is better off than if the other did not exist at all; whereas a 'non-productive' exchange is one where one party would be better off if the other dropped dead. Thus: 'if I pay you for not harming me, I gain nothing from you that I wouldn't possess if either you didn't exist at all or existed without having anything to do with me.' ...
>
> Let us then see how Nozick applies his 'non-productive' ... criteria to the problem of blackmail. Nozick tries to rehabilitate the outlawry of blackmail by asserting that 'non productive' contracts should be illegal, and that a blackmail contract is non-productive because a blackmailee is worse off because of the blackmailer's very existence. In short, if blackmailer Smith dropped dead, Jones (the blackmailee) would be better off. Or, to put it another way, Jones is paying not for Smith's making him better off, but for not making him worse off. But surely the latter is also a productive contract,

---

[81] *See* Berman, *supra* note 1, fn. 127.

[82] Nozick, *supra* note 60, at 84–85.

because Jones is still better off making the exchange than he would have been if the exchange were not made.

But this theory gets Nozick into very muddy waters indeed; some (though by no means all) of which he recognizes. He concedes, for example, that his reason for outlawing blackmail would force him also to outlaw the following contract: Brown comes to Green, his next-door neighbor, with the following proposition: I intend to build such-and-such a pink building on my property (which he knows Green will detest). I won't build this building, however, if you pay me X amount of money. Nozick concedes that this, too, would have to be illegal in his schema, because Green would be paying Brown for not being worse off, and hence the contract would be 'non-productive.' In essence, Green would be better off if Brown dropped dead. It is difficult, however, for a libertarian to square such outlawry with any plausible theory of property rights. ... In analogy with the blackmail example above, furthermore, Nozick concedes that it would be legal, in his schema, for Green, on finding out about Brown's projected pink building, to come to Brown and offer to pay him not to go ahead. But why would such an exchange be 'productive' just because Green made the offer? What difference does it make who makes the offer in this situation? Wouldn't Green still be better off if Brown dropped dead? And again, following the analogy, would Nozick make it illegal for Brown to refuse Green's offer and then ask for more money? Why? Or, again, would Nozick make it illegal for Brown to subtly let Green know about the projected pink building and then let nature take its course: say, by advertising in the paper about the building and sending Green the clipping?[83] Couldn't this be taken as an act of courtesy? And why should merely advertising something be illegal? Clearly, Nozick's case becomes ever more flimsy as we consider the implications.

Furthermore, Nozick has not at all considered the manifold implications of his 'drop dead' principle. If he is saying, as he seems to, that A is illegitimately 'coercing' B if B is better off should A drop dead, then consider the following case: Brown and Green are competing at auction for the same painting which they desire. They are the last two customers left. Wouldn't Green be better off if Brown

---

[83] Shades of Katz's Mildred and Abigail "warning" case. *See* Katz, *supra* note 64.

dropped dead? Isn't Brown therefore illegally coercing Green in some way, and therefore shouldn't Browns participation in the auction be outlawed? Or, per contra, isn't Green coercing Brown in the same manner and shouldn't Green's participation in the auction be outlawed? If not, why not? Or, suppose that Brown and Green are competing for the and of the same girl; wouldn't each be better off if the other dropped dead; and shouldn't either or both's participation in the courtship therefore be outlawed? The ramifications are virtually endless.

Nozick, furthermore, gets himself into a deeper quagmire when he adds that a blackmail exchange is not 'productive' because outlawing the exchange makes on party (the blackmailee) no worse off. But that of course is not true: as Professor Block has pointed out, outlawing a blackmail contract means that the blackmailer has no further incentive not to disseminate the unwelcome, hitherto secret information about the blackmailed party.[84]

Berman also errs in his own critique of Nozick's "drop dead" theory. He states: "But the equivalence between coercion and unproductive exchanges does not always hold. Imagine that your coworker announces that his daughter is selling Girl Scout cookies and that he will be taking orders. You subscribe for four boxes of Thin Mints at $2.50 per box. Although you'd prefer the $10 to the cookies, you estimate that to decline the offer might cause you some reputational harm, and you value the cookies and the preservation of your reputation more highly than $10 plus a possible slight diminution of your office status. This is plainly an unproductive exchange you would have preferred that your coworker had never mentioned his daughter and the cookies. But the offer to sell you Girl Scout cookies is not a threat (because it doesn't put you worse off than your expected or morally deserved baselines)."[85]

To be sure, as Berman observes, your co worker's suggestion is an offer, not a threat. But this is not "because it doesn't put you worse off than your expected or morally deserved baselines." In the absence of a definition or morality, it ill behooves this author to rely on any such justification for his position: we simply have no independent criterion to determine what your deserved baseline is. Even if we blindly accept that this exchange would put you below this level, it is still not a threat, because there are numerous ways in

---

[84] Rothbard, *supra* note 68, at 245–247.

[85] Berman, *supra* note 1, at fn. 127.

which this could occur and yet no threat take place. For example, a bakery could open its doors right next to yours, and attract your customers away from you; your girlfriend could take up a new religion, and leave you on this basis; you could be fired from your job for any number of reasons having nothing to do with a threat. All of these occurrences would leave you "worse off." No, the reason Berman is correct in maintaining that your co-worker's announcement is not a threat is because he has every right[86] to make such an offer.

III. BERMAN'S THEORY

A. Preliminary

After having pretty well demolished virtually all of the arguments of both consequentialists and deontologists in their attempt to solve the paradox of blackmail, Berman now weighs in with his own positive theory to this end. How does he attempt to clear up the mystery? He characterizes this as "evidentiary theory," and makes some pretty ambitious claims in its behalf: "It explains why blackmail is an exception to two general rules: that it should be legal to threaten what it is legal to do, and that voluntary transactions should be lawful."[87]

Specifically, Berman presents his theory in the form of three principles. Behavior should be prohibited by law if:

> (1) it is likely in the aggregate to yield net adverse social consequences (taking into account the costs imposed by the criminal ban itself);

> (2) it (a) tends to cause or threaten identifiable harm and (b) is morally wrongful in itself; or

> (3) it tends both (a) to cause or threaten identifiable harm, and (b) to be undertaken by a morally blameworthy actor."[88]

---

[86] For the libertarian, this means, merely, that his daughter has good title to the cookies, and that no physical violence is in the offing.

[87] Berman, *supra* note 1, at 835.

[88] *Id.* at 837.

Principle (1) is the now by familiar utilitarian or consequentialist criterion, according to which anything reducing wealth, or GDP, or some such measure of well-being, ought to be banned by law. It is more than puzzling that after expending so much ink utterly demolishing such theories Berman adopts it for himself.

Principle (2) is an amalgamation of the consequentialist and deontological theories. The first part, "identifiable harm" focuses attention of the former of these two. In the second, "wrongful in itself" is aimed in the direction of the latter of these two, in that it looks at the act in principle, apart from its effects. Both sections of principle (2), then, are subject to the criticism just made, namely that it is logically inconsistent for Berman to criticize these views, and then to incorporate them into his own explanation.

In addition, Berman nowhere defines, explains, expounds upon or in any way satisfies our curiosity about what he means by "morally wrongful in itself." That this undefined phrase appears in not one but two of his bedrock principles[89] is such a serious lacunae that it well might deserve to be characterized as a philosophical "howler."

Principle (3) is suspect in that it introduces yet another phrase, "morally blameworthy," again without benefit of explanation. How are those who wish to evaluate his three principled theory to do so fairly if we are given no independent criterion of these phrase? Without an explication of words like "moral," "immoral," "blameworthy," etc., the author is free to make things up as he goes along, to create entirely new concepts out of the whole cloth, as a means of precluding reproach.

Then, too, there is no distinction offered as to the difference between "morally wrongful in itself" and "morally blameworthy." If there is no difference between then, then principles (2) and (3) overlap, and one of them may be jettisoned, without loss to the argument. If there is a difference, it is the duty of the author to specify what it is, and he does not. It would appear, at least at the outset, there is no difference between these two concepts. For how else can a morally blameworthy actor be defined other than as a person who from time to time, or often, or more often than most people,[90] does things that are intrinsically wrongful, and of a degree far surpassing the evil deeds of the average? Another consideration which mitigates against there being two separate principles, (2) and (3), is that if an act is not morally wrongful in and of itself, why is it that if X does it, he is morally blameworthy? Alternatively, if the act is indeed morally blameworthy, how can it reasonably be denied that the act is wrong in and of itself?

---

[89] Principle (3) as well.

[90] Even Stalin and Hitler did not *always* act improperly.

Berman offers two arguments in behalf of there being a valid distinction between (2) and (3). Let us consider each in turn.

First, in his opinion: "The distinction between the second and third criteria turns on the claim that an actor is not blameworthy for engaging in a wrongful action if, for example, he lacks information critical to determining its wrongfulness or acts out of a bona fide and reasonable judgment (albeit one a majority of society deems mistaken) that his act is morally justified. For example, a legislator who concludes that euthanasia is morally wrong but also believes that, in practice, the euthanizer rarely acts in a morally blameworthy fashion could vote to criminalize the conduct in accord with the second criterion but not the third."

The difficulty, here, is that if euthanasia is really morally wrong, it is a downright contradiction to assert that "the euthanizer rarely acts in a morally blameworthy fashion." Very much to the contrary, *given* that euthanasia is morally forbidden, akin, indeed, to murder, then it is *impossible* for the euthanasia-murderer to act in a moral manner. It is very much beside the point what the actor believes. He may believe, for example, that murder is justified. This will by not one whit save his act from being immoral.[91] Berman's example sounds more reasonable than it is because of the disputed status of euthanasia, which does not at all apply to murder. But in his premise Berman *stipulates* that this practice is indeed morally wrong. Well, if it is, then it is not possible for anyone, ever, to engage in it without being morally blameworthy.

Secondly, he states: "Conversely, an actor who causes harm for reasons that are not justified is deserving of blame regardless of whether the act is deemed wrongful in itself. To use a familiar example, if someone kills an assailant in a situation where the use of deadly force is justified because necessary for self-defense, but the killer is unaware of the necessity, the killing is justifiably made criminal under the third criterion but not the second."

There are justifications, too, for being dubious about this claim regarding the distinctiveness between (2) and (3). Yes, if Berman is correct in maintaining that such an "unaware" killing is properly criminal, then (2) and (3) yield the results as per Berman. But suppose this author is incorrect in his assessment that "the killing is justifiably made criminal."[92] Then it is *not* the case that (2) and (3) diverge in their implications. For then the act would be nei-

---

[91] If immoral it is; remember, we have not once been vouchsafed a definition of morality by Berman.

[92] It would not be a crime under libertarian law, since the justification for this act exists, whether or not the killer knew about it at the time. But this is, strictly speaking, irrelevant to our attempt to determine whether (2) and (3) are independent or not.

ther morally wrong in itself (2), nor would the actor be morally blameworthy (3). Of course, it is possible that Berman and I are on different wavelengths with regard to these concepts, given that they have not been clarified.

I have criticized Berman for being niggardly with his definitions.[93] This, in spite of the fact that a section of his paper to which we now turn our attention is entitled "the third criterion: defining terms."[94] The main burden of this section, despite its title, is to "endeavor ... to show that blackmail is properly criminal because it satisfies the third criterion."[95] And what of its title? Here, Berman states "Because the argument to follow will necessarily depend on the particular content ascribed to 'harm' and 'moral blameworthiness,' some explication of these notoriously ambiguous terms is in order."[96]

Would that he had followed through on this. Instead, rather than defining harm, he resorts to legal positivism, noting that "the law does recognize as 'harm' injuries to, among other things, bodily integrity (homicide, rape, battery), psychic or emotional wellbeing (assault, stalking, hate speech, child pornography), property interests (theft, vandalism, trespass), public institutions and processes (treason, bribery of public officials, insider trading), and public morals (prostitution, obscenity, drug use, gambling)."[97]

On response to this is that the "law is an ass." Just because it is indeed the law that people be thrown in jail for the "harm" of victimless crimes such as hate speech,[98] insider trading, prostitution, obscenity, drug use and gambling, does not make it right. Another is that Berman himself is already on record as casting aspersions on liberal societies which enact such legislation. How, then, can he come to rely upon such institutions in this context? He states, "criminalization of ... 'victimless' offenses such as gambling, prostitution, and drug use, ... is notoriously suspect on liberal principles."[99] As for bribery of public officials, it all depends upon what they are doing. If they are concentration camp guards, it is perfectly within the libertarian law, if not the law of the land, to bribe them.[100]

"Harm," happily, does not suffer from lack of definition. But it does not follow from this that it is reasonable to embed this concept in the very bowels

---

[93] I have done so more than once, since this is so integral to his theory.

[94] Berman, *supra* note 1, at 838–41.

[95] *Id.* at 838.

[96] *Id.* at 838–39.

[97] *Id.* at 839.

[98] Hate crimes and the outlawry of hate speech are the quintessential thought crimes. On this, *see* George Orwell, Animal Farm.

[99] Berman, *supra* note 1, at 817.

[100] *See* Block, *supra* note 45, "The Dishonest Cop," at 101–106.

of society, the law. Very much to the contrary, if mere harm can suffice for criminalization, then we shall have to ban the following activities: These include, in alphabetical order, to affront, annoy, antagonize, bad mouth, banter, belittle, betray, blame, bother, castigate, challenge, cold shoulder, compete against, condemn, criticize, curse, decry, deprecate, disapprove of, discriminate against, disparage, doubt, embarrass, enrage, flirt with, frown at, frustrate, give the silent treatment to, goad, gossip about, heckle, humiliate, hurt someone's feelings, impugn, insult, inveigh against, insult, irk, irritate, jeer at, laugh at, making jokes at the expense of, be malicious, malign, manipulate, mock, mortify, needle, nettle, pout, provoke, refuse to play with, refuse to befriend, reproach, revile, run up the score against, scoff, sneer at, spite, sulk at, tease, talk behind a friends back, tantalize, tattle tale against, taunt, torment, traduce, trash talk at, treat with contempt, undermine, upbraid, vex, vilify, vituperate against, wear the same dress as, withhold blessing.[101]

Of course, principle (3) is a double edged test. It requires not one but two elements. In addition to being nasty, one must do this with bad motivations.[102] But surely the human condition is such that this is not an insuperable barrier for most people.

A critic might well remark that if a person can't get into a snit and be mean to everyone around him out of bad motives, then life is certainly not worth living. Or, better yet, if the law prohibits on pain of a jail sentence flying off into a passion[103] and exhibiting a nasty temper, then such a law is hopelessly out of touch with human nature.

At the risk of overkill, let us elaborate upon a few of these cases. "Trash talk" has become so disruptive an occurrence in the National Basketball Association that the rules were changed so as to incorporate a prohibition of this behavior. (This is similar to the National Football League player who scores a touchdown, and then does a goal line dance aimed to humiliate the other team; it, too, has been proscribed). Similarly, if a rich woman were to employ spies to find out what kind a dress her victim intended to wear, and then hired a dress maker to copy her wardrobe, she could humiliate the latter.

Then, too, harm is totally subjective, very much in the eyes of the beholder. A deadly insult to one person is something another sloughs off in apathy or non-recognition. If mere harm is to be elevated in law, and included in

---

[101] This is but the tip of the iceberg. Surely there are numerous other legal ways we can make a pain in the neck of ourselves to others.

[102] Whatever these are.

[103] Without, of course, violating the rights of person or property of anyone else through force, fraud, or the threat thereof

the criterion for lawlessness, our legal codes will look very different, and far more arbitrary than at present.

But this does not even begin to cover the difficulties posed in the text. For in addition to failing to define "morality," and to aggrandizing harm eradication into a basic legal principle, Berman also introduces[104] a new concept, "liberal," also without benefit of any definition or explication, and places this, too, at the core of his legal philosophy. He states: "The important question, however, is normative: what types of harms may a liberal society rely on to justify limiting individual liberty?" We shall see, below, just what other liberties (beside the right to engage in blackmail) this author thinks it justified for the state to violate, but the contrasting answer from the libertarian perspective should be clear: none.

Does Berman entirely avoid the question of defining what he means by morality? No. He does state the following:

> Moral blameworthiness' is also a nebulous concept. Although all the factors of which it is a function cannot be fully elucidated in this space, a few guideposts can be marked. In the easiest case, an individual's conduct is morally blameworthy when his objective is to inflict harm such as when he acts out of malice (in the lay sense) or spite. But this does not exhaust the subject. The average thief, after all, steals not in order to impose a loss on his victim, but for the purpose of obtaining a gain for himself. Yet this conduct, too, appears blameworthy even absent a law prohibiting it. The category of 'morally blameworthy' conduct, therefore, must be broad enough to include the conscious willingness to cause harm without adequate moral justification, where the amount and quality of justification required is commensurate with the magnitude of harm caused. Similarly, it should include the conscious willingness to risk harm to others without adequate moral justification.[105]

This, however, creates more problems than it solves. The most serious flaw is that it is a circular definition: it defines "morally blameworthy" in terms of inadequate "moral justification," and thus is of little help to would be critics who are still mystified by the concept. Berman also concedes that the concept is "nebulous." But not nebulous enough to preclude it from being made the guiding light of his legal philosophy in general, and his case against

---

[104] More accurately, he uses this concept all throughout his paper, without every once defining it, or justifying it as the lodestar of law.

[105] *See* Berman, *supra* note 1, at 840

blackmail legalization in particular. Further, not only is harm an integral and presumably independent part of his principle (3), but here, we learn, it also plays a role in defining morality. But if harm (eradication) is a poor bedrock upon which to build a legal system, the same goes for a morality based on this criterion. As well, if morality is defined in terms of harm (abolition), then why does principle (3) require two separate premises, one (a) mentioning harm, and the other (b) articulating moral blame worthiness?

Here is a second attempt at a definition:

> [W]e can articulate moral blameworthiness in terms of the actor's motivations for acting. Thus (as a first and rough pass), an actor has 'morally bad motives' and is therefore morally blameworthy' when he acts with the knowledge that his conduct will cause, threaten, or risk harm to others, unless: (1) he actually believes that his action will produce more good than evil; (2) that belief is a but for cause of his action; and (3) the standards the actor employs for measuring and evaluating 'evil' and 'good' in this case are defensible under common moral standards.[106]

This may not be the first pass at the issue, but it certainly is a "rough" one. It is also circular,[107] defining one concept of morality in terms of another. As well, it underlies yet another difficulty with this entire Berman enterprise: it is very heavy, indeed, on motives, and very light on actual criminal actions. This is wrong, and for several reasons. First, it is notoriously difficult to ascertain what motivates people, particularly if they attempt to disguise their true feelings. Second, motives are no more than thoughts; if we could be incarcerated for our mere cognitions, there probably isn't a one of us who would remain free under such a legal regime.

---

106 *Id.* at 840–41. I would hate to put this to the test under the "common moral standards" prevalent in Nazi Germany, or in the U.S.S.R.

107 Berman offers yet another circular definition of morality when he says "commission of the proscribed conduct is ordinarily morally blameworthy insofar as it reflects the knowing violation of a valid criminal law." *Id.*, fn. 142. But what is a valid law? Presumably one in which morally blameworthy acts are punished.

B. Harm and bad motive

Prof. Berman starts off this section on the interrogatory: "[W]e have reached the critical questions: (a) does blackmail (ordinarily) cause cognizable harm? and (b) does the blackmailer (ordinarily) harbor bad motives?"[109]

The easy answer, at least from this quarter, is yes, blackmail most certainly does cause harm,[109] if compared with the situation in which the secret has not been uncovered. However, assuming that the information has been revealed, blackmail does *not* cause harm, when compared to gossip. And yet, even if blackmail *did* cause harm, there would be no warrant for prohibiting it, unless we also criminalized the other nasty practices mentioned above. As to bad or immoral motives, we stipulate that this is so, but wonder why this should be either necessary or sufficient for criminal behavior.[110]

Berman continues his analysis: "Regardless of whether the third criterion for criminalization rests on consequentialist or retributive justifications, it cannot require that the conduct examined always cause (or threaten) harm and be undertaken with bad motives. Such a requirement would make *ex ante* line drawing impossible. Although one or another more precise qualifiers might appear more apt on further scrutiny, 'ordinarily' serves as a satisfactory placeholder with the important qualification that it not be understood to require that harm or bad motives occur 'more often than not.' There is no *a priori* reason why making certain conduct criminal must be improper when 'only,' say, 40 percent of given conduct is undertaken with bad motives."[111]

But this is almost purposeful obfuscation. Mentioning that an act is motivated by only a certain percentage of bad motivation constitutes a *reductio ad absurdum* of the system better mentioned by a critic than a proponent.[112] "Ordinarily," and "more often than not," in other contexts might full well suffice. At present, however, we are discussing jail sentences for criminals. It seems almost irresponsible to consent to such inexactitude in such a situation.

I am willing to stipulate, if only for the sake of argument, that blackmail is harmful. It appears, though, that Berman is unwilling to do so. In his criti-

---

[108] *Id.* at 841.

[109] To the blackmailee, but perhaps good to the persons who hear the secret (e.g., the cuckolded husband).

[110] If we stipulate that Hitler and Stalin were well motivated and intended to do good (e.g., eliminate vermin) would this save them from criminal charges? Hardly.

[111] Berman, *supra* note 1, fn. 152.

[112] An economics joke (a contradiction in terms?) has it that economists give exact predictions to show they have a sense of humor. But at least economic predictions are in terms of quantities which admit of exact measurement, unlike "bad motives."

cism of Gordon,[113] Berman criticizes her "assertion that 'the blackmailer's end is harm.' What does this mean?," says Berman. "Surely not that his motive is to cause harm, for presumably the average blackmailer's motive, like that of the garden variety thief, is merely to obtain a personal benefit."[114] But doesn't even the "garden variety thief" cause harm? And isn't this why Berman wants to criminalize his acts? One is tempted to ask, doesn't immoral mean not being nice? And whatever the defenders of legalized blackmail have said in its favor, it being nice has never been one of them.

Although hyper critical of Gordon on this point, Berman passes without demur her statement "the blackmailer violates deontological constraints if he threatens disclosure in order to obtain money or other advantage because his intent is directed to the money, not to the [lawfulness of] the disclosure or beneficial side effects that might be produced."[115] But why should a desire to earn money be construed as criminal? Surely, this is done only on the other side of what used to be considered the Iron Curtain?

Suppose my motive in an athletic competition is not the beauty of the enterprise, nor the thrill of physical exertion, nor yet an attempt to engage in sportsmanlike conduct, and not even the joy of participating. Rather, it is to beat the living stuffing out of the opponent, and to humiliate him by running up the score. Presumably, I am guilty of bad motives. If I whip him, especially if I am a "bad winner," I will succeed in my nefarious goal. This will certainly harm my opponent. Should I go to jail for this harmful and immoral behavior? This seems to be Berman's view.

Berman next considers the release of negative information, and how it can harm reputations: "Plainly, the simple disclosure of information likely to injure another's reputation satisfies the harm requirement (at least when the claimed injury is of a sufficiently substantial degree as to warrant society's protection). Injury to reputation is clearly other regarding harm. Moreover, it is a harm that has long been legally cognizable civilly and criminally under both common and statutory law."[116]

But this will not work, and on many levels. A minor point is legal positivism: just because it is indeed the law to punish people who indulge their free speech rights as libelers and slanderers, does not make it right.

The major point is that reputations are simply not the sorts of things that can be owned, by the very nature of things. This is why extant law on this

---

[113] Wendy J. Gordon, *Truth and Consequences: The Force of Blackmail's Central Case*, 141 U. Pa. L. Rev. 1741, 1758 (1993).

[114] Berman, *supra* note 1, at 842.

[115] Gordon, *supra* note 113, at 1758.

[116] Berman, *supra* note 1, at 843.

matter is simply wrong headed. Reputations consist of the thoughts of other people, about a given person. His own views about himself do not count. For example, the reputation of A, consists of the thoughts of other people, B … Z, about him, A. A's opinion of himself counts not one whit in making up his, A's, reputation. Similarly, the reputation of B consists of the thoughts of other people, A, C … Z, about him, B. B's opinion of himself counts not one whit in making up his, B's, reputation. But it is *impossible* to own the thoughts of other people.[117] That being the case, it is also quite inconceivable that C could *steal* D's reputation from him, for to do so would be to change the minds of A, B, E … Z about D. If this be the case, then libel is a victimless crime; it is not at all like stealing someone's wrist watch.[118]

Somewhat paradoxically, people work hard to establish their reputations. They can even sell them, as "goodwill," e.g., when they are attached to a business. Nevertheless, since we each own ourselves, and no one else.

If it were really true that people could have a property right in their reputation, then all sorts of acts that are now legal, and properly so, would become outlawed. For example, negative movie reviews reduce the reputation of their producers and actors; negative book reviews have the same effect on their authors; critical commentary from a radio or television sportscaster can ruin the bankability of a professional athlete. This present Article is critical of that written by Berman; if it succeeds in convincing the legal philosophical fraternity of the errors of his ways, Berman's reputation as a legal philosopher shall suffer. According to the theory now under discussion, all of the "victims" of these critiques would have the right to sue, and to collect, from their detractors.[119]

Berman on libel:

> This is not to say that such conduct should be criminal. Each of the
> three criteria provides only prima facie justification for criminaliz-

---

[117] We are having enough trouble owning our *own* thoughts, e.g., not being punished for them, thanks to hate crimes and hate speech legislation.

[118] For more on the libertarian theory of legalizing libel and slander, *see* Rothbard, *supra* note 68, at 126–28; Block, *supra* note 45, at 59–62.

[119] If the critique in this Article of Berman does not succeed, my reputation will suffer. Would I then have the right to sue and collect from Berman? That would appear to be an implication of his thesis. True, if I fail, it will be no one's fault but my own. On the other hand, assuming this eventuality, Berman will share part of the blame (take it all on?), since if his article were not so brilliant, I might well have succeeded. In any case, my reputation will be tarnished and, according to his theory, he will at least be a causal element in my downfall. Given that we are a litigious society, I think I'll sue him, in that eventuality.

ing conduct; none demands it. A legislature could choose not to criminalize reputation threatening disclosures undertaken with morally bad motives if it concludes that such disclosures advance social welfare. Moreover, other legal norms, including a constitutional guarantee, might mandate non-criminalization. As noted earlier, the Supreme Court has already construed the First Amendment to prohibit criminal punishment of true speech regarding matters of public interest.[120]

Several reactions. First, either these three criteria offered by Berman imply that certain laws are justified, or they do not. If, in his opinion, there merely "provide … only prima facie justification for criminalizing conduct" then they are incomplete, even considering all three together. That is, his criteria are underspecified. Second, the goal of "advanc[ing] social welfare" is the last refuge of the legal philosopher at sea without a rudder. There is no dictator, however totalitarian, who does not hide behind it. Third, while Berman has taken legal positivist positions all throughout his essay, he curiously declines to take this step with regard to libel law. That is, for the legal positivist, the fact that the Supreme Court has made a pronunciamento about an issue should be definitive. Why not in this case? Could it be because that whenever the extant law suits his purpose he is happy to clothe himself in it, and when it does not, not?

How does all of this relate to blackmail? Berman notes that it is "profoundly difficult to obtain direct evidence of an actor's mental state" such as

---

[120] Berman, *supra* note 1, at fn. 180.

"malice," and that a "disclosure made anonymously"[121] would do just fine in this regard.[122] So, too, would blackmail. In Berman's words:

> Surely it is probative. Consider, for example, a criminal libel prosecution (in a jurisdiction where blackmail is legal) involving defendants (D's) disclosure of a husband's (H's) infidelities to his wife (W). Here, D's prior (unaccepted) offer to refrain, for a payment of $1,000, from disclosing the adultery is circumstantial evidence that, when he proceeded to reveal H's secrets, D was not motivated by loyalty to W, or by an interest in achieving some measure of corrective justice, or by devotion to The Truth. A reasonable factfinder could suspect that, had any of these interests motivated D, he would not have offered to sell H his silence. This is not just a covert way of giving effect to the factfinder's own ethical belief that D should not have offered to remain silent for individual gain. It is empirically true that people value goods and interests in diverse and incommensurable ways and, relatedly, that most people have internalized a norm against commodifying certain types of nonmaterial interests and obligations. It is therefore reasonable to assume that most people who recognize morally persuasive grounds for undertaking a given course of action would not offer to sell abstention from it for personal gain."[123]

---

[121], Berman reports on "*Pennsylvania v. Foley*, 292 Pa 277, 141 A. 50, 51–52 (1928) (affirming conviction under statute prohibiting 'the sending of anonymous communications of a … defamatory … nature,' and explain(s) that anonymous publications of defamatory material 'show such a malignity of heart and a desire to do personal injury that the Legislature or the courts may properly hold that such publications are so far malicious or negligent as to be unjustifiable')." *Id.* at fn. 172. I am not so sure about this. My children, now in their early 20's, simply will not listen to me, despite my good intentions with regard to them, and my greater life's experiences, and have not done so for at least the last 5 years. This citation gives me an idea. I will from now on, instead of myself directly telling them of their faults and how to correct them—which I have often done but to no avail—will do so henceforth on an anonymous basis. If I do so, I will be "sending anonymous communications of a … defamatory … nature." Their peccadillos are certainly defamatory, if anything is. But will this "show such a malignity of heart and a desire to do personal injury that the Legislature or the courts may properly hold that such publications are so far malicious or negligent as to be unjustifiable?" Hardly. Remember, I am their loving dad. I mean only what is best for them.

[122] Berman, *supra* note 1, at 845.

[123] Berman, *supra* note 1, at 846.

According to Shakespeare, "There are more things in heaven and earth, Horatio, / Than are dreamt of in your philosophy."[124] In similar manner, we can say of Berman that human motivation is more complex than he incorporates into his analysis. Yes, it is entirely possible that D acted from purely financial motives. But why is this, necessarily, an indication of bad faith, or malevolence? Prof. Berman, himself, accepts a salary in return for his efforts. Are we to impugn his motivations on this ground? Further, cannot motivation be over determined? That is, could not D have been acting out of several motives, some of them good, others bad,[125] like most people on earth? For example, D (the blackmailer) might have intended to punish H for his adultery. And not only that: he might have hoped to double cross the husband and, out of concern for the wife, or for The Truth, told about the secret in any case.[126]

It is also somewhat disquieting to learn that Berman relies heavily on the fact that "most people who recognize morally persuasive grounds for undertaking a given course of action would not offer to sell abstention from it for

---

[124] WILLIAM SHAKESPEARE, HAMLET act 1, sc. 5.

[125] We continue to stipulate, in the absence of any definition of these terms by our author, that we are somehow in any case on the same wavelength with regard to them.

[126] Berman is correct in asserting that "most people have internalized a norm against commodifying certain types of nonmaterial interests and obligations." For a critique of these views, *see* Rothbard, *supra* note 68, at 126–28; Block, *supra* note 45, at 59–62.

personal gain." What "most people" do, or do not do,[127] should surely not be recognized by the criminal law.[128]

All of this, of course, is a bit beside the point. For even if we admit that the blackmailer *was* motivated by selfish pecuniary gains, not devotion to the Truth, nor the wife's interest in knowing of the infidelity, Berman still cannot justify jailing the blackmailer, for he was threatening to do no more than he had every right to do. The fact that he caused "harm" and did this "maliciously" should be of exactly zero moment as far as the law is concerned. For we are all guilty of engaging in malicious harm pretty much every day.[129]

Berman's analysis of the Milverton case is nothing short of superb. This alludes to a fictional character of Arthur Conan Doyle,[130] an arch blackmailer,

---

[127] It is contended by Goldhagen, for example, that most Germans in the pre world war period supported the acts of the Nazi regime. Surely no implications follow from this according to which we must support the views on law of "most people." See, generally, DANIEL JONAH GOLDHAGEN, HITLER'S WILLING EXECUTIONERS : ORDINARY GERMANS AND THE HOLOCAUST (1996).

[128] Berman also states: "the probability that a morally bad disclosure of adultery occurred after the discloser had offered to remain silent for a fee is greater than the probability that a morally good adultery disclosure occurred subsequent to such an offer," and "the conditional threat probably makes it *significantly* more likely that the disclosure was morally blameworthy." Berman, *supra* note 1, at 846–47. The problem, here, is that criminal guilt is supposed to be established by proof "beyond a reasonable doubt," not based on a "balance of the probabilities." Berman is, however, advocating criminalization based on the latter, not the former. Courts are supposed to get at the truth. Maybe not with a capital "T," but truth nonetheless. A defendant is supposed to be *proven* guilty, beyond a reasonable doubt. But here, by the author's own stipulation, there is no proof. If there is none, there can be no guilt. If there is no guilt, if there can be no guilt, this is tantamount to saying that blackmail ought to be legalized. We are here assuming that if there is harm and an indication (not a proof) of malice, there has been a crime committed. But if I open up a store to compete against yours, or seduce your girlfriend, out of bad motives, then there is harm and malice. Jail for me seems to be Berman's implication. If so, it is unwarranted. In another context Berman does mention the concept of reasonable doubt (*see* his footnote 201). But he does not apply this to behavior. Rather, he confines this concern to determining whether or not "the actor would have lacked morally justifying motives for engaging in (an) act."

[129] Block, *supra* note 45, at 101-06. Ok, there are a few saints out there. This doesn't apply to everyone.

[130] ARTHUR CONAN DOYLE, "The Adventure of Charles Augustus Milverton, in1 SHERLOCK HOLMES: THE COMPLETE NOVELS AND STORIES at 791 (Bantam 1986). Milverton is also discussed in MICHAEL HEPWORTH, BLACKMAIL: PUBLICITY AND SECRECY IN EVERYDAY LIFE, AT 46-47 (1975) and in chapter 5, this volume.

who is considered by Sherlock Holmes to be the "worst man" in London. But Berman sees right through this:

> Maybe so, but Milverton could be worse still. Imagine that he is as cunning and ruthless as Conan Doyle represents, but that he is motivated by something other than money. Already rich as Croesus, Milverton acquires information not to blackmail but merely to reveal, for he takes greater pleasure in causing pain and suffering than in aggregating further wealth. This Milverton would never consider offering his victim a choice of harms; he will disclose every bit of embarrassing and discrediting information he obtains at the moment most damaging to its subject."[131]

However, Berman does not draw the obvious and logical conclusion: that if the blabbing Milverton is even worse that the blackmailing Milverton, and the first amendment precludes outlawing the gossip,[132] then *certainly* the blackmailer must be above the law. Instead, he turns things around and opines: "All this suggests that, First Amendment considerations aside, the morally blameworthy disclosure of harmful information could be made criminal."[133]

Berman now moves on to what he calls the solution of the secondary puzzle: showing that blackmail is not really a voluntary trade between money and silence, but rather a coercive act. He starts off by approvingly citing Sullivan[134] to the effect that "coercion 'is inevitably normative .... It necessarily embodies a conclusion about the wrongfulness of a proposal.'"[135]

Continues Berman:

> Surely, then, if a proposed course of action is wrong in itself, the conditional proposal is coercive (at least where the recipient of the proposal views the proposed action as detrimental to her own interests). But normative concerns are not limited to whether a proposal is inherently wrongful in either an objective or conventional sense; they extend as well to considerations of the moral character of an actor's motives for advancing a proposal that is itself morally ambiguous. Although clarity may sometimes be enhanced by term-

---

[131] Berman, *supra* note 1, at 851.

[132] *Id*, at 852.

[133] *Id*.

[134] Kathleen M. Sullivan, *Unconstitutional Conditions*, 102 HARV L. REV. 1413, 1443 (1989).

[135] Berman, *supra* note 1, at 852.

ing an immoral proposal 'wrongful' and an immorally motivated one 'bad,' we should not insist on the distinction at all costs. To the contrary, inasmuch as the conditional offer tends to reveal that the actor would lack morally adequate reasons for engaging in his threatened course of conduct, a refusal to recognize this particular proposal made by this particular actor on this particular occasion as "wrongful" beclouds more than it illuminates. Put otherwise, perhaps we should not rigidly insist that the moral character of acts be judged independently of the motives behind them. It follows that the blackmail victim is just as coerced as the holdup victim.[136]

The last sentence is surely a *non sequitur*. It simply does not follow from the premises. The holdup victim is in a very different position than the blackmailee. It cannot possibly be overemphasized how stark is this difference. Yes, of both are demanded money[137] and each is offered an alternative. But the option offered to the holdup victim is a bullet in the chest, something the gunman has no right to "offer," or, rather, threaten. In very sharp contrast, the blackmailee's alternative is to be subjected to the blackmailer broadcasting from the rooftops information that he would like kept secret. However, the blackmailer *has every right* to engage in such an exercise of free speech! That is, if this needs further elaboration, the holdup man has no right to do what he threatens, while the blackmailer has every right to put into effect the quite different threat he makes.

But Berman is not without a reply. In his view:

> Put otherwise, theorists who deny that blackmail is coercive or that the blackmail victim acts under duress fail to understand or validate the victim's perspective as participant in a particular human drama. Were she to articulate her sense of being coerced, the victim would be more likely to emphasize the particular complaint that her blackmailer ought not to do as he threatens, not the more abstract objection that what the blackmailer threatens ought not be done.[138]

Berman's blackmail victim can complain all she wants that "her blackmailer ought not to do as he threatens," but her complaint would lack validity each time. What is it, after all, that the blackmailer is threatening? No more

---

[136] Berman, *supra* note 1, at 852-853.

[137] Or other valuable considerations

[138] Berman, *supra* note 1, at 852 fn. 197.

than to exercise his rights of free speech to engage in gossip, to put a word in the ear of the people who the blackmailee fears the most. But this right is not contested by anyone, least of all Berman. How, then, can Berman take the side of the blackmailee in this case, and support her complaint?[139]

If we are to sympathetically "understand or validate the victim's perspective as participant in (this) particular human drama," why not in other cases? For example, consider people who pay high rents, receive low wages and do not win the lottery, even though they regularly purchase tickets. It takes no stretch of the imagination to think of them as aggrieved. They, too, like Berman's blackmailee, can "complain." Does this mean we are justified in enacting rent control, a minimum wage law, and a rule mandating that all regular ticket buyers must win the lottery? Hardly. Yet this seems to be implied by Berman's remarks.

Where did Berman go wrong? Although this can only be speculative,[140] it seems to stem from the Sullivan claim that coercion is inevitably wrongful in the moral sense of the word that Berman seems to employ. Take a case in point. I see a man about to jump off a bridge in a suicide attempt. I am bigger and stronger than him, and I use my power to stop him. I do so by use of physical force, or coercion. Yet, normatively, most people, certainly including self-styled "liberals" such as Berman, would undoubtedly approve of my act. Here, then, is a case where coercion is not at all normative, at least in the negative sense.[141]

IV. TESTING THE EVIDENTIARY THEORY

We now arrive at the last section of Berman's paper, where he tests his evidentiary theory against other mainstream[142] views of blackmail. He analyzes seven different types of cases, and we will comment on each.

---

[139] There is an explanation not yet examined by Berman or any other legal theorist who favors the *status quo* on blackmail prohibition as to why blackmailees feel so aggrieved, and filled with outraged and righteous indignation at their treatment. Could this phenomenon be due to their own support for present law in this regard?

[140] I am much more modest about the possibility of seeing into another person's thought processes or motivations than is Berman.

[141] That is, according to what I am able to discern of "liberal" morality. For the libertarian, of course, mine would be a coercive act and therefore unjustified.

[142] He nowhere confronts the libertarian claim that blackmail should be legalized.

1. "Hard" bargains

The hard bargain is a case where the seller jacks up the price when he knows the buyer is desperate. Is this blackmail? One would think that on the basis of "evidentiary theory," it would be. After all, the buyer is harmed by such opportunistic behavior, and the seller certainly can do this out of mean or nasty or immoral motives. But Berman resists this notion. He gives the following example:

> Consider an antique dealer possessed of a cheap and ugly vase that, despite her best efforts, she has been unable to unload for years. One day she receives a visit from an eccentric multimillionaire who announces that the vase is precisely what he needs to complete his collection and cap a lifelong search. When he asks the price, the dealer answers that she will not part with it for a penny less than $10 million. The collector, not a complete fool, is flabbergasted. 'But it's not worth anywhere near that much!' he argues. 'Very true,' the dealer responds. 'Indeed, just before you walked in, I was considering throwing it out to make space for other merchandise. But I know both that you want it and that you can afford my new price. Take it or leave it.'

> Whatever we might think of the dealer's behavior, we could not plausibly condemn it as criminal so long as we (rightly) refrain from imposing price controls or a ban on price discrimination in all its forms. Any satisfactory theory of blackmail must, therefore, coherently explain why the hard bargain is not blackmail. The evidentiary theory provides just such an explanation. It begins by considering the act threatened in this case, to retain ownership of the vase. Very simply, this action could not be criminalized no matter what an observer might infer about the motives of the actor because it would not satisfy the harm requirement. Plainly, the collector has no legally protected interest in the vase; neither does the public at large (though we can imagine systems of property law under which it would). By withholding from the collector a benefit in which he has no legal interest, the dealer cannot inflict legally cognizable harm. Because the dealer's reasons for keeping the vase or even for destroying it, were that her choice are legally immaterial, a conditional threat to do either unless paid off cannot provide any legally relevant information. Therefore, the conditional threat should be as legal as the unconditional performance of the act. In

terms of the evidentiary blackmail test, a 'hard bargain' is not criminal blackmail because, under the second step from Section III.A, the acts threatened (to keep the vase or even to destroy it) would not inflict legal harm.[143]

This argument is fundamentally flawed in several different respects. First, "Vase, schmase" — Berman gives us an example of an aggrieved millionaire, about whom it is difficult for anyone to tug at the heartstrings. As a "liberal" he could have better utilized the example offered by Murphy, which Berman himself cites.[144] Here, it is not a disappointed millionaire and a vase, but rather a little boy, dying of a dread disease, who wants to have a baseball autographed by Babe Ruth, but the owner, unconscionably raises the price almost beyond reach. Here, surely, we can see real *harm*, can we not.[145] And just as certainly, anyone who would tease, abuse, beset and harass a young boy in this condition could not do so out of bad motives?

Second, what is this with not "imposing price controls or a ban on price discrimination?" How is this derived from "evidentiary theory?" Nor is this consistent with Berman's allegiance to "liberalism," at least if this word is understood in its North American 20th and 21st century, not its European and 19th century meaning. Why *shouldn't* a liberal society impose such laws, to protect the weak and downtrodden from "harm" and "malice?"[146]

Third, a minor point. The value of the vase is whatever its owner says it is. Technically, it is equal to the value of the next best opportunity for it, or alternative cost. The value might well have been zero before the advent of the millionaire, but afterward, its value to the owner evidently rose. Berman's view to the contrary bespeaks a Marxist orientation,[147] where the value of items inheres in them, and is not determined by human actor evaluators.

Fourth, coercion. In ordinary parlance we would give short shrift to the argument that the vase or baseball owner "coerced" the buyer, by raising the price of these items. But these are not ordinary times. Berman, himself, is on record as using coercion in an incompatible manner. He supported Sulli-

---

[143] Berman, *supra* note 1, at 852–53.

[144] *Id.* at 866 fn. 204 (referring to Murphy's hypothetical owner of the Babe-Ruth-autographed baseball in G. Murphy Jeffrie, *Blackmail: A Preliminary Inquiry*, 63 MONIST 156 (1980).

[145] Small dying boys can feel real harm about baseballs, but presumably millionaires cannot about vases.

[146] Needless to say, such denigrations of private property rights would not be countenanced under libertarianism.

[147] Here, the value is based on the number of "labor hours" which have gone into its manufacture.

van's[148] claim that coercion is inevitably wrongful in the moral sense of the word. If it is not immoral to jack up the price of a baseball that can make more enjoyable the last days of a dying boy's life, then it is hard to know what is.

Berman has one more arrow in his quiver, however: "It is telling that the hard bargain 'fails' the blackmail test at the second step, rather than the fourth. The hard bargainer may (at least in certain cases) act with motives we might wish to condemn as immoral, though we do not believe her conduct should be made criminal. Put another way, there is a reasonable sense in which our hypothetical millionaire collector might sputter with outrage, 'But that's blackmail!' even though he knows that the dealer's proposition is lawful and believes that it should remain so."[149]

And what, in turn, is "the second step?" It is:

> [I]f the act, y, is not itself criminal, ask whether it causes or threatens legally cognizable harm. If it does not, then it cannot be made criminal (or at least not on the strength of the third criterion of criminalization). Certainly, one might be tempted to call at least some propositions that fall out at this stage "blackmail," and the designation could be appropriate so long as we are speaking of moral rather than legal offenses. However, the purpose of this inquiry is to determine the proper scope of a criminal prohibition. Accordingly, when performing the act threatened would impose a "disutility" that society would not deem a legal harm, this step of the test concludes that the proposition is not blackmail.[150]

This, of course, opens up another inquiry.[151] What is "legally cognizable" harm? Once again, Berman rides to the rescue: "society could (and often does) recognize injury to reputation as legally cognizable harm, a legislature could unproblematically criminalize all disclosures of embarrassing informa-

---

[148] *See* Berman, *supra* note 1, at fn. 193.

[149] *Id.* at 856–57 fn. 205. But the same could be said for any other blackmailee, once he was convinced that to gossip is not a crime, and to threaten that which is not a crime is also not a crime. Berman has appreciated so little of the libertarian case for blackmail legalization that he takes it as a given that if an act is legal, it *cannot* be blackmail. But this argument is odd. Why cannot the millionaire vase collector *both* be a blackmailee, *and* concede "that the dealer's proposition is lawful?"

[150] *Id.* at 854–55.

[151] *Id.* at 858–61.

tion so long as we could reasonably believe that most persons who make such disclosures do so with morally unacceptable motives."[152]

Thus, the case against Berman is straightforward. He says that hard bargaining is not blackmail because of the "second step." This maintains that something should be illegal if it creates "legally cognizable" harm, which means, "done with morally unacceptable motives." But what could be more "morally unacceptable" than immiserating a young boy on his very death bed?

2. Market price blackmail

What is market price blackmail? It is the demand for no more money from the blackmailee than would be obtainable elsewhere, say from a tabloid newspaper, for keeping a secret. Since Berman comes down on the correct (libertarian) side of this issue—it should be legalized—I have no trouble with his conclusion. But his reasoning leaves something to be desired.

First and foremost, the only difference between this type of blackmail and any other is that the blackmailer forbears to ask for as much money as might otherwise be available. He is willing to accept from the blackmailee only the lesser amount he could garner from a tabloid, and forbears to demand the presumably greater amount which might be forthcoming from the blackmailee, were he pushed to the limit. However, this is inconsistent with Ber-

---

[152] *Id.* at 798–99.

man's view that "we (rightly) refrain from imposing price controls."[153] If price controls are illegitimate, it seems farfetched to call legal an otherwise (even for him) licit act the only difference from which is that it occurs at a higher price. Why this prejudice against maximizing profits? Yes, "the seller's purpose is to make a buck," but why is this "not a motivation that makes the harm-causing sale morally justifiable?"[154] What is so wrong with making a buck? Is there no such thing as an honest buck?

Second, Berman opines: "B (the blackmailer) should be permitted to sell T (the tabloid) reputationally harmful information about public figure A, even though ... the class of persons who make the unconditional sale to T are probably not less morally blameworthy than those who make a conditional offer to A."[155] This might well be acceptable coming from almost any other commentator, but from Berman, who makes such a strong case about morality, almost a fetish, it is invalid. Why does his concern vanish in this one case?

---

[153] *Id.* at 856. Berman blatantly contradicts himself when he says "The state can regulate the price B may charge A for non-publication capping it at the market price for the same reason the state engages in price regulation elsewhere. Price regulation is a common way of limiting the monopolist's price to a hypothetical competitive price. And the blackmailer (market price, supramarket price, or otherwise) must be a monopolist (or, at least, an oligopolist) of the information he threatens to reveal, else his offer of secrecy would have little value." *Id.* at 856 fn. 213. At this level of generalization, monopoly abounds. For example, marriage is an example of bilateral monopoly, for each spouse, by law, is the only one who can serve certain needs of the other; on this basis, there is no keeping the government out of the bedroom. For the libertarian case against price control in all so-called cases of "monopoly," *see* DOMINICK T. ARMENTANO, THE MYTHS OF ANTITRUST (1972); DOMINICK T. ARMENTANO, ANTITRUST AND MONOPOLY: ANATOMY OF A POLICY FAILURE (1982); DOMINICK T. ARMENTANO, ANTITRUST POLICY: THE CASE FOR REPEAL (1991); DONALD ARMSTRONG, COMPETITION VERSUS MONOPOLY: COMBINES POLICY IN PERSPECTIVE (1982); WALTER BLOCK, AMENDING THE COMBINES INVESTIGATION ACT (1982); Walter Block, *Austrian Monopoly Theory—a Critique*, 1 J. LIBERTARIAN STUD. 271 (1977); Walter Block, *Total Repeal of Anti-trust Legislation: A Critique of Bork, Brozen and Posner*, 8 REV. AUS. ECON. 35 (1994); Thomas J. DiLorenzo, *The Myth of Natural Monopoly*, 9 Rev. Aus. Econ. 43 (1997); Donald J. Boudreaux and Thomas J. DiLorenzo, *The Protectionist Roots of Antitrust*, 6 REV. AUS. ECON. 81 (1992); Jack High, *Bork's Paradox: Static vs Dynamic Efficiency in Antitrust Analysis*, 3 CONTEMP. POL'Y ISSUES 21 (1984); Fred McChesney, *Antitrust and Regulation: Chicago's Contradictory Views*, 10 CATO J. 775 (1991); Robert McGee, *Mergers and Acquisitions: An Economic and Legal Analysis*, 22 CREIGHTON L. REV. 665 (1998); MURRAY N. ROTHBARD, MAN, ECONOMY AND STATE (1970); William F. Shugart II, *Don't Revise the Clayton Act, Scrap It!*, 6 CATO J. 925 (1987); Fred L. Smith, Jr., *Why not Abolish Antitrust?*, REG. 23 (1983).

[154] Berman, *supra* note 1, at 859.

[155] *Id.* at 859-860.

Third, in his reasoning on this topic, Berman exhibits some strange views of rights enjoyed by public figures vis-à-vis the rest of us. In his view:

> Insofar as public figures have elicited public interest thus creating the market necessary to produce a market price by voluntarily entering the realm of public attention, they have made their private lives, to some extent and in some indistinct sense, public commodities. It could be argued, therefore, that by seeking and achieving celebrity, public figures have assumed the risk of widespread invasions of their privacy. Arguably, then, any harm such invasions may cause should not be legally cognizable.[156]

The objections to this thesis are telling. For one thing, this sets up two castes of people, with different rights: public figures, with lesser recourse to law, and non-public figures, with more.[157] This alone should suffice to sink any such legal doctrine, since all people have the same natural rights. For another, it is by no means true that all public figures "have elicited public interest." Some of the now famous may have achieved that "exalted" status from having been brutalized, or raped, or victimized in any number of other ways. As another example, it is difficult to see how Elian Gonzalez, or his mother for him, sought any public notoriety. [158]

To treat public figures differently in law from non-public figures is arbitrary and capricious. Such a doctrine would imply that different people have different rights, depending upon their status or class. This is not an aspect of the free society, but rather earmarked by the caste system. If a commoner punches the nose of a public figure, or the reverse occurs, it makes not the slightest bit of difference as a matter of law, at least under libertarianism; both

---

156 *Id.* at 858 fn. 208.

157 This pernicious doctrine, of course, emanates from libel case law. But as we have seen, in the free society there would be no interferences with free speech of this variety; hence, there is reason for such a distinction to even arise.

158 In the 2000 Olympics, Nancy Johnson the gold medal in the 10 meter air rifle competition. NEWSWEEK at 58 (Sept. 25, 2000). She finished 36th in the Atlanta Olympics of 1996 in this same event. Presumably, however, she tried equally hard on both occasions. Thus, she can hardly be said to have sought out her status as a public figure in a way that she had not, before. On the other hand, outside of the target shooting community, there is probably not person in a thousand who will recognize her name. Is she a public figure? Numerous teachers, doctors, lawyers, researchers, academics, work in obscurity all their lives, whereupon some medal or accolade is bestowed upon them. It cannot be said that any of them have "elicited" their subsequent public figure-hood in a way that millions of others, just like them apart from the recognition, have not.

are exactly treated alike. There is simply not one rule for the rich (or public figures) and another for the poor (those not in the limelight.) And this holds true, at least ideally[159] not only for a punch in the nose, but for murder, rape, theft, trespass, fraud, fender benders, indeed for virtually all laws. How, then, can there be one and only one exception: regarding libel and slander?

3. Crime exposure blackmail

Here the threat is not to reveal an embarrassing secret about the black-mailee, but rather to expose his criminal behavior to the authorities. As can be expected, Berman maintains it "should be both a crime and a ... serious offense."[160]

But why? Again, we have a jeremiad against "pure selfishness."[161] And, also, a focus on good intentions for the person who refuses to come forward with information of this sort: "Her silence may be motivated largely by fear of retaliation, by friendship and loyalty toward the criminal, and by fear of the police. Our sympathy for these motivations provides an explanation for the lenient treatment."[162]

But it seems artificial that (what could easily be construed as) cowardice, or radically misplaced[163] allegiance is considered morally good, while at-tempting to earn an honest dollar is denigrated on ethical grounds.

However, let the person who refuses to notify the police of a crime try to blackmail the criminal, and her motives take a sharp turn for the worse; then, Berman can throw the book at him.

The problem with this analysis is that there are no positive obligations. Good Samaritan laws are a violation of individual freedom. This being the case, the person with knowledge of a crime is not obliged to share that infor-mation with the police. As the owner of this data, he may do with it as he wishes, as long as he does not threaten or initiate violence against person or property. If he blackmails the criminal with what he has (legally) unearthed, he is not guilty of extortion. It matters not one whit who this harms or hurts. It should be legal to do this to anyone, except through physical violence,

---

[159] Yes, the rich public figures can afford better lawyers, but that is an entirely separate matter. Juries and judges are supposed to treat them in an identical manner, despite their very different backgrounds. But with the doctrine of the "public figure," this is not the case.

[160] Berman, *supra* note 1, at 863.

[161] *Id.*

[162] *Id.* at 862.

[163] We assume, now, that the crime in question is a real one (e.g., murder, rape, assault) and not a victimless one (such as drug trafficking, or prostitution or pornography).

threat, fraud or theft. Nor are motives of any consequence. At best intentions and thoughts can provide a modicum leniency (or not); they cannot, by themselves, or even in tandem with harms, determine whether an act is criminal or not.

4. Victim blackmail

What if the person who knows of the crime was the victim of it? Would this change matters? For once, Berman and I are in agreement: this will not make any difference whatsoever. From the libertarian perspective, blackmail should be legal in either case; for the "evidentiary theory," neither.

According to Berman: "Consequently, if we believe that all members of the community have a civic duty to report crime, then it cannot be morally acceptable for a victim to offer to ignore her obligation for personal gain— even if that gain is in some sense compensatory."[164]

But this rings hollow. Berman, as we have seen, was willing to mitigate such a duty in cases of fear or misplaced loyalty. How can he then rely upon civic duty in his analysis? Further, Berman approvingly cites Justice Marshall to the effect that: "It may be the duty of a citizen to accuse every offender, and to proclaim every offence [sic] which comes to his knowledge; but the law which would punish him in every case for not performing this duty is too harsh for man."[165] No truer words could ever be said. For if it really were a positive obligation it would be unending.

Berman and I do agree, however, that the fact that victim blackmail "is in some sense compensatory" is of no moment. He because he maintains it is not exculpatory, me because I take the position that anyone, victim or not, has a right to blackmail the criminal. Thus, compensation does not arise as a defense for either view.

5. Public interest blackmail

Berman starts off this section with the observation that "The typical blackmailer demands from his victim a cash payment to which he has no legitimate claim."[166] This sounds ominous, but it is not. It applies to each and

---

[164] *Id.* 863.

[165] *Id.* at 861–62 fn. 220 (*quoting* Chief Justice Marshall in *Marbury v. Brooks*, 20 U.S. 556, 557–76 (1822)). True, Berman qualifies this for a father-in-law concealing a forgery of a son-in-law, and for a case of treason where a father does not turn in a son, but this does not appear to be relevant to the present case.

[166] Berman, *supra* note 1, at 865.

every market transaction that has, or ever will, take place. For example, I buy a newspaper for $1. I have "no legitimate claim" to the newspaper, yet I "demand" it, in return for my $1. The vender is in the same position: He has "no legitimate claim" to my dollar, yet he, too, "demands" it, as payment for his newspaper. No, I as blackmailer have "no legitimate claim" to your $1,000, and yet I "demand" it, if you want me to keep secret the fact that you take a bath with a rubber duckie. On the other hand, you, too, have "no legitimate claim" to the information in my head[167] (about you and the duckie). And yet you "demand" that I keep quiet about it, in return for the $1,000 you give me.

Berman's main concern in this section is the analyze the situation when the object of desire of the blackmailer is not private gain, but public good. Will this impinge upon its legality?

For the libertarian view, it matters not what the goal is; blackmail is blackmail is blackmail, and it should be legal in any and all of its varieties. For the evidentiary theory, legal status depends upon the specifics of the case. The key, though, is whether the motives are moral:

> We can solve the puzzle of 'public interest blackmail' by examining what is presumed to be one of the most common blackmail threats, 'homosexual blackmail.' Assume B threatens to expose A's homosexuality (or homosexual acts) unless A pays B $1,000. This is an unproblematic case of criminal blackmail. And quick application of the evidentiary test explains why. The key (step 3) is to identify the morally justifying reasons B might have for exposing A. Different observers will have widely differing intuitions regarding which reasons do in fact supply moral justification for outing A. Most persons, I suspect, would recognize few if any motives as morally legitimate beyond protecting a benighted spouse or suitor. Others might endorse a more general interest in exposing homosexuals, perhaps as a means to discourage homosexual activity. B's conditional offer of silence (step 4) should have evidentiary significance to individuals who fall near either pole, however. B's willingness to remain silent for personal gain suggests that his motives for exposing A would satisfy neither the social liberal nor the cultural conservative.[168]

---

[167] We obviate an objection here by assuming I came to this knowledge legitimately, e.g., no trespass.

[168] Berman, *supra* note 1, at 865.

This seems a bit too narrow. Why consider only the moral sensibilities of the "social liberal" and "the cultural conservative?" There can be no doubt that neither would find "morally justifying reasons" in sheer naked greed, or the quest for the unholy buck. However, there are other perspectives from which these motives would be interpreted as fully acceptable.[169] Berman is willing to consider "widely differing intuitions" stretching all the way from the "social liberal" to the "cultural conservative," but no further. Pity. More generally, the fact that he consults only *some* systems of morality, but eschews others, without giving any reasons why the former should be ranked higher than the latter, is a difficulty with his system

Another problem is that his theory seems almost infinitely malleable, and inclusive. If one view doesn't fit, try another. He states: "Some people might conclude that outing is categorically unjustifiable. This view does not, however, undermine the evidentiary theory. One who believes there are no morally acceptable reasons for exposing an individual's homosexuality should, I submit, favor making outing illegal (on the second or third criteria of criminalization). They can then approve criminalizing homosexual blackmail on the grounds that it is (or should be) simple extortion."[170]

There would appear to be a one size fits all mentality, here. The theory can satisfy pretty much *any* view of morality. If so, it is "too good," in that it makes no distinctions between correct and incorrect perspectives. It is only saved from this fate by Berman's incomprehensible refusal to consider systems of morality such as ethical egoism.

6. Non-informational blackmail

Sometimes, what the blackmailer offers[171] to refrain from is not the disbursement of information which he has every right to disburse, but rather to engage in other acts which would be perfectly legal, but for the fact he is asking for money or other valuable consideration to refrain from undertaking them.

---

[169] Such as libertarianism, and objectivism. For the latter, any of the works of Ayn Rand.

[170] Berman, *supra* note 1, at 864 fn. 225.

[171] I could say, instead of "offers," "threatens." But it would amount to the same thing. For a "threat" to do something I have every right to do should be as legal as an "offer" to undertake the same act. On the other hand, suppose I "offer" to punch you in the nose. (We are not in a boxing ring, in which context this "offer" would be unexceptionable.) This, too, is illicit, despite being couched in the language of "offer" rather than "threat" since I do not have a right to carry through on this physically invasive act.

Katz[172] offers a few examples of this variety of blackmail, which are cited by Berman:

> 'Pay me $10,000, or I will seduce your fiancée'; 'Pay me $10,000, or I will persuade your son that it is his patriotic duty to volunteer for combat in Vietnam'; 'Pay me $10,000, or I will give your high-spirited, risk-addicted 19-year-old daughter a motorcycle for Christmas'; 'Pay me $10,000, or I will hasten our ailing father's death by leaving the Catholic Church.'[173]

Although Berman acknowledges that all these acts are "perfectly legal,"[174] he nevertheless persists is calling for their prohibition when coupled with offers to refrain, if paid off to do so. (As a good politically correct[175] "liberal,"[176] Berman would presumably also object to the request for sexual services of a woman by a man in lieu of refraining from the act which would otherwise be undertaken by the blackmailer. It is unclear as to what his position would be were the sexes reversed.) Why? Because "they also cause (or risk) cognizable harm,"[177] and are undertaken with bad motives. But Berman never calls for the abolition of hang gliding, or chocolate, or cigarettes, or other dangerous activities. As well, his analysis continues to be marred by the fact that he will accept practically anything under the sun as a good motive, with the exception of asking for (or demanding)[178] money. For example, if the thought of the blackmailer is that it is the son's "duty" to enlist, or that he will "profit from the experience,"[179] that is all well and good.

Berman even goes so far as to accuse the blackmailer who threatens to leave the Catholic Church a "murder[er] by religious conversion." This, if the threat was motivated by a desire to inherit from the father. But in this case the blackmail was not even the precipitating factor. Rather, the proximate cause of the father's death was the the departure of the son from the church.

The difficulty with this, from my critic's point of view, is that it is not easy to come up with as telling a *reductio ad absurdum* as this one, furnished by

---

[172] Berman, *supra* note 1, at 866, (*quoting* Katz, *supra* note 64, at 1567–68).
[173] *Id.* at 867.
[174] *Id.*
[175] There is no sexist language in his article. Berman does not adopt the traditional convention that "he" actually stands for "he or she."
[176] In the 20th century, not the 19th century sense.
[177] *Id.* at 867.
[178] The distinction between "asking for" and "demanding" is pretty much the same as between an "offer" and a "threat."
[179] *Id.*

Berman. But I'll try: I seduce your fiancée, and marry her myself. You commit suicide. I am guilty of murder. All I can say to this one is, "c'mon, give me a break." Here is another try. I marry someone I know my parents will hate. They will die of grief. I will inherit. Thus we have murder by marriage.

No, no, no. It pains me to have to say this, and I would never have thought to do so but for Berman, but no one should be found guilty of murder by merely leaving the church, buying a Christmas present, convincing someone to enter the army, marrying an "unsuitable" spouse in the eyes of one's parents, or seducing an adult woman.

7. Bribery

A bribery contract, in this context, is exactly the same as one for blackmail, only it is initiated by the blackmailee, not the blackmailer. Berman and I are in accord on this: when the blackmailee approaches a potential gossip, and pays him off not to tell the secret, this should be legal. As per usual, however, our respective reasoning is different. For me, this should be legal because it does not violate the libertarian axiom proscribing aggression. For Berman, this conclusion is justified because it does not involve "blameworthy, harm-causing conduct."[180]

But suppose a married woman commits adultery. I innocently witness it. She approaches me with an offer of $1,000 if I will keep my lips sealed about this event. Berman considers her innocent of any crime. However, this is a false analysis, inconsistent with his own evidentiary theory. For the woman did do something that, at least according to one moral code acknowledged by Berman, would be considered blameworthy. Namely, for the "cultural conservative,"[181] adultery is blameworthy. And so would be her attempt to cover up this sin by bribing me to keep quiet about the event. As well, at least a *prima facie* case can be made out that this attempted bribery on the part of the woman would be "harm-causing." For if I spill the beans to her husband, he may be able to take steps to improve his own situation. If he is kept in the dark on this, he will not. True, we might also interpret this as not "harm-causing." Perhaps ignorance is bliss, and the husband will be better off not knowing of his wife's infidelity. But Berman is very "liberal" in his interpreta-

---

[180] *Id.* at 869.

[181] *Id.* at 865.

tions; pretty much any "reasonable" interpretation[182] will do for him.[183] It is difficult, then, to see why he interprets his own evidentiary theory as unambiguously supportive of legalization for the unfaithful wife's attempt at bribery.

So much for the woman adulterer briber. What of the bribee–blackmailer? For Berman, this all depends upon: "(1) does the bribe taker cause legally cognizable harm? and (2) if so, does he have morally blameworthy motives?"[184] This is more than passing curious in that although they are the essence of his evidentiary theory, Berman has just eschewed them in the case of the briber. Here, he once again resorts to them. However, they will avail him little, in that they can be interpreted, as we have soon, in numerous ways, and can be tailored to fit just about any perspective. Yes, Berman will not apply these criteria in a way that incorporates moral perspectives with which he is not in sympathy, but this need not stop the rest of us. The briber and the bribee are equally likely to create "harm." Indeed, the one is the opposite side of the same coin as other. That Berman interprets them 180 degrees apart only indicates the arbitrary way he wields his own principles. And not only capricious. Berman's own language—"This is probably not legally cognizable harm," "not likely enough to have ... acted with morally blameworthy motives as to justify criminal punishment,"[185]—leaves something to be desired. If even the proponent of the theory cannot use it to answer questions of guilt, of what value is it to others?

Berman also is guilty of an elementary mistake in economic theory. He states that "B ... [can] profit at A's expense,"[186] where B is the bribee and possible blackmailer, and A is the adulterer briber. But trade, of whatever variety, shape or manner, including barter and those intermediated with money, must of necessity be *mutually* beneficial in the *ex ante* sense of anticipations, otherwise it would scarcely take place. That is, in the market, no one can ever "profit" at anyone else's "expense," in the sense that denies that such acts necessarily benefit both parties. If I purchase a newspaper for $1, then at the time of purchase I *must* rate the periodical itself, or at least something about[187]

---

[182] Berman states: "Different observers will have widely differing intuitions regarding which reasons do in fact supply moral justification for outing A." *Id.*

[183] Anything but ethical egoism, selfishness, making a buck, objectivism, Randianism or libertarianism.

[184] Berman, *supra* note 1, at 869.

[185] *Id.* at 870.

[186] *Id.*

[187] In another context, that having to do with Girl Scout cookies, Berman correctly notes that it need not be this dessert itself which is of definitive value. It could be, in the case he mentions, an attempt to curry favor with the girl scout's father. *Id.* at 831 fn. 127.

having it, more highly than the coin; as a mirror image, the vendor *cannot but* make the opposite ranking, namely, for him, the money is worth more than the newspaper. It is the same with A and B and bribery blackmail. If *both* parties did not value what they were to receive more than what they were to give up, the deal would never have been agreed to.

V. CONCLUSION

Berman's thesis can be neatly summarized by use of his principle (3), which stipulates that any act should be criminalized if it tends both (a) to cause or threaten identifiable harm, and (b) to be undertaken by a morally blameworthy actor.[188]

To this I say two things. First, "Harm, schmarm:" just because something is harmful does not mean it should be illegal. We do altogether too many things to each other that hurt one another. We have a right to do these things, since not a one of them violates the libertarian non-aggression axiom; e.g., initiates violence or the threat thereof to person or property, nor constitutes an unwarranted border crossing. Second, it is much the same thing with being morally blameworthy. To the extent this phrase has any meaning whatsoever, we are all guilty of it: we all forget to tell our loved ones how much we love them, we are all boorish from time to time, we omit birthday cards, and do many of the other acts mentioned above.[189]

Borrowing a leaf from Berman's book, I could with as much sense set up principle (4), which states that any act should be criminalized it if tends both (a) to begin with the letter "B," and (b) to be undertaken by a person sporting a pair of shoes. This would capture blackmail, alright, but it would also place in the net baseball, eating beans, and being boring. I suggest that Berman's principle (3) has much the same effect.

None of the acts such as publicly revealing embarrassing secrets, which are threatened by blackmailers, would earn a jail sentence from Berman, in and of themselves. But when they are "threatened" unless the "victim" pays off the initiator not to undertake them, and to add insult to injury, it could be somehow proven that they were enacted with malice aforethought, then, these become criminal acts for Berman. But this would be wildly over inclusive in any rational system of law. In fact, it would not be an exaggeration to say that under such a legal system, there would be no one left to condemn or imprison anyone, since we would all long since have been incarcerated. Which of us,

---

[188] *Id.* at 837.

[189] Block, *supra* note 45, at 101–06.

apart from a Mother Teresa, could be innocent of any of these acts for an entire lifetime?

How many of us have said things like the following hurtful (in a nasty mood, to cover malice) things which constitute blackmail: "If you don't clean up your room, you can't get the car keys!" "If you are not nice to me, there will be no sex tonight!" "If you don't give me that $1, I won't give you this *newspaper!*" "If you don't give me that newspaper, I won't give you this $1!"

Blackmail is not a paradox for the libertarian perspective; only for the mainstream commentators, who have not yet, any of them, nor will they, solve it. This is because it is not a paradox at all; rather, there is the fallacy of blackmail: twist and turn as they might, there is no way to turn two legal whites into a legal black.

If there is any paradox, it is this: how can so many otherwise smart people contort themselves into so many different fallacious positions in order to solve the nonexistent paradox of blackmail?

Chapter 15.

A Reply to Wexler: Libertarianism, Blackmail and Decency

Wexler's[1] vision of libertarianism is a hellish one indeed. Were it a correct rendition of this philosophy, I would join with him in not embracing it either. Perhaps he has attained his interpretation from reading only my article on blackmail[2] and from no other source. In my own defense, I was there concerned not with articulating libertarianism, but merely with applying it to the issue of blackmail. Let us clear up a few of his misconceptions, and perhaps thereby assure him that this perspective is not a diabolical one.[3]

1. Atomistic fallacy. Wexler characterizes as "anathema" law constructed on the vision that each person is "an island"[4] living in splendid isolation from all others. Apart from hermits' rights, that is not at all the essence of libertarianism. Societies, voluntary associations, churches, clubs, or any other consensual interactions are the order of the day for this philosophy. Markets are also instances of togetherness.[5] What advocates of this philosophy oppose, however, are some people forcing their will on others, in a totalitarian manner, in the name of "society."

2. Profit. Yes, libertarians advocate allowing businessmen to "profit from someone else's extreme need."[6] This sounds horrible. But profit is a far better motivator than political or bureaucratic institutions. The more extreme the need, the greater the profit, and the more alacrity with which firms will satisfy that need. It is no accident that the poor in countries which rely on monetary incentives to provide goods and services do far better than those in nations where private profit is regulated, or prohibited outright. If you want a vision

---

[1] Steve Wexler, *My Enemy's Enemy, But Not My Friend*, 34 U.B.C. L. Rev. 39 (2000).

[2] Reproduced at chapter 13 , this volume

[3] Seldom in the annals of scholarly discourse has an author actually admitted to irrationality, indeed, reveled in it. And yet Wexler's footnotes 4 and 14 hardly admit of any other interpretation. A similar analysis applies to his view that legal theory can never consistently explain the law. If he sticks to his guns in this regard, he will not even read what I say, let alone be convinced by it. However, I don't for a moment believe Wexler's protestations of irrationality. His brilliant writing style, his ability to see the fallacies of the "economic approach," not to mention his appreciation of my previous work in this regard, his keen understanding of Mill, render this stance, in my view, mere playacting.

[4] Wexler, *supra* note 1 at 39.

[5] Nozick calls them "capitalist acts between consenting adults." Robert Nozick, Anarchy, State and Utopia at 163 (1974)

[6] Wexler, *supra* note 1, at 40.

of hell, go to public housing projects in the U.S. where profits have been banned, or go to North Korea.

3. Duty. Libertarianism does not at all wish to "minimize the duties that people have," let alone is this its "sole goal."[7] Very much to the contrary, the tenets of this philosophy are adamant that people have all sorts of duties: to refrain from murder, rape, theft, fraud, assault, kidnapping, car jacking, the list goes on and on. We all have the negative right not to be molested in any way in our persons or property, and everyone has a correlative duty to respect this. As for so-called positive rights, e.g. the "right" to food, clothing or shelter to be taken from others at the point of a governmental gun, there are no such things. This is merely a prettified veneer for theft.

4. Direction of danger. Contrary to Wexler, libertarians see dangers to liberty emanating from two directions, both a paternalistic one of protecting man from himself (e.g. forced seat belts, helmets, social security, worker's compensation, unemployment insurance, laws against drugs and tobacco, etc.), and also from others, coercing good Samaritanism (e.g. welfare, equalization grants to poor provinces, etc.) As for the first, if people are smart enough to vote, they ought not be treated like children and told to save for their retirement, or how to dress for bicycle riding. Regarding the second, welfare is no way to "help others."[8] Rather, as the experience of eviscerating the initiative of Indians on reservations, of poor people on welfare, or third world countries through foreign "aid," these programs are all counterproductive.[9] It is not only paternalistic, it is condescending. What the poor need to lift themselves up by their bootstraps is not a handout, but freedom. Witness the economies of the five "tigers" of the far east in the last several decades, and compare them with those of Africa or South America.

5. Labor. The libertarian theory of how rights to property arise is based, roughly, on Lockean[10] homesteading theory. Here, just titles are gained by mixing one's *labour* with virgin land. So labour, far from "not [being] a prominent feature of libertarianism,"[11] is at its very core. Trade, too, includes

---

7 *Id.* at 41.

8 *Id.* at 42.

9 CHARLES MURRAY, LOSING GROUND: AMERICAN SOCIAL POLICY FROM 1950 TO 1980 (1984); PETER T. BAUER AND BASIL S. YAMEY, THE ECONOMICS OF UNDER-DEVELOPED COUNTRIES (1957); PETER T. BAUER, EQUALITY, THE THIRD WORLD, AND ECONOMIC DELUSION (1981).

10 John Locke, "An Essay Concerning the True Origin, Extent and End of Civil Government," at 27-28, in TWO TREATISES OF GOVERNMENT (1960); JOHN LOCKE, SECOND TREATISE OF CIVIL GOVERNMENT (1955).

11 Wexler, *supra* note 1, at 43.

the swap of labour for a wage. As for being a "wage slave,"[12] this is a veritable contradiction in terms. Working as an employee is a *voluntary* act, even if you need a job in order to live;[13] in very sharp contrast, slavery is a *coercive* state of affairs. Anyone who does not appreciate this distinction ought to take a time trip back to Alabama about two hundred years ago.

6. Privilege. Contrary to Wexler, libertarianism defends the "poor and powerless"[14] against those who would undermine their chances for happiness. Henry Ford, Bill Gates and Ray Croc have done more for the poor than any one million politicians, bureaucrats and social workers. Yes, they are wealthy, but they earned every penny of their money, and in so doing immeasurably enriched the lives of the poor and middle class. In contrast, tin pot dictators the world over with their hidden Swiss bank accounts are highly affluent, but their money comes at the *expense* of the poor.

7. Inheritance. In attacking bequests, Wexler is actually denigrating the labour he thinks he is championing. Most people work hard to make a better life for their kids. Take that away from them, and you make labour that much less satisfying. And what of inherited wealth in the form of intangibles such as love and learning? The only way to preclude these intergenerational transfers is to break up the family. Inheritance is just one kind of gift, and people have a right to give their property to those they wish. To disallow this is to commit theft.

8. Starve. The only way that "those who grew the wheat and baked the bread starve"[15] is when someone, invariably government, takes it from them by coercive means. The most massive historical case in point was the forced starvation of the grain growing kulaks by Stalin.[16] Does Wexler think libertarians support Soviet communism?

9. Social need. There is no such thing as "social need."[17] This is simply a way to disguise stealing when done by government. Nor does majority rule

---

[12] *Id.*

[13] That is hardly the fault of the employer. He is the benefactor of the worker, not his exploiter, as the Marxists would have it. For a vaccination against the labor theory of value, *see* EUGEN BOHM-BAWERK, CAPITAL AND INTEREST (George D. Hunke and Hans F. Sennholz, trans., 1959) (particularly Part I, Chapter XII, "Exploitation Theory of Socialism-Communism.").

[14] Wexler, *supra* note 1, at 43.

[15] *Id.*

[16] STEPHANE COURTOIS et al., THE BLACK BOOK OF COMMUNISM: CRIMES, TERROR, REPRESSION (Jonathan Murphy and Mark Kramer, trans. 1999); R. J. RUMMEL, DEATH BY GOVERNMENT (1996); ROBERT CONQUEST, THE GREAT TERROR (1990); ROBERT CONQUEST, THE HARVEST OF SORROW (1986).

[17] Wexler, *supra* note 1, at 43.

justify any such act. Hitler came to power through a democratic system. No one would be rash enough to absolve his acts on that ground.

10. Devil. Libertarians, in their opposition to the forced transfer of funds by government, do not at all advocate that the "devil take the hindmost."[18] On the contrary, theft, even when done in the name of majorities by government, is the devilish act. It does not have good effects. In contrast, libertarians advocate free enterprise, the last best hope for the poor of the world, and voluntary charity.

11. Hell. According to Wexler, "Libertarianism even suggests you can push people into hell, so long as you are not interfering with their 'rights.'"[19] He is correct. I fall in love with a lady. She spurns me. I am in hell unless I can possess her. Yet, she has every right[20] to choose another. Surely Wexler would agree I have no right to override her choice in the matter. In hell I must stay.

Conclusion. Libertarianism is not the bogeyman depicted by Wexler. A bit of reading in this subject ought to convince him of this. I hope and trust his native rationality will lead him in that direction.

---

[18] *Id.* at 44.

[19] *Id.* Why the quotation marks around "rights?" Surely Wexler agrees with the libertarian rights not to be murdered, raped, enslaved, assaulted, robbed?

[20] No quotation marks.

Chapter 16.

The Crime of Blackmail: A Libertarian Critique

There is something deeply paradoxical about laws that criminalize blackmail. How is it that, as Glanville Williams put it, "two things that taken separately are moral and legal whites together make a moral and legal black?"[1] For the crime of blackmail involves the criminalization of two otherwise legal acts when they occur in combination—for example, the threat to disclose damaging information about another, and the offer to refrain from disclosing it for some valuable consideration. Were Alfred to (threaten to) disclose damaging information concerning Bill's extramarital affairs, no offense recognized by law would be involved (even if there were something distasteful about such gossip); were Alfred to ask Bill for $5,000, again there would be no contravention of any proper law (even if it displayed a degree of chutzpah). But were Alfred to threaten Bill that he would disclose information concerning Bill's extramarital affairs unless Bill paid him $5,000, his two-part act would—under current laws—constitute the crime of blackmail. Why should the conjunction of such otherwise legal acts have an entirely different legal status?[2]

The paradox is heightened when we consider the reverse situation. Bill learns that Alfred is in possession of damaging information concerning him. He seeks Alfred out, and offers him $5,000 to keep silent. If Alfred accepts Bill's offer, and subsequently keeps mum, he should not be held to have blackmailed Bill. Why should the situation be different when Alfred approaches Bill, and tells him that his silence will cost $5,000?

This is the heart of the libertarian critique of blackmail laws, and in this essay I propose to defend that critique against a number of arguments that have been advanced to justify them. Although my critique of such laws depends ultimately on my belief that criminal prohibitions are justified only

---

[1] Glanville Williams, *Blackmail*, CRIM. L. REV. 79, 163 (1954). It was Williams who originally spoke of "the paradox of blackmail." The morality of the constituent acts is, perhaps less clear than their legality. But my concern here is with the justification of blackmail's criminalization, not with its morality *per se*.

[2] It might be claimed that using the example of extramarital affairs—though typical—unfairly prejudices the case in favor the opponent of blackmail. Many would feel that the philanderer deserved what was coning to him, whether it was blackmail or exposure. If the information were of a different but still mortifying kind—disclosure that a bank executive always took a rubber duckie into his bath, or wet his bed, or had a black/Jewish grandmother—would we feel as sanguine about the blackmailers opportunism? Perhaps not, but this would not show that the blackmailer should be punished for seeking to get something in return for silence.

when some material threat is posed to another (by means of force, fraud, or theft), my arguments here will show that various attempts to avoid or account for the paradox do not succeed, even on their own terms. Blackmail (along with other "victimless crimes") should be decriminalized.

I. SOME DEFINITIONAL PRELIMINARIES

Although standard instances of blackmail involve a threat to disclose damaging information if some monetary payment is not made, the range of possibilities is somewhat wider. Leo Katz, for example, suggests as alternative threats:

> Pay me $10,000—or I will: cause some really bad blood at the next faculty meeting, ... seduce your fiancé, ... persuade your son that it is his patriotic duty to volunteer for combat in Vietnam, ... give your high-spirited, risk-addicted 19-year-old daughter a motorcycle for Christmas, hasten our father's death by leaving the Catholic church.[3]

Demands as well as threats may vary: usually it is for money, but it could also be for sexual favors or some other valued consideration. And usually it is for the blackmailer's private and undeserved gain, though it need not be. Imagine, writes Eric Mack,

> that you can deter a factory owner from (safely) burning his plant to the ground (and thus thoroughly eliminating many employment opportunities) for the sake of destructive glee only by threatening to reveal his secrets. Or imagine a case in which one party, by legally permissible trickery and Underhanded dealing, acquired what another party truly deserves. Wouldn't it be perfectly moral for the morally deserving party to blackmail the first party into transfer-

---

[3] Leo Katz, *Blackmail and Other Forms of Arm Twisting*, 4 U. PA. L. REV. 1567, 1567–68 (1993). Sometimes the threat may take the form of an offer—though of a form that Hillel Steiner refers to as a "throffer"—in which failure to take it up is associated with threatened consequences. *See* Hillel Steiner, *Individual Liberty*, 75 ARISTOTELIAN SOC'Y PROC. 33, 39 (1974–75).

ring that valued good—especially if what was threatened was pre-cisely the [revelation] of the trickery and underhandedness?[4]

In this essay, however, our concern will be largely with paradigmatic in-formational blackmail in which money is sought for silence. Blackmail should not be confused with extortion. In the latter, a threat to do something that would otherwise be illegal is made in demanding something from another: If Charles threatens to break David's knees or burn down his house if David does not give him $5,000, Charles is guilty of extortion, not blackmail, Extor-tion is properly considered illegal.

II. IS THERE REALLY A PARADOX OF BLACKMAIL?

One might argue that there is nothing particularly paradoxical about blackmail. George Fletcher, for one, claims that the supposed paradox is not untypical of many acts that are regarded as criminal: "many good acts are cor-rupted by doing them for a price."[5] Fletcher instances bribery, prostitution, and payment for confessing to a crime. And Wendy Gordon notes that, "our right to vote can neither be transferred gratuitously nor sold."[6]

But are these plausible counter instances? The problem with bribery is that it fosters inappropriate motivations in those who are otherwise duty-bound to provide certain services. Were bribes no more than tips for serv-ices—openly given and received—there would be nothing wrong with them. What makes bribery problematic is not the conjunction of service and money, but the fact that money given secretly becomes an incentive to forgo duty and/or to do it only when more is giver than one is contractually obliged to accept. Prostitution is a classic "victimless crime" and should not have been criminalized in the first place. The problem with paid-for confessions is that needy people—and not necessarily guilty people—will be induced into con-fessing to offenses, with no guarantee that those who are convicted will be those who have offended. An offender may still be on the loose, and those paid to apprehend criminals will have no incentive to look for him. As for the

---

[4] Eric Mack, *In Defense of Blackmail*, 41 PHIL STUD. 274, 277. To counter the response that these are cases in which the blackmailees are being blackmailed only into not doing something,
Mack suggests that the factory owner might be blackmailed into donating money for Cambo-dian relief. *Id.* at 278.

[5] George P. Fletcher, *Blackmail: The Paradigmatic Case*, 141 U. PA. L. REV. 1617 (1993).

[6] Wendy J. Gordon, *Truth and Consequences: The Force of Blackmail's Central Case*, 141 U. PA. L. REV. 1741, 1744 (1993).

right to vote, it could have been otherwise. The only reason that political votes (unlike votes in publicly traded corporations) cannot be sold is that a majority has agreed not to commodify them.

III. BLACKMAIL AND OTHER COMMERCIAL TRANSACTIONS

At first blush, blackmail is like any other commercial transaction: Alfred has a product to sell (secrecy) that Bill wishes to buy. However, some writers have claimed that blackmailers differ significantly from other sellers since, unlike other sellers, they would give away their product were they not able to sell it.[7] Perhaps so, perhaps not![8] In any case it is not easy to see any significance to the difference. For other sellers, perhaps, the product to be sold represents all investment on their part, and therefore something they would be unlikely to give away, whereas the incriminating information that the blackmailer possesses is much more likely to have been gained without significant investment.

May be the difference lies in motivation, Wendy Gordon suggests that blackmail should be outlawed because "the blackmailer acquires information *for the sole purpose of obtaining money or advantage from the victim, and ... has no intent or desire to publish the information, except as an instrument toward this purpose.*"[9] But why should the blackmailer's intent be of any interest to the law unless the conduct in question has independently infringed another's rights? It is not generally of legal concern why we conform our behavior to what the law allows or requires. Intent only becomes an issue once the law is broken. But since Alfred's disclosure of Bill's infidelities does not constitute conduct of a kind the law would ordinarily prohibit, it should not be of any legal interest to know why Alfred may or may not choose to disclose the information he has about Bill.[10]

---

[7] Scott Altman, *A Patchwork Theory of Blackmail*, 141 U. Pa. L. Rev. 1639, 1641 (1993).

[8] Restaurants and supermarkets often donate "day old" food to the poor.

[9] Gordon, *supra* note 6, at 1746. Mack's counter-examples cast some doubt on the generality of this claim. *See, generally,* Mack, *supra* note 4.

[10] In actual fact, a blackmailer's motives might be much more complicated. Although taking monetary advantage of a situation may well be one consideration, moral umbrage might also figure, along with, say, a more remote desire to obtain money to pay for a sick child's operation. Gordon's characterization of the blackmailer's intent might—in certain cases, at least—apply equally to many other currently legal commercial ventures that people may undertake.

Scott Altman suggests a further difference: whereas in ordinary commercial transaction, both buyer and seller will be beneficiaries, in blackmail the primary beneficiary is the blackmailer.[11] But why should the person who buys silence not also be seen as benefiting from the transaction? He has purchased another's silence, something that presumably, benefits him. It is true that, antecedent to the blackmailer's approach, the blackmailee was not seeking to purchase the silence of others, but that was because he believed that his secret was safe, and did not need to be secured through purchase.

IV. BLACKMAIL AND COERCION

Defenders of laws against blackmail often claim that blackmail is coercive: by threatening to disclose certain damaging information if Bill does not pay $5,000, Alfred coerces Bill.[12] Or so it is said. However, the idea of coercion cannot clearly be extended to such cases. In paradigm cases, Alfred coerces Bill into parting with $5,000 if he tackles Bill and steals his wallet containing $5,000, or if he puts a gun to Bill's head and threatens to pull the trigger should Bill refuse to hand over $5,000. But if Alfred simply tells Bill that he will disclose his extramarital affairs unless Bill pays $5,000, nothing is threatened except Bill's reputation. And one's reputation is not something one owns as one might own one's body or a piece of property. Reputation is a form of social recognition to which one does not have a right as one might have a right to one's property.[13] Should Alfred spread the information without making any claim for money, he will have done nothing illegal. Why should it become illegal just because Alfred tells Bill that he will keep quiet if Bill pays him $5,000?

---

[11] Altman, *supra* note 7, at 1641.

[12] The simple fact of a threat is not sufficient to make the act coercive (and hence illegitimate). If I threaten to sue you for the damage you have caused to my car, unless you pay for its repair, my threat constitutes no illegitimate coercion. Should it be argued that some threats one has a right to make (as in the latter case) whereas others one has no right to make (as in blackmail), the libertarian will reply that this begs the question: Why should Alfred not threaten to reveal Bill's extra-marital affairs unless some payment is made?

[13] Should it be objected that the destruction of reputation by means of disclosure of information about one does constitute a violation of rights (as is sometimes allowed by laws against libel and defamation), the libertarian will respond that the question is begged. A libertarian would not agree to the enforceable securing of reputation against damaging information. On this *see* WALTER BLOCK, DEFENDING THE UNDEFENDABLE at 59–62 (1976); MURRAY N. ROTHBARD, ETHICS OF LIBERTY at 121–22 (1998).

Perhaps the argument from coercion can be expressed as follows: The blackmailer's act is coercive because he proposes to reveal information that he is obligated not to disclose.[14] But this will not do either. Even if Alfred were obligated not to reveal the information, it would still not show the threat to reveal it to be blackmail; rather, it would be a coercive threat, for example, extortion. It would indeed be legally wrong for Alfred to reveal what he told Bill in confidence, but the threat to disclose it unless Bill pays Alfred to keep quiet would be a legal wrong not because it is blackmail, but because it breached Alfred's contractual obligation to Bill. But if there is no obligation for Bill to keep the damaging information to himself, then and only then would there be no coercion involved in making it known, Should Alfred accidentally find out about Bill's extramarital affairs, he is under no obligation at all regarding its disclosure.[15] Why, then, should his informing Bill that he will reveal what Bill has been up to be coercive.

Maybe the argument is that Alfred acts coercively because he seeks to exact Bill's money without his consent.[16] Although no literal gun is being pointed at Bill's head, something else is—serious damage to his life, reputation, job prospects, or whatever—should he refuse to pay. This account, of course, would not work with cases in which Bill, on hearing that Alfred possesses (and is likely to reveal) the information, seeks him out to offer him "hush money, but perhaps the supporter of blackmail laws may not mind cutting these cases adrift from the scope of such legislation. Once again, however, we need to remind ourselves of the disanalogy with the gunman. Absent monetary considerations, if the gunman pulls the trigger a legally significant wrong is done to his victim, whereas, if Alfred spills the beans on Bill's philandering no crime is committed.

Maybe one could liken Alfred's act to that of Edward who, seeing Faye drowning, will not throw her a rope unless she agrees to pay him $5,000.[17] This is surely exploitative of Faye's situation, but is it coercive? Were Edward to have pushed Faye into the water in the first place, there would indeed be an argument for saying that the demand for $5,000 was coercive; but *ex hypothesi* he did not, and so, given that he does not violate a legal obligation in not

---

[14] For this argument, see Altman, *supra* note 7, at 1642 fn. 11. For a rejoinder, *see* chapter 4, this volume.

[15] That may be too strong: perhaps there is a moral or religious obligation not to gossip about others. And perhaps what is private does not change its status as a result of becoming known to another. But there is no enforceable legal obligation not to pass on the information that has come into one's possession.

[16] Katz, *supra* note 3, at 1599.

[17] *See* Altman, *supra* note 7, at 1643.

throwing a rope to her, it is hardly coercive for him to demand something for his assistance.[18] Bill's follies, likewise, are his own doing, and not the result of a "set up" by Alfred, and if Alfred has come into possession of information that could be Bill's undoing, may he not offer to withhold it on his own terms?

V. BLACKMAIL AND EXPLOITATION

Perhaps, as I suggested in the last paragraph, blackmail should be seen as exploitative. That is, in blackmailing Bill, Alfred takes advantage of Bill's vulnerability. If so, should this justify its legal proscription?

Note, first of all, that the notion of exploitation is none-too-clear; it is, for example, used by Marxist writers to characterize ordinary capitalist labor relations: in making a profit, employers of labor are said to return to their employees less than the full value of their labor. Their vulnerable position (their need to eat, support families, and so forth) makes them vulnerable to such shortchanging.

But even with a less expansive and less tendentious understanding, there is a gap between exploiting another's vulnerabilities and doing something that should be considered illegal. If George exploits Harold's generosity to get a loan, or Ivan exploits John's poor management of a rival business or even John's sudden and debilitating illness to gain a larger share of the market or to put John out of business, neither George nor Ivan have done anything illegal, however opportunistic they may have been. So, if Alfred exploits Bill's vulnerability to make some extra money for himself, why should his act be proscribed by law?

VI. BLACKMAIL AND PRIVACY

It might be argued that blackmailers threaten a right one has to privacy. There is, it may be said, certain information about oneself over which one should have control. It is "one's own business," and not the business of others. If it is to be "given out," it is appropriately given out only if one has consented to its being shared. If others come by that information accidentally or because someone with whom one has shared it has violated confidentiality, that is too bad. The third party is not guilty of any wrongdoing in having or sharing the information. However, if the third party, realizing that one wanted to keep the

---

[18] I am, of course, assuming that there is no "Good Samaritan" law requiring that assistance be given. Were there such a law, a libertarian would of course oppose it.

information to oneself, now chooses to use it as leverage for self-enrichment then that person is violating the privacy rights of another no less improperly than the person who taps one's telephone or bugs one's house or looks in one's personal files.

But there are significant differences between these various cases. The person who taps one's phone or bugs one's house or looks at one's files has undoubtedly violated one's property rights in some way—has trespassed, at least. Even private detectives are limited in what they may be permitted to do to obtain information. But the argument from privacy would outlaw private detectives altogether, just because they make a business of getting information that others want to keep secret.[19] The blackmailer need not violate any so-called privacy rights[20] to obtain his information: a sharp eye, an open ear, and a little advantageous positioning may be all that is necessary. Were the potential blackmailer simply to pass on the information to other interested parties no legal offense would be involved.[21] Why should that change if the blackmailer seeks to take advantage of what he knows by seeking cash for silence?

VII. REPEAT BLACKMAIL

Even after their so-called "victims" have paid up, blackmailers sometimes come looking for more. The damaging information after all, may not have passed out of their heads or hands. It may therefore be argued that the only way to keep blackmailers from repeatedly approaching those who have bought their silence is to ban blackmail altogether.[22]

But repeated attempts at blackmail may be prevented much more easily if blackmail is decriminalized. All that is required is that blackmailers sign a contract with the blackmailee that stipulates the blackmailers' permanent silence in return for a payment of $X. Then, if the blackmailer breaks his

---

[19] That surely goes for investigative reporters, newshounds, and gossip columnists as well. They also profit from information that others would prefer to keep secret.

[20] Libertarians reject privacy rights that are not reducible to property rights, e.g., rights not to have one's property bugged or phone tapped. *See* Rothbard, *supra* note 13, at 121–22.

[21] Although some jurisdictions do recognize torts for "violation of privacy," libertarians are opposed to such constraints, because such torts must allow—what I challenge—that people can have property rights in their reputation.

[22] *See, e.g.,* Fletcher, *supra* note 5, at 1623, 1627. *See also* Altman, *supra* note 7, at 1648. Fletcher sees the possibility of the blackmailer's coming back for more as constituting a permanent domination of the blackmailer over the blackmailee. But that is only if no contract is made between the blackmailer and blackmailee forbidding any further claims.

agreement (something he can do even when blackmail is illegal), he can be held liable for whatever damages might be stipulated or otherwise determined by the courts. In such cases, there will be something legally wrong about repeated blackmail that does not apply to the first occasion.

What is more, to outlaw blackmail in the first instance because blackmail demands may be repeated in the future is not to punish someone for a past crime done but for a (potential) future crime—hardly what we have in mind when we speak of criminal justice. If this were allowed to be a general legal principle, moreover, we would have to entrench in the law the concept of preventive detention, for all members of groups statistically over represented in the criminal category.

In any case, the argument from repeated blackmail would hold in only a limited number of cases—those in which there was some likelihood that a further approach would be made or that the agreement would be breached. It would hardly provide a general argument against blackmail.

VIII. THE CONSEQUENCES OF BLACKMAIL

Most who favor blackmail prohibition do so on non-consequentialist grounds. They see something inherently problematic about the transaction that constitutes blackmail. Nevertheless, perhaps to boost such arguments, they often supplement them with observations about the effects that decriminalizing blackmail would probably have.

Richard Epstein, for example, suggests that were blackmail to be legalized, it would encourage the formation of corporations such as his hypothetical "Blackmail, Inc.," an organization devoted to ferreting out embarrassing (or worse) information on people and then blackmailing them to have it kept quiet.[23] Assuming the profitability of such an enterprise, a blackmailee might find himself the target of numerous independent approaches and, to meet the financial obligations incurred by this, might be led (or even encouraged) into committing crimes to pay for his chronic secrecy need.

But are such fears well founded? Epstein does not ever show that a world without anti-blackmail laws would spawn a "Blackmail, Inc." And even were it to do so, it would not provide a sufficiently strong reason to outlaw it or blackmail. The tastelessness or unseemliness of a social institution is not a sufficient reason to ban it or enterprises that exploit it. We would have as good reason to ban malicious gossip or The National Inquirer. And the social pressure that might lead a person into committing crimes to pay for secrecy

---

[23] Richard Epstein, *Blackmail, Inc.*, 50 U. CHI. L. REV. 553 (1983).

would not differ substantially from the social pressure to "be somebody" or "impress others," motivations that may be just as likely to lead people to commit crimes.[24]

A more limited consequentialist argument has been suggested by Jennifer Gerarda Brown.[25] She suggests that were blackmail in cases of incriminating information legalized, there would likely be a reduction of crime. The criminally inclined would face the real possibility that they would have to "split" the profits of their criminality or otherwise pay to cover up their crimes, and such "costs" would constitute a significant deterrent to criminal activity. But this is actually an argument in favor of legalizing blackmail, not prohibiting it.

IX. BUYING SILENCE

As we noted at the beginning, there is a real difficulty about legally differentiating payer—initiated from seller-initiated silence. If Bill learns that Alfred possesses damaging information that he might be inclined to disclose to others, and offers Alfred $5,000 to keep quiet, it is hard to argue that Alfred has either coerced or exploited Bill, or that the transaction should be outlawed.

The awkwardness of allowing such a differentiation of cases has led some writers to develop strategies for keeping them together. Thus Scott Altman has claimed:

> Evidentiary and definitional problems with payer initiation can undermine any power it has to separate coercive from non-coercive transactions. Some bargains appear payer-initiated because the payer initially suggests the deal. But the payer might only learn of the other party's intent to reveal the embarrassing information after that party discloses this intent in order to elicit an offer or payment. Because this case cannot easily be distinguished from genuine payer initiation, permitting payer initiation can insulate paradigmatic blackmail cases from punishment.[26]

Similar arguments used to be employed against all forms of euthanasia, lest it should become a cloak for murder. The solution, were we to persist in outlawing seller-initiated silence, would be essentially the same: the develop-

---

[24] For an extended discussion, *see* chapter 13, this volume.

[25] Jennifer Gerarda Brown, *Blackmail as Private Justice*, 141 U.PA. L. REV. 1935 (1993).

[26] Altman, *supra* note 7, at 1649.

ment of procedures that would allow—for most cases—clearer discriminations to be made. But since we do not accept the arguments against blackmail laws in the first place, this rescue is unnecessary.

X. BLACKMAIL AND VICTIMIZATION

Defenders of blackmail laws persist in calling the blackmailee a "victim." Once seen as such, blackmailers are easily tarred with wrongdoing. Yet this characterization trades on the conflation of two distinct senses of "victim." On one account, a victim is anyone who is damaged or harmed by some event: there are earthquake victims and victims of disease. Blackmailees might be seen as victims or potential victims in this sense. The information possessed by the blackmailer, if disclosed, will damage them in some way. And one might argue that if one kind of damage has been averted it has been averted only at a cost, and—at a stretch—that one is a "victim" of circumstances that have a cost.

But the term "victim" may also be used in a more restricted sense—as when we speak of someone being victimized. Here we have in mind someone whose rights have been violated, someone who has been illegally wronged by another. Is the person who is blackmailed a "victim" in this second sense? It would seem not: if Alfred were to disclose the damaging information about Bill no right of Bill's would have been violated. That he should refrain from doing what he had a right to do in exchange for some monetary consideration does not change the matter.[27]

Those who persist in speaking of blackmailees as "victims" can mean "victim" only in the first sense. Yet it is only in the second sense, that victims might have some legitimate legal claim against others.

---

[27] Indeed, one might be inclined to argue that the blackmailer displays a kind of decency toward the blackmailee by offering him a way out of his predicament (the blackmailer's opportunity to damage the potential blackmailee by disclosing, as he has a right to do, the information he has on him). The gossip provides no such injury-averting option. *See* chapter 13, this volume ("In contrast to the gossip, who tells the secret without even affording the victim the opportunity of purchasing silence, the blackmailer can be seen as a benefactor.").

XI. HARD CASES

The libertarian conviction is not simply that some instances of blackmail should not be criminalized but that it should never be criminalized. The libertarian therefore needs to confront some hard cases.

(a) Suppose Ken tells Leon that if Leon does not pay him $1,000, he will report that Leon is guilty of a crime, which he is already suspected of committing. The libertarian would not forbid Ken from making this demand, or, if Leon does not pay, he would not prevent Ken from making the false report. Ken has free speech rights, including the right to speak falsely about another. True, the police-and courts-may subsequently accept Ken's word about Leon, so that Leon is unjustly punished, but if they do that, that injustice is on them for failing thoroughly to investigate Ken's report. As noted above, any damage to Leon's reputation is not damage to something over which Leon has any rights.[28]

While the foregoing is perfectly compatible with libertarian theorizing, it will strike many as repugnant. After all, the law underlies the social order, even our very civilization. If one may with impunity place a spoke in the wheel of justice in this manner, it bespeaks ill of the libertarian philosophy. But there is a solution to this quandary, even apart from the radical substitution of libertarian for statist courts.[29] And that is to pay or "tie up" witnesses so that they are contractually obligated to tell the truth upon pain of contract violation. One of the great injustices of our present court system is that witnesses are in effected drafted into testifying, and, so, for that matter, are jurors. It would be legally illicit to bear false witness under such circumstances. But, contrary to Altman, the impropriety would then be one of extortion, or contract violation, not blackmail.

(b) What if Michael learns that Nicholas has embezzled $1 million from his company, but suggests to Nicholas that for a payment of $56,000 he will not report it? Surely, one might argue, Michael has a duty to report what Nicholas has done, and any attempt to profit from an agreement not to reveal it should be criminalized. Although some libertarians might balk at cases of this kind, it is certainly open to others—myself included—to argue that whatever moral duty might be claimed to report the crimes of another (and not to profit from them), nevertheless there is no basis for legally requiring that the crimes of another should be reported. Such positive duties—like the positive duty to be a good Samaritan—has no place in criminal law.

---

[28] *See* Block, *supra* note 13, at 59–62; Rothbard, *supra* note 13, at 126–27.

[29] *See* MURRAY ROTHBARD, FOR A NEW LIBERTY (1973).

XII. CONCLUSION

Blackmail laws are often taken for granted. Indeed, such is the moral objectionableness of blackmail in many people's minds that they cannot imagine how the decriminalization of blackmail could possibly be supported. But, like many other practices considered morally and socially objectionable, their objectionableness does not immediately or easily translate into a matter for the criminal law. It has been my contention that this is true of blackmail. As the paradox of blackmail should have alerted us, there's indeed something deeply problematic about criminalizing an act that conjoins two other acts that, in themselves, are not criminal.

Chapter 17.

Replies to Levin and Kipnis on Blackmail

I appreciate the care that both Michael Levin[1] and Kenneth Kipnis[2] have taken to understand and respond to my paper. Both concede much—even most—of what I want to argue, yet both refuse to draw my conclusions. Even though there is some overlap in their concern about blackmail contracts, their different approaches make it more convenient if I respond separately to each.

I. MICHAEL LEVIN'S CRITIQUE

In allowing that the blackmailer violates no right of a blackmailee,[3] Levin concedes just about all I have ever argued. The absence of any rights-violation, I have wanted to claim, is sufficient to justify blackmail's decriminalization. So his suggestion that it should *still* be prohibited presents a novel challenge.

(a) *Anxiety.* As Levin expresses it, legal blackmail "would create too much anxiety:"[4] a world in which decriminalized blackmail existed is not one in which he would choose to live.

A response to Levin's claim might take anyone of several tacks. One might be to deny that blackmail causes anxiety, or that its decriminalization would. Because criminals and other wrongdoers would also be exposed to the possibility of blackmail, the effect of its decriminalization might be to reduce the general level of crime and other wrongdoing. Levin himself acknowledges as much: "People who do not wish to be spied on ... can guarantee invulnerability to petty blackmail by leading blameless lives—an incidental benefit to the rest of us."[5]

A second tack would be to argue that any (or at least some of the) anxiety caused might be a good thing. Taking our lead from the passage just quoted, anxiety over the possibility of blackmail might keep us keep us "in line." In

---

[1] Michael Levin, *Blockmail*, 18 CRIM. JUST. ETHICS 11–18 (1999). I am charmed and flattered by the pun.

[2] Kenneth Kipnis, *Blackmail as a Career Choice: A Liberal Assessment*, 18 CRIM. JUST. ETHIS 19–22 (1999).

[3] Levin, *supra* note 1, at 12.

[4] *Id.*

[5] *Id.*

any case, anxiety is not necessarily bad: anxiety frequently spurs us to greater achievement.

But these responses are not wholly satisfactory: they are consequentialist in character and subject to all the shortcomings of consequentialist arguments. A better tack is simply to deny the relevance of anxiety to the issue of criminalization. Causing anxiety is not, *per se*, a ground for criminal prohibition. A great number of human activities—from exams to hang gliding to investing in the stock market to being "victimized" by "hate" speech—are anxiety-producing, but we do not see such anxiety as a legitimate reason for seeking to prevent such activities. Almost any change is potentially anxiety-producing, and a policy of anxiety reduction would be a prescription for maintaining the *status quo*. If anxiety is the problem, it is better to see a psychiatrist.

Might Levin object that he does not intend the outlawing of all anxiety-producing activities but only those that are not associated with greatly valued benefits? I think not. Assertions of this kind presume, contrary to fact, that we can make interpersonal comparisons of utility. But considerations of justice trump those of utility, if only because interpersonal comparisons of happiness are impossible to make. The libertarian position on blackmail is grounded in considerations of justice: the rights of blackmailers and blackmailees. These rights cannot be overridden by utilitarian concerns about anxiety production.

(b) *Blackmail Contracts.* Levin notes that I "sometimes write ... as if commercial blackmail would sometimes coalesce into one large Blackmail, Inc."[6] I did so simply as a convenience and as part of my criticism of Epstein. I am agnostic on the question of how blackmailers would work, if legalized. The critical question is whether they should be. And that is why the peculiarities of blackmail contracts deserve attention.

Despite the inventiveness of his discussion, I remain unconvinced that the problems Levin points out are at all telling. Given that such contracts do not violate rights *per se*, the issue is simply a practical one of implementation, not a theoretical one of principle. And the problem is not one that would emerge *de novo* with decriminalization, because blackmail agreements—albeit illegal—currently exist, and those who are parties to them have already to wrestle with the issue of trust. In many cases they appear to have done so satisfactorily. Blackmail contracts may differ from contracts of other kinds, but

---

[6] *Id.* at 13.

nothing that Levin says establishes that they are "unique"[7] in any sense that would make them impossible or inappropriate.[8]

One strategy for ensuring better compliance might be to rent—rather than sell—silence: I offer you my silence for one month for $100. An arrangement of this kind—renewable or renegotiable after a month—would be less likely to generate the problem that Levin envisages: a blackmailer coming back for more after an initial agreement.

Levin's claim that I "must reject" legally mandated memory erasure for blackmailers,[9] though correct, does not rule it out of question as part of a voluntary contract and, absent some further argument, I do not see why an honest blackmailer should resist agreeing to such memory erasure provided that the technology for achieving it has no other (for example, ill) effects.

(c) *Libertarianism and the Sufficiency of Rights.* In my original paper, I saw my purpose to be that of establishing that blackmail violated no rights and, therefore, given my libertarian premises, concluding that it ought not to be criminalized. Levin accepts that no rights are violated, but then rejects the libertarian framework that would have allowed my conclusion to be drawn. So I must now venture into territory that I originally took for granted.

For the libertarian, *aggression presupposes property rights.* Levin's critique of libertarianism begins from a rejection of Locke's account of the origin of property rights. But libertarianism is erected on something more primordial—the ownership we each have over our own bodies. The libertarian position is that we are each rightfully self-owners of our persons. The only alternatives are that somebody else owns us—we are his slaves and owe him obedience—or that each of us owns an equal fraction of the other. Since the last position would result in an impossible coordination problem (even a right to scratch my nose would become impossible), that leaves only enslavement or self-ownership. Only self-ownership is sustainable.

Why is this so? Hans-Hermann Hoppe has argued the point as follows.[10] The only way in which any conclusion can be established is through argumentation. And no conclusion can be accepted that would require a rejection of the prerequisites of argumentation. Argumentation cannot go on without the human body and its functions. To claim, therefore, that one does not own one's body would be to undermine the prerequisites for argument. Ergo, one must own one's self. Once that has been granted, it is then possible to move

---

[7] *Id.* at 14.

[8] Levin's discussion of blackmail insurance (*Id.*) is clever, but beyond my brief. My purpose was simply to establish that blackmail would not violate rights.

[9] Levin, *supra* note 1, at 14.

[10] HANS-HERMANN HOPPE, THE ECONOMICS AND ETHICS OF PRIVATE PROPERTY 204–07 (1993).

convincingly into the world of property: not only does argumentation require bodies but a place for them to be—a chair, house, land, or whatever. Some private property rights are assumed by the very possibility of argument.

From this we can see that Levin's objection to the libertarian right to speak is incoherent. Were it the case that your speaking—"by agitating my body and ambient air without my consent"[11]—violated my property rights, then it would be impossible for us to argue.[12] A libertarianism based on argumentation makes no such claim. Rothbard, for example, distinguishes the invasion of property rights when A trespasses onto or places an object on B's land from the case in which radio waves cross our properties without our consent.[13] In one case the boundary crossing affects the other person's exclusive possession, use, or enjoyment of his property. In the other case it does not.

A more sympathetic interpretation of Levin's homesteading theory might be the following: I breathe on my property and Levin, 100 yards away, breathes on his. Neither of us violates the property rights of the other because when we homesteaded our respective lands, we did so subject to the fact that the other was already breathing air and would continue to do so. We came to own our properties subject to the condition that the other had a continuing right to breathe.

Admittedly, the distinction between aggression and non-aggression is not always clear: it is not always easy to discern whether a boundary crossing affects another's rights. But that is not an argument against or even a problem exclusive to libertarianism.[14]

Important as the nonaggression axiom is to libertarianism, Levin misconstrues it by seeing it as fundamental. That way he can erect his straw-man arguments about the loaf of bread and the person dangling from the cliff. Al-

---

[11] Levin, *supra* note 1, at 14.

[12] More sympathetically, homesteading our persons is always subject to the proviso that others may continue to homestead theirs.

[13] Murray N. Rothbard, *Law, Property Rights, and Air Pollution*, 2 (1) CATO J. (1982).

[14] Murray Rothbard asks:

> When is an act held to be an assault? Frowning would scarcely qualify. But if Jones had whipped out a gun and pointed it in Smith's direction without firing, this is clearly a threat of imminent aggression, and would properly be countered by Smith plugging Jones in self defense. ... The proper yardstick for determining whether the point of assault had been reached is this: Did Jones initiate an 'overt act' threatening battery?

Id. at 239.

though he is right to see that if non-aggression is taken to be fundamental a circular argument will arise if rights are specified in terms of aggression—since "aggression pre-supposes the idea of a right"[15]—he is wrong to see this as the basic libertarian claim. For the libertarian, aggression *presupposes* property rights. Aggression is quintessentially the violation of property rights, and property rights are essential to Levin's very speaking, writing, and publishing in opposition to libertarianism, or anything else.

Once this is recognized, Levin's examples can be easily addressed. In the dispute over the loaf of bread,[16] the violator of the non-aggression axiom was the ex-owner who refused to hand over the bread that no longer belonged to him. He was not justified in striking the new owner "defensively." Similarly, in the cliff example,[17] once you had been paid $1 for the help, I owned the service that you had agreed to, and your failure to act constituted a theft of the service. The case of the woman who allows her newborn to starve in the crib[18] is, however, more complicated. Here libertarians, along with others, make a firm distinction between adults and children.[19] Although there is some disagreement about this in libertarian circles, I take the view that—in the case of her child—the woman owes more than passive non-aggression. She has a duty to notify others of her intention not to care for the child, even if—as was traditionally done—only by placing it in the town square or on the church steps. Then, if no one else was willing to care for it, no rights violation would be involved were it allowed to die.[20]

(d) *Levin's Sociobiological Ethics.* Fascinating though I found Levin's sociobiological insights, I was puzzled as to how his "moral antirealism"—his denial "that anything is objectively good, bad, right or wrong"[21]—left him with the tools to question my claim that blackmail ought to be legalized. At best he is left with a way of explaining why we do or do not have rules to that effect.[22]

---

[15] Levin, *supra* note 1, at 15.

[16] *Id.*

[17] *Id.*

[18] *Id.*

[19] Recognizing, of course, that in practice there is a continuum—a problem for every theory of crime.

[20] *See* Walter Block, *Woman and Fetus: Rights in Conflict?*, REASON 18–19 (April 1978).

[21] Levin, *supra* note 1, at 16.

[22] He writes: "Given antirealism, the most that can be done by way of finding a foundation for ethics is to identify the most general moral rules prevalent in particular societies .... and then to explain why these rules exist." *Id.*

I have some sympathy for Darwinistic explanations of our moral (and other) senses, but believe that these are compatible with there also being true claims in morality (as well as in science and history). Not that all such claims are absolute: the bully may be lied to, since he has no property right to the truth. Some moral claims, however, function as side-constraints: we may not torture the child of a mad bomber, even if it would have greatly beneficial consequences. Here there is a victim whose rights have been invaded, and these are not subject to some utilitarian calculus.[23]

For this reason I have some difficulty with the view that Levin attributes to me in his note 24.[24] As I recall it, my position was that the torture of a child would violate the private property rights it has in its own person. Period. Given the choice between torturing the child and standing by while a city was consumed by a nuclear conflagration, however, I might well hope that some-one—even I—might torture the child. But this would not be prompted by lib-

---

[23] Note Rothbard's discussion of a related issue:

> Similar principles hold in innocent-bystander cases. Jones assaults and attacks Smith; Smith, in self defense, shoots. The shot goes wild and accidentally hits Brown, an innocent bystander. Should Smith be liable? Unfortunately, the courts, sticking to the traditional "reasonable man" or "negligence" doctrine, have held that Smith is not liable if indeed he was reasonably intending self defense against Jones. But, in libertarian and in strict liability theory, Smith has indeed aggressed against Brown, albeit unintentionally, and must pay for this tort. Thus, Brown has a proper legal action against Smith. …
>
> One of the great flaws in the orthodox negligence approach has been to focus only on one victim's (Smith's) right of self defense in repelling attack, or on his good faith mistake. But orthodox doctrine unfortunately neglects the other victim—the man frowning across the street, the plainclothesman trying to save someone, the innocent bystander. The plaintiff's right of self-defense is being grievously neglected. The proper focus in all these cases is: Would the plaintiff have had the right to plug the defendant in his self defense? Would the frowning man, the plainclothesman, the innocent bystander [Levin's infant son of the terrorist], if he could have done so in time, have had the right to shoot the sincere but erring defendants [Levin's authorities] in self defense? Surely, whatever our theory of liability, the answer must be "yes."

Rothbard, *supra* note 13, at 240 (material in brackets is my own).

[24] Levin, *supra* note 1, at 18 fn. 24.

ertarian considerations, and were someone to do that he would have to pay for it under a libertarian code.[25]

Even allowing Levin's sociobiological approach, I might have expected him to adopt an account more closely attuned to a libertarian one. The extreme example he uses is just that: an extreme example. He would surely agree that the world would be a better place, better suited to our "happiness, productivity and, ultimately, reproductive fitness"[26] were we to adopt the libertarian proscription against aggression and its respect for property rights.

In sum, interesting though I find Levin's position to be, I do not think that he has succeeded either in refuting libertarianism or in establishing anxiety-reduction as a basis for retaining the current laws against blackmail.

II. KENNETH KIPNIS'S CRITIQUE

Kipnis has clearly grasped the central thrust of my argument. And for the most part he leaves it unquestioned. Furthermore, he provides a valuable analysis of the prerequisites of being a blackmailer's "mark."[27] Even so, he fails to understand what drives my position when he asserts that contract is central to libertarian theory. Important as it is, it is not as central as the private property right we have in our own persons and things." And it is because blackmail violates no such private property right that it should be decriminalized. The problems with blackmail contracts are not central.

Blackmail Overkill. Although I did not explicitly deny it in my original paper, I did not "assume [that] blackmailers [must] limit themselves to a sin-

---

[25] Matthew Block has suggested the following criticism of the rejoinder. Suppose an All Powerful Being then sent out a message that if we (libertarians) punished the "heroic" murderer of the mad bomber's son, he would blow up the entire world. To this I would respond that if someone is determined to construct an example that will drive a wedge between libertarian rights and consequentialist values, then he may well succeed. But such an example would not be about the world in which we live: there are no such All Powerful Beings running around. Consider a different example. It is undeniable that 2+2=4. Suppose the All Powerful Being threatened to blow up the world if anyone stated that 2+2=4. Even though no one might ever say 2+2=4 again, it would still be true. No matter how serious the threat, it would constitute a rights violation to kill the mad bomber's innocent son, and it would be just to punish the boy's murderer even though he killed to save the city.

[26] Levin, *supra* note 1, at 17.

[27] Kipnis, *supra* note 2, at 19–20. My only hesitation concerns his suggestion that "mere hearsay" may be sufficient for gossip journalism but not for blackmail. *Id.* at 20. Though this may be true of some journalism, many newspapers require more than their gossip counterparts.

gle payment based on the mark's present financial means."[28] In earlier writings I had explicitly suggested an ongoing payment schedule.[29]

Kipnis contends that because the blackmailer will milk the mark for whatever he can, it may "now become necessary for the mark to supplement income in risky, questionable, and illegal ways."[30] I certainly agree that the blackmailer my exact a high fee from a blackmailee. But whether this should be seen as "unconscionably extortionate" is quite another matter. For one thing—as I made clear in my original article[31]—extortion involves the threat of an intrinsically criminal (*malum in se*) retaliation, whereas the disclosure involved in blackmail would be—leaving the issue of money aside—perfectly legal.

But there is another problem with his claim. Blackmailers are not the only people who charge what some see as unconscionable prices. So do most tradesmen and professionals. Should we consider criminalizing their fees-for-service? The same applies to his concern about the potential rage of blackmailees: that may be a reason for caution on the blackmailer's part, but not a ground for outlawing blackmail. Some sports fans become enraged when their team loses. Yet we would hardly ban all athletic contests.

Justice is not synonymous with openness, and sometimes closed proceedings will do more for justice than open ones.

Blackmail Contracts. The heart of Kipnis's case, however, is to be found in his critique of blackmail contracts. His initial questions, about their longevity and heritability,[32] the possibility of public scrutiny and report after a blackmailer's death, and so on, are interesting, but basically unproblematic. And even were it impossible to keep the secret after the blackmailer's death, that would be unfortunate but not a rights violation: the blackmailer offered silence for the term of his life; the blackmailee had no right to more.[33]

---

[28] *Id.* at 21.

[29] Walter Block, Defending the Undefendable 55 (1976). The cartoon which appears there answers one of Kipnis's later questions: If the blackmailer died, would "the cache of valuable dirt … properly belong to the estate, the income stream passing to the blackmailer's heirs? Kipnis, *supra* note 2, at 21. It might, should the blackmailer bequeath it. In the cartoon, the blackmailer says to the blackmailee: "This is my kid, Mr. T. He'll be blackmailing you from now on. I'm going to Florida."

[30] *Id.* at 21.

[31] Reprinted as chapter 16, this volume.

[32] See discussion above in note 29.

[33] *See* Dick Francis, Reflex (1981), for a case of blackmail which survives the death of the initial blackmailer.

The key issue concerns their enforceability without jeopardizing the blackmailee's secret. Kipnis believes that our judicial system—in the case of an action (here, against a blackmailer)—depends for its justice on the fact "its proceedings [are] generally public and that parties can be called upon to testify truthfully."[34] But this is to elevate form over substance. No doubt it is generally true that open hearings will do more for justice than closed ones (a point that Kipnis's own wording concedes). But justice is not synonymous with openness, and sometimes closed proceedings will do more for justice than open ones. If, as Kipnis admits, "the courts will very occasionally accede to closed proceedings—in child abuse and trade secret cases,"[35] why not also for blackmail? He claims that "the weighty justifications for those exceptions do not apply in the disputes under review here"[36] but fails to say why. Kipnis's failure to provide reasons why breaches of blackmail contracts should not be considered in closed court leaves the onus on him. Blackmail secrets are in fact not so different from trade secrets. In both cases, there are dangers that attempts to force a contractual partner to live up to his obligations will boomerang.

Kipnis thus recasts the blackmail "paradox:" "while the bilateral agreement guarantees the mark an urgently needed secrecy, the mark must waive the very secrecy he ... is contractually entitled to in order judicially to secure an entitlement to secrecy. In other words, one must waive one's right to secrecy in order to secure one's entitlement to that same secrecy."[37]

But even were it true (a claim I dispute) that the blackmailee would have to give up his secret in order to hold the blackmailer to his contractual obligations, the former would gain a potent hold over the blackmailer. To be publicly held to have reneged on his contract, the blackmailer would undermine the basis for whatever credibility he has as a blackmailer. His ability to make a profitable blackmail deal will be diminished. Of course, this will still require a blackmailee who is willing to have his secret made known, and he cannot be expected to undertake this lightly.

Consider Kipnis's worst case scenario: "post-disclosure remedies are characteristically worthless to the client in that the entire game will have been decisively lost by then.[38] "Why does this vitiate the argument for blackmail

---

[34] Kipnis, *supra* note 2, at 22.

[35] *Id.*

[36] *Id.*

[37] *Id.* Kipnis is not the first to draw attention to this issue: *see* Sidney W. Delong, *Blackmailers, Bribe Takers, and the Second Paradox*, 141 U. PENN. L. REV. 1663 (1993); *but see also* chapter 3, this volume.

[38] Kipnis, *supra* note 2, at 22.

legalization? According to Kipnis: "When it is plain, as it is here, that the very structure of a contract precludes the possibility of fair judicial review, that, it seems, justifies treating such contracts as invalid. Contracts calling for the concealment of guilty secrets have precisely this flawed structure."[39] Not at all. Contracts calling for the concealment of *any* secrets have precisely this structure. And, just as fair judicial review of trade secrets may require a different form of oversight, so also should this be possible for blackmail secrets.

I am puzzled by the intended force of Kipnis's position. He writes that even if "the blackmailer's contract should be seen as void, it does not establish that what the blackmailer does in initiating and participating in such an arrangement should be a criminal offense."[40] His rough "sketch" of an argument that would yield the latter conclusion barely acknowledges what was the central point of my own essay, namely, the impropriety of criminalizing blackmail. As it is, his sketch must beg the question that has been at issue between us—the capacity of civil law to accommodate blackmail contracts. His further contention—that we must devise systems of justice that can secure the blessings of peace—then stands on its head one of the central tenets of libertarianism: justice is the mother of utility, not the daughter. If we violate rights to reduce strife, we will attain neither.

Finally, if Kipnis thinks we are debating about a legal "blessing" for blackmail, he misconstrues the exercise. As is the case with most victimless "crimes," those who defend the decriminalization of blackmail hardly advocate this practice. One need not actually *favor* prostitution, pornography, homosexuality, gambling, addictive drugs, and so on, to support their decriminalization. It is enough that these activities do not violate what Kipnis correctly sees as the libertarian "triad" of force, fraud, or theft. There is no question of officially "blessing" blackmail, any more than any of these others.

---

[39] *Id.*

[40] *Id.*

Afterword

I. BLACKMAIL

In the United States, blackmail is a crime. Blackmail, like extortion, is a threat coupled with a demand for money or other valuable consideration. In blackmail, however, what the blackmailer threatens to do is perfectly legal, such as spreading gossip or building a spite fence. In extortion, by contrast, the threat is very different. Here, it is to do something that is illegal such as killing the victim, or kidnapping his children, or burning down his business.

The classic example of blackmail is an offer to refrain from speaking ill of someone in return for compensation, usually money or sexual services. For example, one man tells another that unless the second man gives him $1,000 he will tell the man's wife and his prudish employer about his adultery. Or, a man tells his neighbor that unless the neighbor pays him $100 he will build a fence that blocks the neighbor's view and reduces the value of his property.

One of the more interesting debates among legal scholars is whether or not blackmail should be classified as criminal behavior. There is no debate about extortion as all people seem to agree that such behavior should be considered criminal. But for blackmail, a furious debate is taking place between those who favor keeping it classified as a crime and libertarians who argue for legalization.

For Decriminalization—The Libertarian Perspective

Libertarianism is the political, economic, and legal philosophy that maintains that crime should be defined so as to prohibit only threats or actual initiation of force against persons or their private property. Extortion clearly falls under this rubric, but blackmail does not. In the libertarian view, blackmail is a victimless crime, akin to other capitalist acts between consenting adults such as drug use, gambling, prostitution, pornography, homosexuality, and so forth. Strictly speaking, there are no victims in any of these cases, unless paternalism is seen as the basic political philosophy.

How can one argue that blackmail is a consensual commercial interaction? It appears that there is a perpetrator, the blackmailer, and a victim, the blackmailee. But, is the adulterous husband who is threatened by exposure really a victim? From his point of view, he may well be better off meeting the threat of the blackmailer than being exposed by a gossip who demands nothing from him to keep quiet. The gossip would expose the adulterer and the man might lose his wife and job. But with the blackmailer, the man has a chance of keeping his secret and his marriage and job by making a mutually beneficial deal in which the amount paid the blackmailer is worth less than the cost of being exposed.

For example, suppose that keeping his wife and employer in the dark is worth $16,000 and the blackmailer demands only $1,000 per year, which at an assumed interest rate of 10% translates, very roughly, into a present discounted value of $10,000. If the man agrees to the deal, he can earn an actual profit of $6,000 ($16,000 minus $10,000). The blackmailer also makes a profit, $10,000, if one assumes that the costs of transacting this deal were negligible. In contrast, with his secret on the lips of the gossip, the man loses something valued at $16,000.

Even if the target of the blackmailer is better off than the object of the gossip, it still does not follow that society is better off by legalizing blackmail. But, in the libertarian view, society can also benefit. Let us assume that the law actually has some effect, and discourages at least some blackmail activity that might otherwise take place. When it becomes legal, more people enter the "profession," and each of them is more active. Society as a whole might actually be better off as a result, and for several reasons.

First, there might be less adultery and other acts about which people are ashamed and are considered by many to be immoral and destructive to society. With blackmail legalized, and more blackmailers at work, it is more likely that people who engage in these behaviors will be found out. And they will have to pay more-for the service and for the blackmailer's silence. And, because economic theory shows that the more something costs, the less people will buy of it, immoral activities that are subject to blackmail might well become less frequent as less people pay for them and those who pay, engage in such behaviors less often.

A second, possible societal benefit is less crime. Like many other things, robbery, carjackings, murder, etc., are often better accomplished by groups of criminals, rather than individuals. Sometimes more people are needed to overpower a victim; sometimes, there are specialties (e.g., safe cracking, dynamiting, get-a-way car driving, planning, strong-arm tactics) that no one criminal can master. Given that legalizing blackmail will likely produce more blackmailing, the costs of cooperating with other criminals will also rise, because of the increased likelihood of being blackmailed by a fellow gang member after the fact. The result will be a decrease in the number of people in any one gang, and with it a decrease in the effectiveness of the gang. This means that there will be less crime, since criminals will have economic incentives to operate on their own, where they are less effective.

Objections to Libertarian Assumptions

Despite claiming benefits to both parties, no one denies that the black-mailer threatens the blackmailee, as most people do not like to be threatened. But, from the libertarian point of view, threats in and of themselves are innocuous, and not a clear indication of a crime. Threats are part of daily life in a capitalist society as every commercial transaction is in some sense a series of implicit threats. For example a customer threatens the grocer that unless he gives him food, he will not give him money. The grocer makes a "counter-threat" that unless he is given money, he will not give the customer food. These threats are typically implicit, not explicit, but they are threats despite the veneer of nicety that underlies virtually all commercial interaction.

A second objection is that blackmail ought to be banned by law since it leads to economic waste. It's as if de-criminalizing blackmail would create two industries, the creation of glass windows and the encouragement of shooting bullets through them. If both are prohibited, society will be better off. Under blackmail decriminalization, some people would be encouraged to spy on others, to get the goods on them, and then also stimulating others to hide their secrets.

The libertarian response to this objection is that even if it could be shown that blackmail is economically wasteful, it still does not logically follow that it should be prohibited by law. If it did, we would also have to ban other economically wasteful activities such as goofing off, lying in a hammock, taking a siesta, etc. For that matter, society should criminalize all incompatible industries, such as glass making and gun-smithing. Yes, the blackmailee might be better off if the blackmailer didn't exist at all or dropped dead, but the same might be said in a host of other situations

Libertarians see their case for the decriminalization as a strong one. The blackmailer does utter a "threat," but this occurs, also, in ordinary commerce. Yes, there are some parallels between this practice and extortion, but the differences are dramatic and crucial. No, it cannot be denied that blackmail may well be immoral, but if all non-ethical acts were crimes, with the exception of a few saints everyone would be a criminal.

The Other Side

If the case in favor of legalizing blackmail is so strong, why is it that every civilized society has prohibited it by law? This is because, as even many advocates for legalization admit, it is a nasty business. One commentator goes so far as to characterize blackmail as "moral murder." The bottom line is that most members of society see a great wrong in the practice and, since the laws of a relatively free society (and even some that are not so free) tend to reflect the beliefs of the overwhelming majority of the population, it should occasion little surprise that blackmail is everywhere prohibited by law. The bottom line is that acts considered highly immoral by most people tend to be outlawed, whether or not they comprise the actual use of physical violence or the threat thereof.

II. THE BLACKMAILER AS HERO

Is blackmail really illegitimate? At first glance it is not hard to answer this question. The only problem it would seem to pose is why it is being asked at all. For do not blackmailers well, … blackmail people? And what could be worse? Blackmailers prey on your most hidden deep dark secrets, they threaten to publicize them, they bleed you white, they can even drive you to suicide. Blackmail is so evil that even to consider its legitimacy will strike many as an unmitigated evil; even those scholars who would otherwise favor the spirit of free and untrammeled inquiry.

We push on in any case. And we find that the critique of the blackmailer falls like a house of cards; we find that the case against blackmail is based on a tissue of unexamined shibboleths, blown out of all proportion, and on deep philosophical misunderstandings.

What, exactly, is blackmail? Blackmail is the offer of a trade; it is the offer to trade something, usually silence, for some other good, usually money. If the offer of the blackmail trade is accepted, then the blackmailer maintains his silence and the blackmailee pays the agreed amount of money. If the black-mail offer is rejected, then the blackmailer may exercise his right of free speech, and perhaps announce and publicize the secret. Notice that there is nothing amiss here. All that is happening is that an offer to maintain silence is being made. If the offer is rejected, the blackmailer does no more than exer-cise his rights of free speech, something he has a complete right to do in the first place, whether or not the offer is made or accepted.

The only difference between a gossip or blabbermouth and the black-mailer is that the blackmailer will refrain from speaking—for a price. In a sense the gossip or the blabbermouth is much worse than the blackmailer, for the blackmailer at least gives you a chance to shut him up. The blabbermouth and gossip just up and spill the beans. A person with a secret he wants kept will be much better off if a blackmailer rather than a gossip or blabbermouth gets hold of it. With the blabbermouth or gossip, as we have said, all is lost. With the blackmailer, one can only gain, or at worst, be no worse off. If the price required by the blackmailer for his silence is worth less than the secret, the secret-holder will pay off, and accept the lesser of the two evils. He will gain the difference to him between the value of the secret and the price of the blackmailer. It is only in the case that the blackmailer demands more than the secret is worth that the information gets publicized. But in this case the secret-keeper is no worse off with the blackmailer than with the inveterate gossip. (He may still be better off with the blackmailer, even here, because the typical blackmailer gains nothing if he publicizes the secret—except the dubious value of making sure that the secret-keeper knows he is not bluffing—so the secret keeper may well be able to bargain down the blackmailer's price.) It is indeed difficult, then, to account for the vilification suffered by the blackmailer, at least compared to the gossip, who is usually dismissed with merely slight contempt.

Blackmail need not entail the offer of silence in return for money. This is only the most well known form. More generally, blackmail may be defined as threatening to do something, anything, (which is otherwise entirely legal) *unless* the blackmailer's demands, financial or otherwise, are met. In its more general form there are several acts which qualify as blackmail but interestingly enough, far from receiving the vilification associated with blackmail, have even attained respectability among certain segments of the population. As an example, let us consider the lettuce boycott, beloved of every liberal or progressive worthy of his limousine.

The lettuce boycott is (a form of) blackmail!! What is being done in the lettuce boycott (and every other boycott, for that matter), what the lettuce boycott consists of, is making threats to various retailers and wholesalers of fruits and vegetables. These threats are that if the retailer or wholesaler handles non-union lettuce, people will be asked not to patronize their establishments. The not inconsiderable energies, time, and money of the lettuce boycott movement will be brought to bear on all handlers of non-union lettuce.

Now, there are plenty of reasons to oppose the boycott of non-union lettuce. But I am here concerned to show that the lettuce boycott is indeed blackmail, and that, as a form of blackmail, it is entirely legitimate. We can see that the lettuce boycott conforms perfectly to the more general definition of blackmail as a threat that something otherwise entirely legal will take place unless the blackmailer's demands are met. In this case, the threat is to withhold patronage from establishments unless they refuse to handle non-union lettuce. Although it is not legal to threaten this, it is perfectly legal not to patronize establishments that one, for any reason, does not like. So the lettuce boycott is legitimate, and blackmail as well, a pair of strange bedfellows if ever there was one.

Let us consider the question of the threats involved in blackmail, because perhaps more than anything else, it is this aspect of blackmail that is most misunderstood and feared. Now threats are usually considered evil, and rightly so. The usual dictum against aggression warns of aggression against non-aggressors as well as the threat of such aggression.

And the reason is not hard to fathom. If a highwayman were to accost us, it is usually the threat of aggression that will get us to do his bidding. It is the threat of aggression that will relieve us of our possessions. If the highwayman actually had to use aggression against us, as opposed to the threat thereof, it would be practically an admission of defeat. So the threat of aggression is entirely illegitimate.

But notice that the threat involved in blackmail is entirely different. In aggression, what is being threatened is aggressive violence, something that the aggressor has no right to do. In blackmail, however, what is being "threatened" is something that the blackmailer most certainly does have a right to do! To exercise his right of free speech, to gossip about our secrets, or in the case of the lettuce boycott, to threaten not to patronize certain stores.

One can hardly call the "threat" in blackmail a real threat. When contrasted to the real threat of the highwayman, the "threat" of the blackmailer can only be characterized as an offer to keep silent, and not as a real threat at all. The blackmailer never threatens bodily violence or any type of violence. If he did, he would no longer be a legitimate blackmailer; he would be an illegitimate aggressor, who uses threats as a means of coercion.

There is one case where blackmail would not be legitimate, but not because it is blackmail. It would rather be illegitimate because it would be in violation of a contract. For instance, if the secret-keeper takes a lawyer or a private investigator into his confidence on the condition that, among other things, the confidence be maintained in secrecy, then, if the lawyer or private investigator turns around and tries to blackmail him, it would be in violation of the contract, and therefore illegitimate. It is only when the blackmail violates an agreement that it is illegitimate. If there is no contract, if it is a perfect stranger who holds the secret, then the blackmail is legitimate because perfect strangers have free speech rights. It is only someone who has sold his right to speak freely (about the secrets of his client) like the lawyer or the private investigator who then has no right to engage in blackmail.

In addition to being a legitimate activity, blackmail has many good effects, the litanies to the contrary notwithstanding. And once we get over the shock that there is anything at all that can be said in favor of blackmail, it is not too surprising that this should be so. For apart from some innocent victims that get caught in the net, who does the blackmailer prey upon? There are two groups. On the one hand we have the murderer, the thief, the swindler, the embezzler, the cheater, the rapist, etc., all criminals and violators of the stricture against aggression upon non-aggressors. On the other hand we have people who engage in activities which are not illegitimate themselves, but go against the mores and habits of the majority of the people. There are the homosexuals, the sadomasochists, the sex perverts, the communists, the adulterers, etc. It is my contention that the institution of blackmail has beneficial, but different, effects on each of these groups, none of which seem to have been realized by writers on the subject. Let us consider them each in turn.

In the case of the criminals, blackmail, the threat of blackmail, and the very existence of the institution of blackmail serves as a hindrance. It makes the payoff to the criminal less certain and less rewarding because if caught, the criminal must now share some of his "hard won" loot with the blackmailer, with the risk that the blackmailer can always turn him in. Even with blackmail illegal, this can have a much greater effect than many people would believe possible. How many of the anonymous "tips" received by the police can be traced, directly or indirectly, to blackmail?

And the value of these tips cannot be over estimated. How many criminals are led to pursue crime on their own, eschewing the aid of fellow criminals in "jobs" that call for cooperation—out of fear of possible later blackmail? Since there are always some people on the verge of committing crimes, or at the margin of criminality, as the economist would say, where the least factor will propel them one way or another, the additional fear of crime-related blackmail may be enough, in many cases, to dissuade them from crime.

Imagine then how much more effective blackmail would be in curtailing real crime if blackmail itself were legalized! Then the blackmailer would not have to worry about possible legal steps being taken against him because of his public-spirited preying on criminals. This would undoubtedly encourage the quantity and quality of such blackmail efforts, with attendant depredations upon our criminal class.

It is sometimes said that what diminishes crime is not the penalty attached to the crime but the certainty of being caught. Although this controversy rages with great relevance in the debates on capital punishment, we need not enter into it here. For our purposes it will suffice to point out that the institution of blackmail does both. It increases the penalty associated with crime, since criminals are forced to share a part of their loot with the blackmailer. It also raises the probability of being caught, as the blackmailers are now added to the police, private citizens, vigilantes and others whose function if not purpose it is to suppress crime. And let it be added that blackmailers who can often be members of the criminal gang in good standing are in an especially good position to foil crimes Their "inside" position surpasses even that of a spy or infiltrator. who is forced to play a part. The blackmailer can live the part of the criminal, for until he turns against the gang as a blackmailer, he really is a criminal. Legalizing blackmail also will at one fell swoop allow us to take advantage of not one but two crime-fighting adages: "divide and conquer," and "take advantage of the lack of honor among thieves." So it is pretty clear that one effect of legalizing blackmail will be to diminish crimes of aggression.

The legalization of blackmail will also have good effects upon actions which may be illegal but are not criminal in the sense that they involve aggression but are at variance with the mores of the majority of the people. Far from suppressing them, the legalization of blackmail will have a liberating effect.

Even now, with blackmail still illegal, we are witnessing some of its beneficial effects. Let us take homosexuality as an example. Homosexuality may be illegal but is not really criminal since it involves no aggression. For individual homosexuals, we must admit, blackmail causes untold harm and can hardly be considered beneficial. But for the group as a whole, or rather, for each individual as a member of the group, blackmail has helped. Blackmail has helped the gay community as a whole by making homosexuality more widely known, by making the public more accustomed to homosexuality, and by placing the homosexual in a more open light. In so doing, the blackmailer has contributed to forcing the homosexuals to make themselves more known. Let it be repeated. Forcing individual members of a downtrodden group out into the open, or "out of the closet," can by no stretch of the imagination be considered doing them a favor. Forcing anyone to do anything can usually only violate rights; and forcing someone to do something "for his own good" is a particular rung in hell reserved for liberals. But still it must be realized that practically the only way a downtrodden group of people can attain liberation is by being known to each other so that they can cooperate with each other. And it must be realized that one important effect of blackmail is to force people out into the open where they will be able to know each other. In this way blackmail can legitimately claim some small share in the credit for the liberation of groups whose only crime is to deviate from the norm in some non-criminal way.

It is not surprising that this should be so when we reflect upon the old aphorism that "the truth shall make you free." For the only "weapon" at the disposal of the blackmailer is the truth. If it were not for the truth, the blackmailer would be in no position to be able to blackmail. But in using the truth to back up his threats, as upon occasion he must, without any intention on his part he sets the truth free to do whatever good, as well as whatever bad, it is capable of doing.